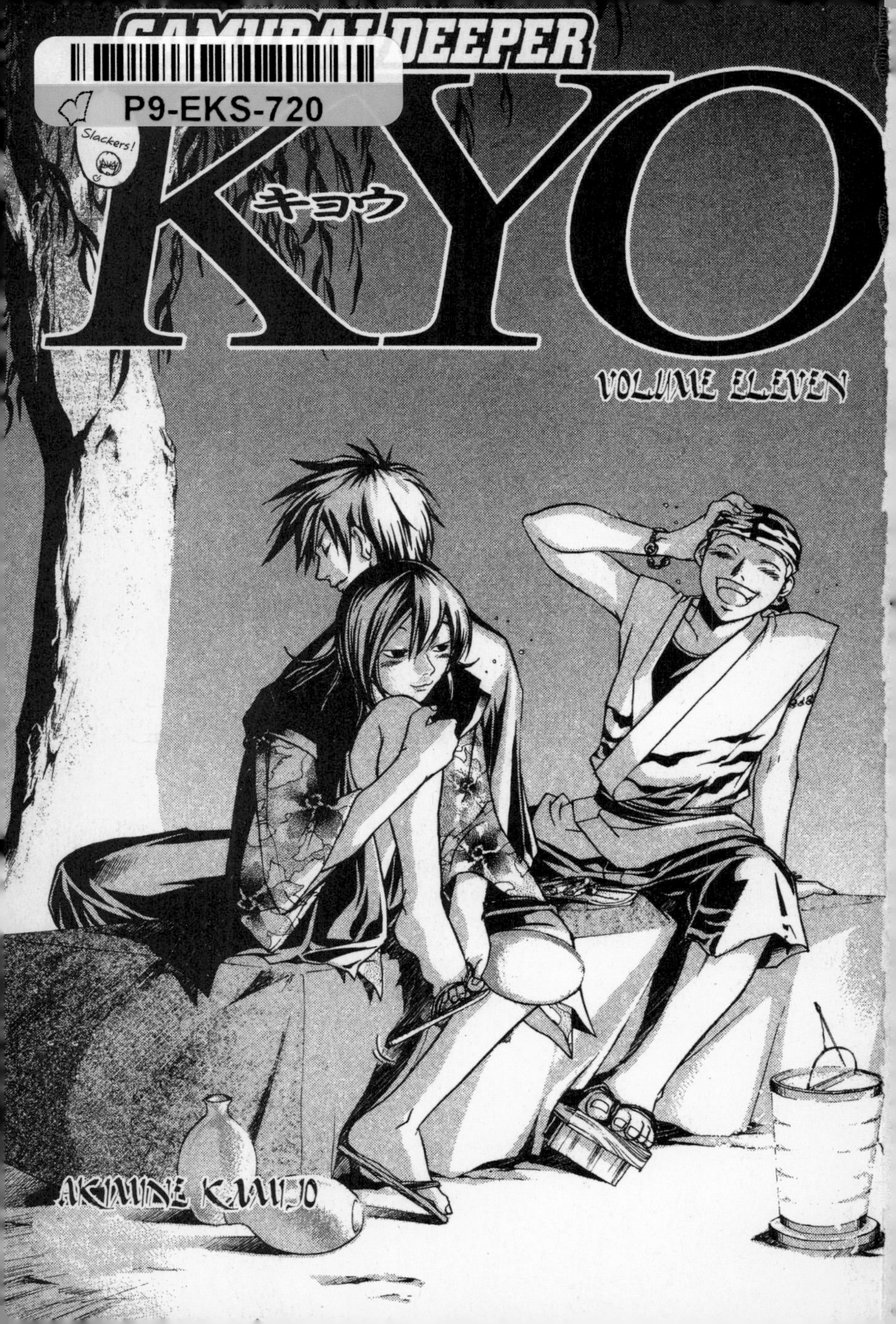
SAMURAI DEEPER
KYO
キョウ
Slackers!
VOLUME ELEVEN
AKIMINE KAMIJO

Samurai Deeper Kyo Vol. 11
Created by Akimine Kamijyo

Translation - Alexander O. Smith
Script Editor - Rich Amtower
Copy Editor - Peter Ahlstrom
Retouch and Lettering - Patrick Tran
Production Artists - Jose Macasocol, Jr.
Cover Design - Seth Cable

Editor - Aaron Suhr
Digital Imaging Manager - Chris Buford
Pre-Press Manager - Antonio DePietro
Production Managers - Jennifer Miller and Mutsumi Miyazaki
Art Director - Matt Alford
Managing Editor - Jill Freshney
VP of Production - Ron Klamert
Editor-In-Chief - Mike Kiley
President and C.O.O. - John Parker
Publisher and C.E.O. - Stuart Levy

A  Manga

TOKYOPOP Inc.
5900 Wilshire Blvd. Suite 2000
Los Angeles, CA 90036

E-mail: info@TOKYOPOP.com
Come visit us online at www.TOKYOPOP.com

ISBN: 1-59532-451-8

First TOKYOPOP printing: February 2005
10 9 8 7 6 5 4 3 2 1
Printed in the USA

SAMURAI DEEPER Kyo

Vol. 11
by Akimine Kamijyo

HAMBURG // LONDON // LOS ANGELES // TOKYO

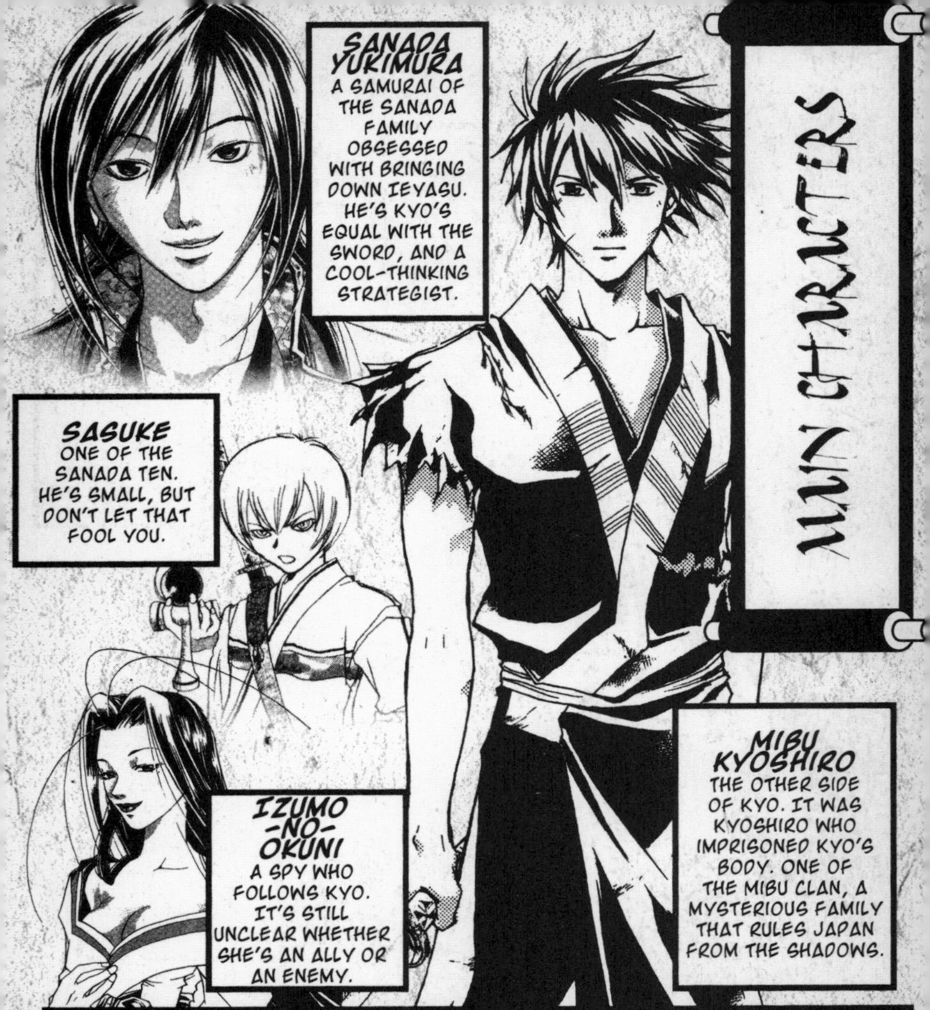
MAIN CHARACTERS
SANADA YUKIMURA
A SAMURAI OF THE SANADA FAMILY OBSESSED WITH BRINGING DOWN IEYASU. HE'S KYO'S EQUAL WITH THE SWORD, AND A COOL-THINKING STRATEGIST.
SASUKE
ONE OF THE SANADA TEN. HE'S SMALL, BUT DON'T LET THAT FOOL YOU.
MIBU KYOSHIRO
THE OTHER SIDE OF KYO. IT WAS KYOSHIRO WHO IMPRISONED KYO'S BODY. ONE OF THE MIBU CLAN, A MYSTERIOUS FAMILY THAT RULES JAPAN FROM THE SHADOWS.
IZUMO-NO-OKUNI
A SPY WHO FOLLOWS KYO. IT'S STILL UNCLEAR WHETHER SHE'S AN ALLY OR AN ENEMY.

THE STORY

FOUR YEARS HAVE PASSED SINCE THE BATTLE OF SEKIGAHARA. YUYA AND KYOSHIRO MEET AND BEGIN TO TRAVEL TOGETHER, BUT YUYA SOON LEARNS THAT KYOSHIRO HAS ANOTHER SIDE: THE CRUEL AND POWERFUL SAMURAI KYO. AS THE TWO KYOS FIGHT FOR DOMINANCE, THEY PICK UP TWO MORE TRAVELING COMPANIONS, BENITORA AND YUKIMURA, AND LEAVE EDO, HEADING WEST. THEIR DESTINATION: THE AOKIGAHARA FOREST AT THE BASE OF MT. FUJI, WHERE KYO'S BODY LIES HIDDEN...BUT ON THE WAY, THEY ARE ASSAILED BY THE SIXTH DEMON KING, ODA NOBUNAGA, AND HIS TWELVE GOD SHOGUNS! A BATTLE ENSUES, AND BLOOD IS SPILLED UPON BLOOD. JUST AS KYO SEEMED ABOUT TO RECLAIM HIS BODY, IT WAS SNATCHED AWAY BY AN OLD FRIEND--AKIRA. THE PARTY SETS OUT TOWARD KYOTO, HOT ON AKIRA'S TRAIL...WHEN THEY ENCOUNTER THE MAN KNOWN AS DATE MASAMUNE, WHO CALLS HIMSELF "BONTENMARU." WHAT COULD HE WANT?

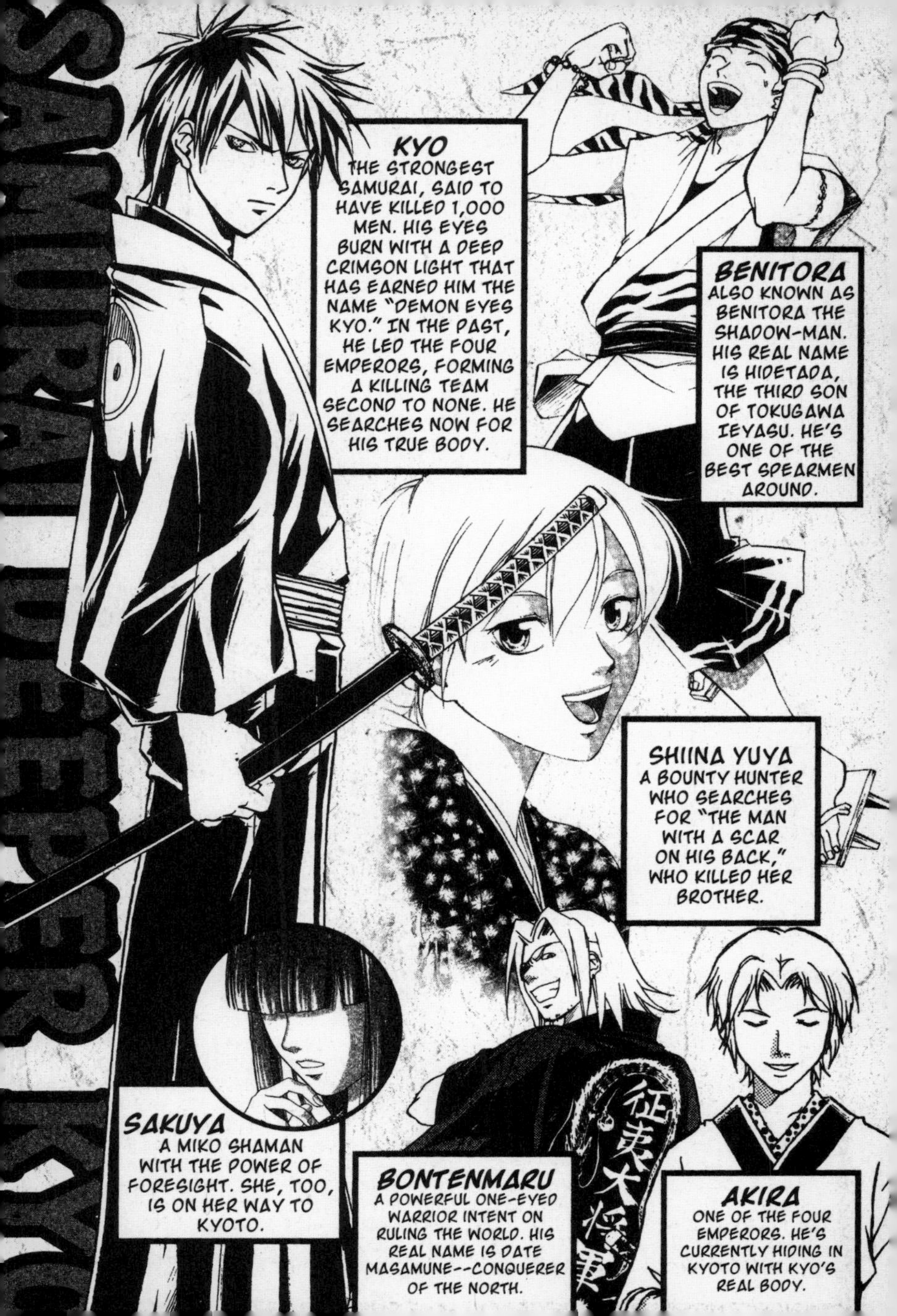

SAMURAI DEEPER KYO
KYO
THE STRONGEST SAMURAI, SAID TO HAVE KILLED 1,000 MEN. HIS EYES BURN WITH A DEEP CRIMSON LIGHT THAT HAS EARNED HIM THE NAME "DEMON EYES KYO." IN THE PAST, HE LED THE FOUR EMPERORS, FORMING A KILLING TEAM SECOND TO NONE. HE SEARCHES NOW FOR HIS TRUE BODY.
BENITORA
ALSO KNOWN AS BENITORA THE SHADOW-MAN. HIS REAL NAME IS HIDETADA, THE THIRD SON OF TOKUGAWA IEYASU. HE'S ONE OF THE BEST SPEARMEN AROUND.
SHIINA YUYA
A BOUNTY HUNTER WHO SEARCHES FOR "THE MAN WITH A SCAR ON HIS BACK," WHO KILLED HER BROTHER.
AKIRA
ONE OF THE FOUR EMPERORS. HE'S CURRENTLY HIDING IN KYOTO WITH KYO'S REAL BODY.
BONTENMARU
A POWERFUL ONE-EYED WARRIOR INTENT ON RULING THE WORLD. HIS REAL NAME IS DATE MASAMUNE--CONQUERER OF THE NORTH.
SAKUYA
A MIKO SHAMAN WITH THE POWER OF FORESIGHT. SHE, TOO, IS ON HER WAY TO KYOTO.

SAMURAI DEEPER

KYO

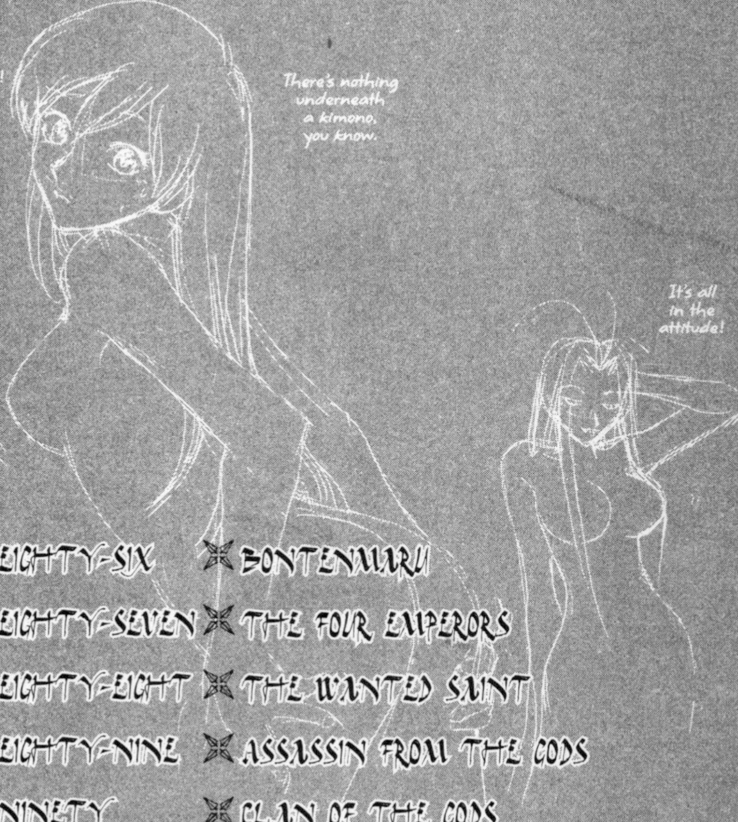
How... convenient!
There's nothing underneath a kimono, you know.
It's all in the attitude!

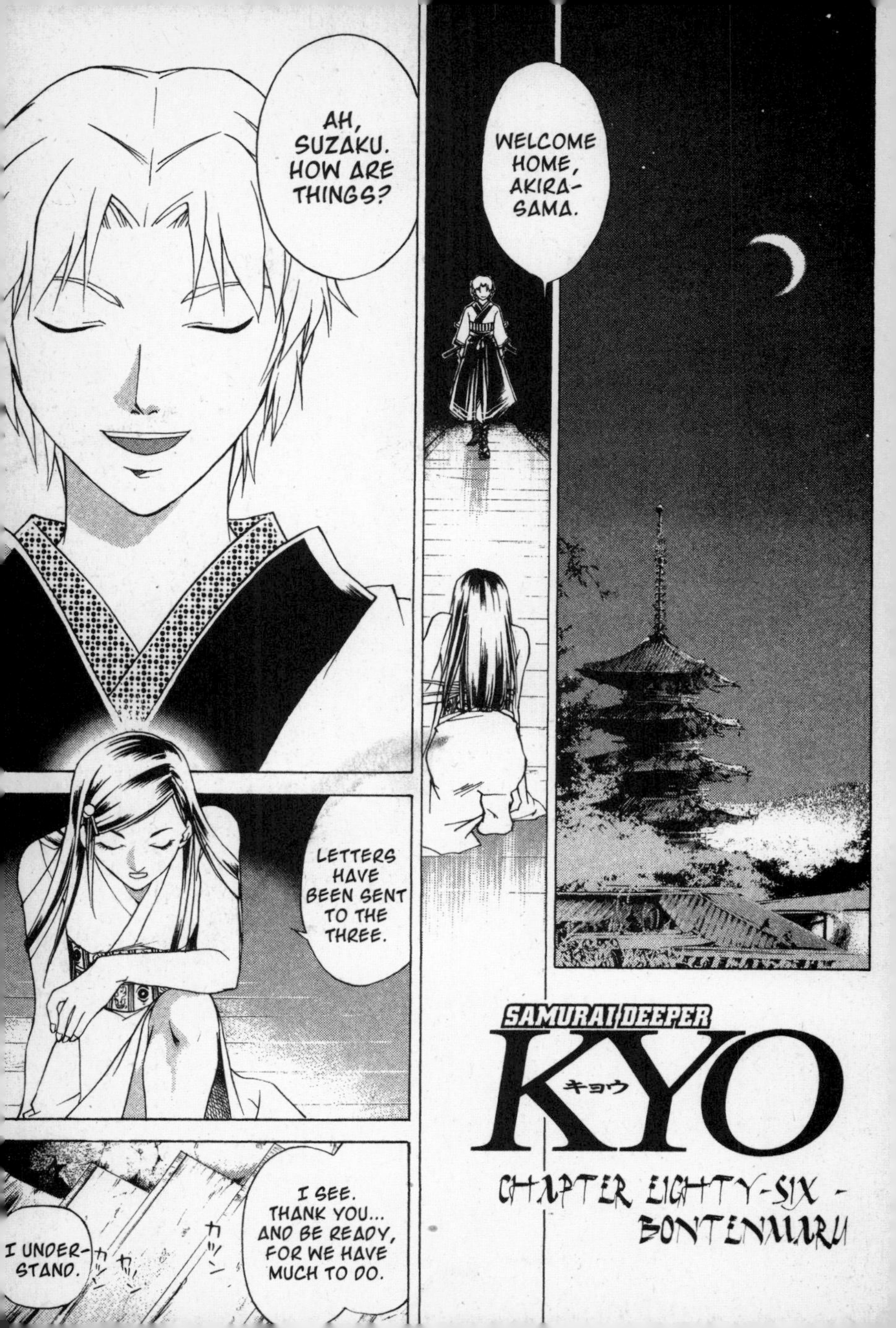
WELCOME HOME, AKIRA-SAMA.
SAMURAI DEEPER
KYO
キョウ
CHAPTER EIGHTY-SIX - BONTENMARU
AH, SUZAKU. HOW ARE THINGS?
LETTERS HAVE BEEN SENT TO THE THREE.
I SEE. THANK YOU... AND BE READY, FOR WE HAVE MUCH TO DO.
カツン
I UNDER-STAND.
カツン
カツン

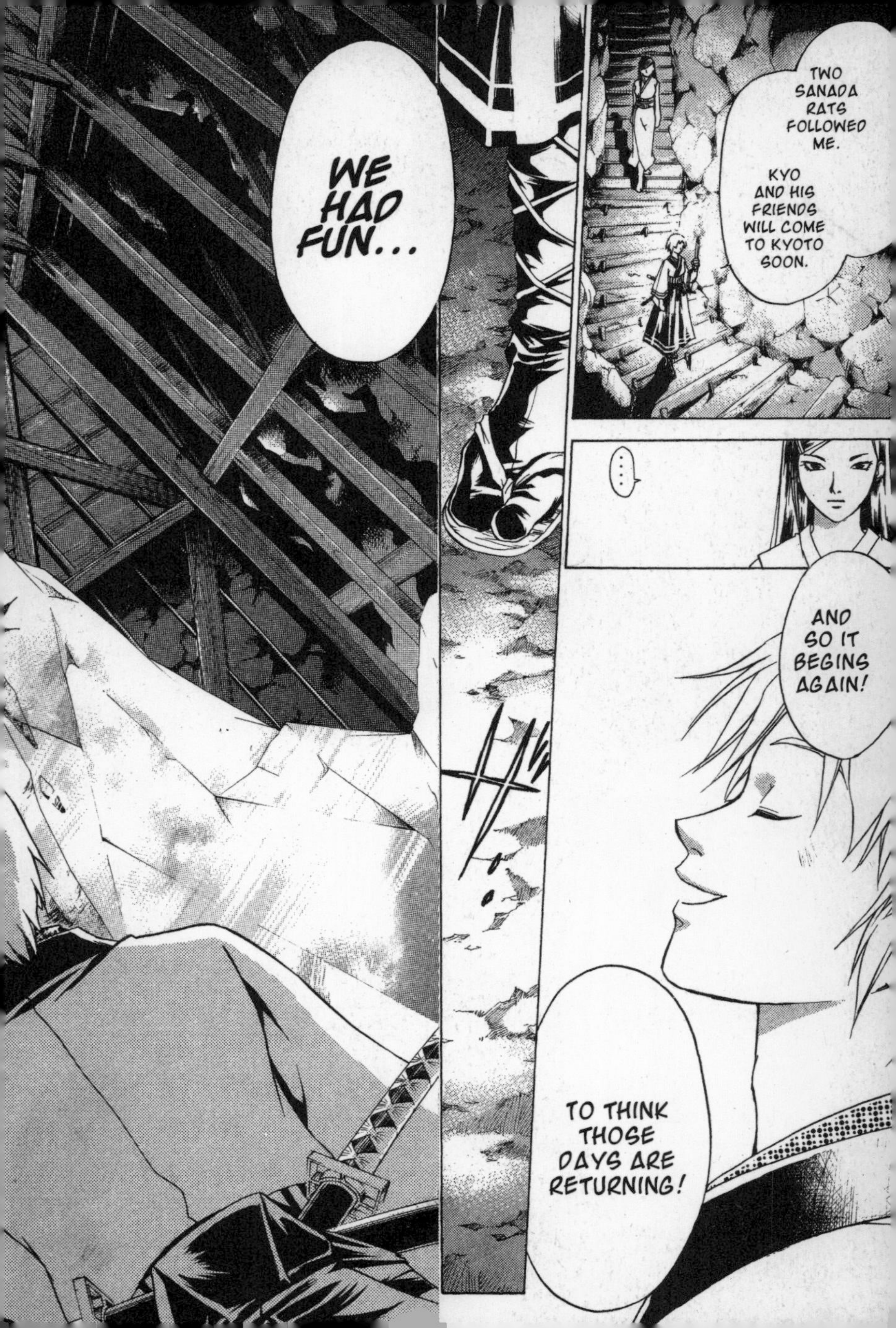
TWO SANADA RATS FOLLOWED ME.
KYO AND HIS FRIENDS WILL COME TO KYOTO SOON.
...
AND SO IT BEGINS AGAIN!
TO THINK THOSE DAYS ARE RETURNING!
WE HAD FUN...

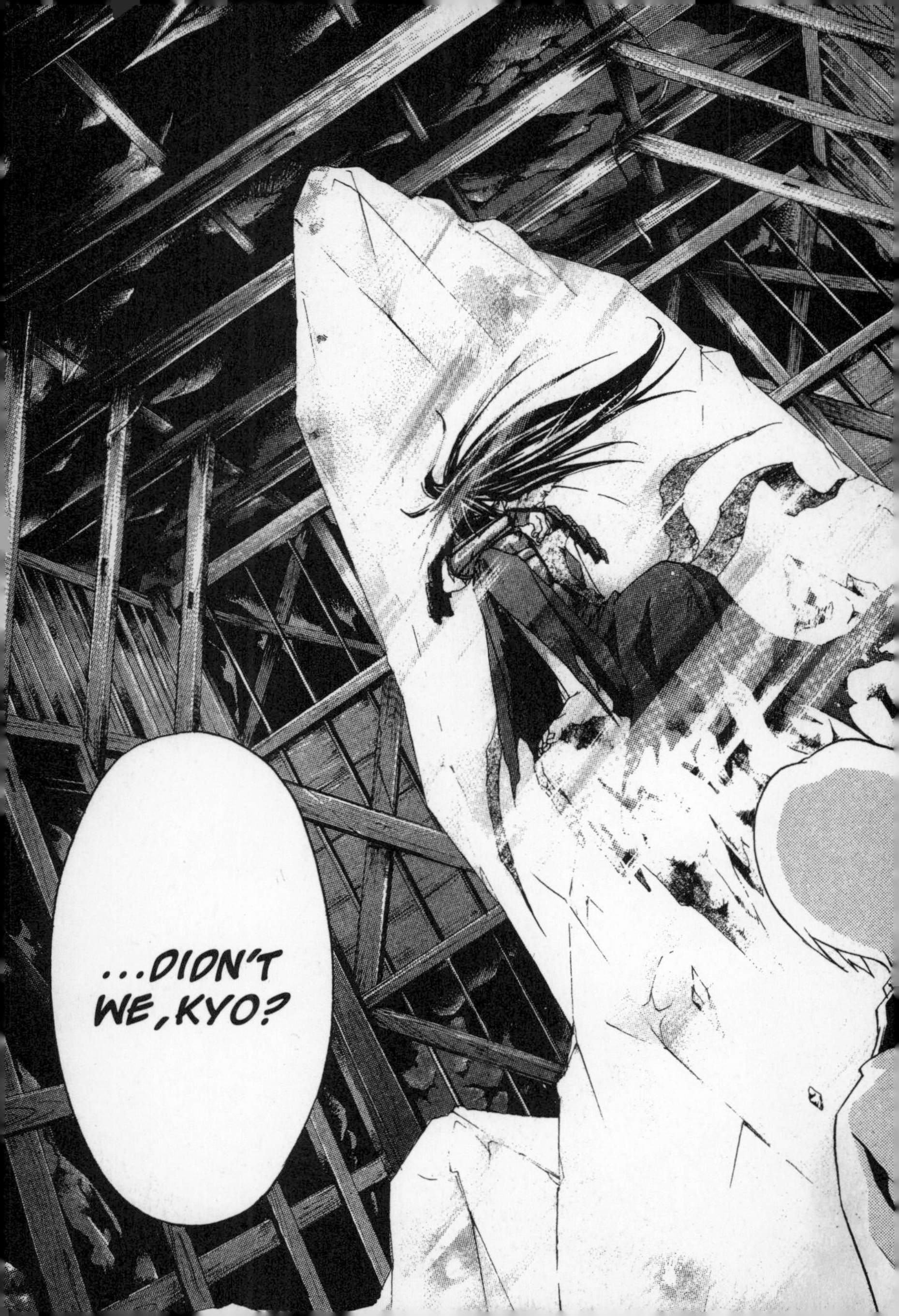
...DIDN'T WE, KYO?

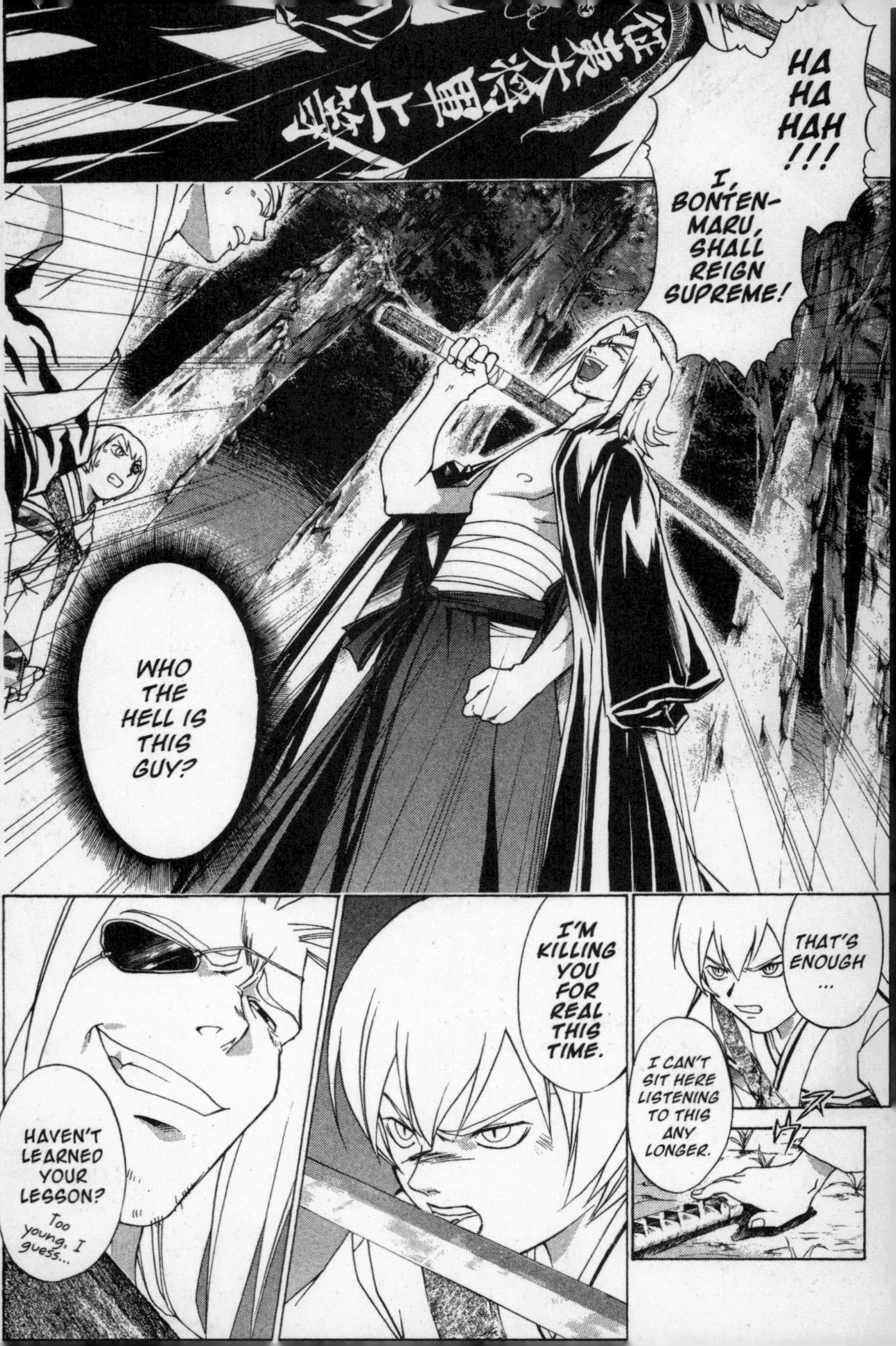
HA HA HAH!!!
I, BONTEN-MARU, SHALL REIGN SUPREME!
WHO THE HELL IS THIS GUY?
THAT'S ENOUGH...
I CAN'T SIT HERE LISTENING TO THIS ANY LONGER.
I'M KILLING YOU FOR REAL THIS TIME.
HAVEN'T LEARNED YOUR LESSON?
Too young, I guess...

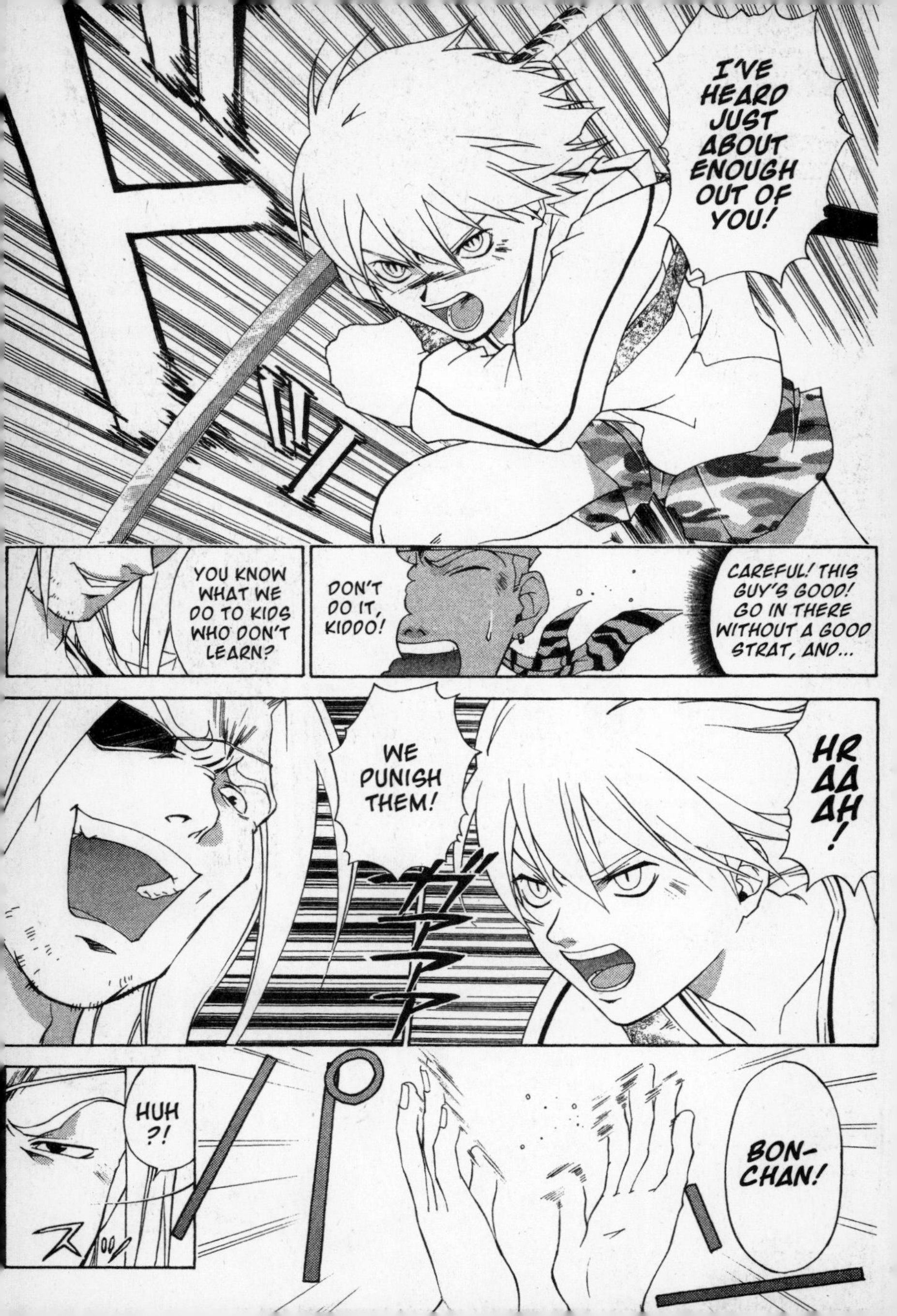
I'VE HEARD JUST ABOUT ENOUGH OUT OF YOU!
CAREFUL! THIS GUY'S GOOD! GO IN THERE WITHOUT A GOOD STRAT, AND...
DON'T DO IT, KIDDO!
YOU KNOW WHAT WE DO TO KIDS WHO DON'T LEARN?
HRAAAH!
WE PUNISH THEM!
BON-CHAN!
HUH?!

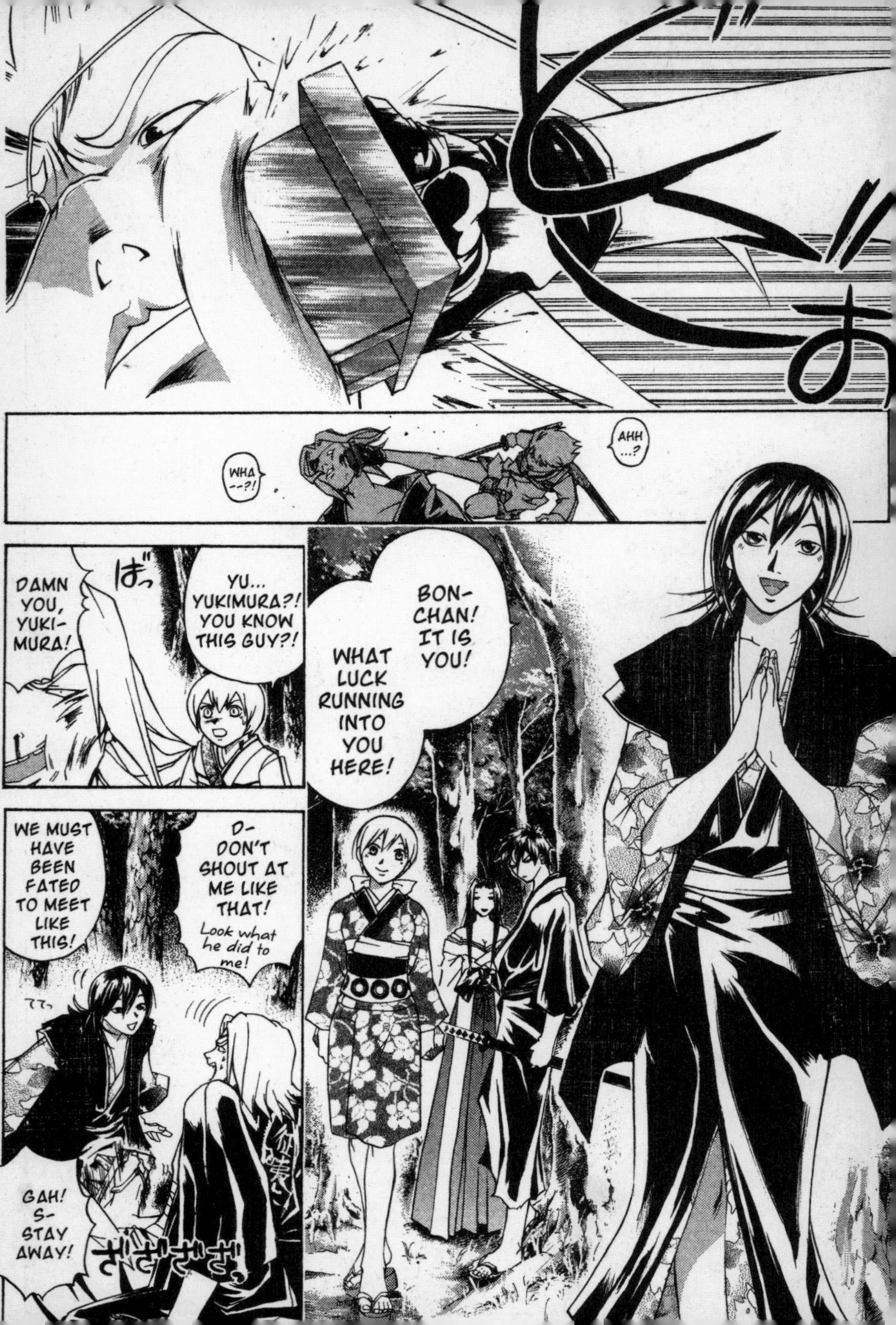
どお
AHH ...?
WHA --?!
BON-CHAN! IT IS YOU!
WHAT LUCK RUNNING INTO YOU HERE!
YU... YUKIMURA?! YOU KNOW THIS GUY?!
ばっ
DAMN YOU, YUKI-MURA!
D-DON'T SHOUT AT ME LIKE THAT!
Look what he did to me!
WE MUST HAVE BEEN FATED TO MEET LIKE THIS!
てて
GAH! S-STAY AWAY!
ざざざざ

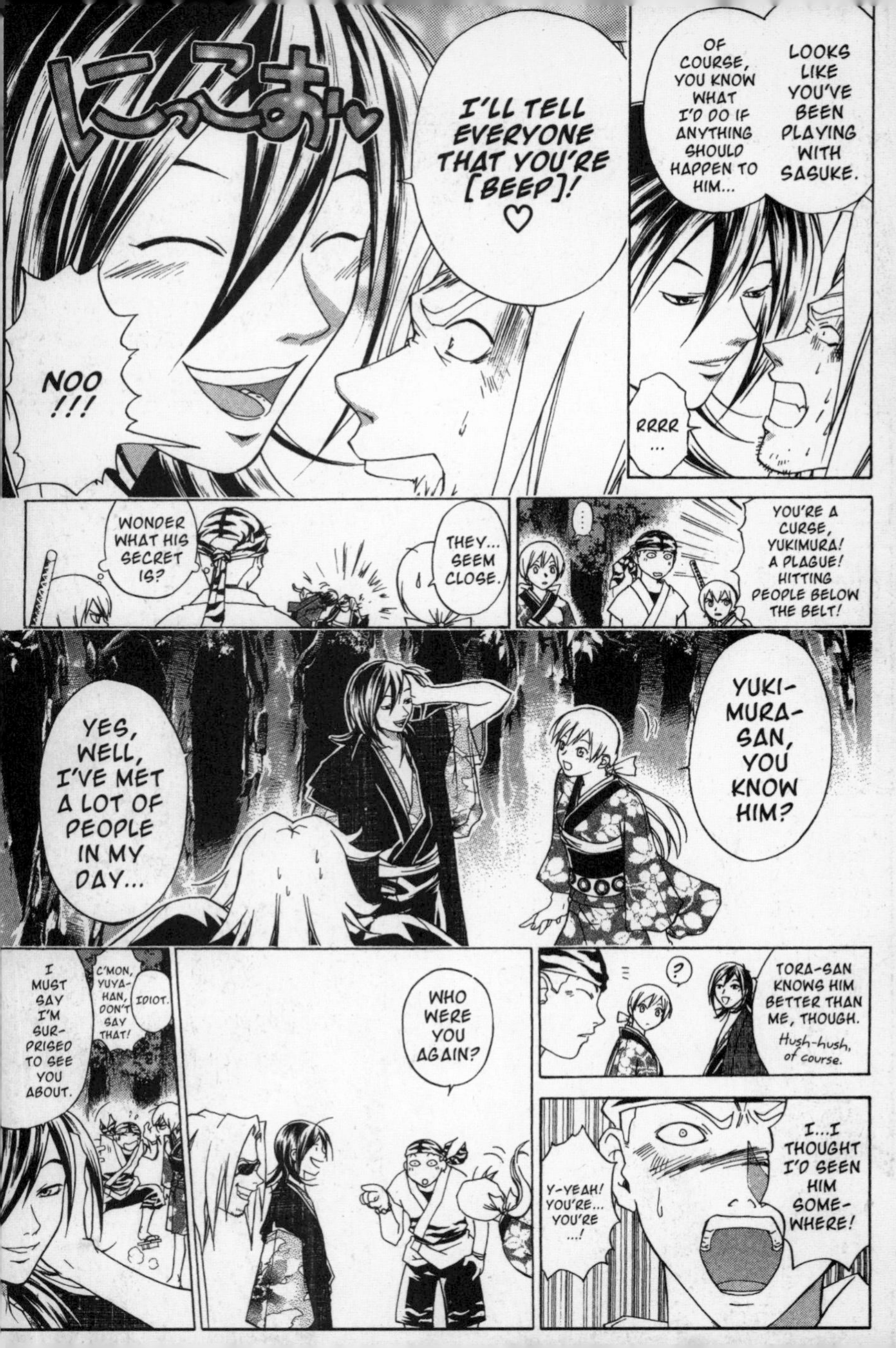
LOOKS LIKE YOU'VE BEEN PLAYING WITH SASUKE.
OF COURSE, YOU KNOW WHAT I'D DO IF ANYTHING SHOULD HAPPEN TO HIM...
RRRR ...
I'LL TELL EVERYONE THAT YOU'RE [BEEP]! ♡
にっこお♡
NOO !!!
YOU'RE A CURSE, YUKIMURA! A PLAGUE! HITTING PEOPLE BELOW THE BELT!
...
THEY... SEEM CLOSE.
WONDER WHAT HIS SECRET IS?
YUKI-MURA-SAN, YOU KNOW HIM?
YES, WELL, I'VE MET A LOT OF PEOPLE IN MY DAY...
TORA-SAN KNOWS HIM BETTER THAN ME, THOUGH.
Hush-hush, of course.
?
I...I THOUGHT I'D SEEN HIM SOME-WHERE!
Y-YEAH! YOU'RE... YOU'RE ...!
WHO WERE YOU AGAIN?
IDIOT.
C'MON, YUYA-HAN, DON'T SAY THAT!
I MUST SAY I'M SUR-PRISED TO SEE YOU ABOUT.

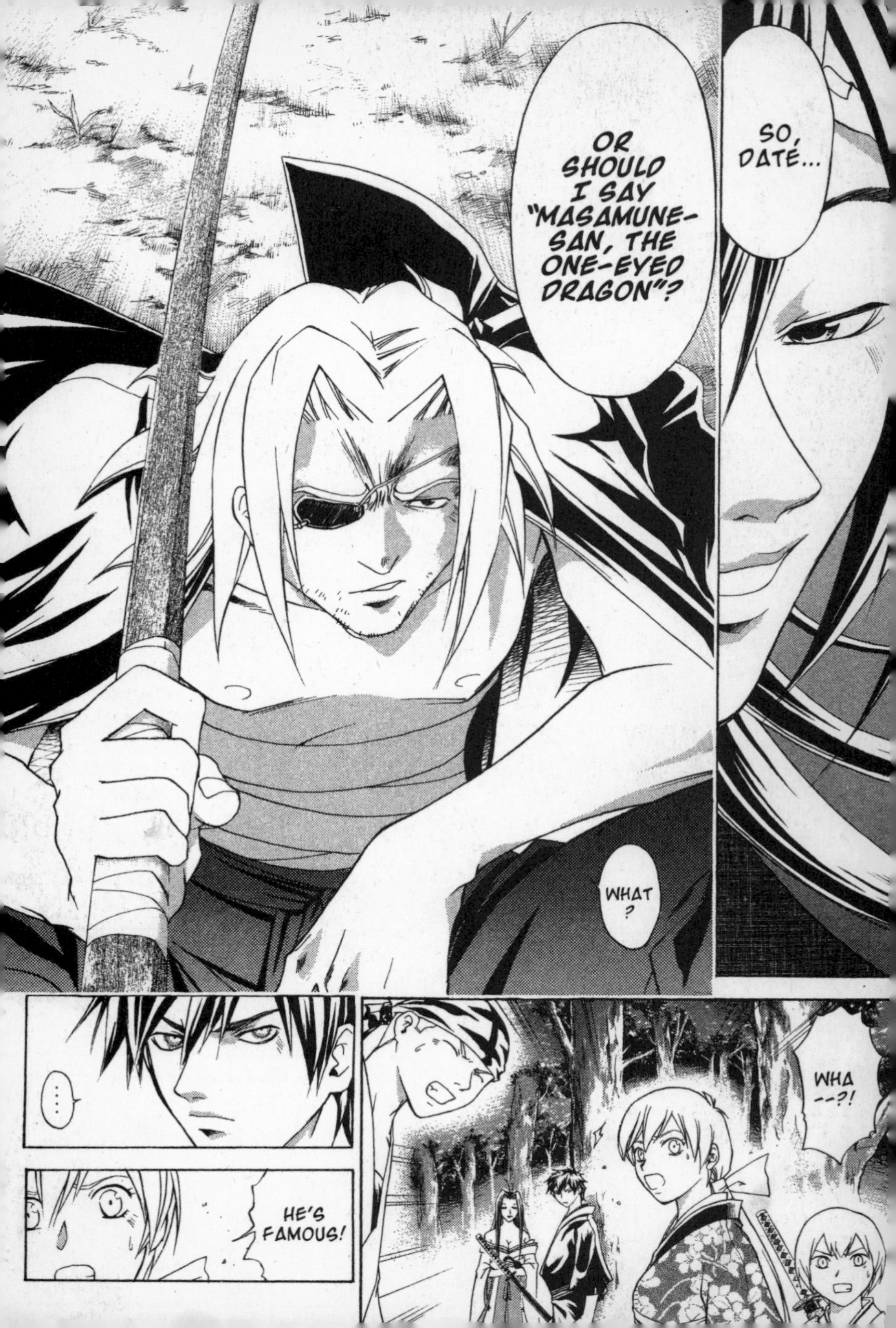
SO, DATÉ...
OR SHOULD I SAY "MASAMUNE-SAN, THE ONE-EYED DRAGON"?
WHAT?
WHA--?!
...
HE'S FAMOUS!

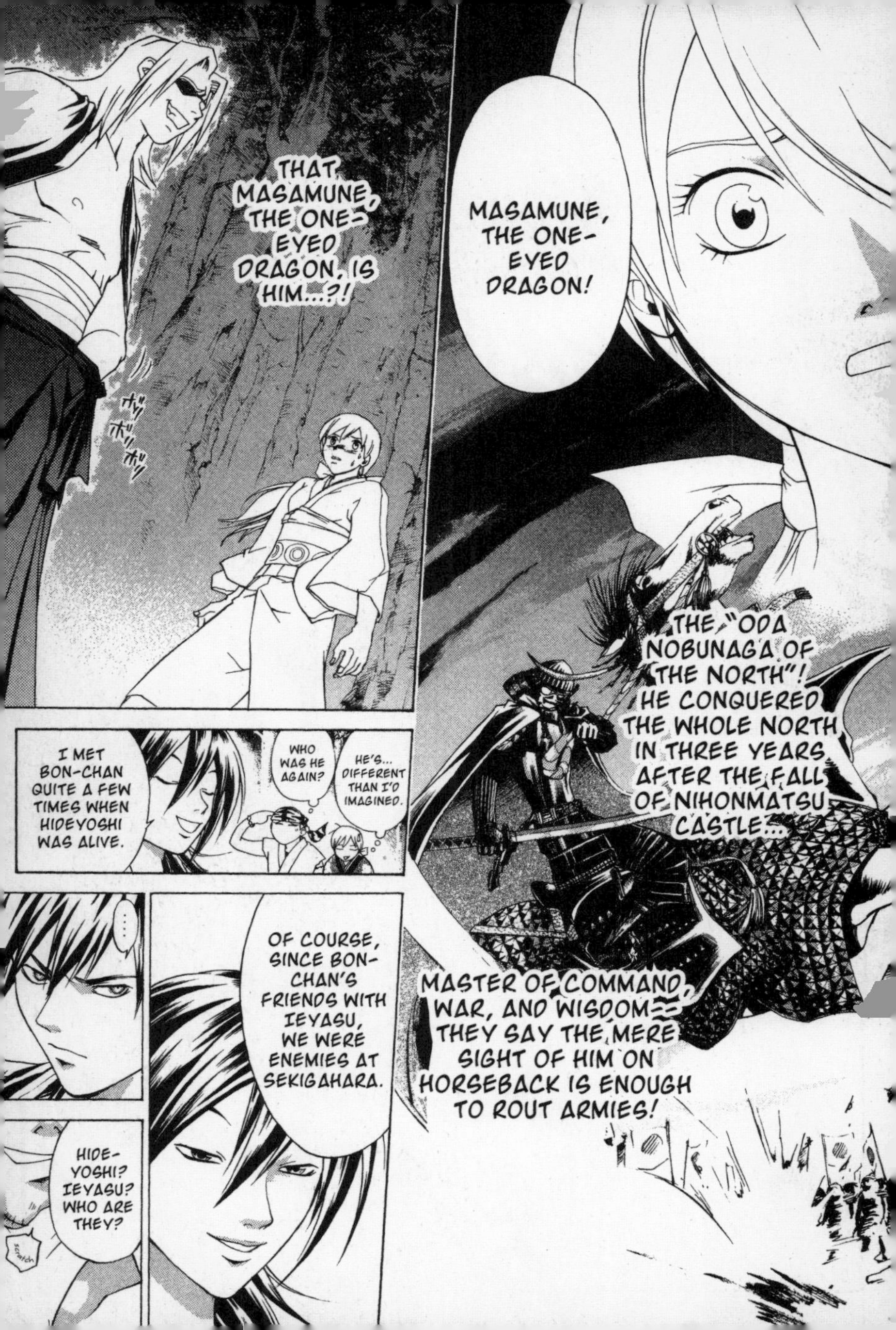

MASAMUNE, THE ONE-EYED DRAGON!
THE "ODA NOBUNAGA OF THE NORTH"! HE CONQUERED THE WHOLE NORTH IN THREE YEARS AFTER THE FALL OF NIHONMATSU CASTLE...
MASTER OF COMMAND, WAR, AND WISDOM-- THEY SAY THE MERE SIGHT OF HIM ON HORSEBACK IS ENOUGH TO ROUT ARMIES!
THAT MASAMUNE, THE ONE-EYED DRAGON, IS HIM...?!
HE'S... DIFFERENT THAN I'D IMAGINED.
WHO WAS HE AGAIN?
I MET BON-CHAN QUITE A FEW TIMES WHEN HIDEYOSHI WAS ALIVE.
OF COURSE, SINCE BON-CHAN'S FRIENDS WITH IEYASU, WE WERE ENEMIES AT SEKIGAHARA.
...
HIDE-YOSHI? IEYASU? WHO ARE THEY?
scratch

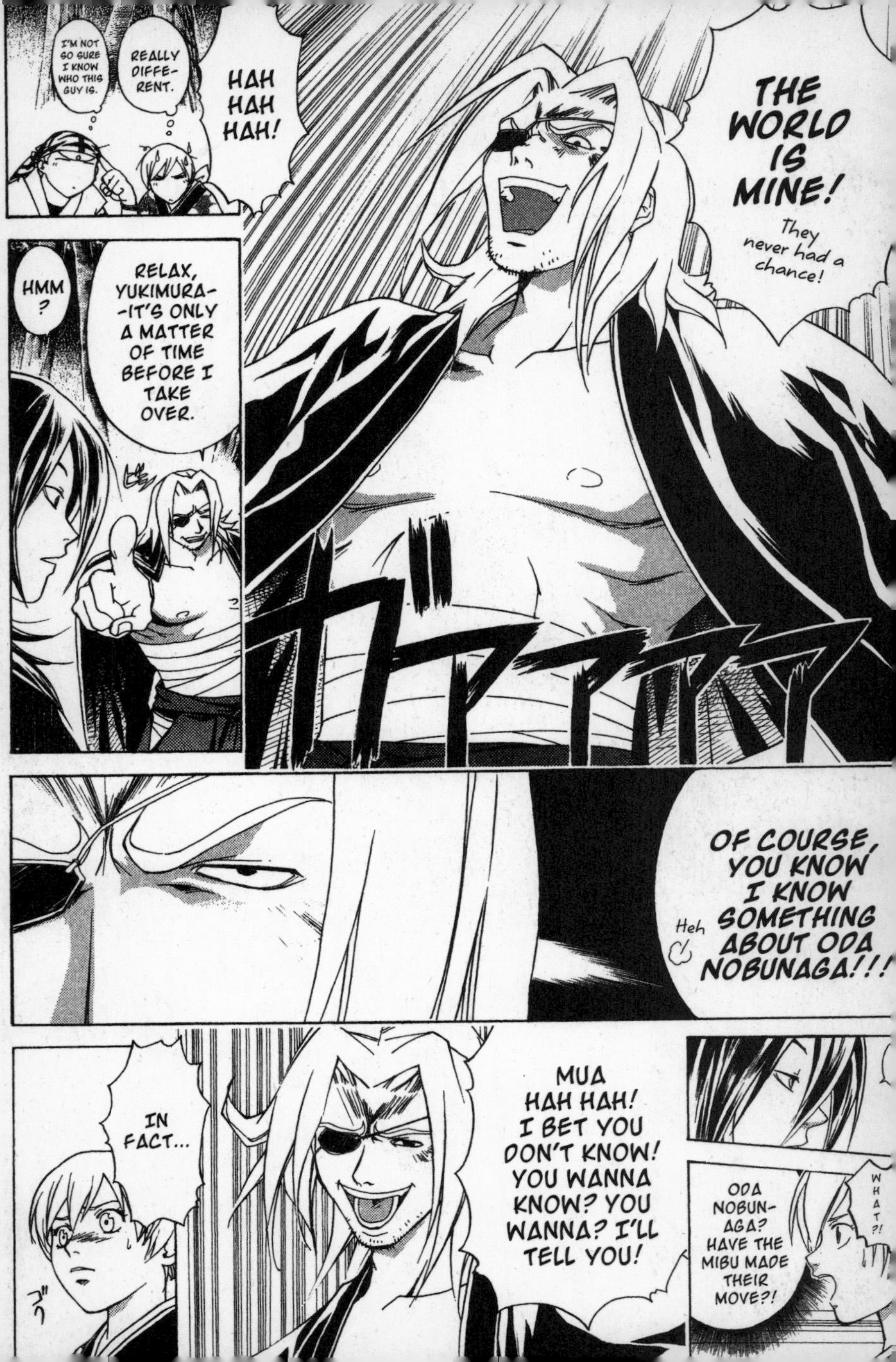
THE WORLD IS MINE!
They never had a chance!
HAH HAH HAH!
REALLY DIFFE-RENT.
I'M NOT SO SURE I KNOW WHO THIS GUY IS.
RELAX, YUKIMURA--IT'S ONLY A MATTER OF TIME BEFORE I TAKE OVER.
HMM?
OF COURSE, YOU KNOW I KNOW SOMETHING ABOUT ODA NOBUNAGA!!!
Heh
WHAT?!
ODA NOBUN-AGA? HAVE THE MIBU MADE THEIR MOVE?!
MUA HAH HAH! I BET YOU DON'T KNOW! YOU WANNA KNOW? YOU WANNA? I'LL TELL YOU!
IN FACT...

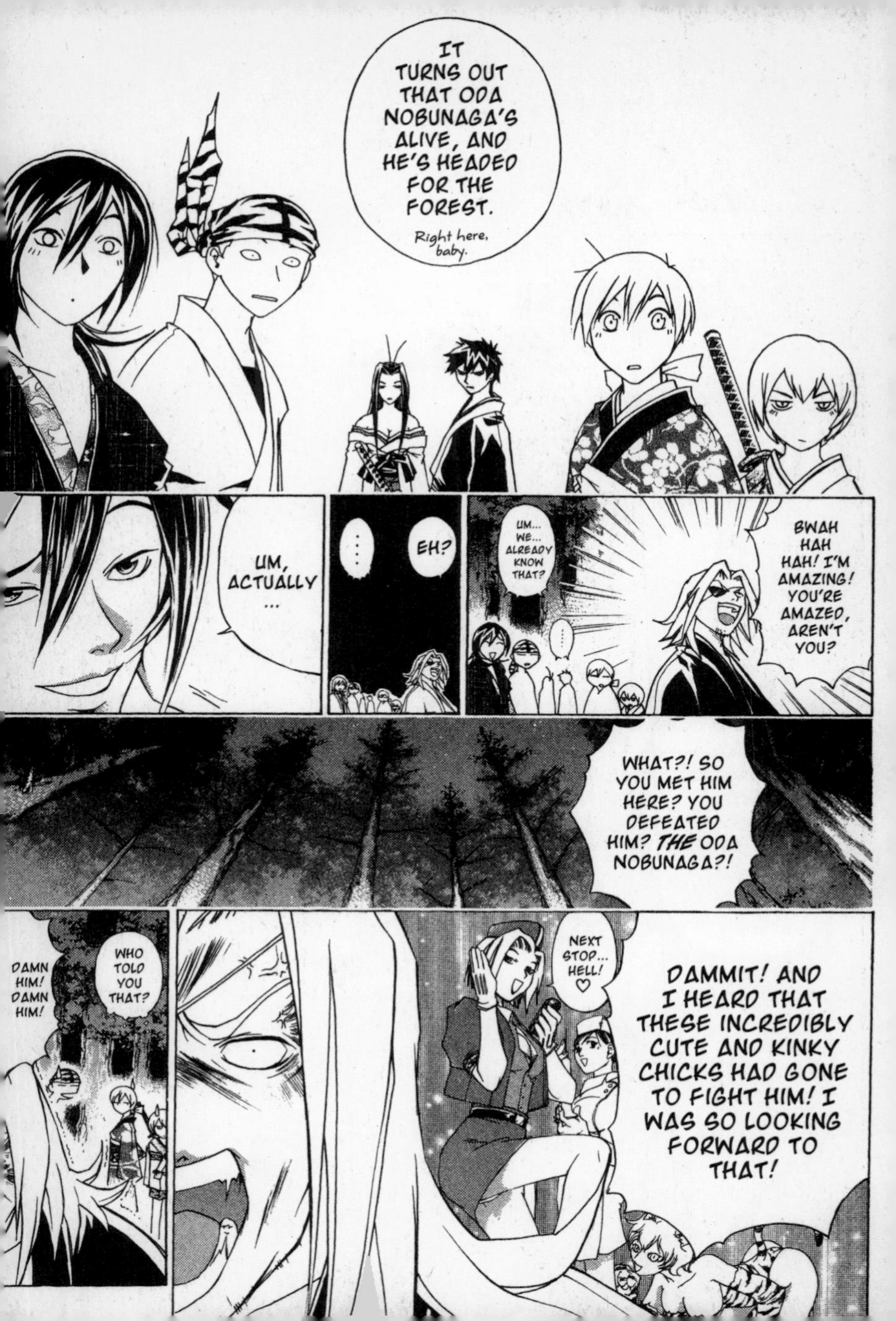
IT TURNS OUT THAT ODA NOBUNAGA'S ALIVE, AND HE'S HEADED FOR THE FOREST.
Right here, baby.
BWAH HAH HAH! I'M AMAZING! YOU'RE AMAZED, AREN'T YOU?
UM... WE... ALREADY KNOW THAT?
...
EH?
....
UM, ACTUALLY ...
WHAT?! SO YOU MET HIM HERE? YOU DEFEATED HIM? THE ODA NOBUNAGA?!
DAMMIT! AND I HEARD THAT THESE INCREDIBLY CUTE AND KINKY CHICKS HAD GONE TO FIGHT HIM! I WAS SO LOOKING FORWARD TO THAT!
NEXT STOP... HELL! ♡
WHO TOLD YOU THAT?
DAMN HIM! DAMN HIM!

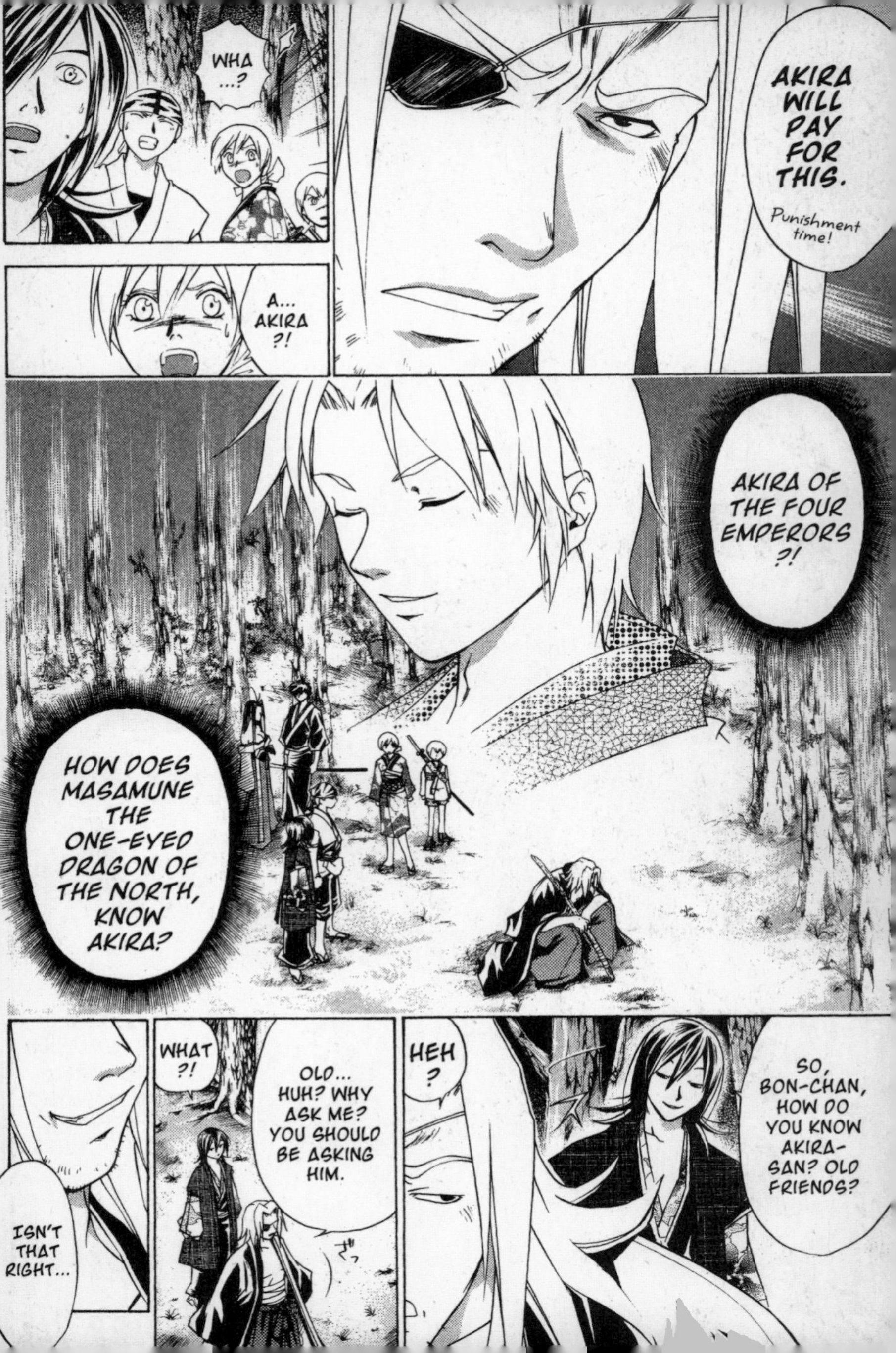
AKIRA WILL PAY FOR THIS.
Punishment time!
WHA ...?
A... AKIRA ?!
AKIRA OF THE FOUR EMPERORS ?!
HOW DOES MASAMUNE THE ONE-EYED DRAGON OF THE NORTH, KNOW AKIRA?
SO, BON-CHAN, HOW DO YOU KNOW AKIRA-SAN? OLD FRIENDS?
HEH ?
WHAT ?!
OLD... HUH? WHY ASK ME? YOU SHOULD BE ASKING HIM.
ざっ
ISN'T THAT RIGHT...

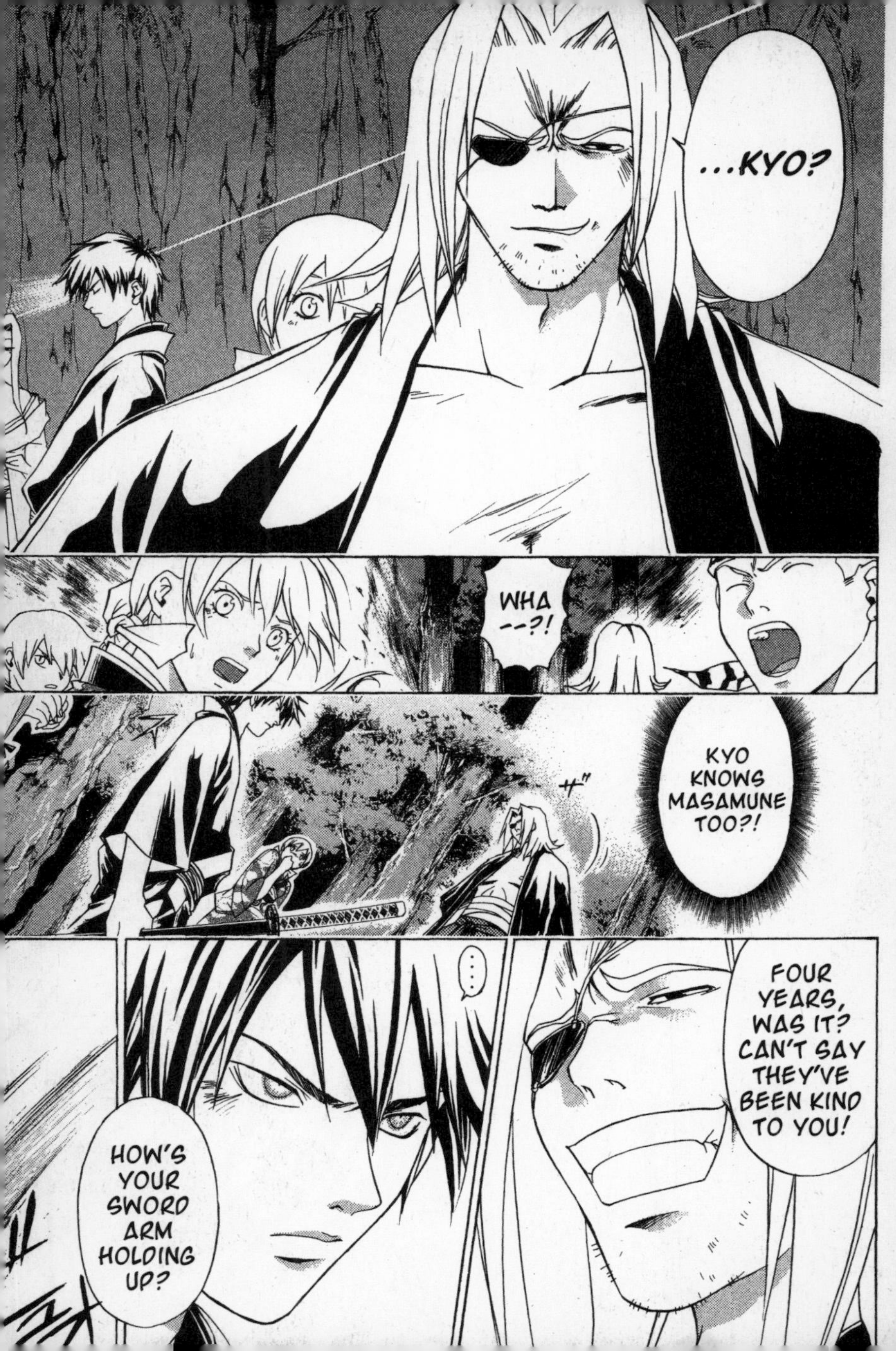
...KYO?
WHA--?!
KYO KNOWS MASAMUNE TOO?!
FOUR YEARS, WAS IT? CAN'T SAY THEY'VE BEEN KIND TO YOU!
...
HOW'S YOUR SWORD ARM HOLDING UP?

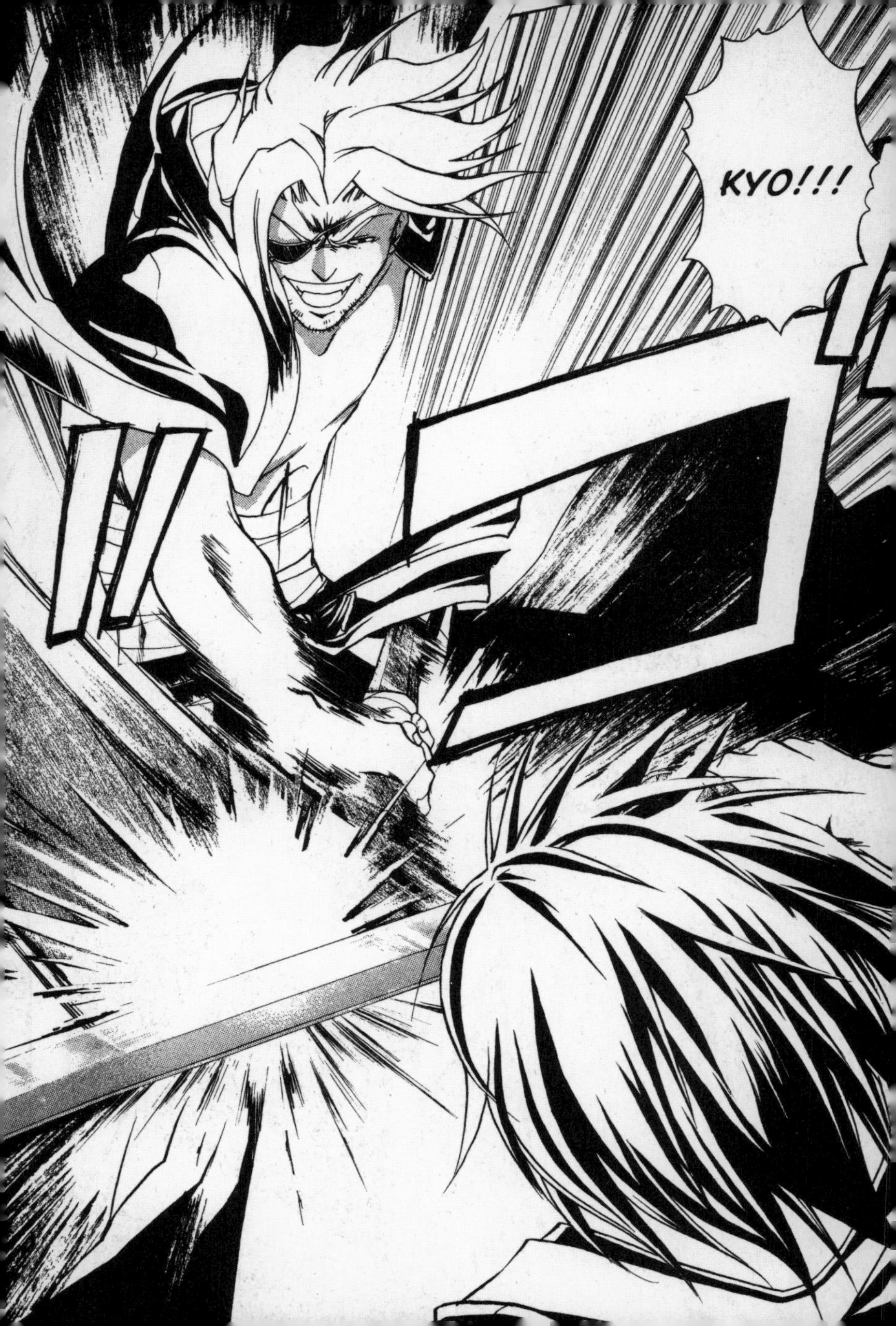
KYO!!!

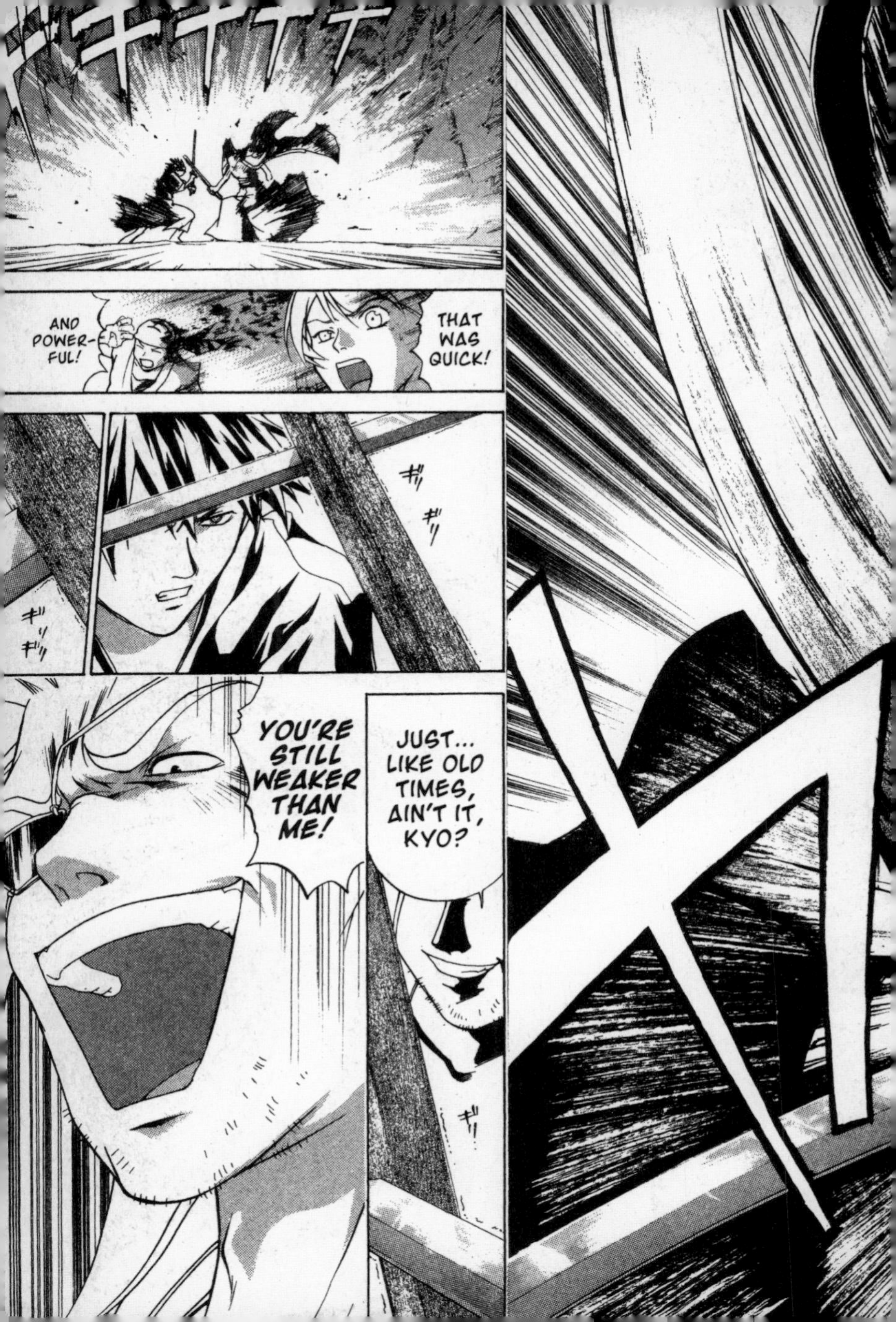
THAT WAS QUICK!
AND POWER-FUL!
ギリ
ギリ
ギリギリ
JUST... LIKE OLD TIMES, AIN'T IT, KYO?
YOU'RE STILL WEAKER THAN ME!
ギリ

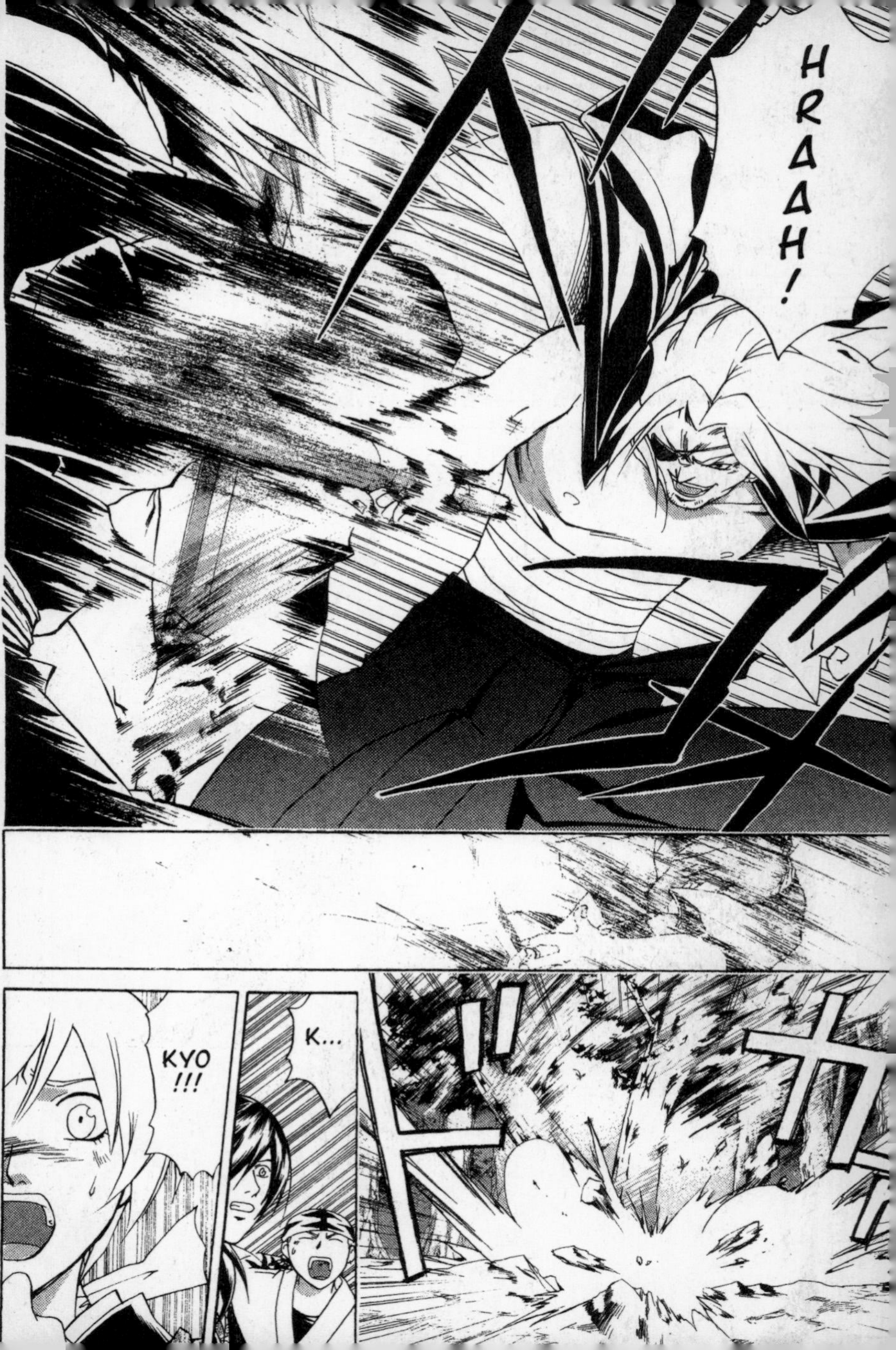
HRAAH!
K...
KYO !!!

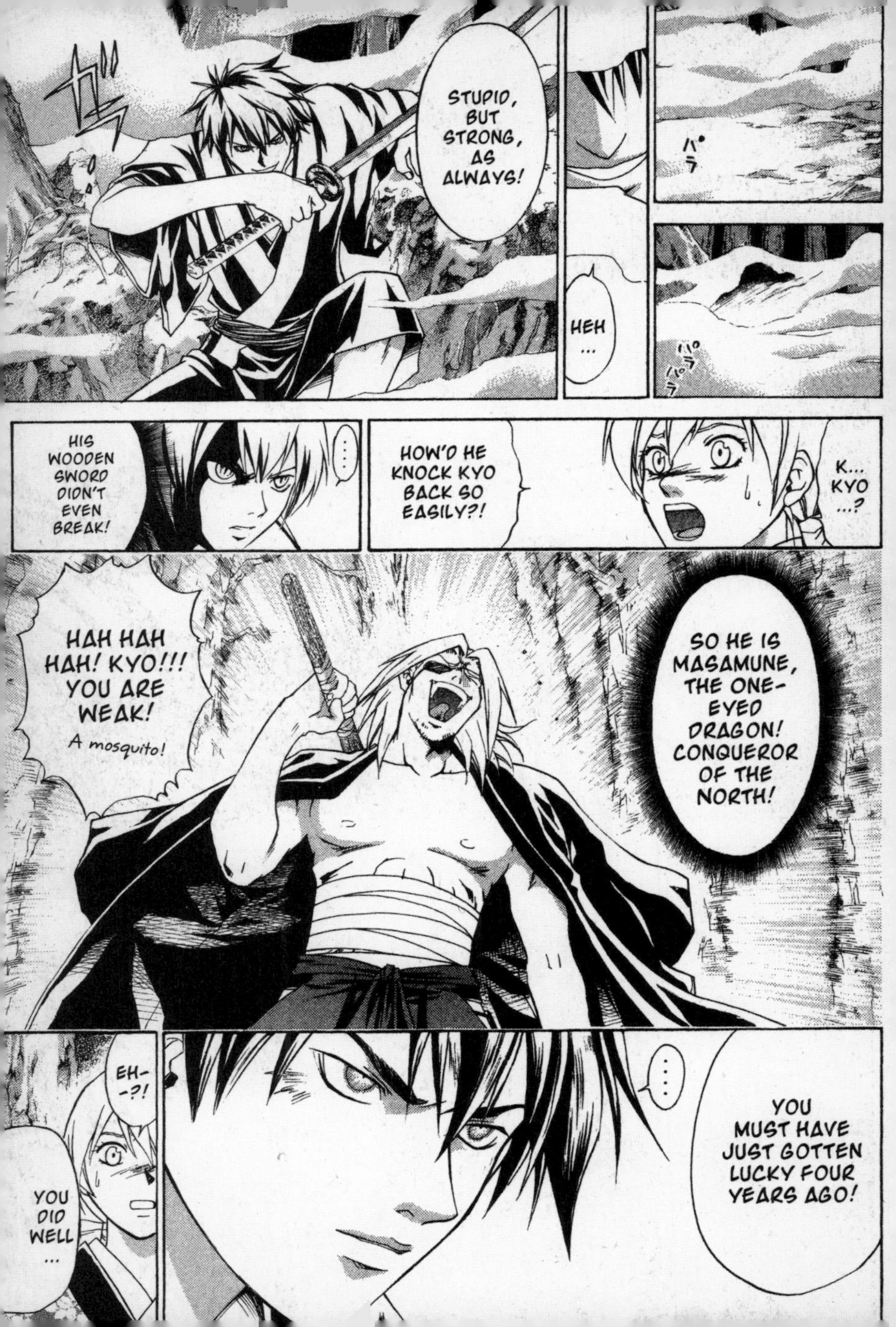
パラ
パラパラ
HEH ...
STUPID, BUT STRONG, AS ALWAYS!
K... KYO ...?
HOW'D HE KNOCK KYO BACK SO EASILY?!
....
HIS WOODEN SWORD DIDN'T EVEN BREAK!
SO HE IS MASAMUNE, THE ONE-EYED DRAGON! CONQUEROR OF THE NORTH!
HAH HAH HAH! KYO!!! YOU ARE WEAK!
A mosquito!
YOU MUST HAVE JUST GOTTEN LUCKY FOUR YEARS AGO!
....
EH--?!
YOU DID WELL ...

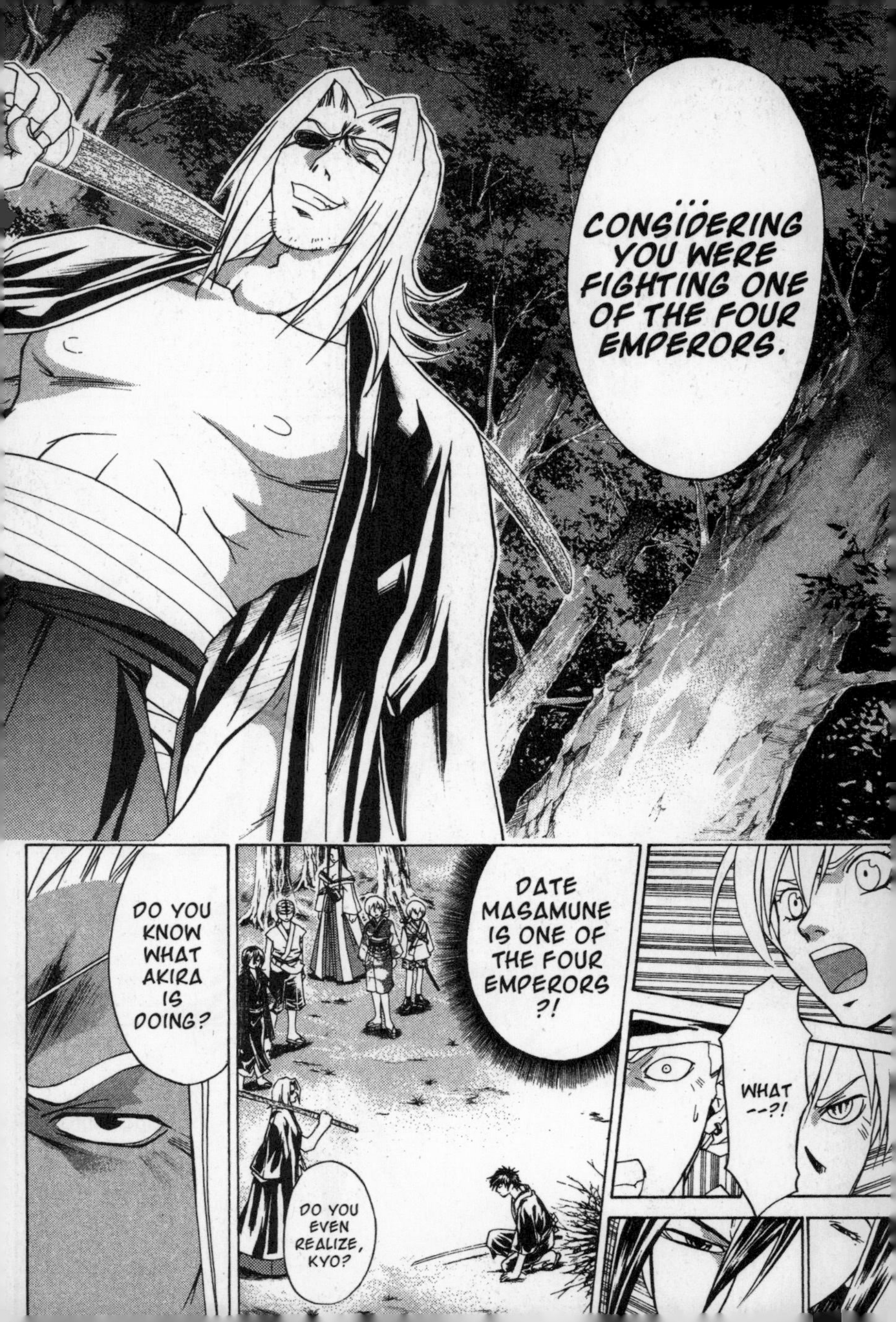
...CONSIDERING YOU WERE FIGHTING ONE OF THE FOUR EMPERORS.
WHAT --?!
DATE MASAMUNE IS ONE OF THE FOUR EMPERORS ?!
DO YOU EVEN REALIZE, KYO?
DO YOU KNOW WHAT AKIRA IS DOING?

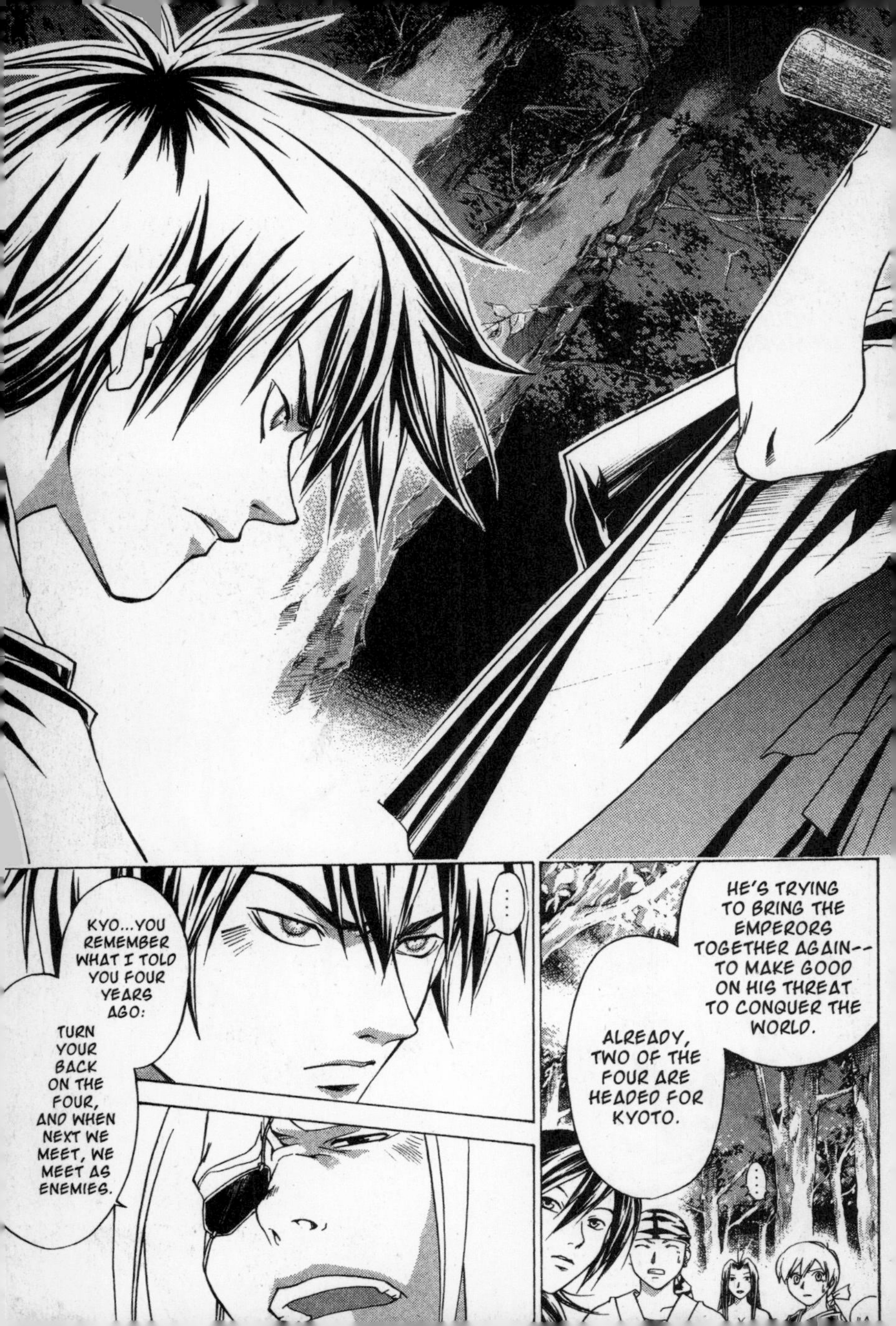
HE'S TRYING TO BRING THE EMPERORS TOGETHER AGAIN--TO MAKE GOOD ON HIS THREAT TO CONQUER THE WORLD.
ALREADY, TWO OF THE FOUR ARE HEADED FOR KYOTO.
...
...
KYO...YOU REMEMBER WHAT I TOLD YOU FOUR YEARS AGO:
TURN YOUR BACK ON THE FOUR, AND WHEN NEXT WE MEET, WE MEET AS ENEMIES.

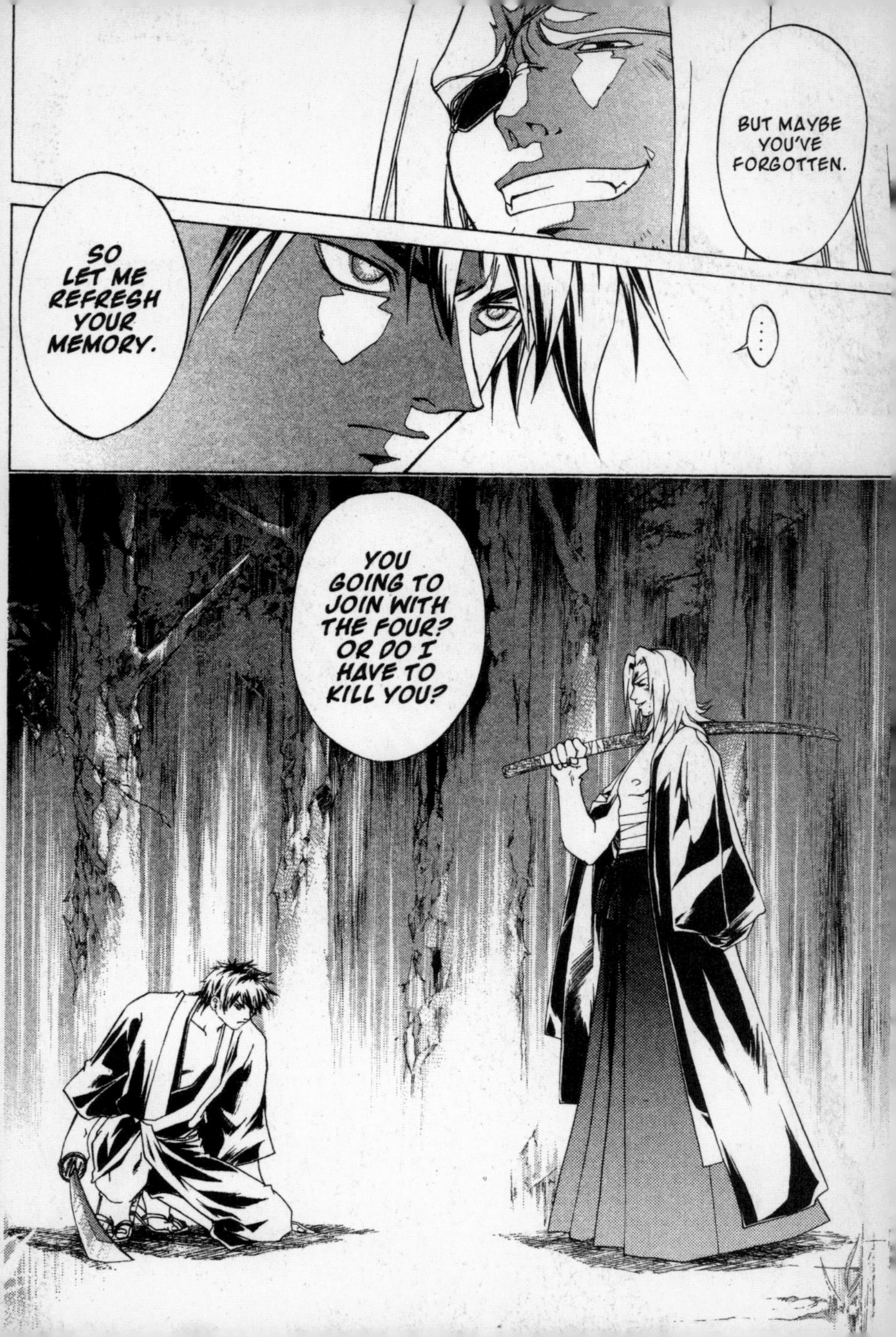
BUT MAYBE YOU'VE FORGOTTEN.
SO LET ME REFRESH YOUR MEMORY.
...
YOU GOING TO JOIN WITH THE FOUR? OR DO I HAVE TO KILL YOU?

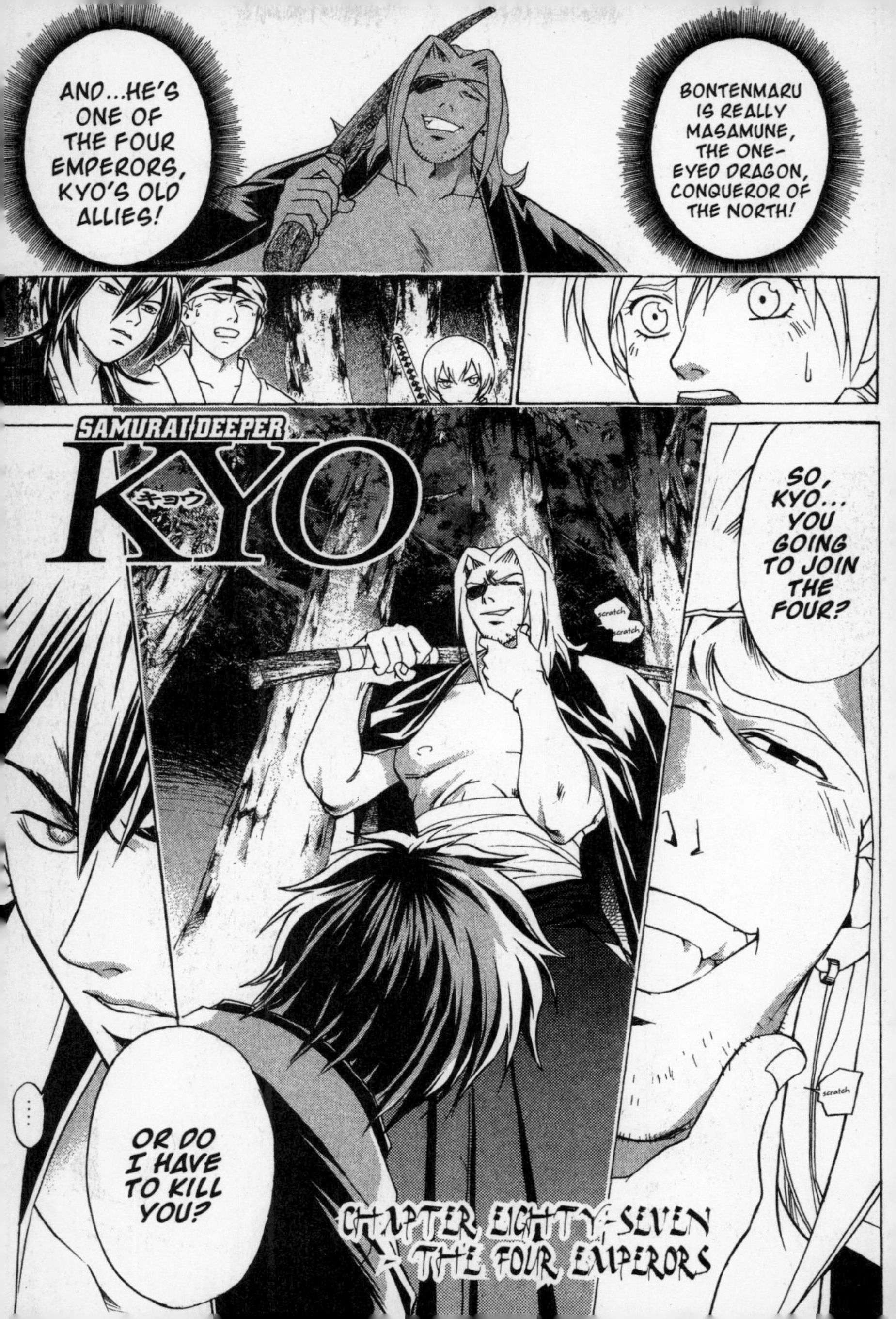
BONTENMARU IS REALLY MASAMUNE, THE ONE-EYED DRAGON, CONQUEROR OF THE NORTH!
AND...HE'S ONE OF THE FOUR EMPERORS, KYO'S OLD ALLIES!
SAMURAI DEEPER KYO キョウ
SO, KYO... YOU GOING TO JOIN THE FOUR?
scratch scratch
scratch
...
OR DO I HAVE TO KILL YOU?
CHAPTER EIGHTY-SEVEN - THE FOUR EMPERORS

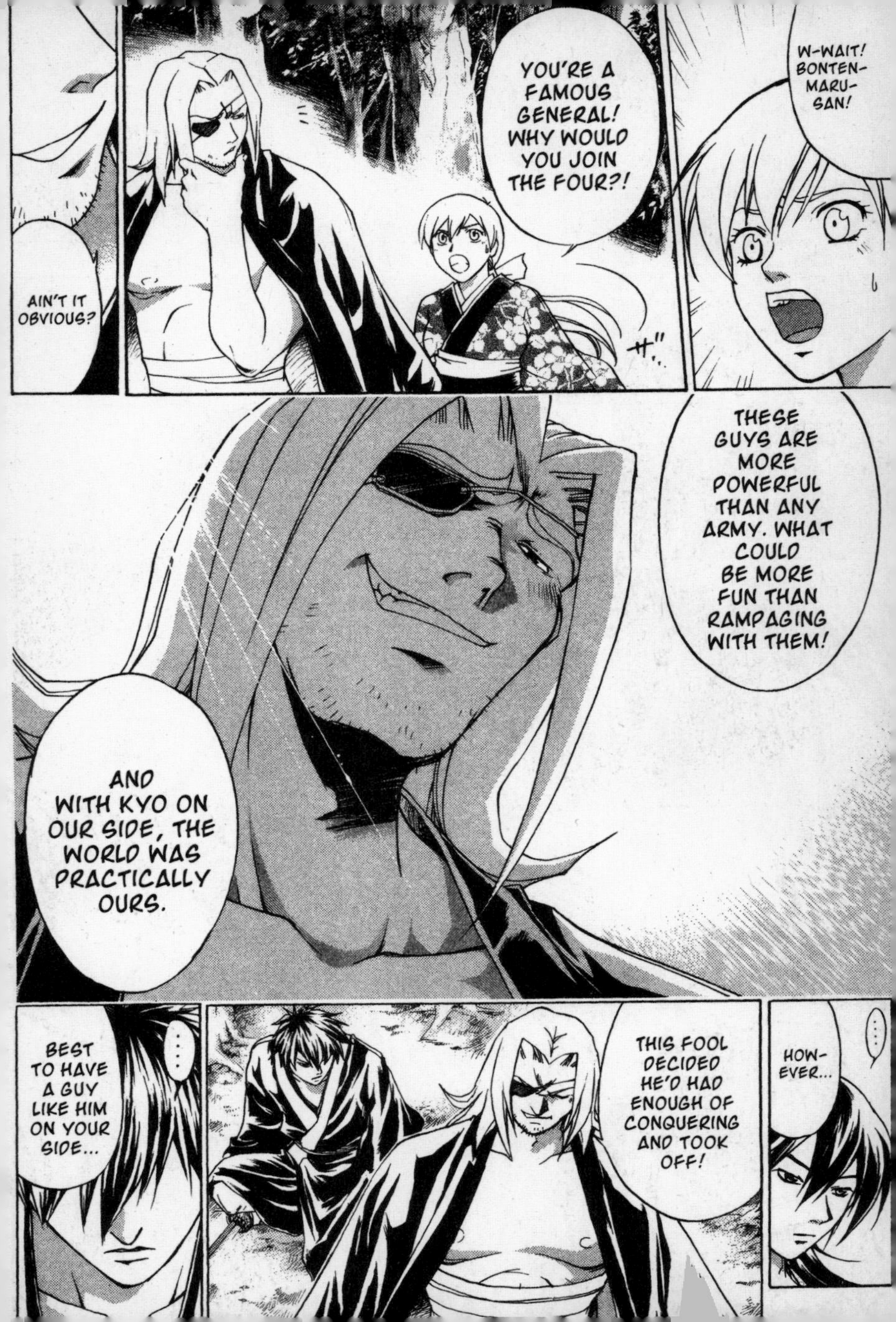
W-WAIT! BONTEN-MARU-SAN!
YOU'RE A FAMOUS GENERAL! WHY WOULD YOU JOIN THE FOUR?!
AIN'T IT OBVIOUS?
THESE GUYS ARE MORE POWERFUL THAN ANY ARMY. WHAT COULD BE MORE FUN THAN RAMPAGING WITH THEM!
AND WITH KYO ON OUR SIDE, THE WORLD WAS PRACTICALLY OURS.
....
HOW-EVER...
THIS FOOL DECIDED HE'D HAD ENOUGH OF CONQUERING AND TOOK OFF!
....
BEST TO HAVE A GUY LIKE HIM ON YOUR SIDE...

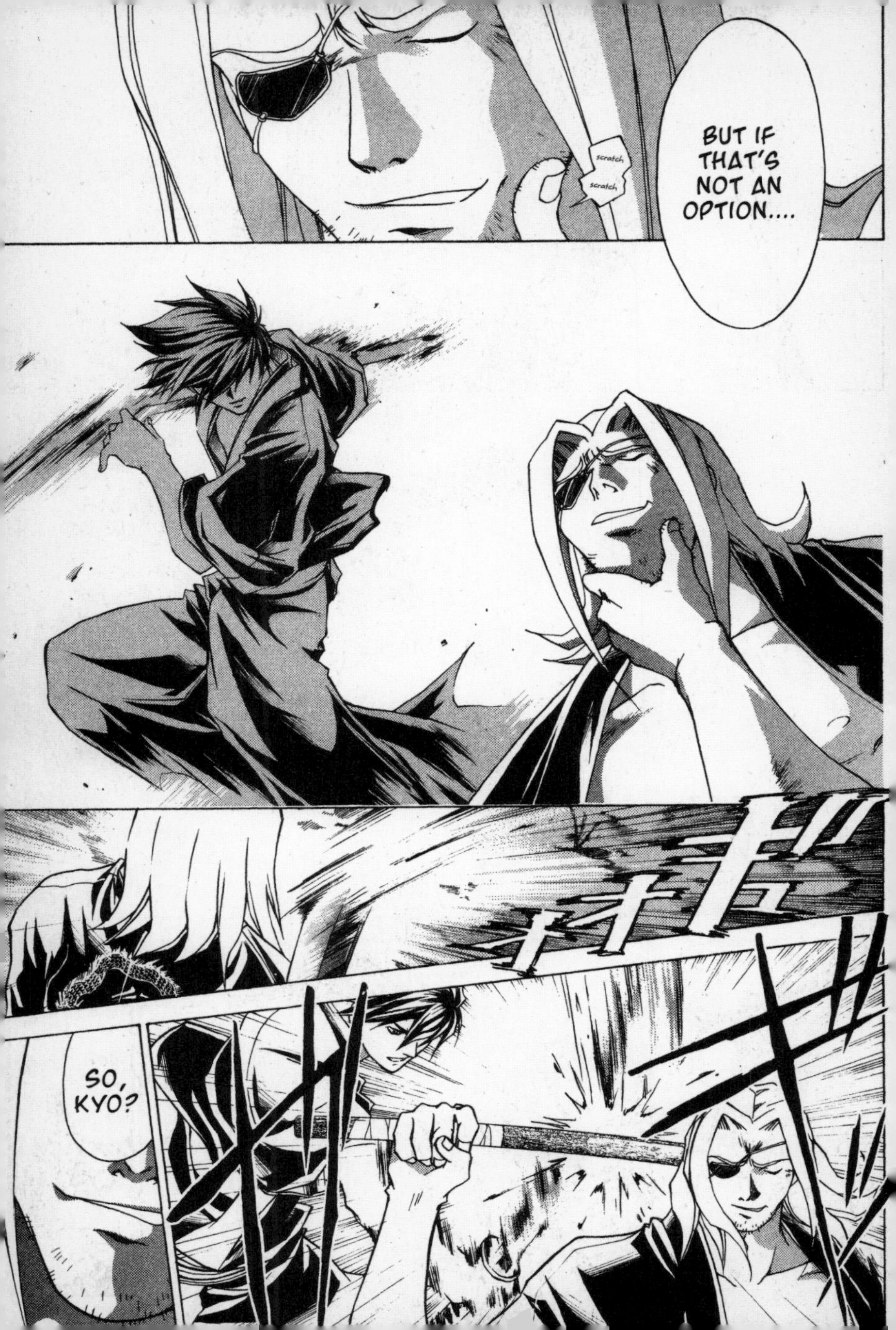
BUT IF THAT'S NOT AN OPTION....
scratch
scratch
SO, KYO?

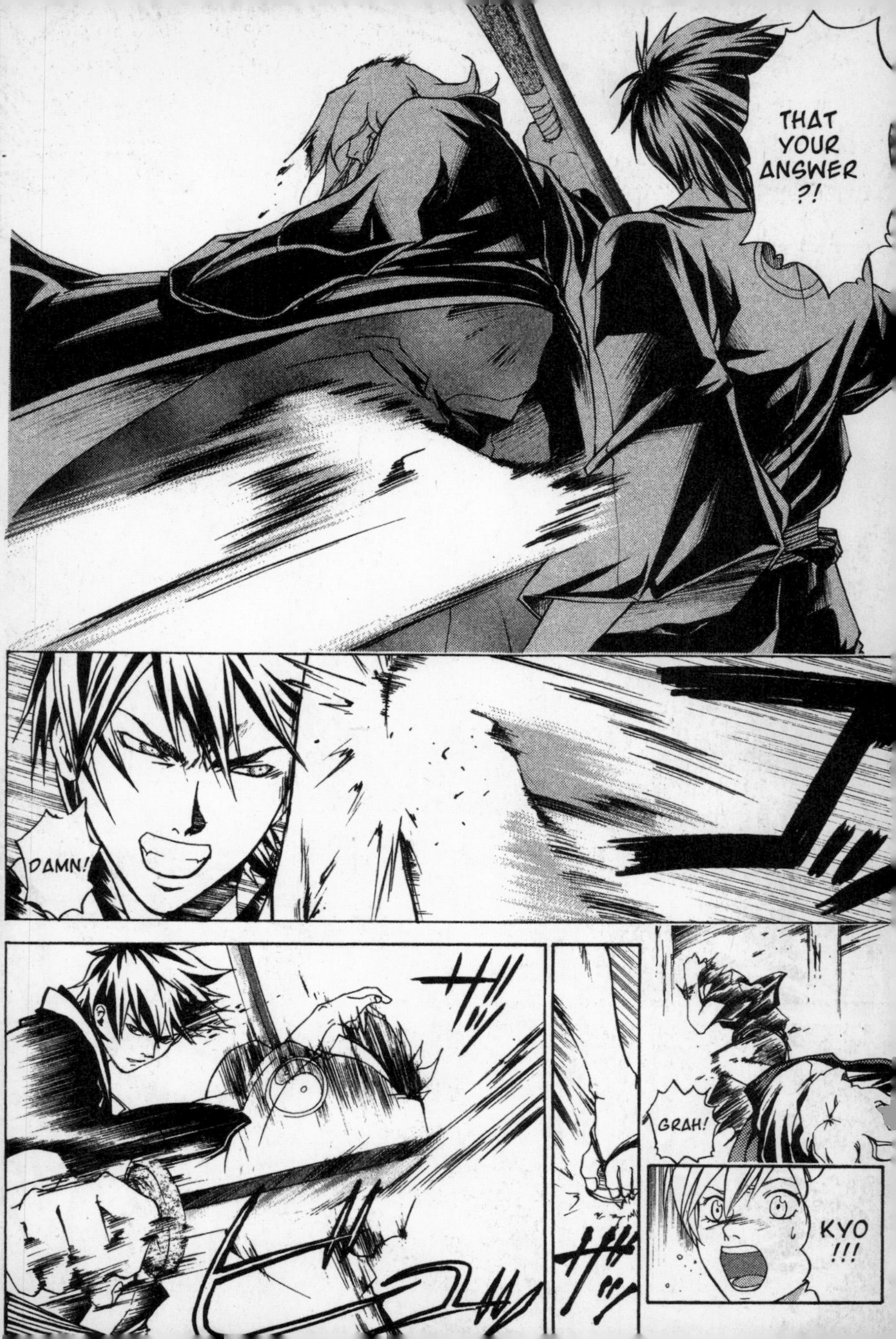

THAT YOUR ANSWER ?!
DAMN!
GRAH!
KYO !!!

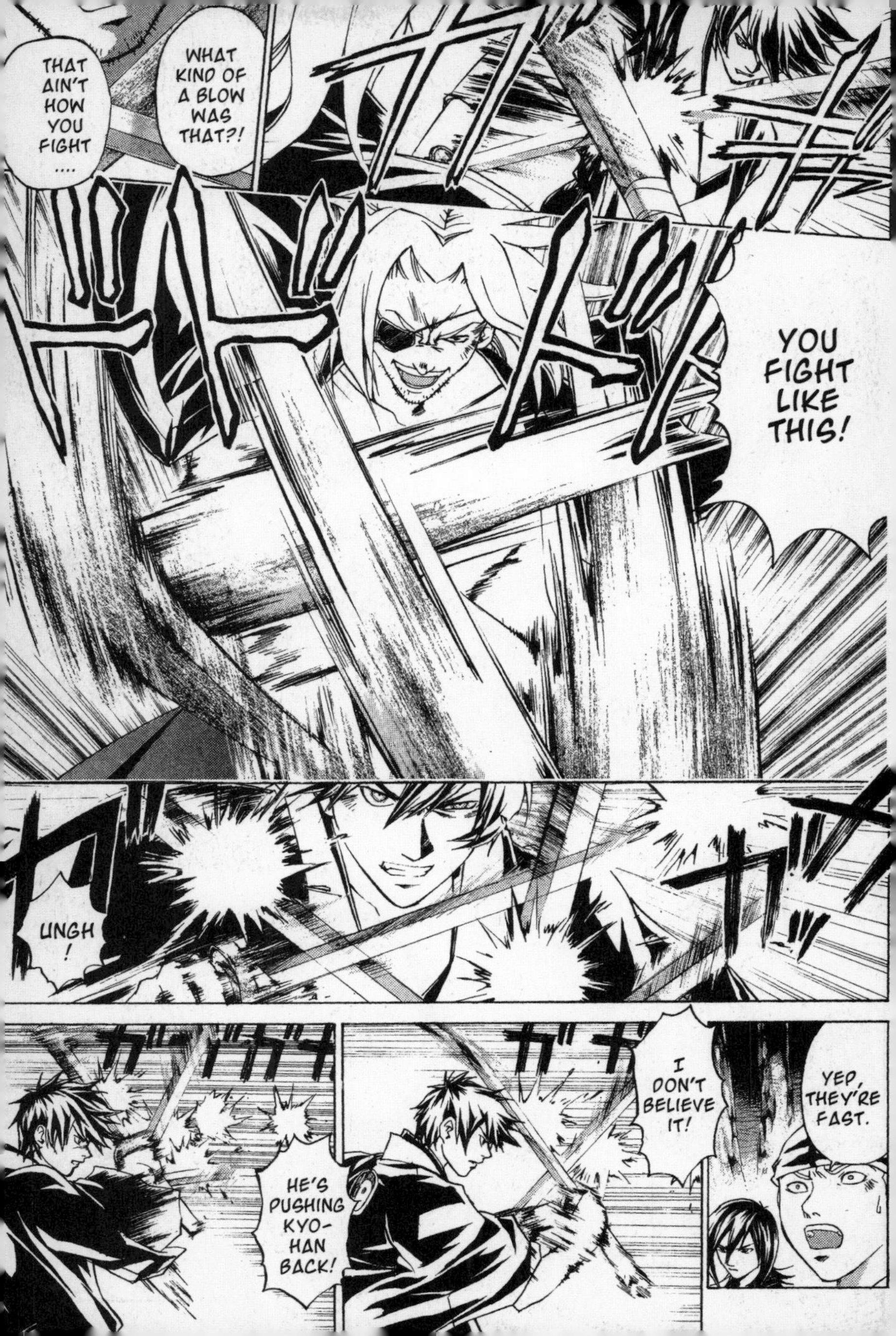
WHAT KIND OF A BLOW WAS THAT?!
THAT AIN'T HOW YOU FIGHT ....
YOU FIGHT LIKE THIS!
UNGH!
YEP, THEY'RE FAST.
I DON'T BELIEVE IT!
HE'S PUSHING KYO-HAN BACK!

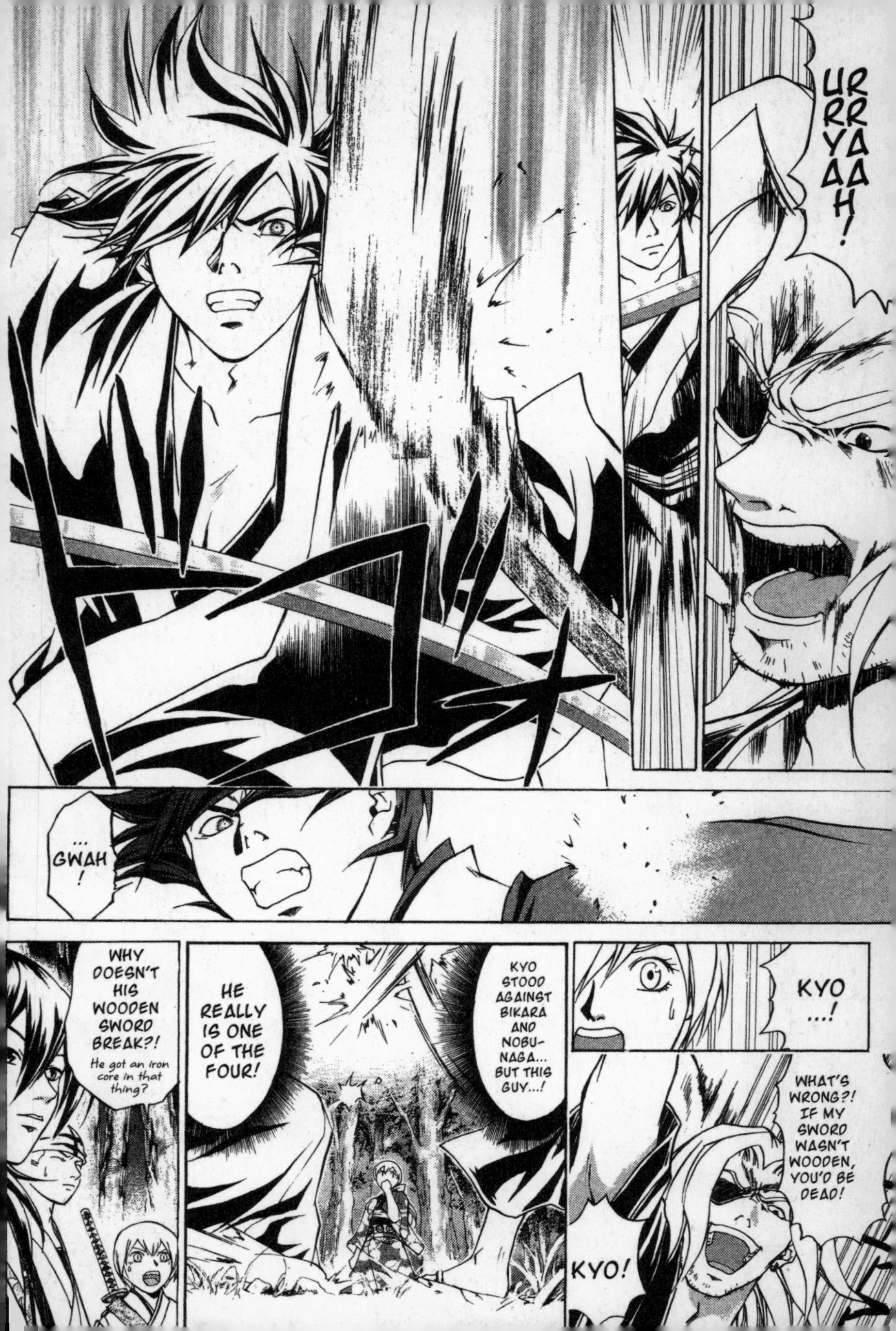
URRYAAAH!
...GWAH!
KYO...!
WHAT'S WRONG?! IF MY SWORD WASN'T WOODEN, YOU'D BE DEAD!
KYO!
KYO STOOD AGAINST BIKARA AND NOBUNAGA... BUT THIS GUY...!
HE REALLY IS ONE OF THE FOUR!
WHY DOESN'T HIS WOODEN SWORD BREAK?!
He got an iron core in that thing?

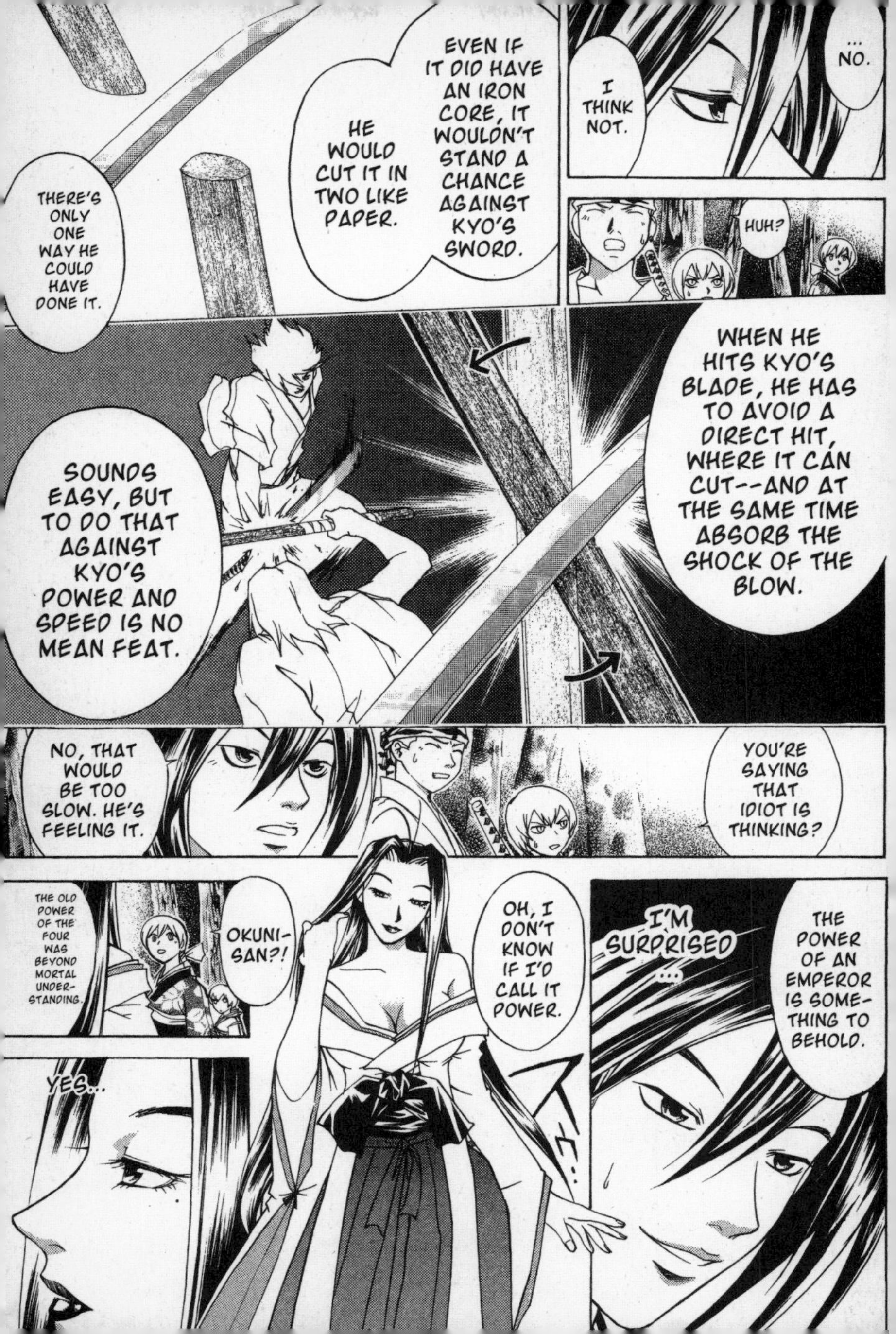
... NO.
I THINK NOT.
HUH?
EVEN IF IT DID HAVE AN IRON CORE, IT WOULDN'T STAND A CHANCE AGAINST KYO'S SWORD.
HE WOULD CUT IT IN TWO LIKE PAPER.
THERE'S ONLY ONE WAY HE COULD HAVE DONE IT.
WHEN HE HITS KYO'S BLADE, HE HAS TO AVOID A DIRECT HIT, WHERE IT CAN CUT--AND AT THE SAME TIME ABSORB THE SHOCK OF THE BLOW.
SOUNDS EASY, BUT TO DO THAT AGAINST KYO'S POWER AND SPEED IS NO MEAN FEAT.
YOU'RE SAYING THAT IDIOT IS THINKING?
NO, THAT WOULD BE TOO SLOW. HE'S FEELING IT.
THE POWER OF AN EMPEROR IS SOMETHING TO BEHOLD.
I'M SURPRISED...
OH, I DON'T KNOW IF I'D CALL IT POWER.
OKUNI-SAN?!
THE OLD POWER OF THE FOUR WAS BEYOND MORTAL UNDERSTANDING.
YES...

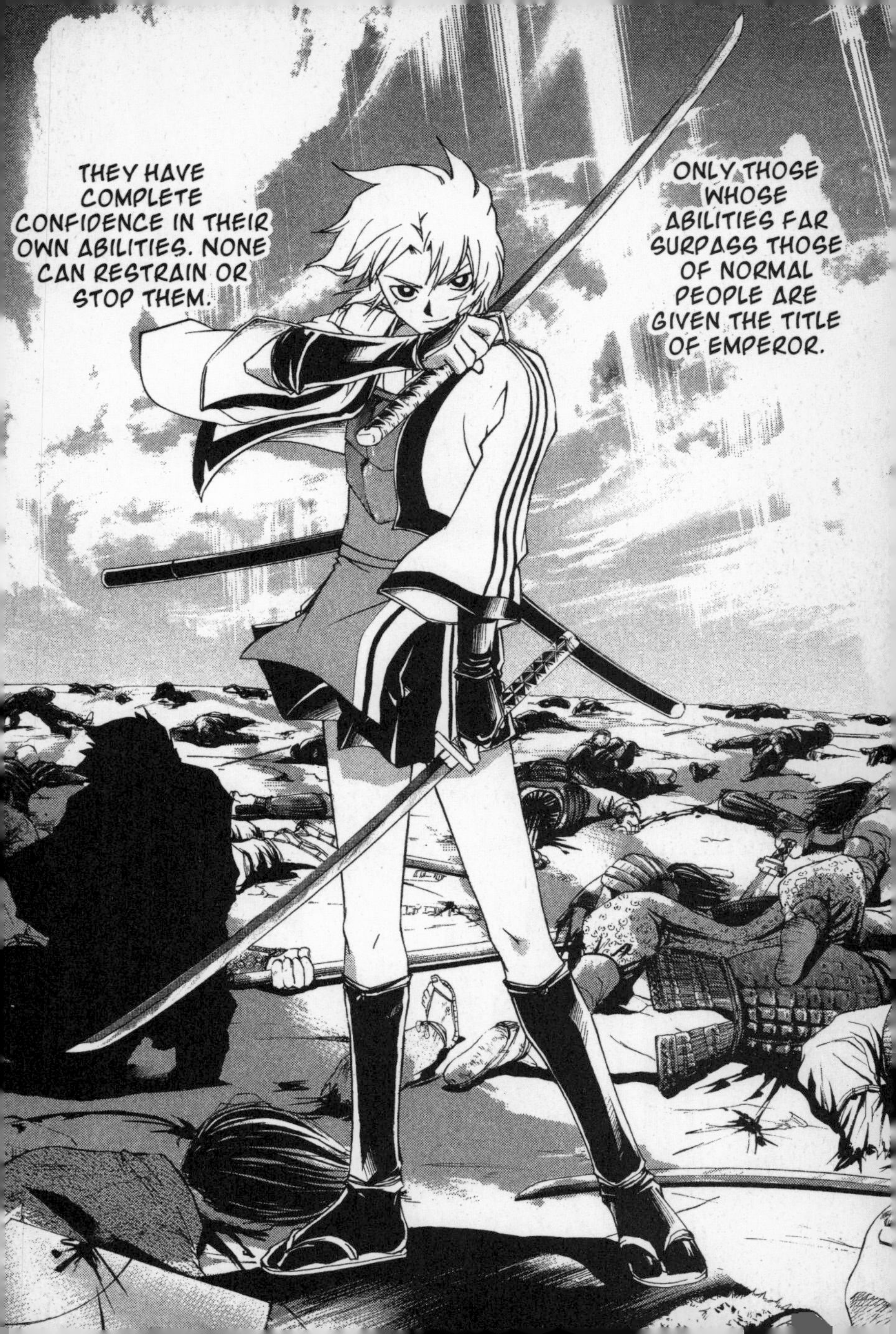
ONLY THOSE WHOSE ABILITIES FAR SURPASS THOSE OF NORMAL PEOPLE ARE GIVEN THE TITLE OF EMPEROR.
THEY HAVE COMPLETE CONFIDENCE IN THEIR OWN ABILITIES. NONE CAN RESTRAIN OR STOP THEM.

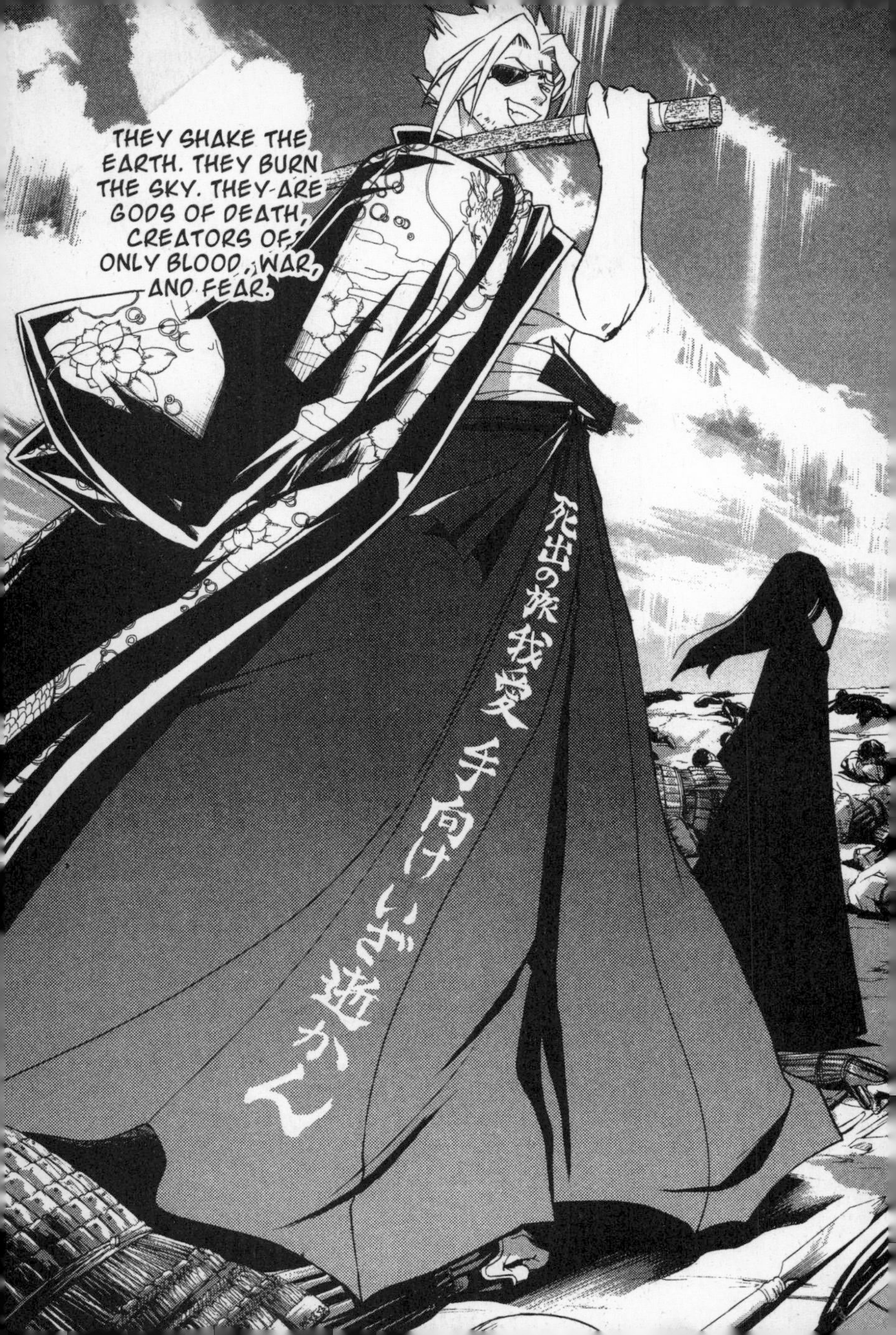
THEY SHAKE THE EARTH. THEY BURN THE SKY. THEY ARE GODS OF DEATH, CREATORS OF ONLY BLOOD, WAR, AND FEAR.
死出の旅 我愛
手向け いざ逝かん

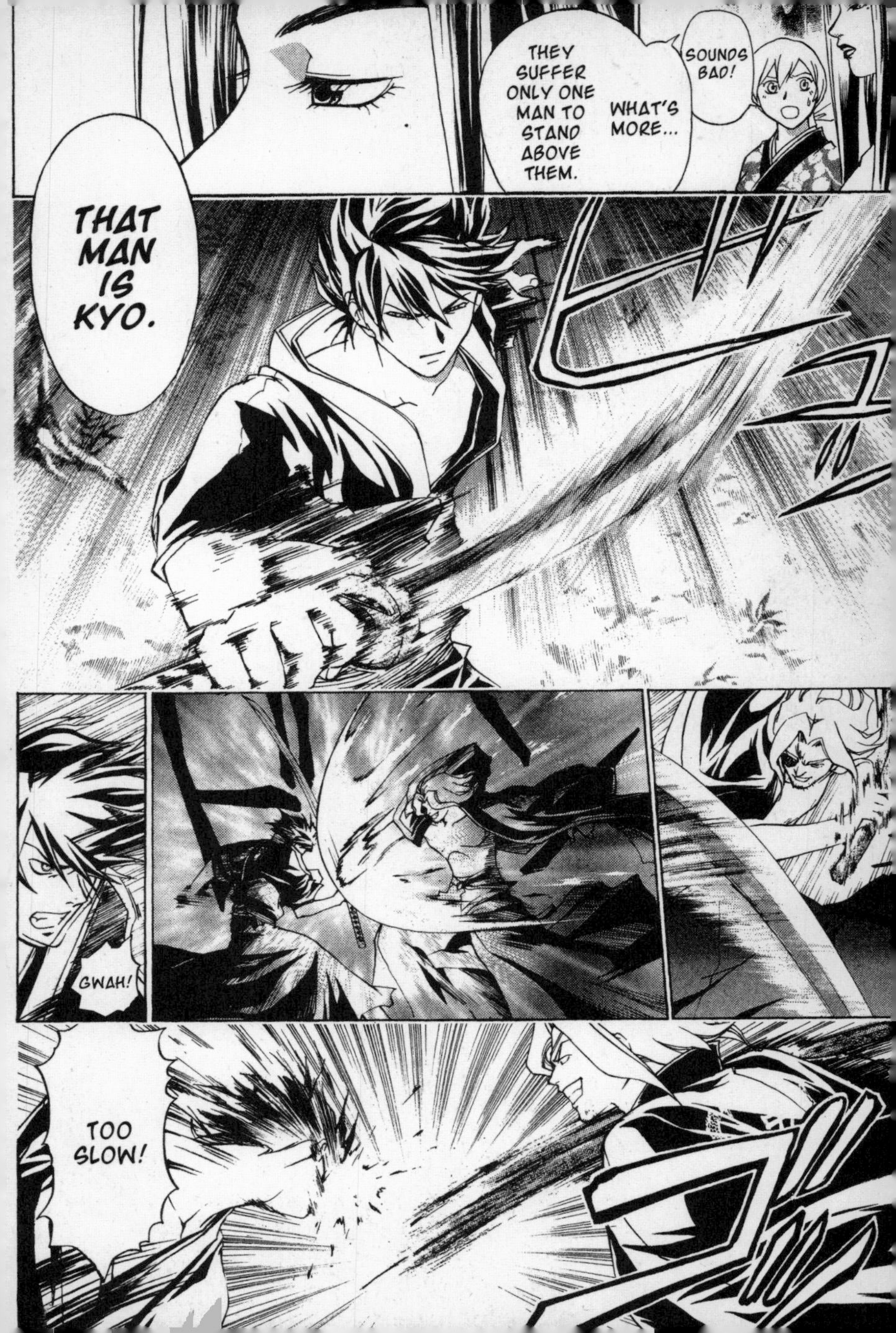
SOUNDS BAD!
WHAT'S MORE...
THEY SUFFER ONLY ONE MAN TO STAND ABOVE THEM.
THAT MAN IS KYO.
GWAH!
TOO SLOW!

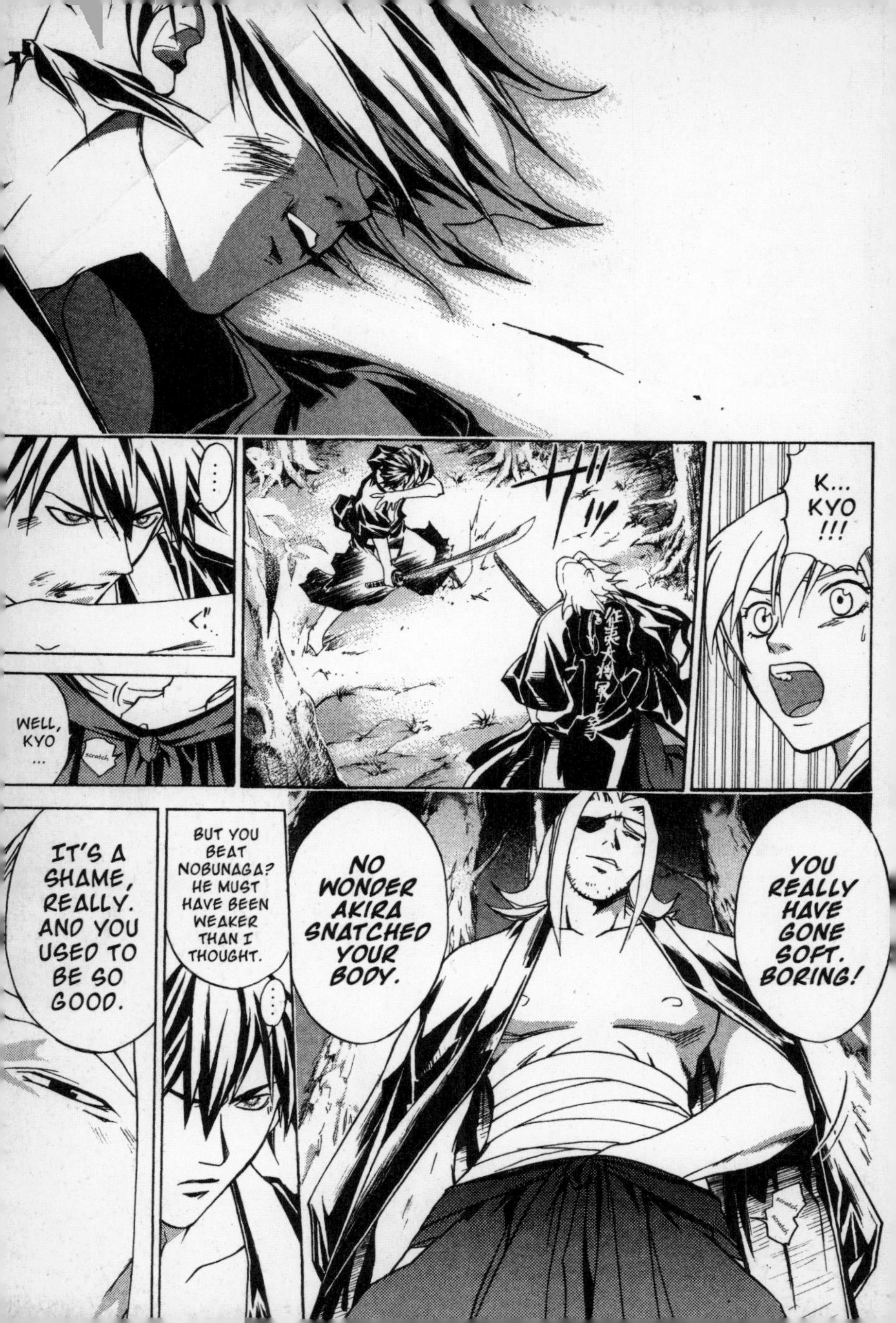
K... KYO !!!
....
WELL, KYO ...
scratch
YOU REALLY HAVE GONE SOFT. BORING!
NO WONDER AKIRA SNATCHED YOUR BODY.
BUT YOU BEAT NOBUNAGA? HE MUST HAVE BEEN WEAKER THAN I THOUGHT.
IT'S A SHAME, REALLY. AND YOU USED TO BE SO GOOD.
....
scratch scratch

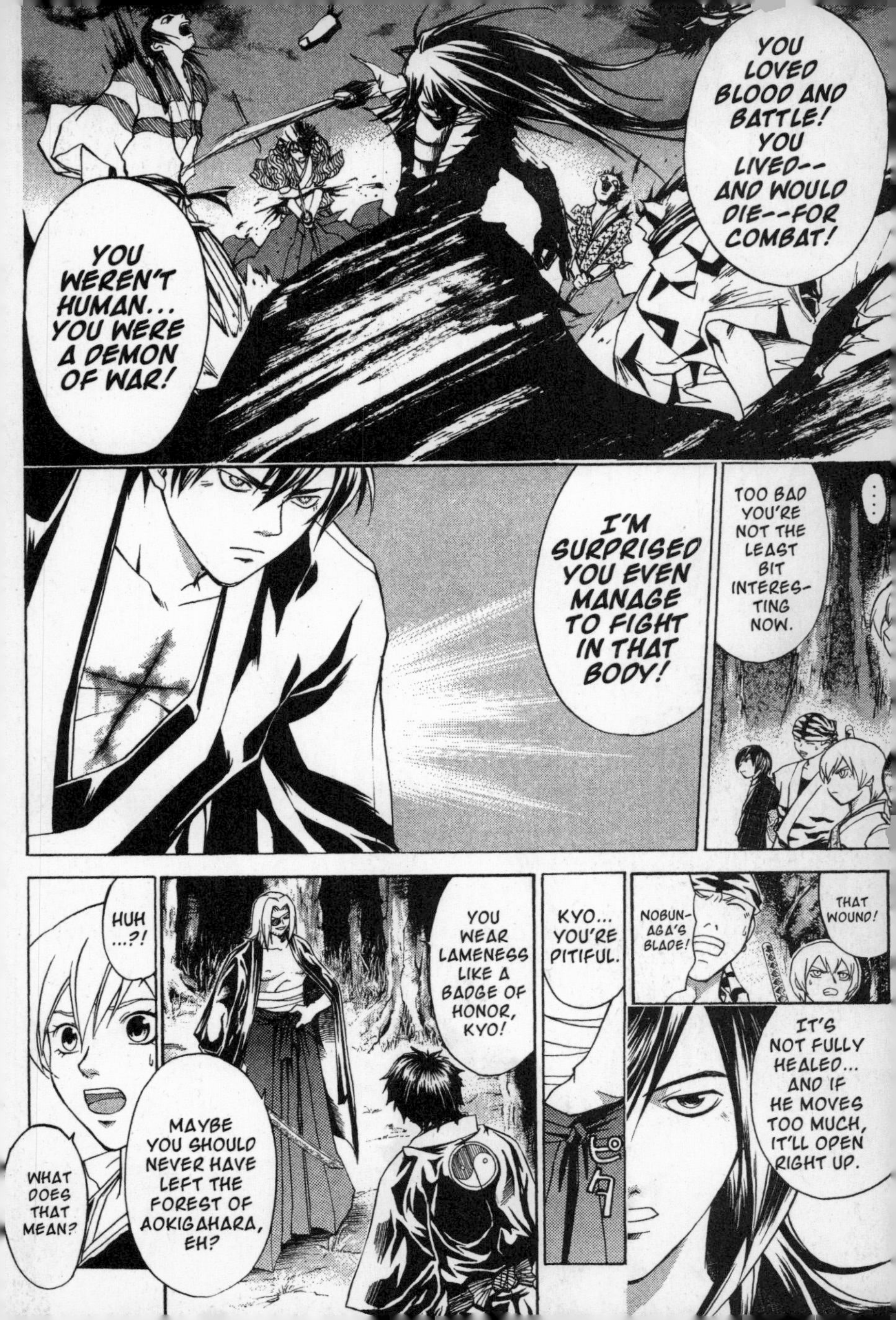
YOU LOVED BLOOD AND BATTLE! YOU LIVED--AND WOULD DIE--FOR COMBAT!
YOU WEREN'T HUMAN... YOU WERE A DEMON OF WAR!
...
TOO BAD YOU'RE NOT THE LEAST BIT INTERES-TING NOW.
I'M SURPRISED YOU EVEN MANAGE TO FIGHT IN THAT BODY!
THAT WOUND!
NOBUN-AGA'S BLADE!
IT'S NOT FULLY HEALED... AND IF HE MOVES TOO MUCH, IT'LL OPEN RIGHT UP.
KYO... YOU'RE PITIFUL.
YOU WEAR LAMENESS LIKE A BADGE OF HONOR, KYO!
MAYBE YOU SHOULD NEVER HAVE LEFT THE FOREST OF AOKIGAHARA, EH?
HUH ...?!
WHAT DOES THAT MEAN?

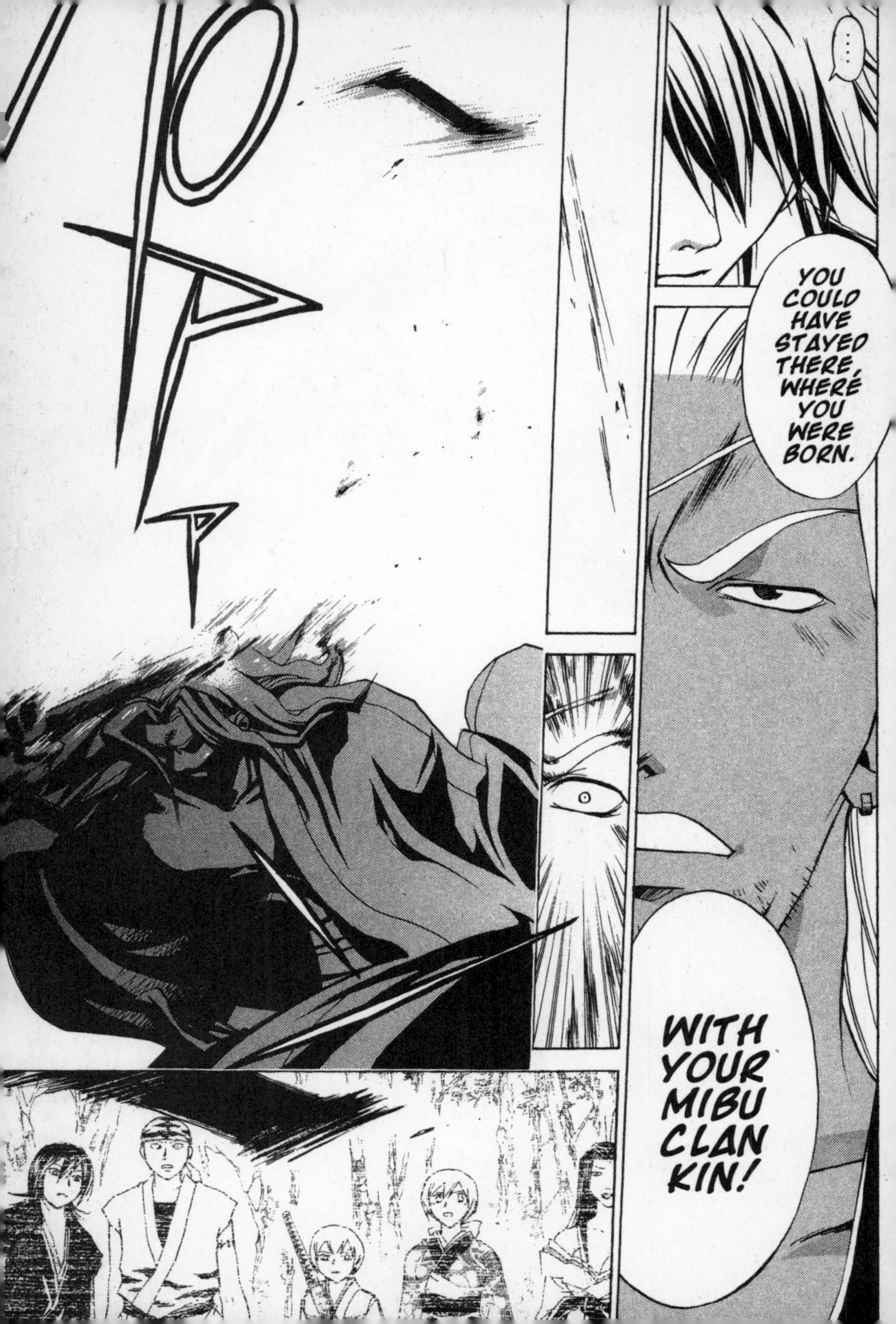
....
YOU COULD HAVE STAYED THERE, WHERE YOU WERE BORN.
WITH YOUR MIBU CLAN KIN!

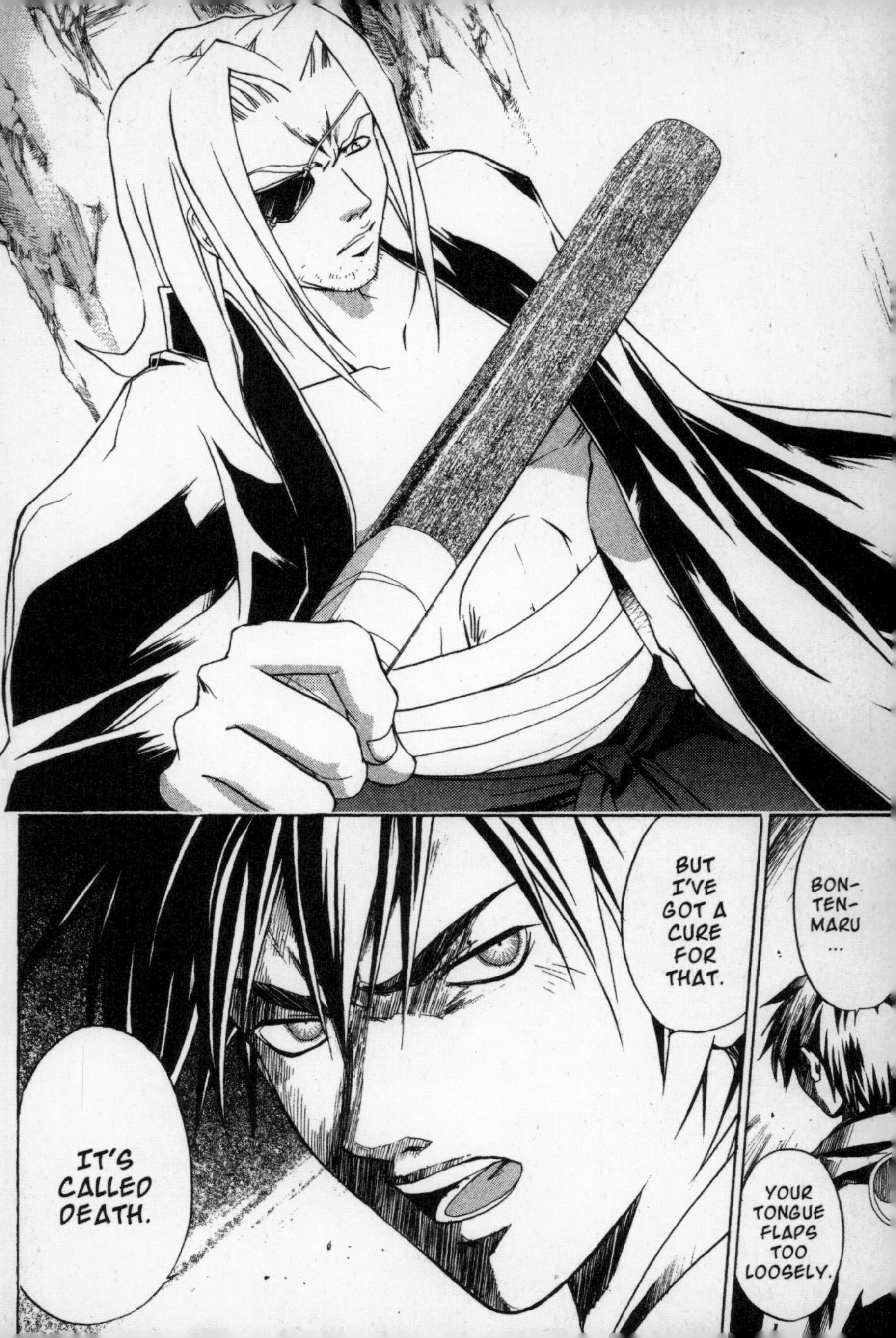
BON-TEN-MARU...
YOUR TONGUE FLAPS TOO LOOSELY.
BUT I'VE GOT A CURE FOR THAT.
IT'S CALLED DEATH.

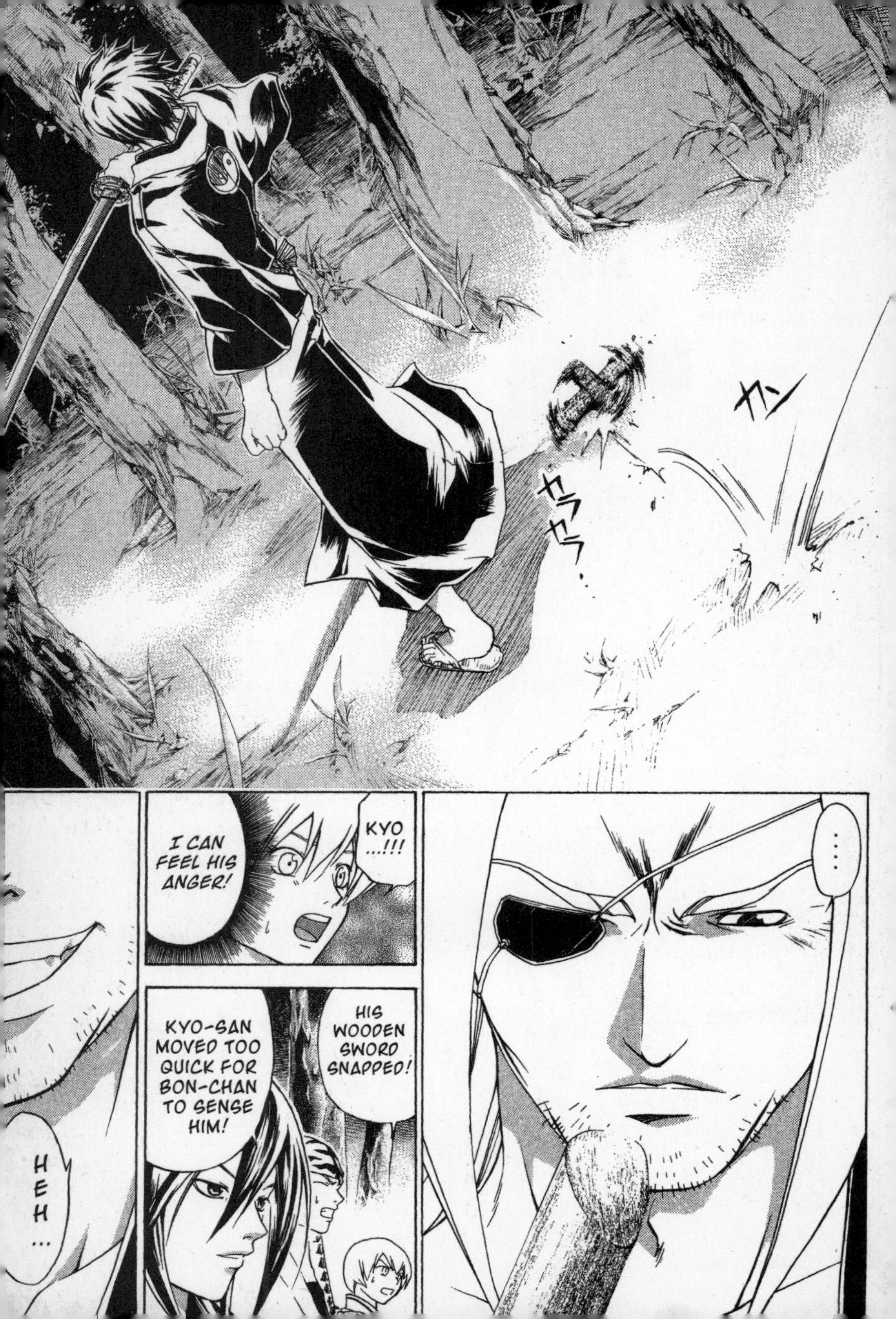
カン
カラカラ…
....
KYO ...!!!
I CAN FEEL HIS ANGER!
HIS WOODEN SWORD SNAPPED!
KYO-SAN MOVED TOO QUICK FOR BON-CHAN TO SENSE HIM!
HEH ...

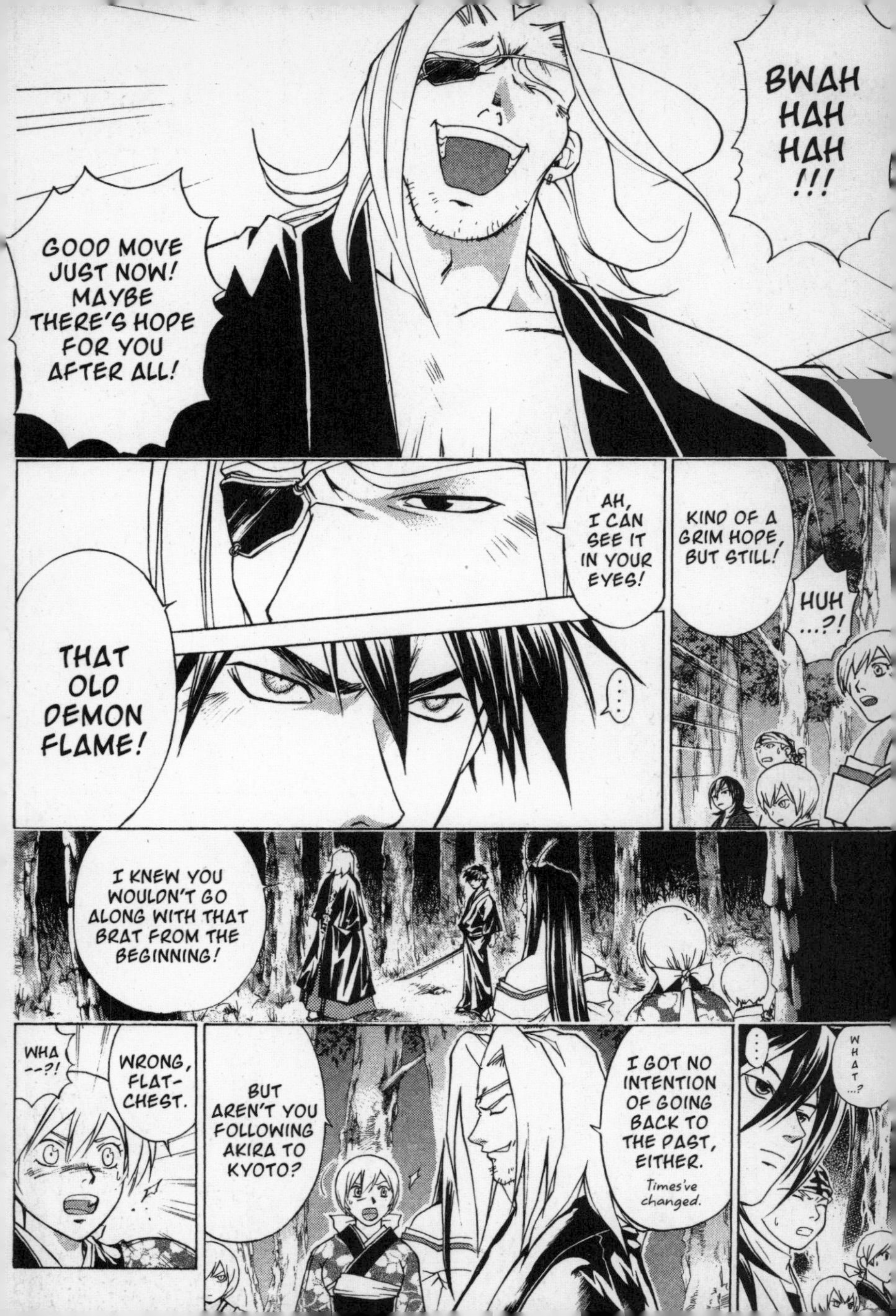
BWAH HAH HAH !!!
GOOD MOVE JUST NOW! MAYBE THERE'S HOPE FOR YOU AFTER ALL!
KIND OF A GRIM HOPE, BUT STILL!
HUH ...?!
AH, I CAN SEE IT IN YOUR EYES!
...
THAT OLD DEMON FLAME!
I KNEW YOU WOULDN'T GO ALONG WITH THAT BRAT FROM THE BEGINNING!
...
WHAT ...?
I GOT NO INTENTION OF GOING BACK TO THE PAST, EITHER.
Times've changed.
BUT AREN'T YOU FOLLOWING AKIRA TO KYOTO?
WRONG, FLAT-CHEST.
WHA --?!

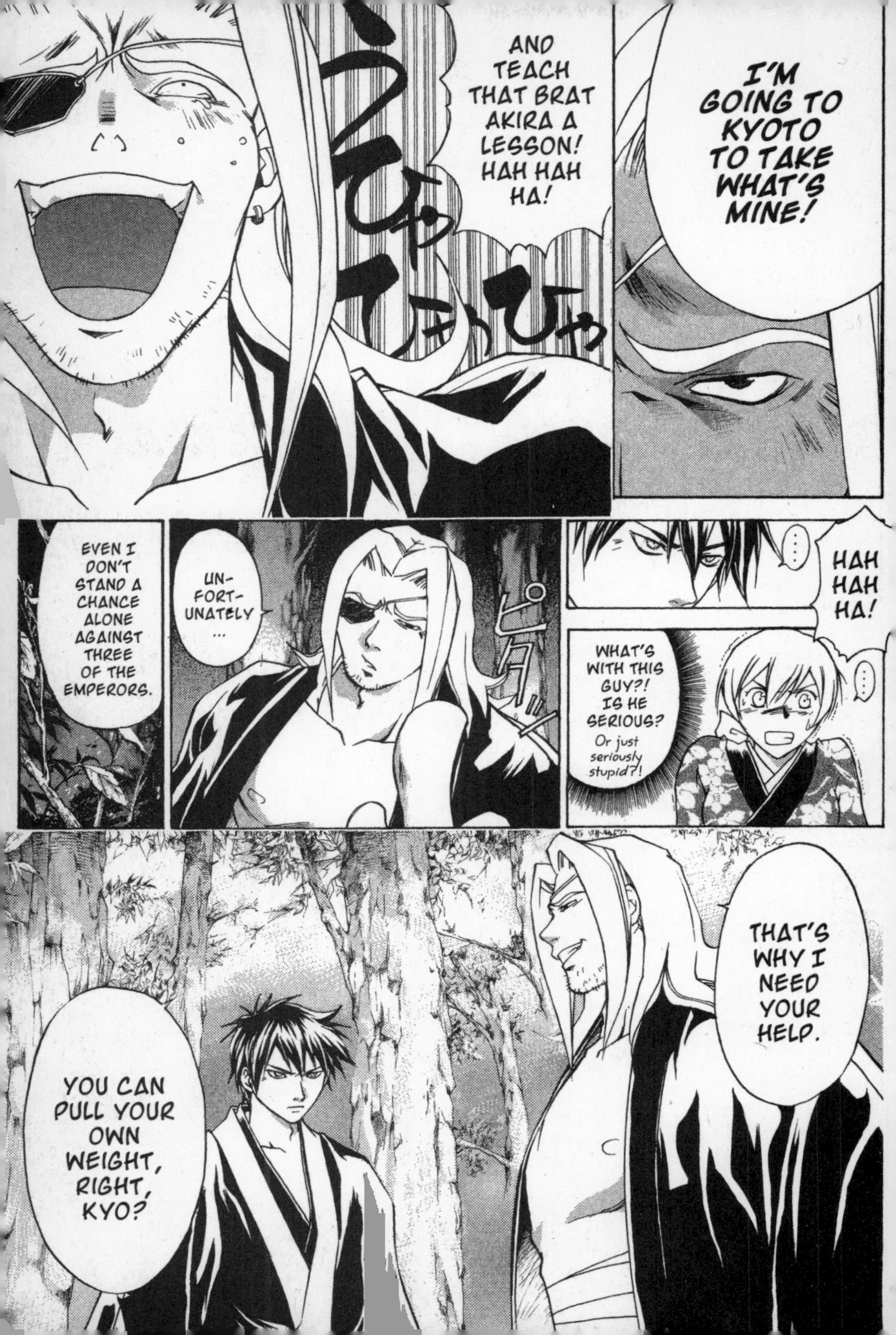
I'M GOING TO KYOTO TO TAKE WHAT'S MINE!
AND TEACH THAT BRAT AKIRA A LESSON! HAH HAH HA!
...
HAH HAH HA!
...
WHAT'S WITH THIS GUY?! IS HE SERIOUS?
Or just seriously stupid?!
UN-FORT-UNATELY ...
EVEN I DON'T STAND A CHANCE ALONE AGAINST THREE OF THE EMPERORS.
THAT'S WHY I NEED YOUR HELP.
YOU CAN PULL YOUR OWN WEIGHT, RIGHT, KYO?

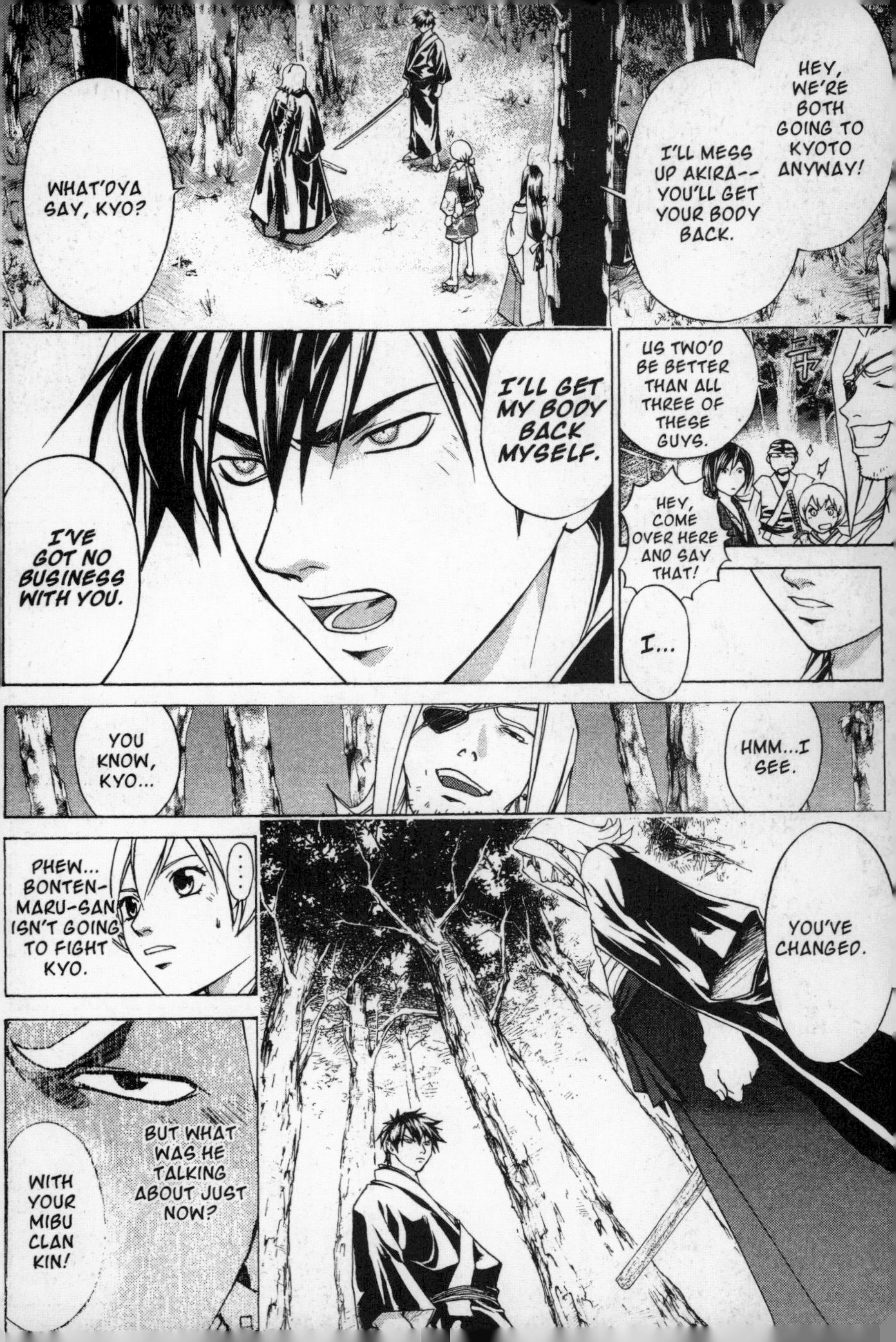
HEY, WE'RE BOTH GOING TO KYOTO ANYWAY!
I'LL MESS UP AKIRA-- YOU'LL GET YOUR BODY BACK.
WHAT'DYA SAY, KYO?
US TWO'D BE BETTER THAN ALL THREE OF THESE GUYS.
HEY, COME OVER HERE AND SAY THAT!
I...
I'LL GET MY BODY BACK MYSELF.
I'VE GOT NO BUSINESS WITH YOU.
HMM...I SEE.
YOU KNOW, KYO...
YOU'VE CHANGED.
....
PHEW... BONTEN-MARU-SAN ISN'T GOING TO FIGHT KYO.
BUT WHAT WAS HE TALKING ABOUT JUST NOW?
WITH YOUR MIBU CLAN KIN!

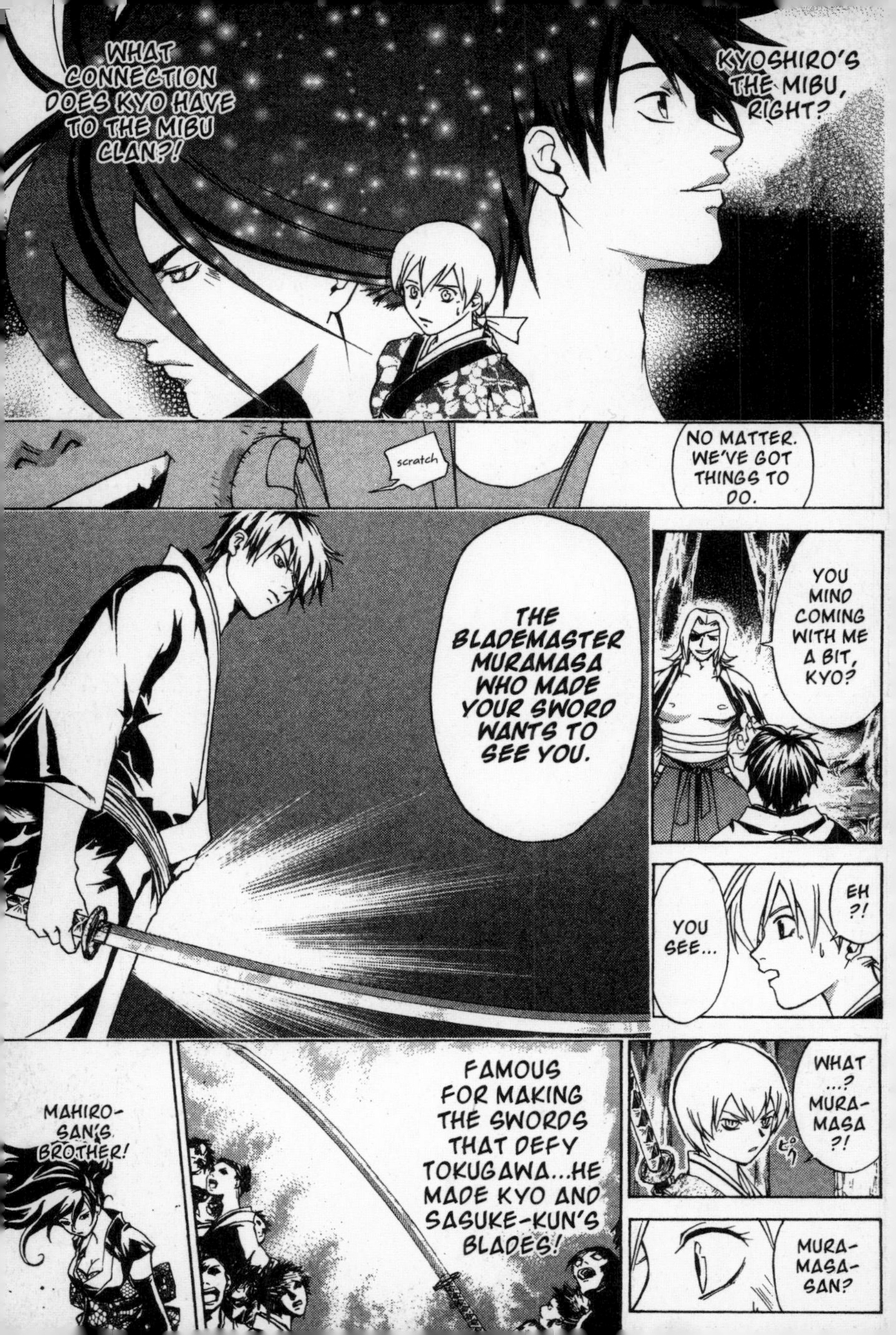
KYOSHIRO'S THE MIBU, RIGHT?
WHAT CONNECTION DOES KYO HAVE TO THE MIBU CLAN?!
NO MATTER. WE'VE GOT THINGS TO DO.
scratch
YOU MIND COMING WITH ME A BIT, KYO?
EH?!
YOU SEE...
THE BLADEMASTER MURAMASA WHO MADE YOUR SWORD WANTS TO SEE YOU.
WHAT...? MURA-MASA?!
MURA-MASA-SAN?
FAMOUS FOR MAKING THE SWORDS THAT DEFY TOKUGAWA...HE MADE KYO AND SASUKE-KUN'S BLADES!
MAHIRO-SAN'S BROTHER!

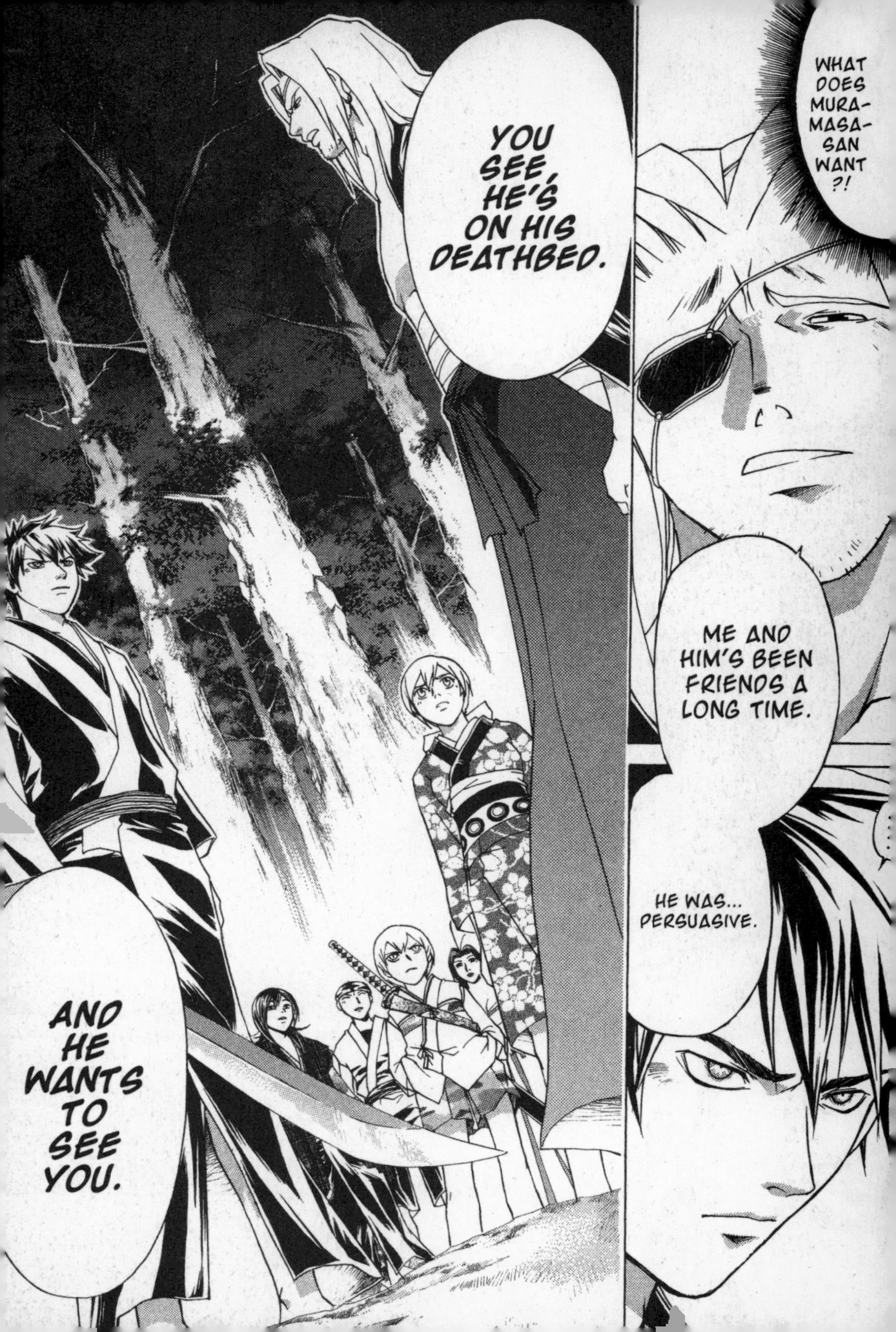
WHAT DOES MURA-MASA-SAN WANT?!
ME AND HIM'S BEEN FRIENDS A LONG TIME.
HE WAS... PERSUASIVE.
YOU SEE, HE'S ON HIS DEATHBED.
AND HE WANTS TO SEE YOU.

Kyo and his band head toward Kyoto, where Akira has gone into hiding.

They unexpectedly encounter Bontenmaru--sworn enemy of Tokugawa Ieyasu.

He is none other than Date Masamune, Conqueror of the North!

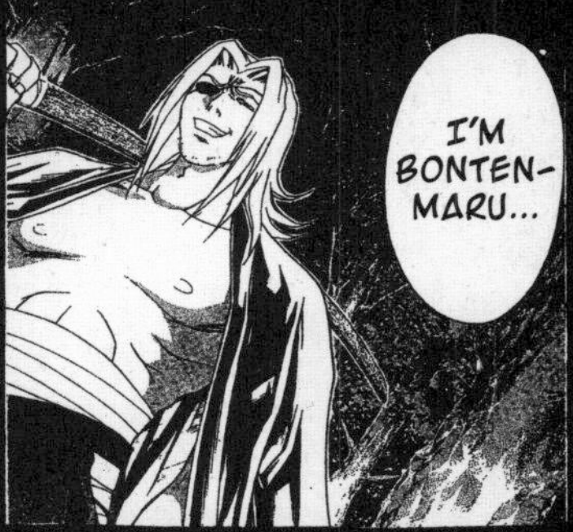
I'M BONTEN-MARU...

With only a wooden sword, he seems unstoppable!

Led by Bontenmaru, they go to the side of the great Muramasa, who has called for Kyo from his deathbed!

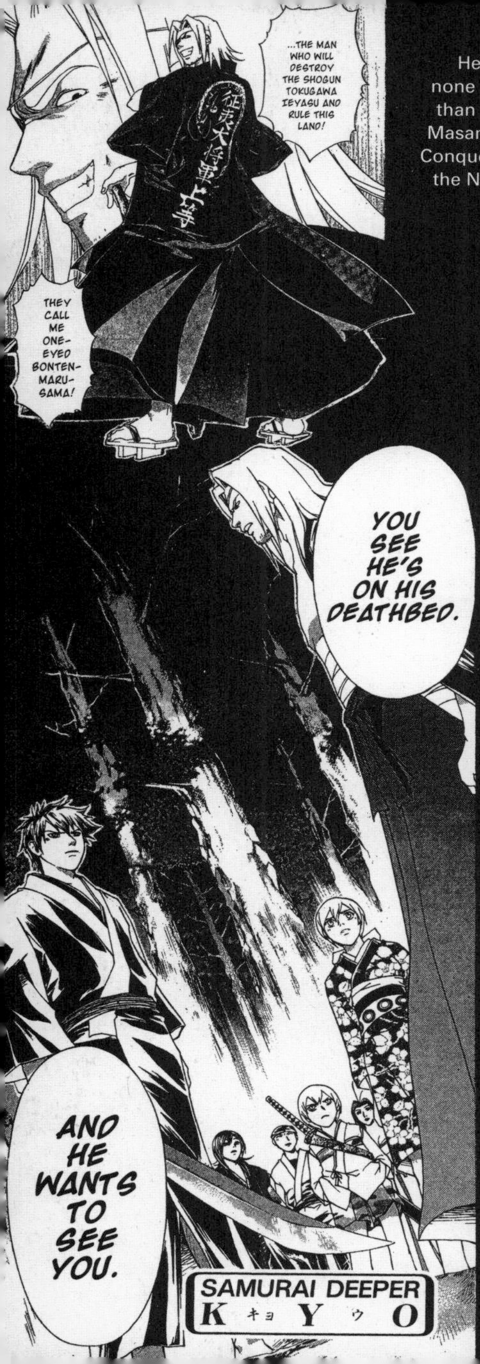
...THE MAN WHO WILL DESTROY THE SHOGUN TOKUGAWA IEYASU AND RULE THIS LAND!
THEY CALL ME ONE-EYED BONTEN-MARU-SAMA!
YOU SEE HE'S ON HIS DEATHBED.
AND HE WANTS TO SEE YOU.
SAMURAI DEEPER
K キョ Y ウ O

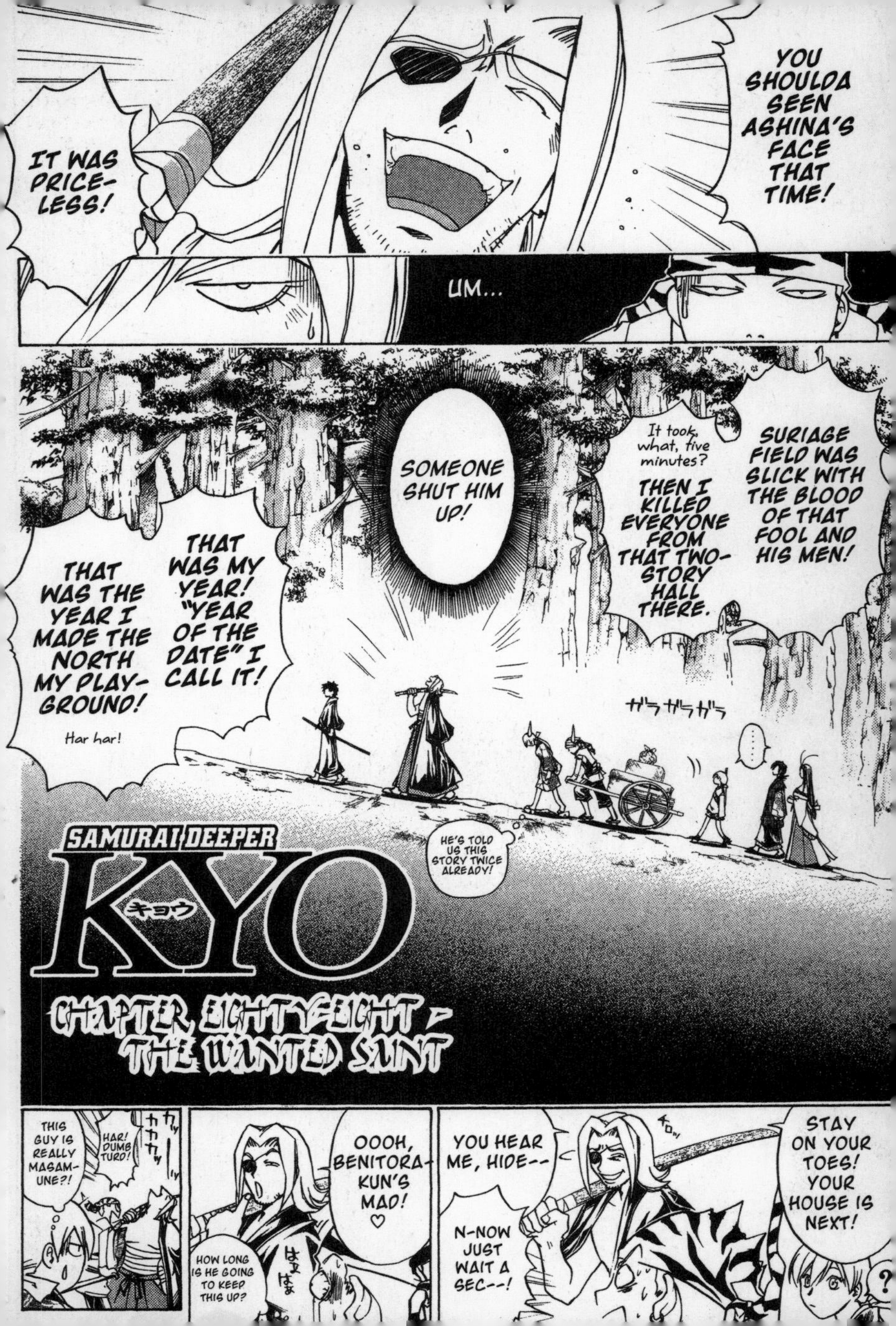
YOU SHOULDA SEEN ASHINA'S FACE THAT TIME!
IT WAS PRICELESS!
UM...
SURIAGE FIELD WAS SLICK WITH THE BLOOD OF THAT FOOL AND HIS MEN!
It took, what, five minutes?
THEN I KILLED EVERYONE FROM THAT TWO-STORY HALL THERE.
SOMEONE SHUT HIM UP!
THAT WAS MY YEAR! "YEAR OF THE DATE" I CALL IT!
THAT WAS THE YEAR I MADE THE NORTH MY PLAYGROUND!
Har har!
ガラガラガラ
....
HE'S TOLD US THIS STORY TWICE ALREADY!
SAMURAI DEEPER
KYO
キョウ
CHAPTER EIGHTY-EIGHT - THE WANTED SAINT
STAY ON YOUR TOES! YOUR HOUSE IS NEXT!
?
YOU HEAR ME, HIDE--
N-NOW JUST WAIT A SEC--!
OOOH, BENITORA-KUN'S MAD! ♡
HOW LONG IS HE GOING TO KEEP THIS UP?
HAR! DUMB TURD!
THIS GUY IS REALLY MASAMUNE?!

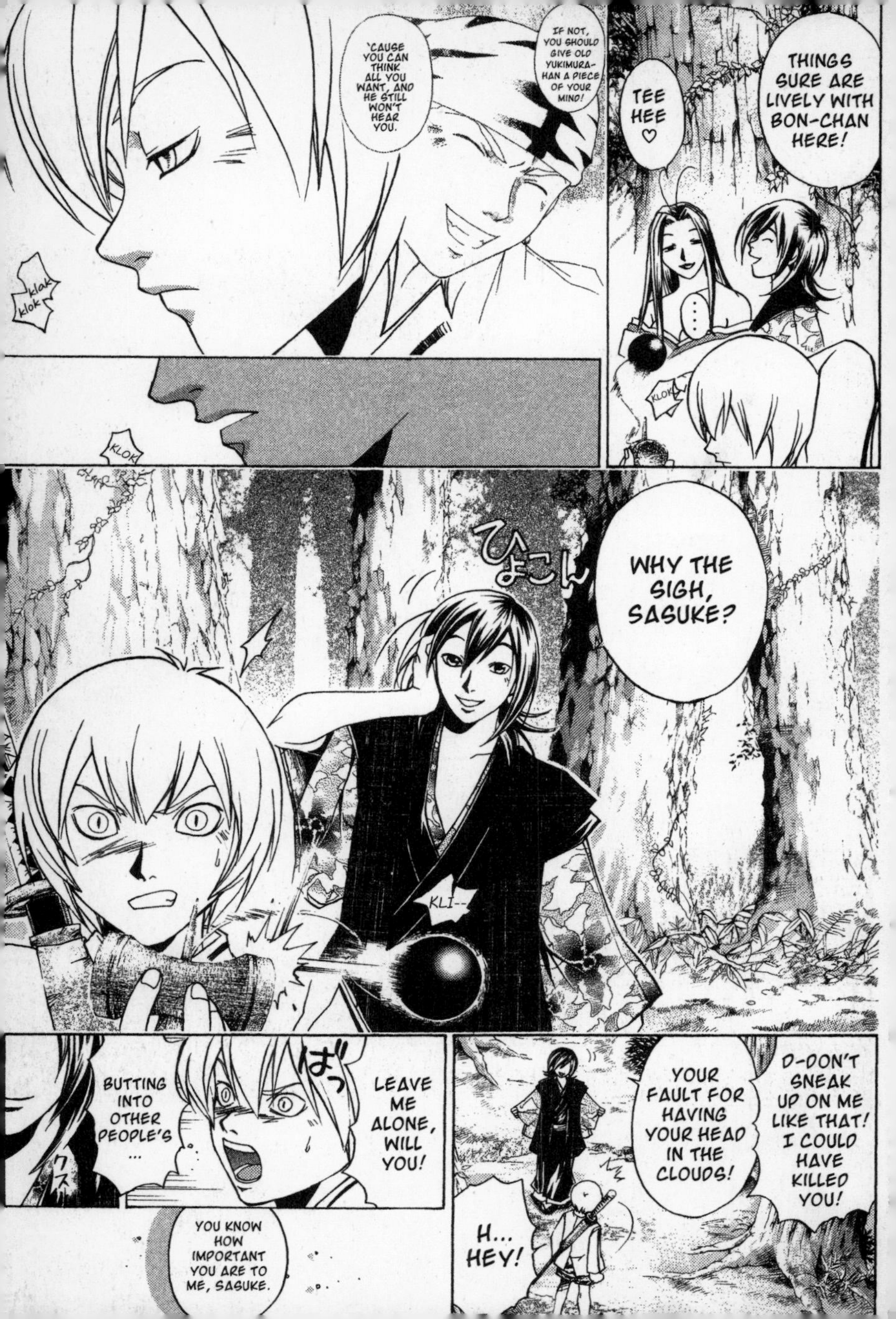
THINGS SURE ARE LIVELY WITH BON-CHAN HERE!
TEE HEE ♡
...
KLOK
IF NOT, YOU SHOULD GIVE OLD YUKIMURA-HAN A PIECE OF YOUR MIND!
'CAUSE YOU CAN THINK ALL YOU WANT, AND HE STILL WON'T HEAR YOU.
klak klok
KLOK
ひょこん
WHY THE SIGH, SASUKE?
KLI--
D-DON'T SNEAK UP ON ME LIKE THAT! I COULD HAVE KILLED YOU!
YOUR FAULT FOR HAVING YOUR HEAD IN THE CLOUDS!
H... HEY!
ばっ
LEAVE ME ALONE, WILL YOU!
BUTTING INTO OTHER PEOPLE'S ...
クス
YOU KNOW HOW IMPORTANT YOU ARE TO ME, SASUKE.

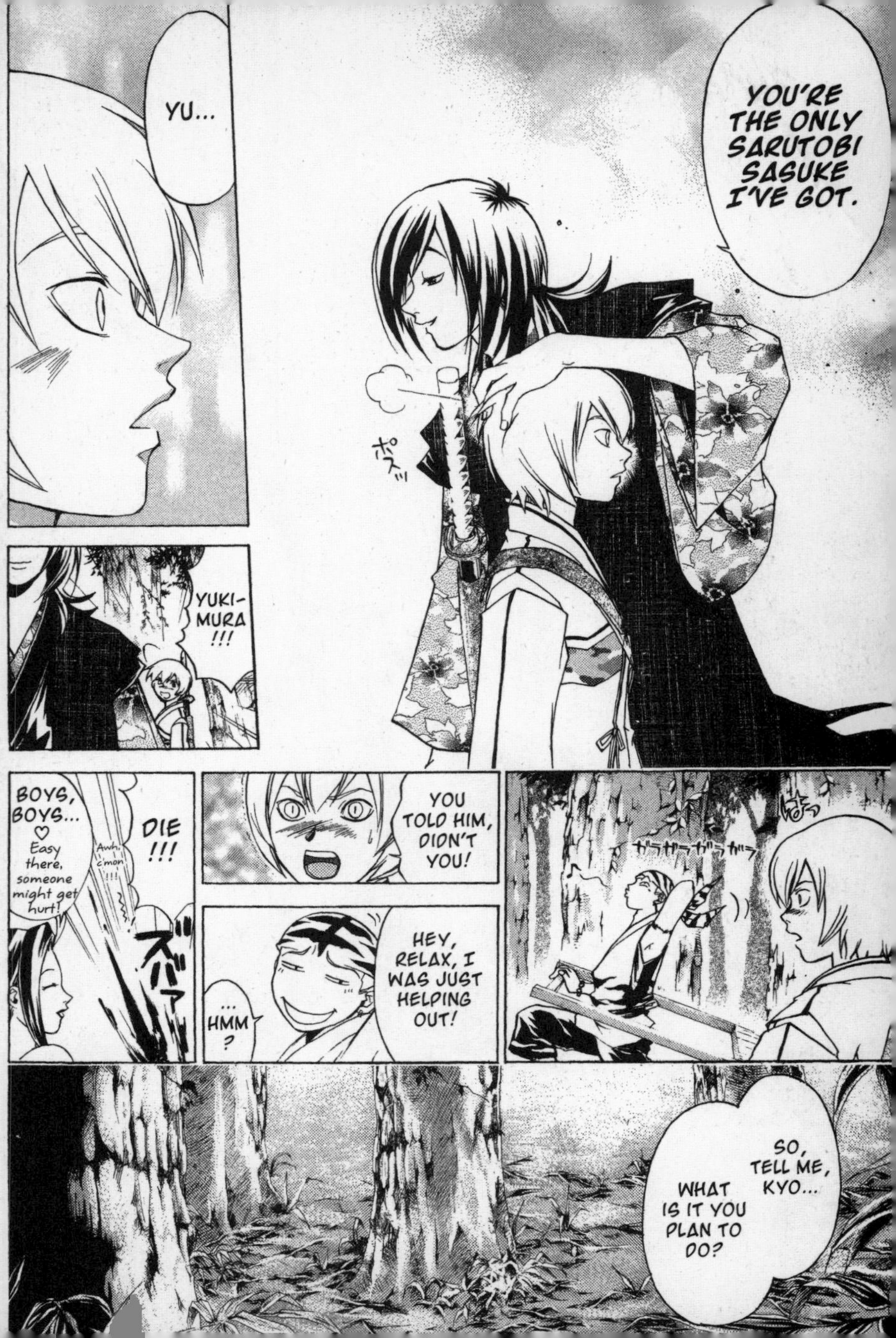
YOU'RE THE ONLY SARUTOBI SASUKE I'VE GOT.
ポスッ
YU...
YUKIMURA!!!
ガラガラガラガラ
YOU TOLD HIM, DIDN'T YOU!
HEY, RELAX, I WAS JUST HELPING OUT!
...HMM?
BOYS, BOYS... ♡
Easy there, someone might get hurt!
DIE!!!
Awh, c'mon!!!
ズバァ
SO, TELL ME, KYO...
WHAT IS IT YOU PLAN TO DO?

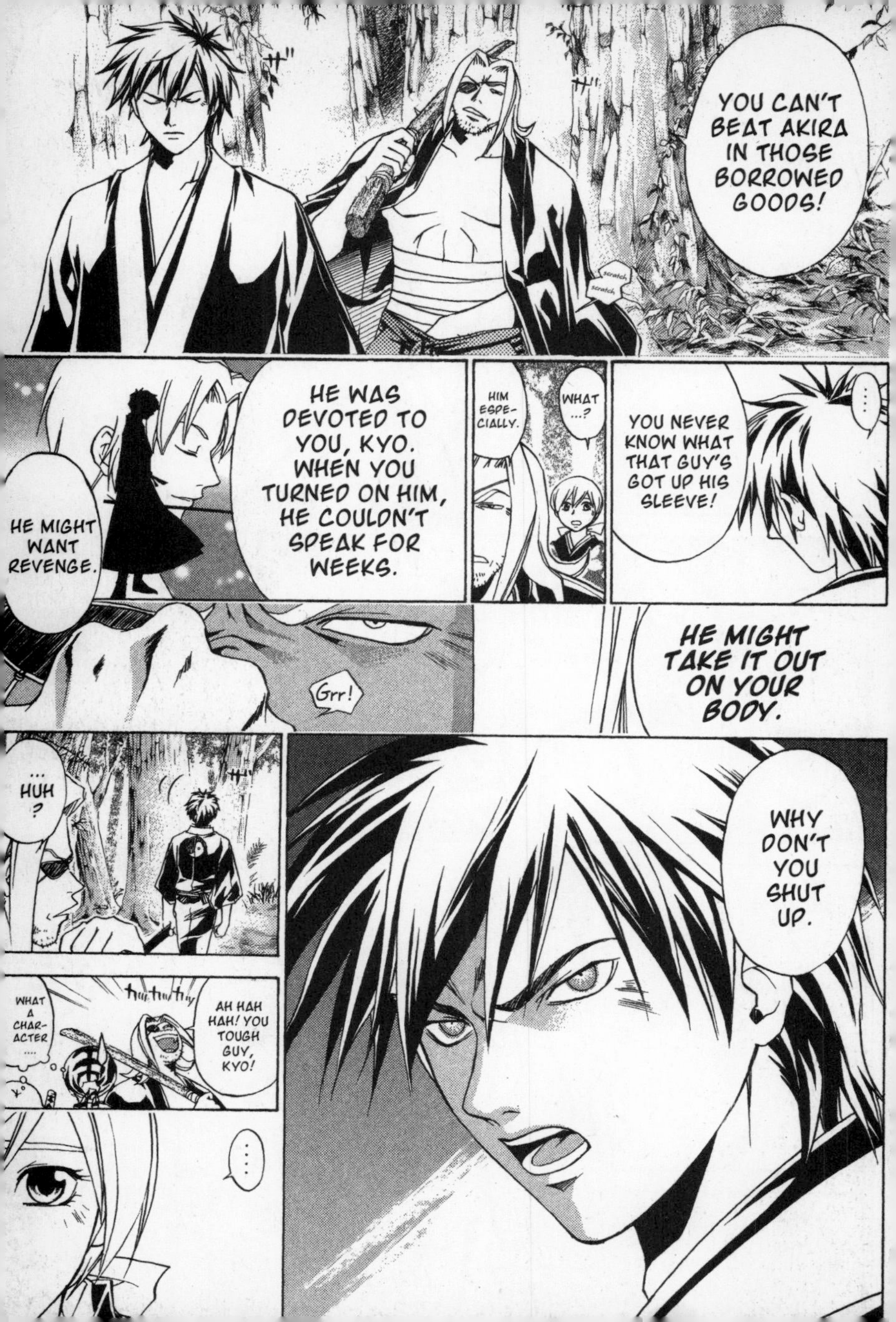
YOU CAN'T BEAT AKIRA IN THOSE BORROWED GOODS!
scratch
scratch
...
YOU NEVER KNOW WHAT THAT GUY'S GOT UP HIS SLEEVE!
WHAT ...?
HIM ESPE-CIALLY.
HE WAS DEVOTED TO YOU, KYO. WHEN YOU TURNED ON HIM, HE COULDN'T SPEAK FOR WEEKS.
HE MIGHT WANT REVENGE.
HE MIGHT TAKE IT OUT ON YOUR BODY.
Grr!
WHY DON'T YOU SHUT UP.
... HUH ?
AH HAH HAH! YOU TOUGH GUY, KYO!
WHAT A CHAR-ACTER ....
....

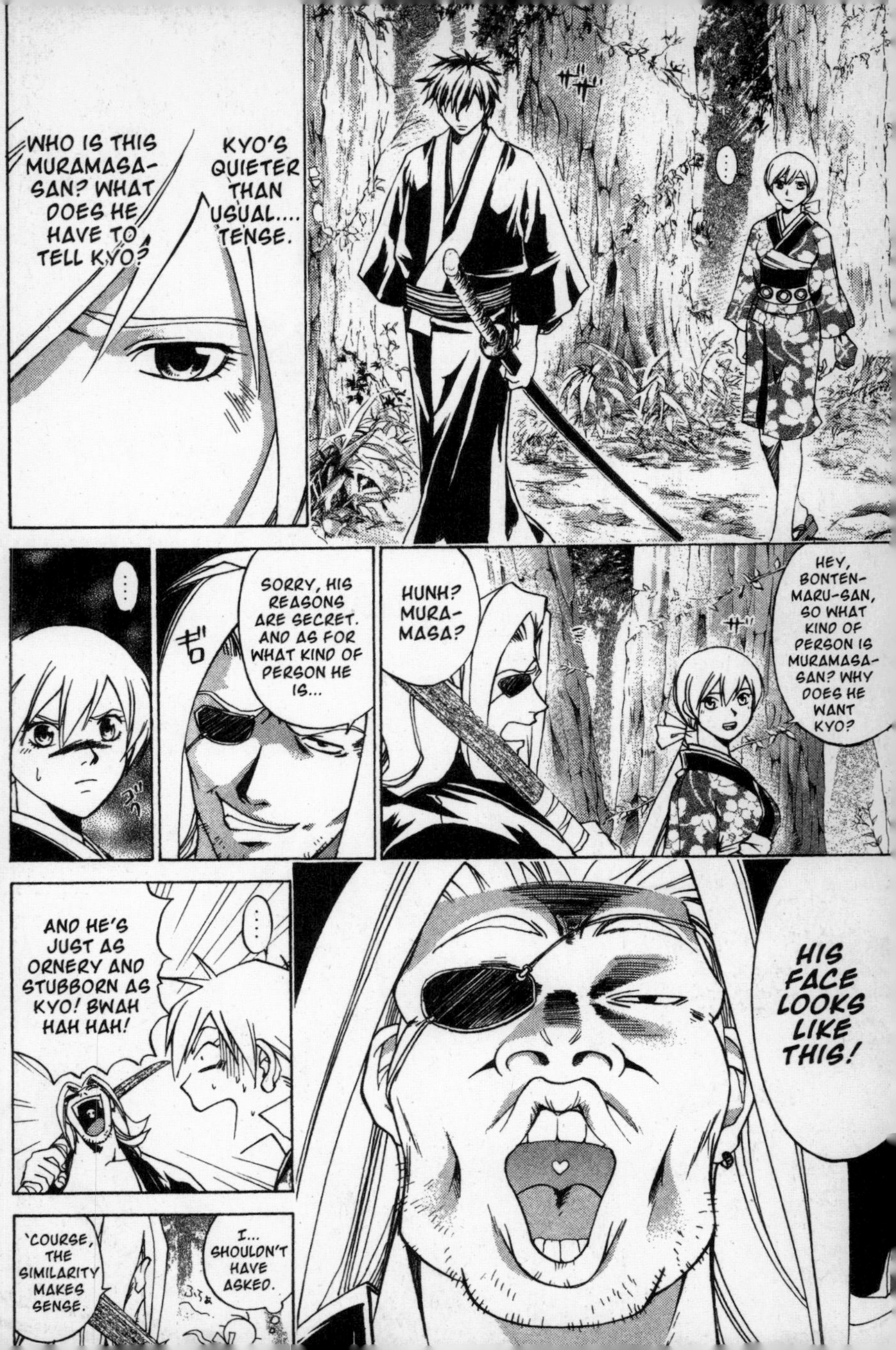
...
KYO'S QUIETER THAN USUAL.... TENSE.
WHO IS THIS MURAMASA-SAN? WHAT DOES HE HAVE TO TELL KYO?
HEY, BONTEN-MARU-SAN, SO WHAT KIND OF PERSON IS MURAMASA-SAN? WHY DOES HE WANT KYO?
HUNH? MURA-MASA?
SORRY, HIS REASONS ARE SECRET. AND AS FOR WHAT KIND OF PERSON HE IS...
...
HIS FACE LOOKS LIKE THIS!
...
AND HE'S JUST AS ORNERY AND STUBBORN AS KYO! BWAH HAH HAH!
I... SHOULDN'T HAVE ASKED.
'COURSE, THE SIMILARITY MAKES SENSE.

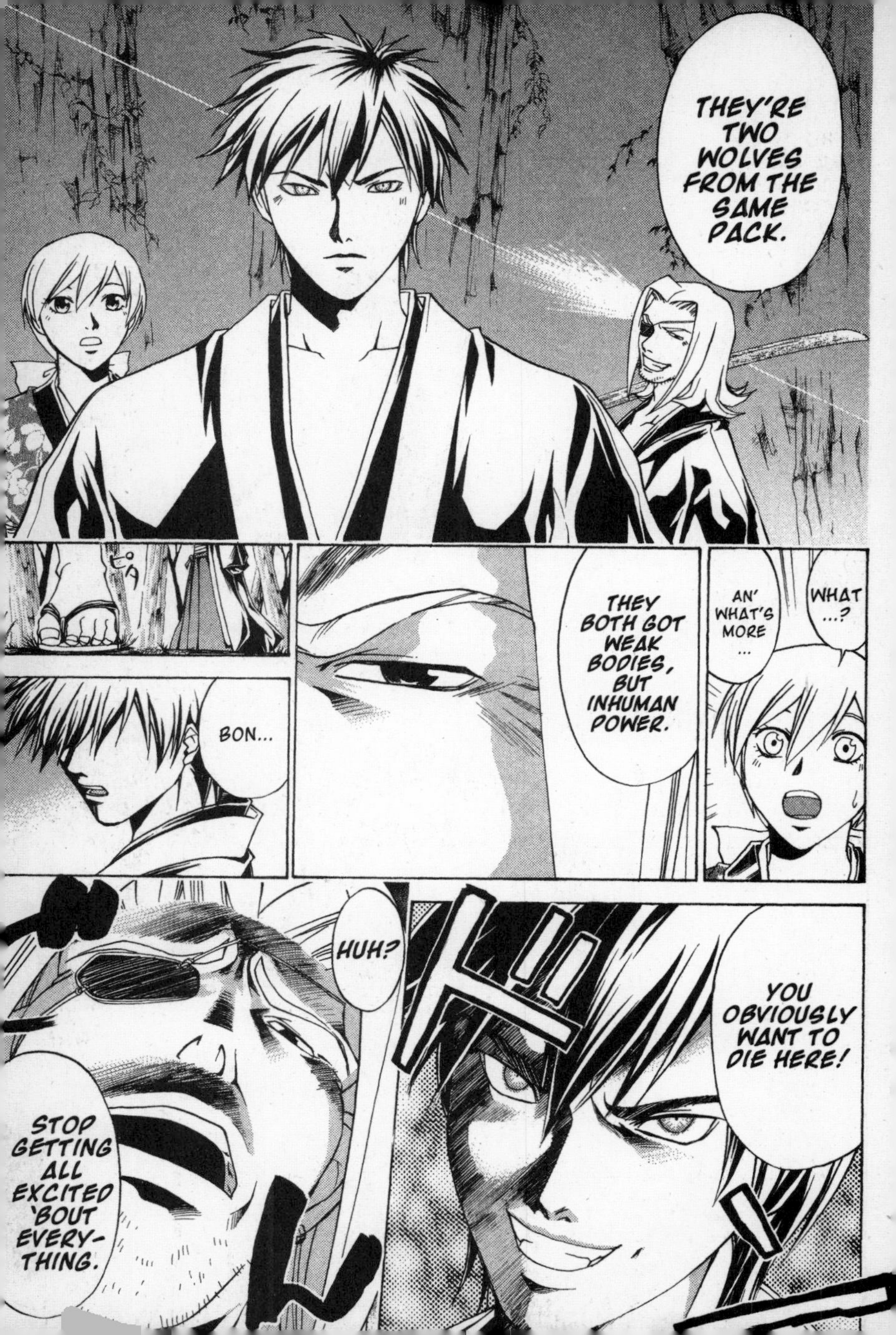
THEY'RE TWO WOLVES FROM THE SAME PACK.
WHAT ...?
AN' WHAT'S MORE ...
THEY BOTH GOT WEAK BODIES, BUT INHUMAN POWER.
BON...
YOU OBVIOUSLY WANT TO DIE HERE!
HUH?
STOP GETTING ALL EXCITED 'BOUT EVERY-THING.

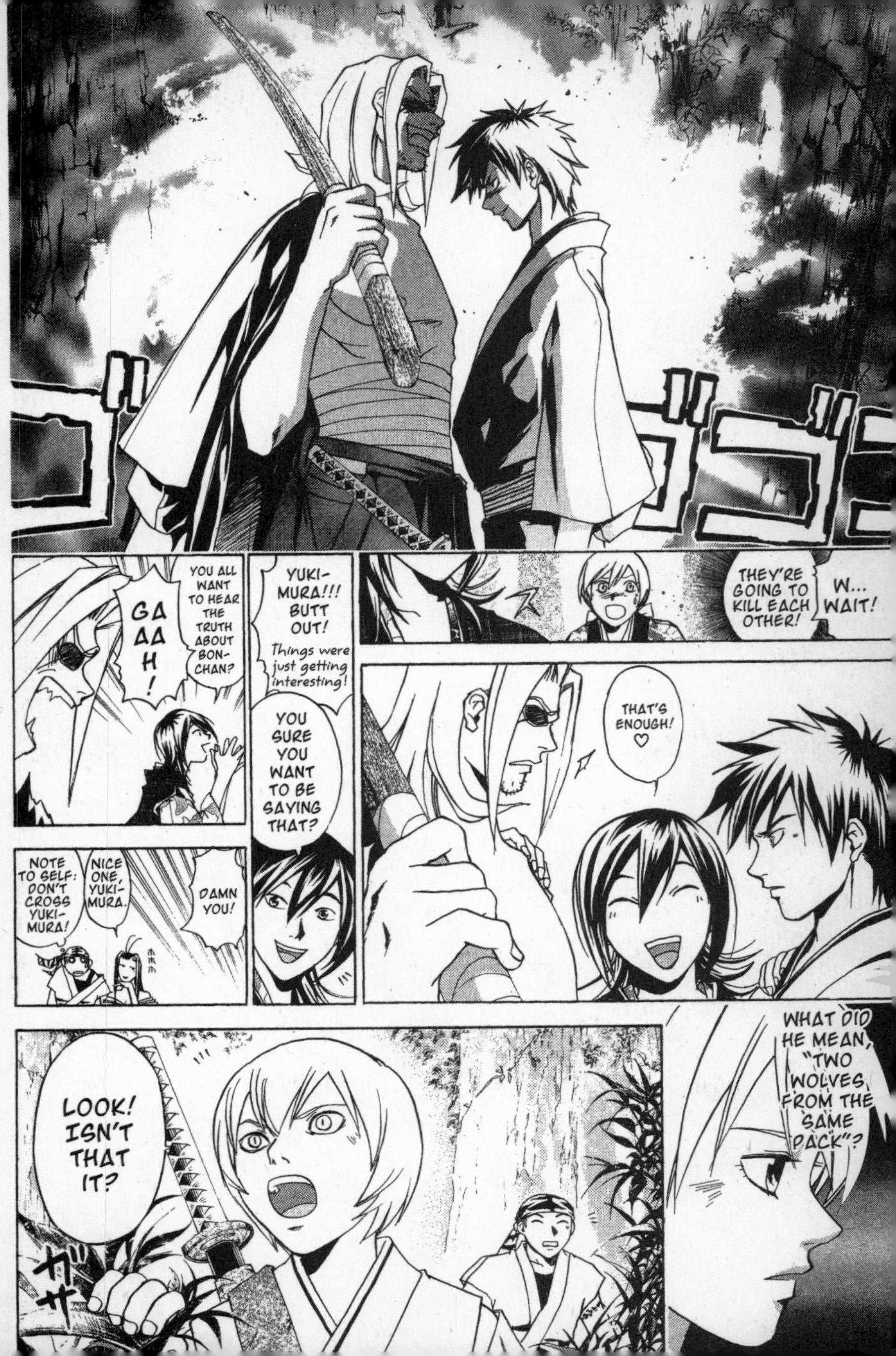
W... WAIT!
THEY'RE GOING TO KILL EACH OTHER!
THAT'S ENOUGH! ♡
YUKI-MURA!!! BUTT OUT!
Things were just getting interesting!
YOU SURE YOU WANT TO BE SAYING THAT?
YOU ALL WANT TO HEAR THE TRUTH ABOUT BON-CHAN?
GAAAH!
DAMN YOU!
NICE ONE, YUKI-MURA.
NOTE TO SELF: DON'T CROSS YUKI-MURA!
WHAT DID HE MEAN, "TWO WOLVES FROM THE SAME PACK"?
LOOK! ISN'T THAT IT?

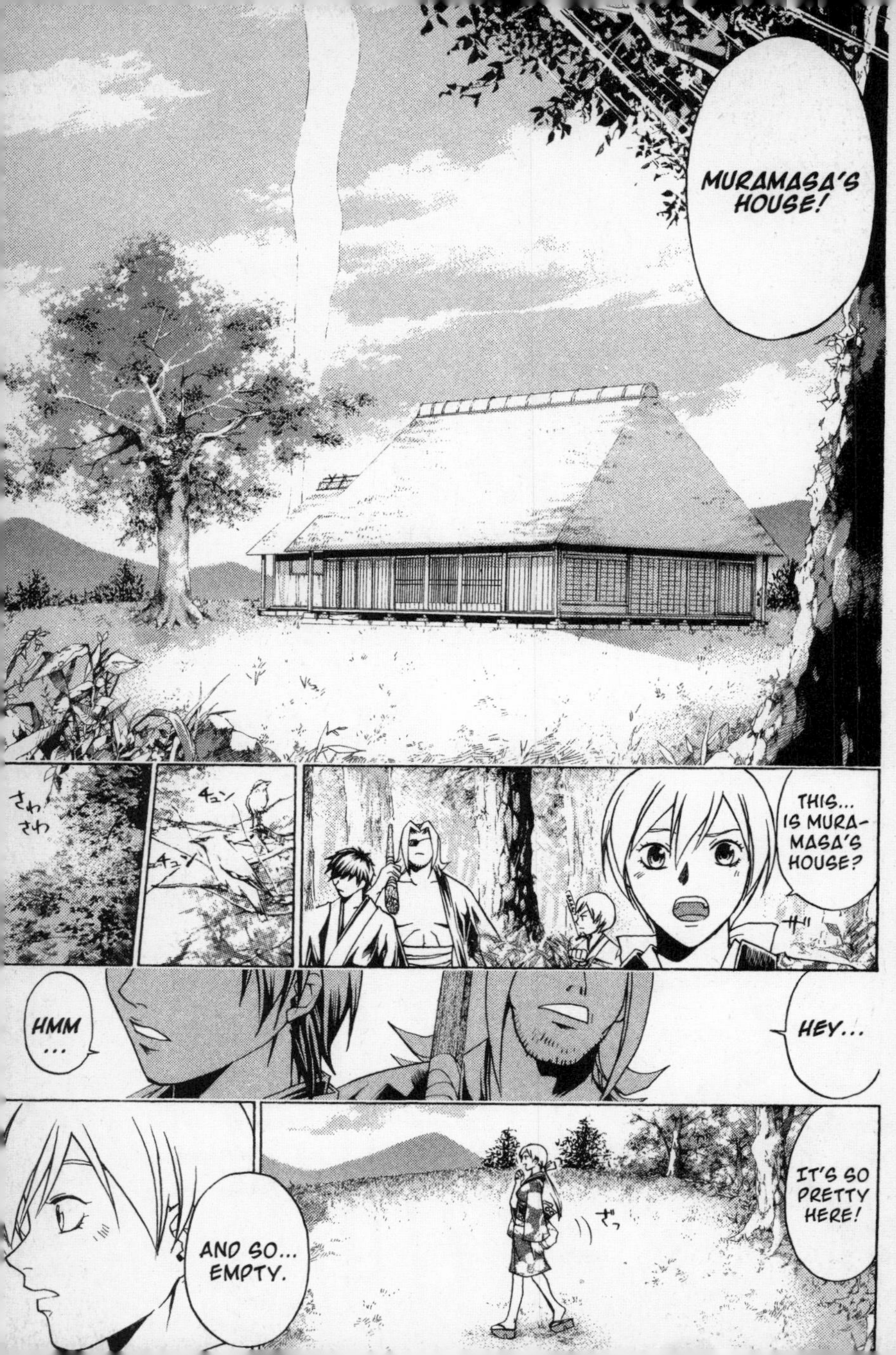

MURAMASA'S HOUSE!
THIS... IS MURA-MASA'S HOUSE?
ザ
チュン
チュン
さわ さわ
HEY...
HMM ...
IT'S SO PRETTY HERE!
ざっ
AND SO... EMPTY.

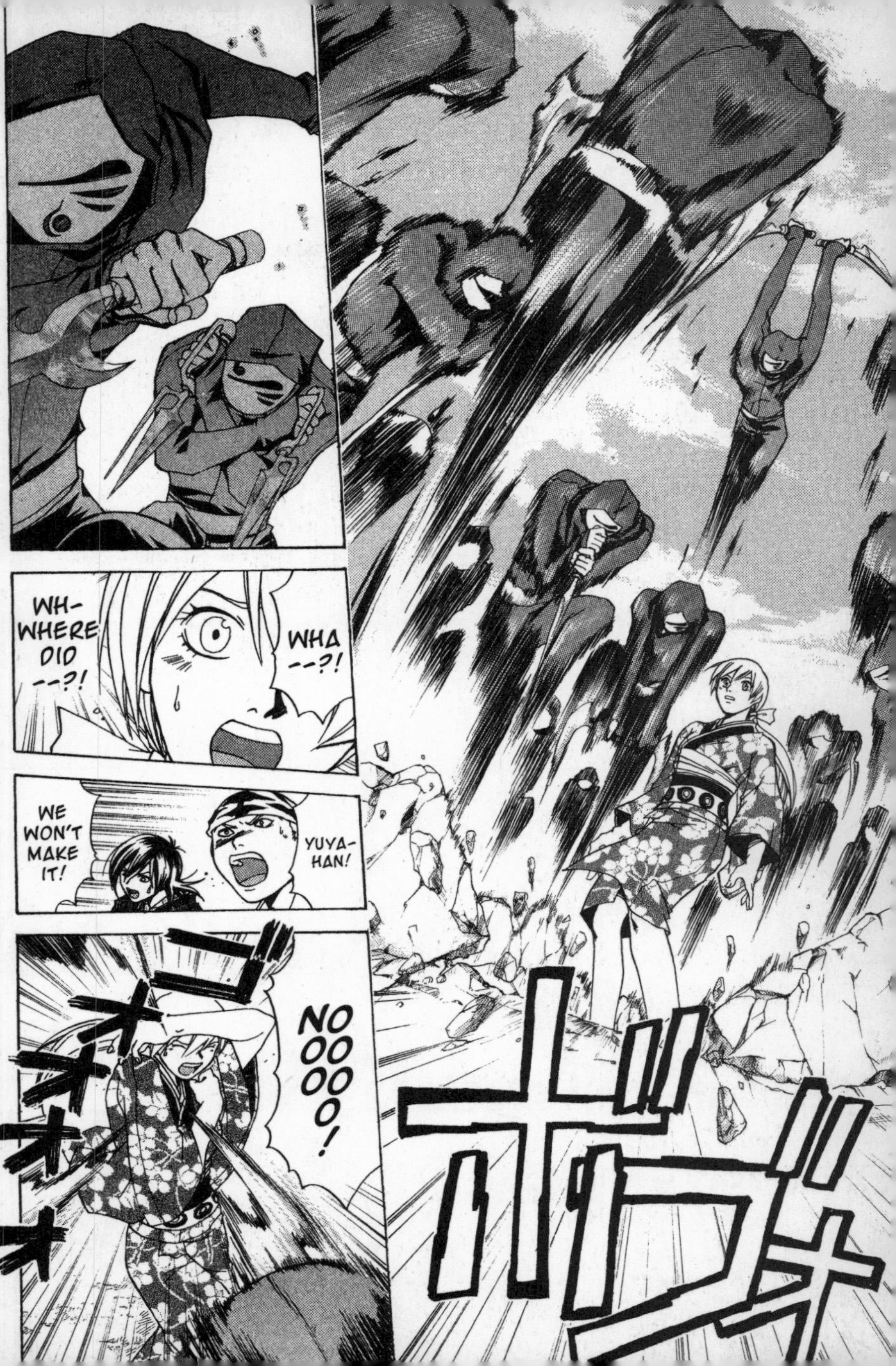
ボゴォ
WHA--?!
WH-WHERE DID--?!
YUYA-HAN!
WE WON'T MAKE IT!
ゴォォォォ
NOOOOOOO!

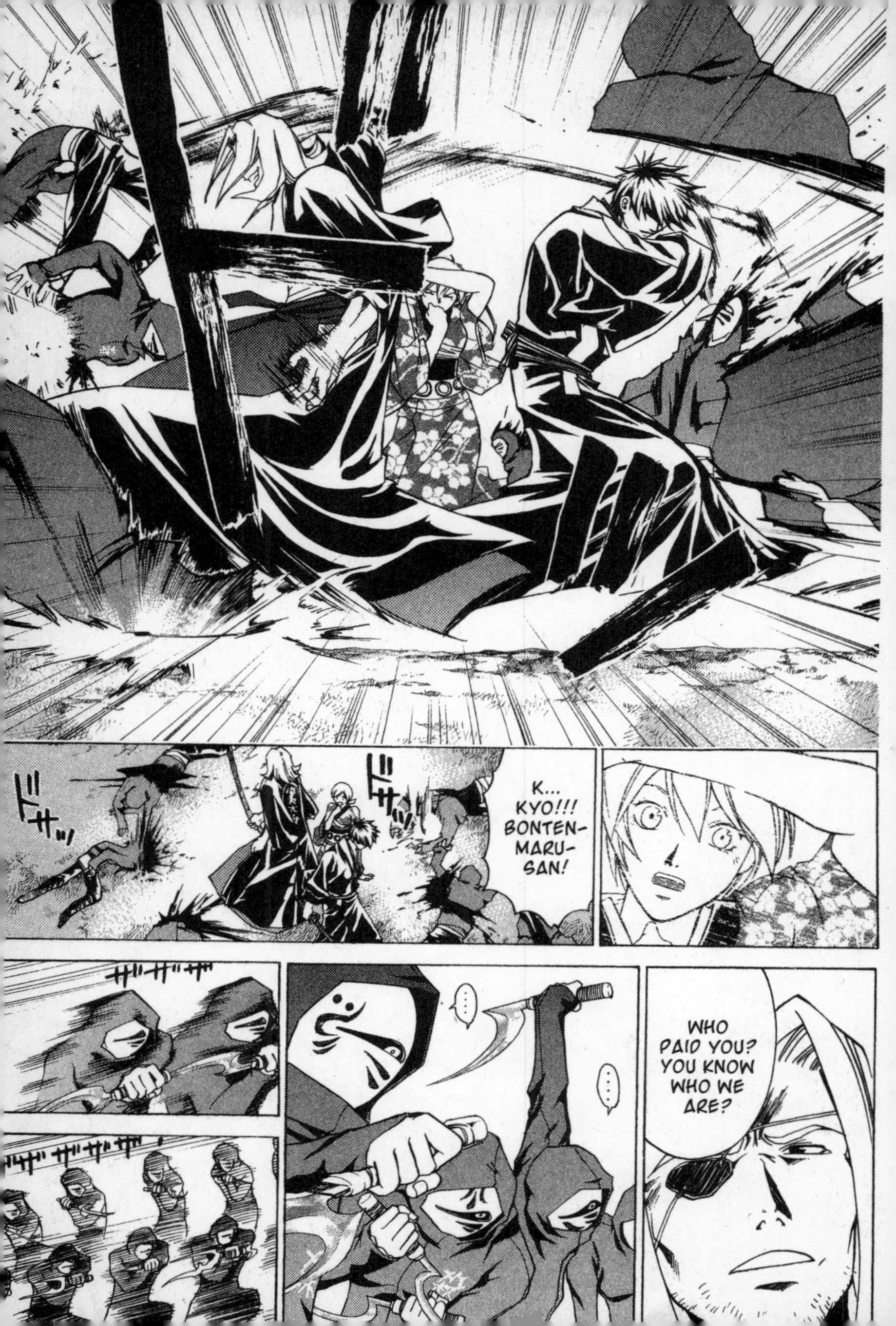
K... KYO!!! BONTEN-MARU-SAN!
WHO PAID YOU? YOU KNOW WHO WE ARE?
....
....

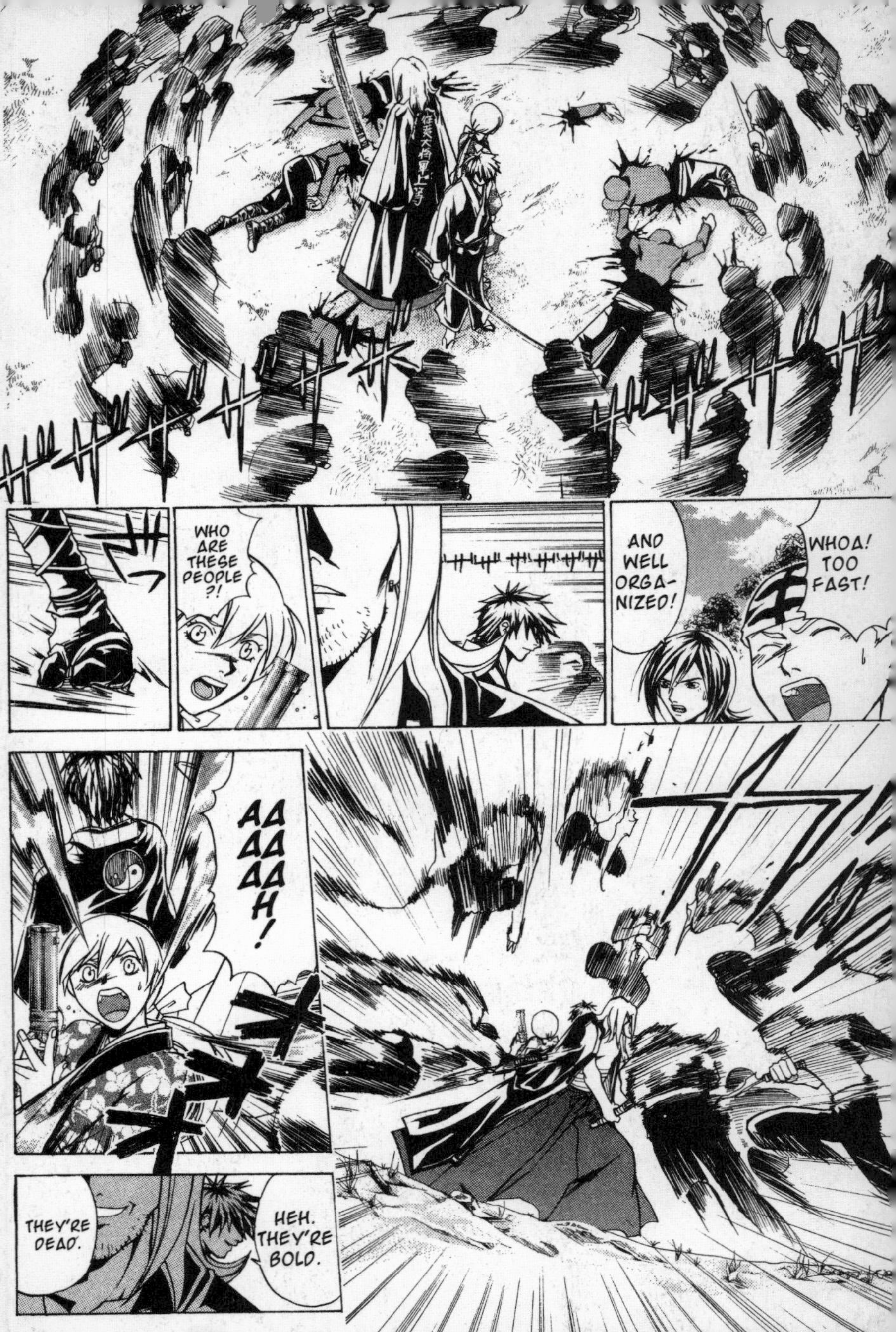
WHOA! TOO FAST!
AND WELL ORGANIZED!
WHO ARE THESE PEOPLE?!
AAAAAAH!
HEH. THEY'RE BOLD.
THEY'RE DEAD.

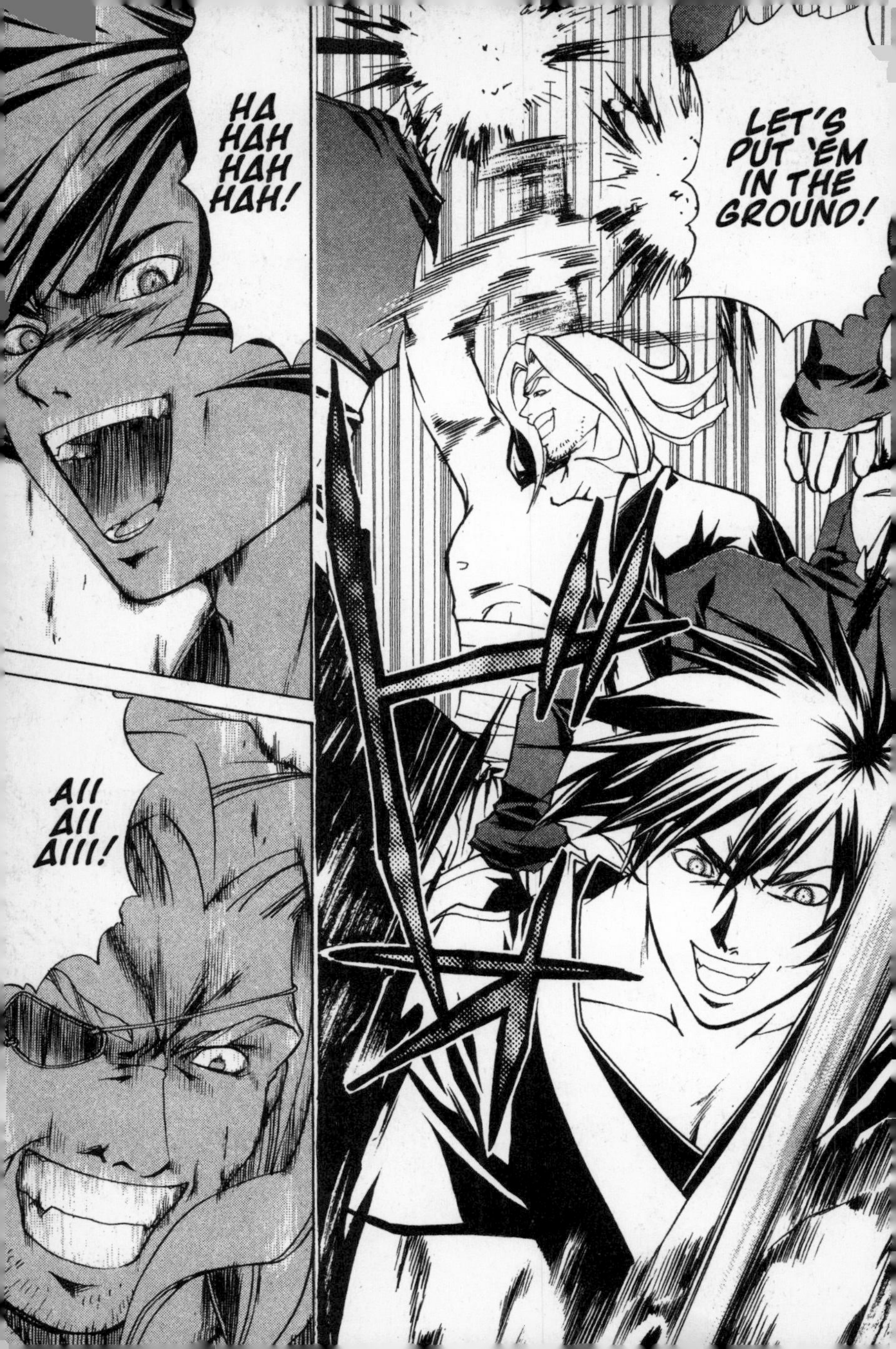
LET'S PUT 'EM IN THE GROUND!
HA HAH HAH HAH!
AII AII AIII!

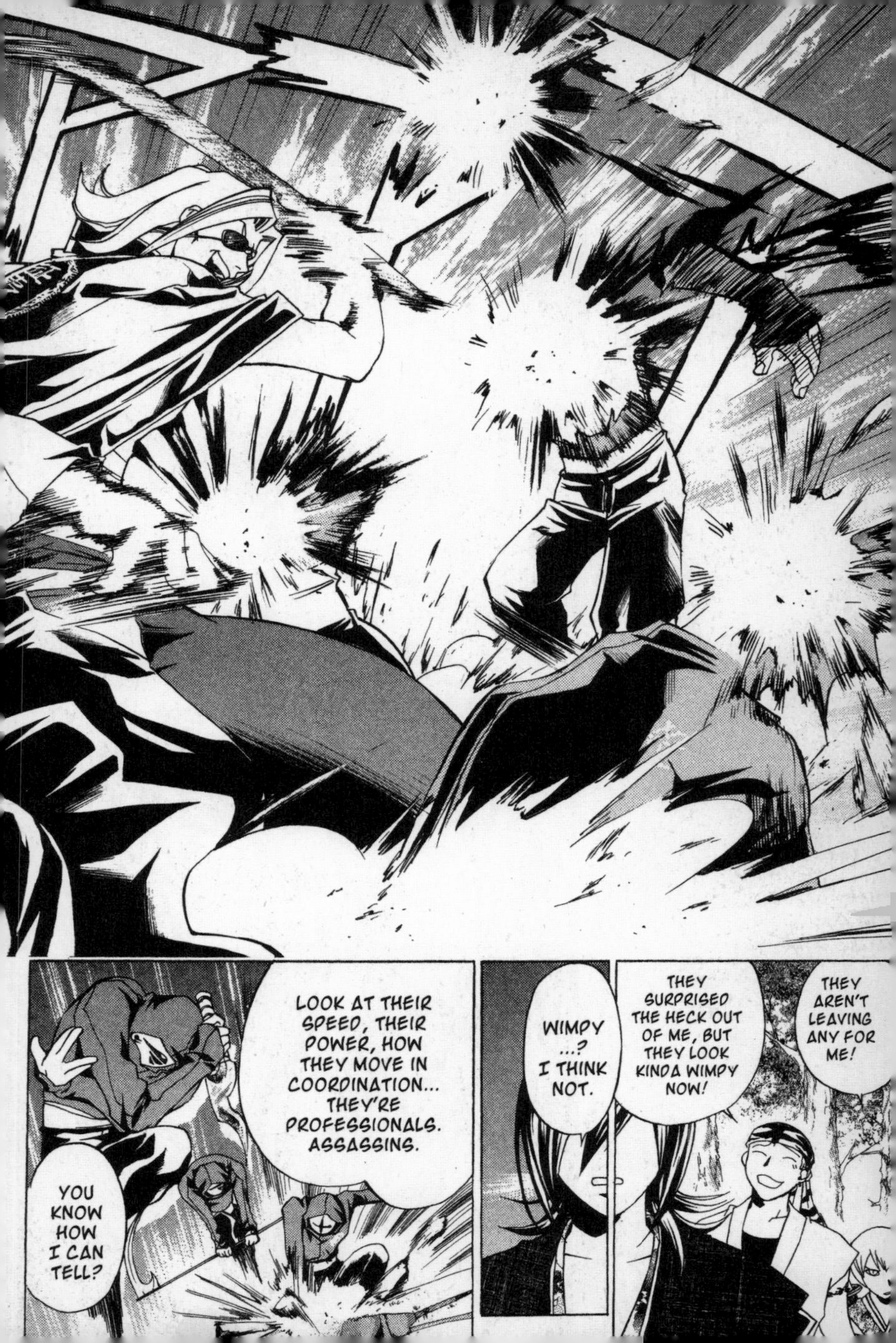
THEY AREN'T LEAVING ANY FOR ME!
THEY SURPRISED THE HECK OUT OF ME, BUT THEY LOOK KINDA WIMPY NOW!
WIMPY ...? I THINK NOT.
LOOK AT THEIR SPEED, THEIR POWER, HOW THEY MOVE IN COORDINATION... THEY'RE PROFESSIONALS. ASSASSINS.
YOU KNOW HOW I CAN TELL?

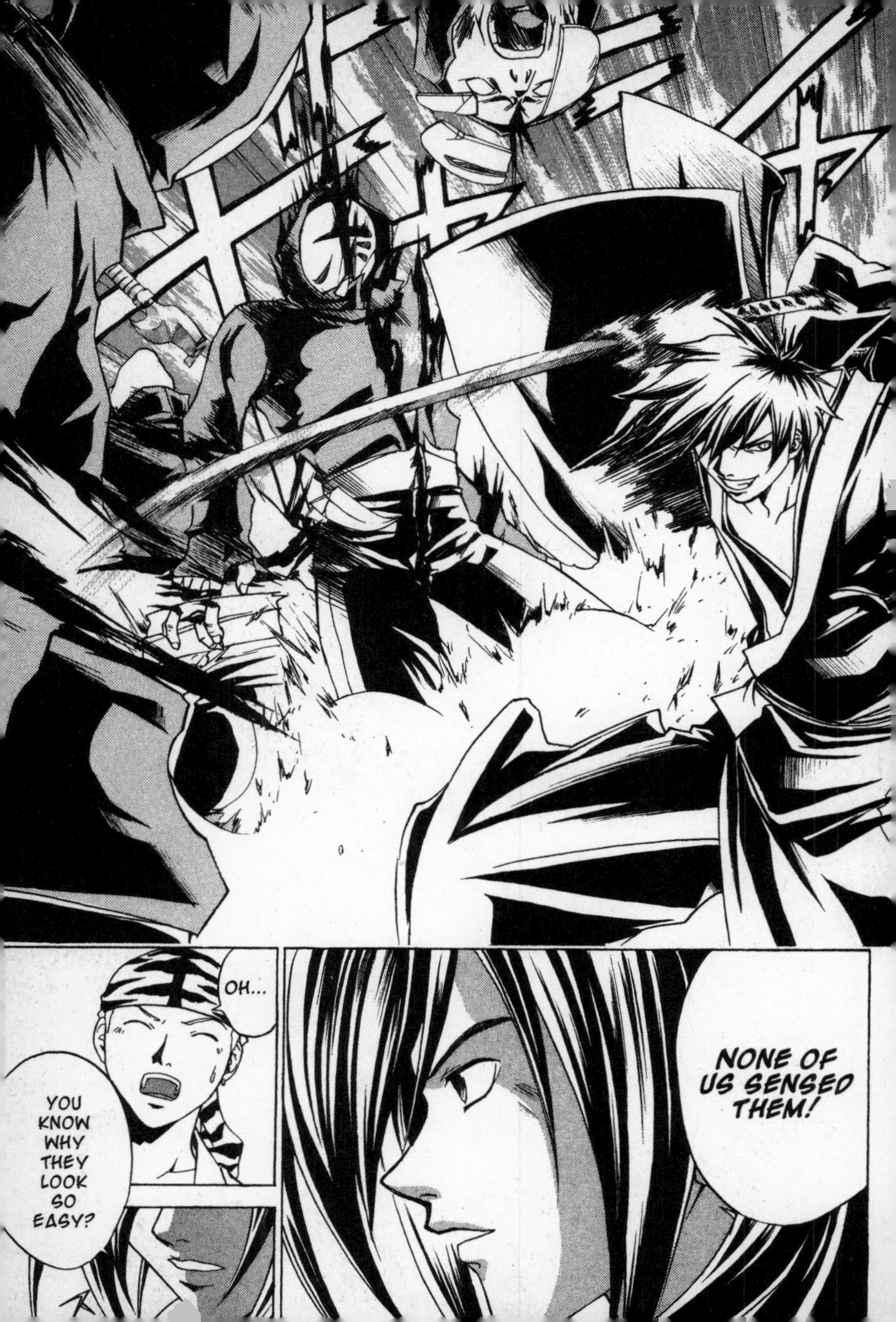
NONE OF US SENSED THEM!
OH...
YOU KNOW WHY THEY LOOK SO EASY?

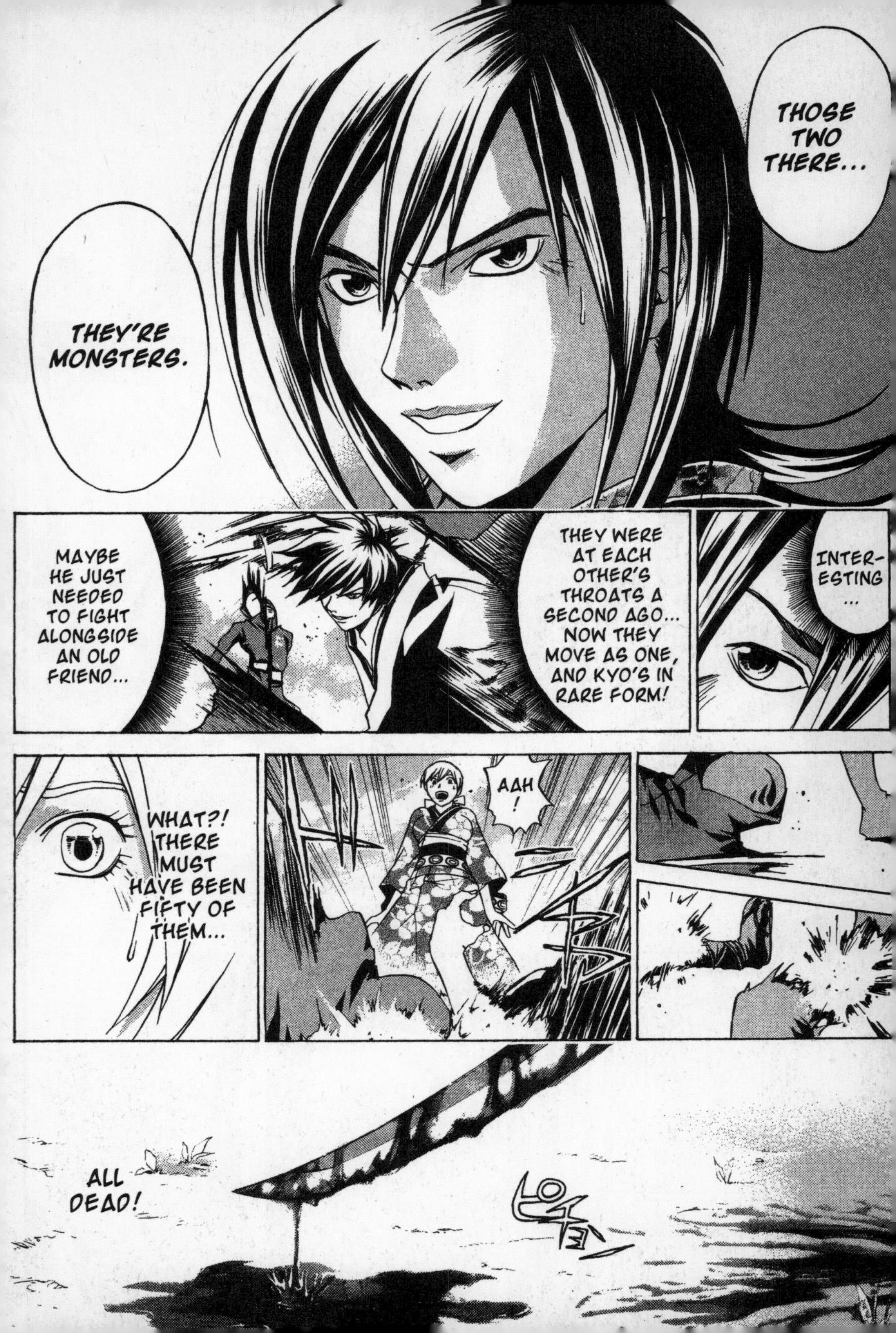
THOSE TWO THERE...
THEY'RE MONSTERS.
INTER-ESTING...
THEY WERE AT EACH OTHER'S THROATS A SECOND AGO... NOW THEY MOVE AS ONE, AND KYO'S IN RARE FORM!
MAYBE HE JUST NEEDED TO FIGHT ALONGSIDE AN OLD FRIEND...
AAH!
WHAT?! THERE MUST HAVE BEEN FIFTY OF THEM...
ALL DEAD!

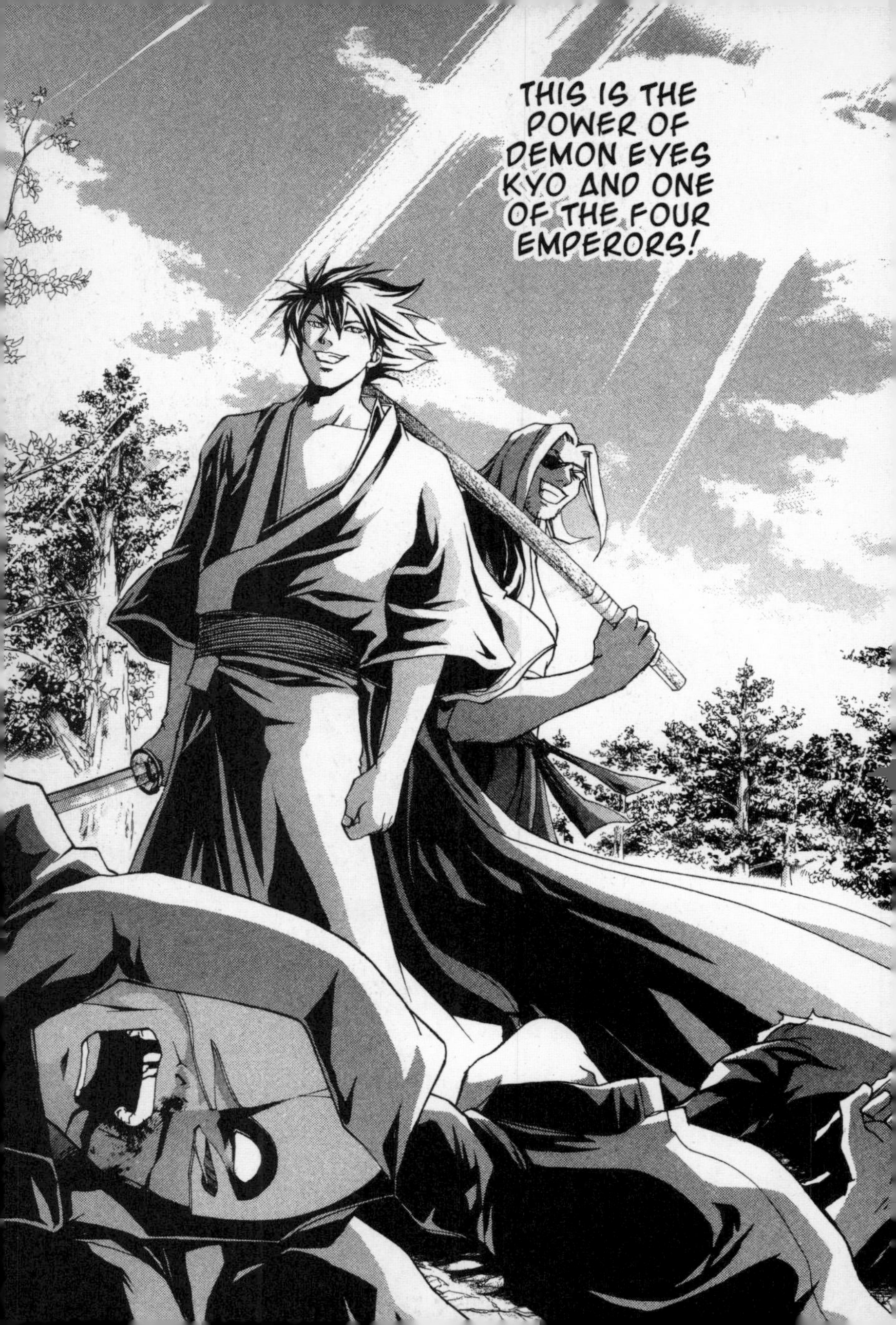
THIS IS THE POWER OF DEMON EYES KYO AND ONE OF THE FOUR EMPERORS!

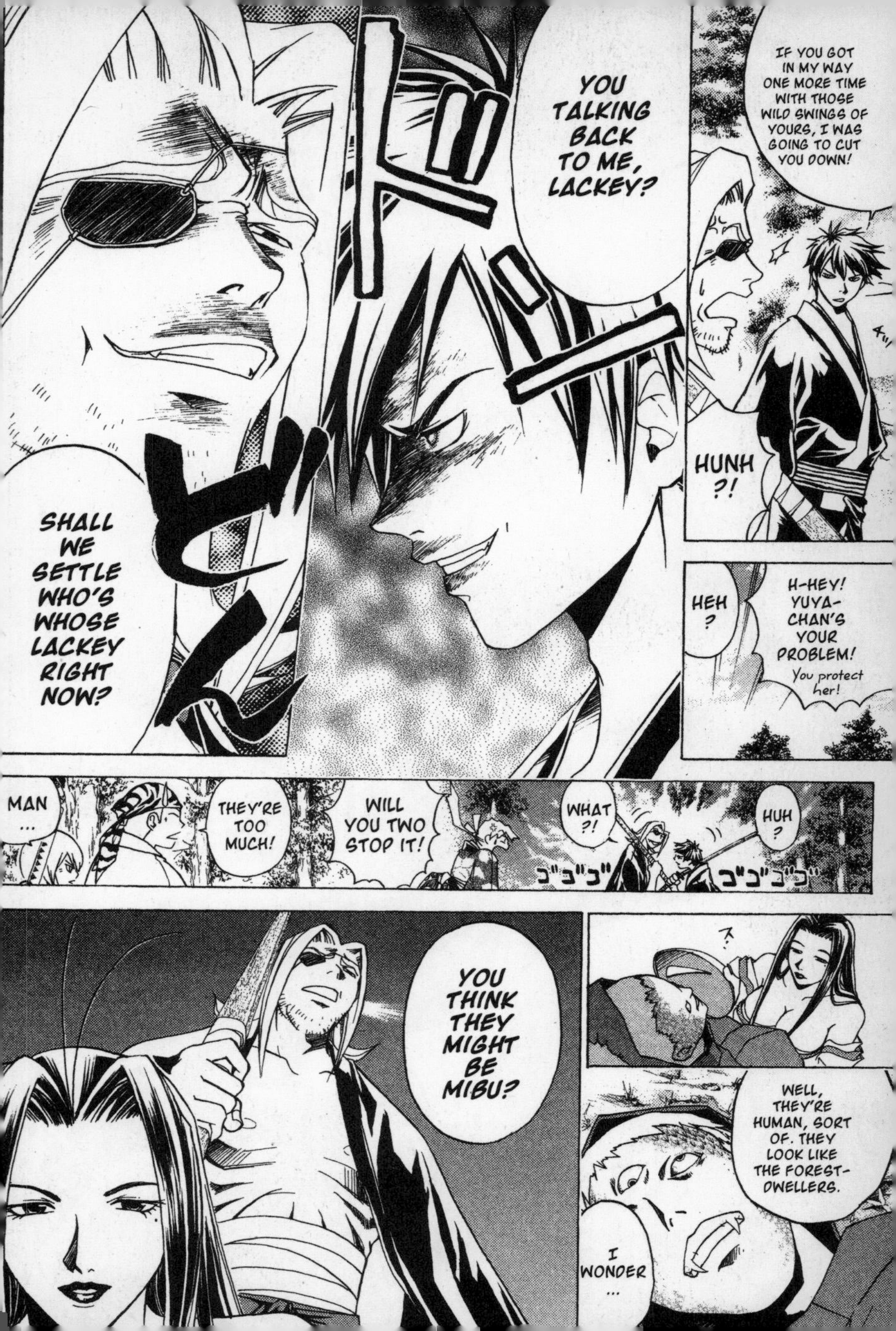
IF YOU GOT IN MY WAY ONE MORE TIME WITH THOSE WILD SWINGS OF YOURS, I WAS GOING TO CUT YOU DOWN!
HUNH ?!
H-HEY! YUYA-CHAN'S YOUR PROBLEM!
You protect her!
HEH ?
YOU TALKING BACK TO ME, LACKEY?
SHALL WE SETTLE WHO'S WHOSE LACKEY RIGHT NOW?
HUH ?
WHAT ?!
WILL YOU TWO STOP IT!
THEY'RE TOO MUCH!
MAN ...
WELL, THEY'RE HUMAN, SORT OF. THEY LOOK LIKE THE FOREST-DWELLERS.
I WONDER ...
YOU THINK THEY MIGHT BE MIBU?

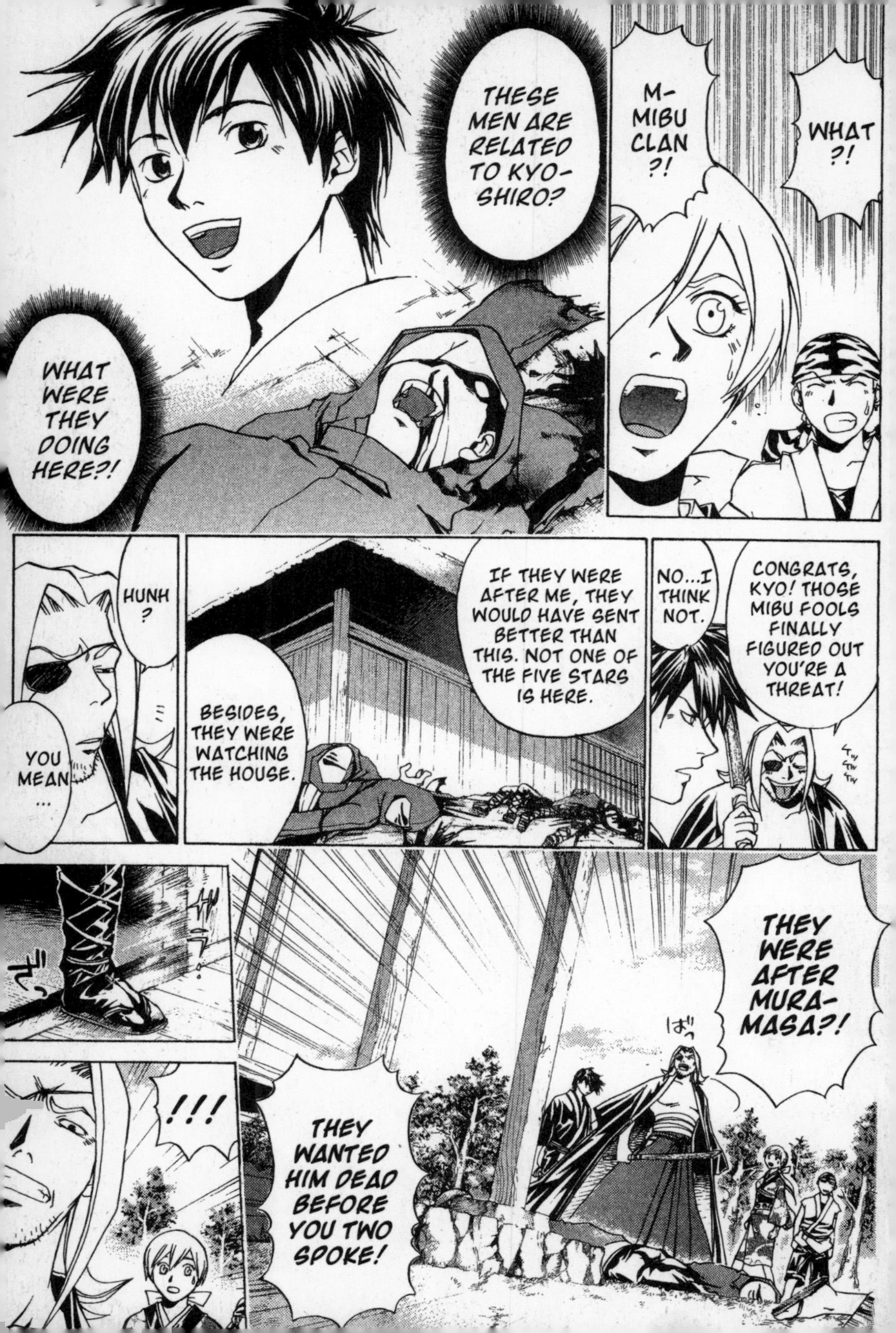
WHAT?!
M-MIBU CLAN?!
THESE MEN ARE RELATED TO KYO-SHIRO?
WHAT WERE THEY DOING HERE?!
CONGRATS, KYO! THOSE MIBU FOOLS FINALLY FIGURED OUT YOU'RE A THREAT!
NO...I THINK NOT.
IF THEY WERE AFTER ME, THEY WOULD HAVE SENT BETTER THAN THIS. NOT ONE OF THE FIVE STARS IS HERE.
BESIDES, THEY WERE WATCHING THE HOUSE.
HUNH?
YOU MEAN ...
THEY WERE AFTER MURA-MASA?!
THEY WANTED HIM DEAD BEFORE YOU TWO SPOKE!
!!!

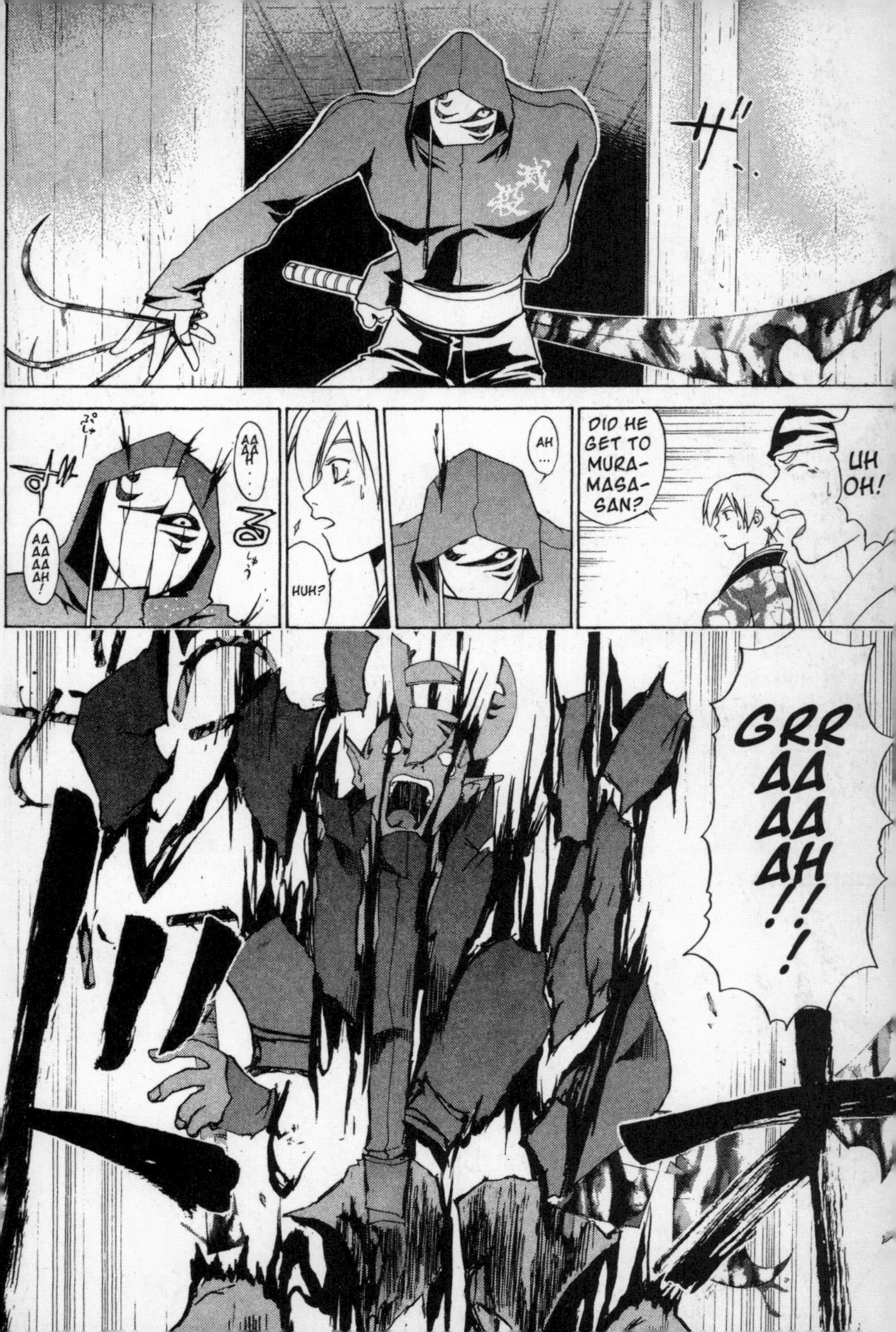
UH OH!
DID HE GET TO MURAMASA-SAN?
AH ...
HUH?
AAAAH...
AAAAAAAAH!
GRRAAAAAAH!!!

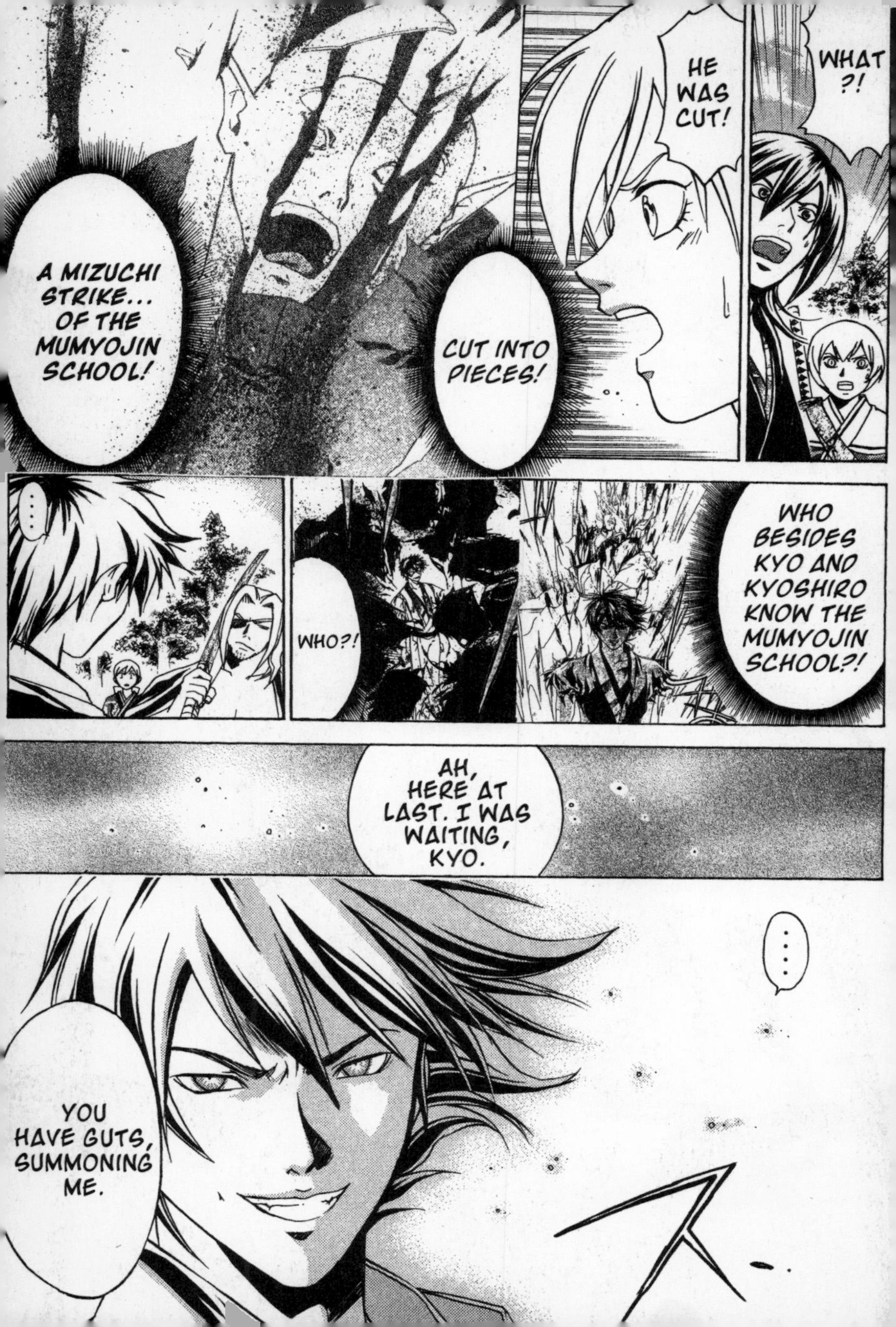
WHAT?!
HE WAS CUT!
CUT INTO PIECES!
A MIZUCHI STRIKE... OF THE MUMYOJIN SCHOOL!
WHO BESIDES KYO AND KYOSHIRO KNOW THE MUMYOJIN SCHOOL?!
WHO?!
.....
AH, HERE AT LAST. I WAS WAITING, KYO.
.....
YOU HAVE GUTS, SUMMONING ME.

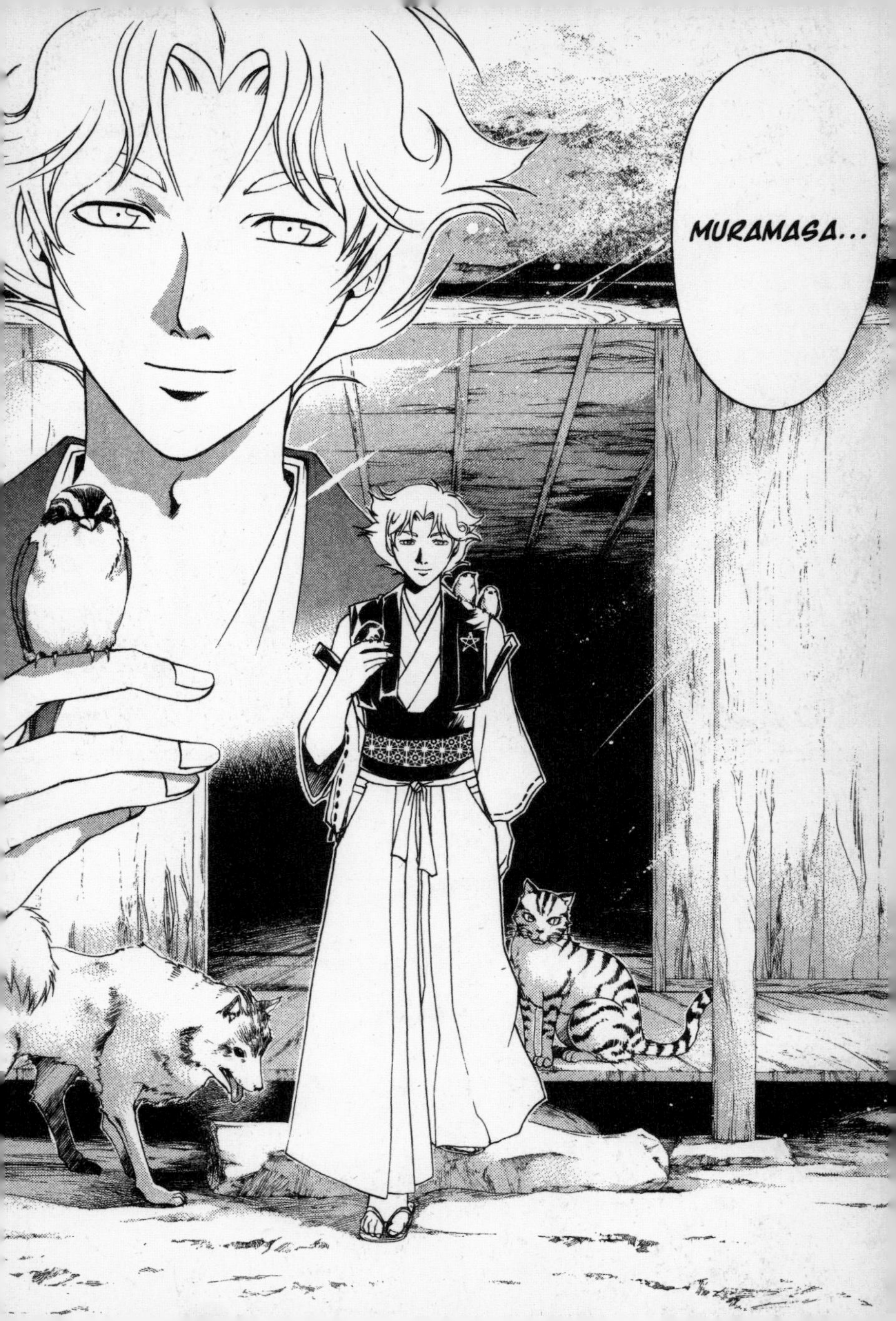
MURAMASA...

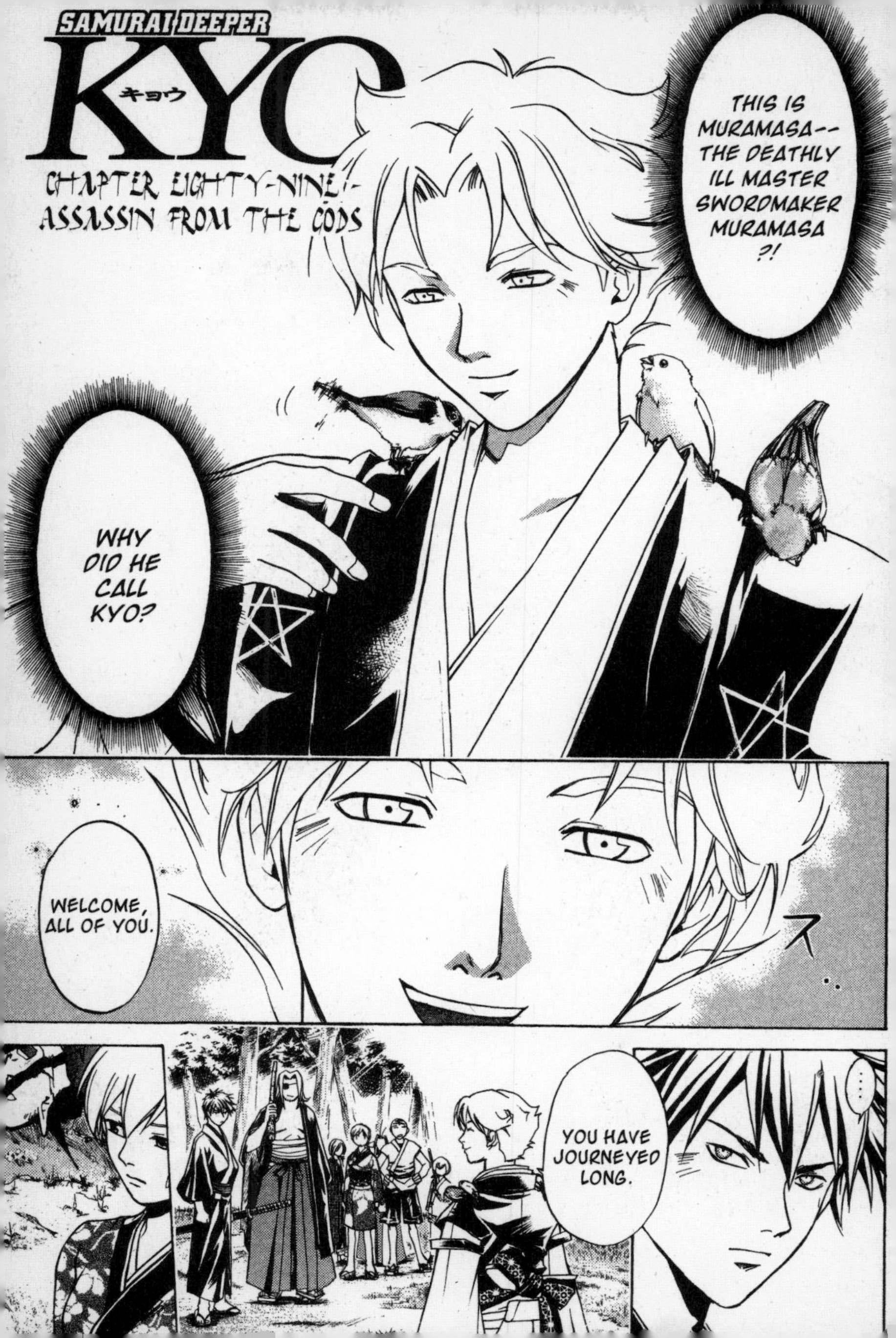
THIS IS MURAMASA-- THE DEATHLY ILL MASTER SWORDMAKER MURAMASA ?!
SAMURAI DEEPER KYO
キョウ
CHAPTER EIGHTY-NINE: ASSASSIN FROM THE GODS
WHY DID HE CALL KYO?
WELCOME, ALL OF YOU.
...
YOU HAVE JOURNEYED LONG.

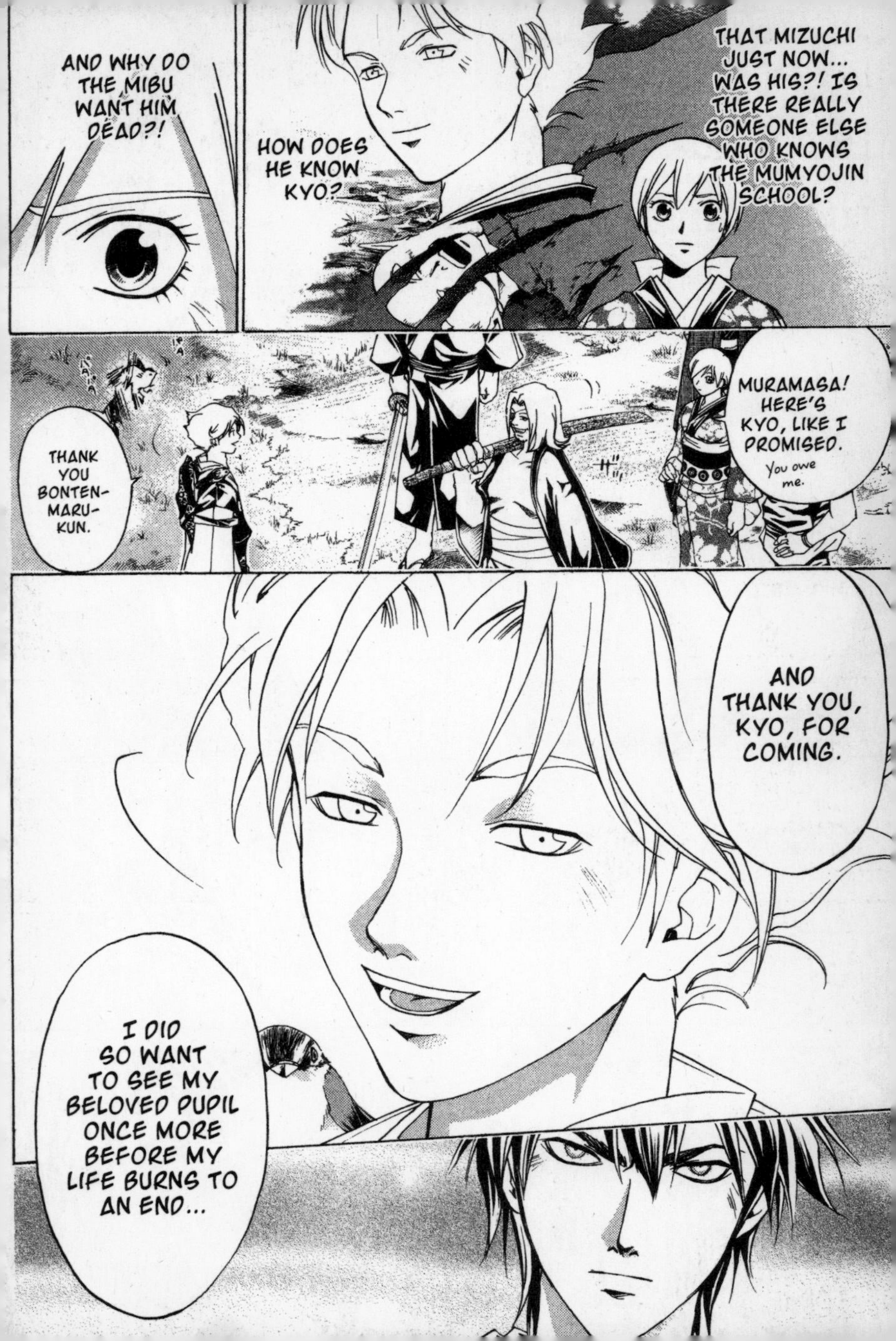
THAT MIZUCHI JUST NOW... WAS HIS?! IS THERE REALLY SOMEONE ELSE WHO KNOWS THE MUMYOJIN SCHOOL?
HOW DOES HE KNOW KYO?
AND WHY DO THE MIBU WANT HIM DEAD?!
MURAMASA! HERE'S KYO, LIKE I PROMISED.
You owe me.
THANK YOU BONTEN-MARU-KUN.
AND THANK YOU, KYO, FOR COMING.
I DID SO WANT TO SEE MY BELOVED PUPIL ONCE MORE BEFORE MY LIFE BURNS TO AN END...

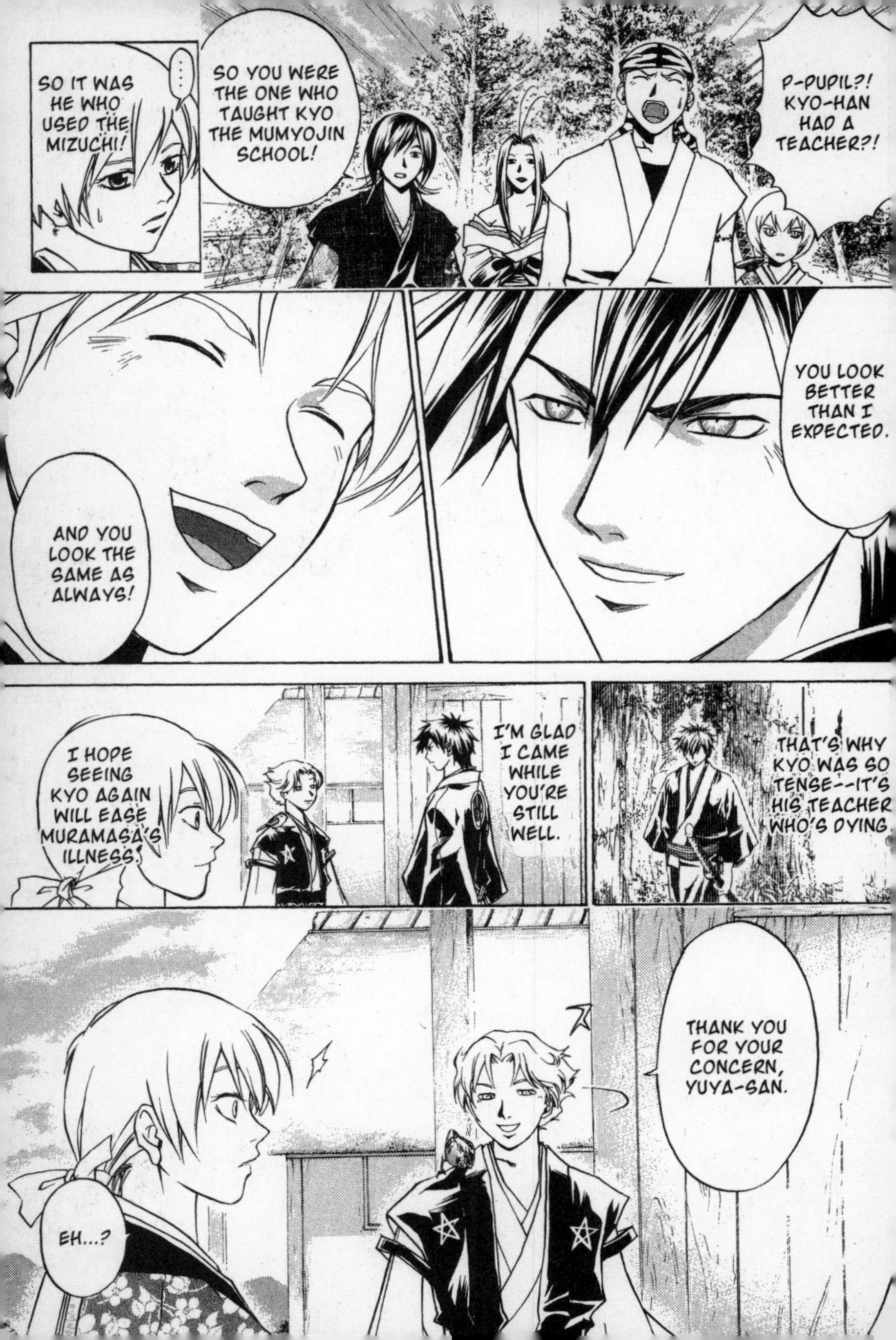
P-PUPIL?! KYO-HAN HAD A TEACHER?!
SO YOU WERE THE ONE WHO TAUGHT KYO THE MUMYOJIN SCHOOL!
...
SO IT WAS HE WHO USED THE MIZUCHI!
YOU LOOK BETTER THAN I EXPECTED.
AND YOU LOOK THE SAME AS ALWAYS!
THAT'S WHY KYO WAS SO TENSE--IT'S HIS TEACHER WHO'S DYING.
I'M GLAD I CAME WHILE YOU'RE STILL WELL.
I HOPE SEEING KYO AGAIN WILL EASE MURAMASA'S ILLNESS.
THANK YOU FOR YOUR CONCERN, YUYA-SAN.
EH...?

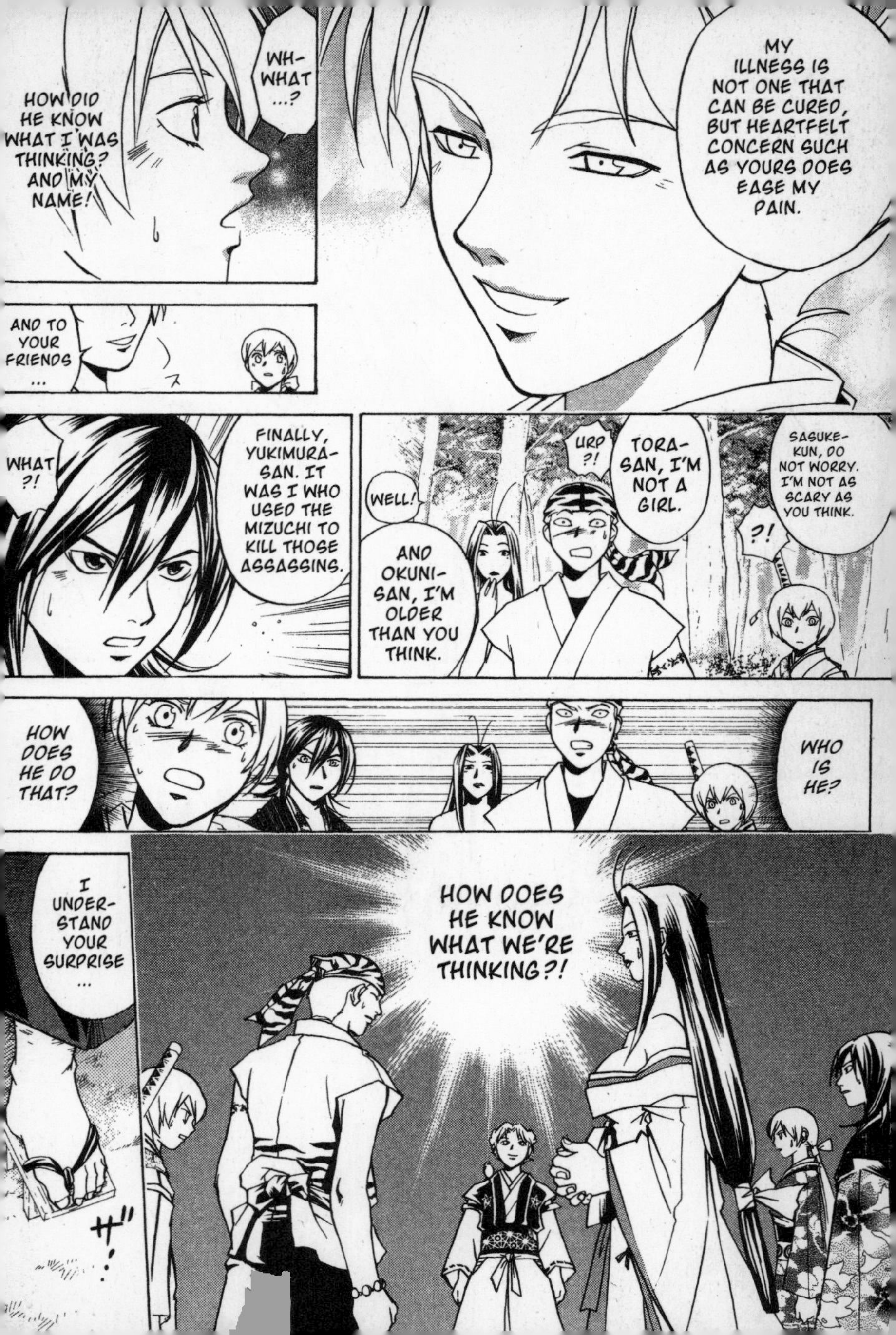
MY ILLNESS IS NOT ONE THAT CAN BE CURED, BUT HEARTFELT CONCERN SUCH AS YOURS DOES EASE MY PAIN.
WH- WHAT ...?
HOW DID HE KNOW WHAT I WAS THINKING? AND MY NAME!
AND TO YOUR FRIENDS ...
SASUKE-KUN, DO NOT WORRY. I'M NOT AS SCARY AS YOU THINK.
?!
TORA-SAN, I'M NOT A GIRL.
URP ?!
WELL!
AND OKUNI-SAN, I'M OLDER THAN YOU THINK.
FINALLY, YUKIMURA-SAN. IT WAS I WHO USED THE MIZUCHI TO KILL THOSE ASSASSINS.
WHAT ?!
WHO IS HE?
HOW DOES HE DO THAT?
HOW DOES HE KNOW WHAT WE'RE THINKING?!
I UNDER-STAND YOUR SURPRISE ...

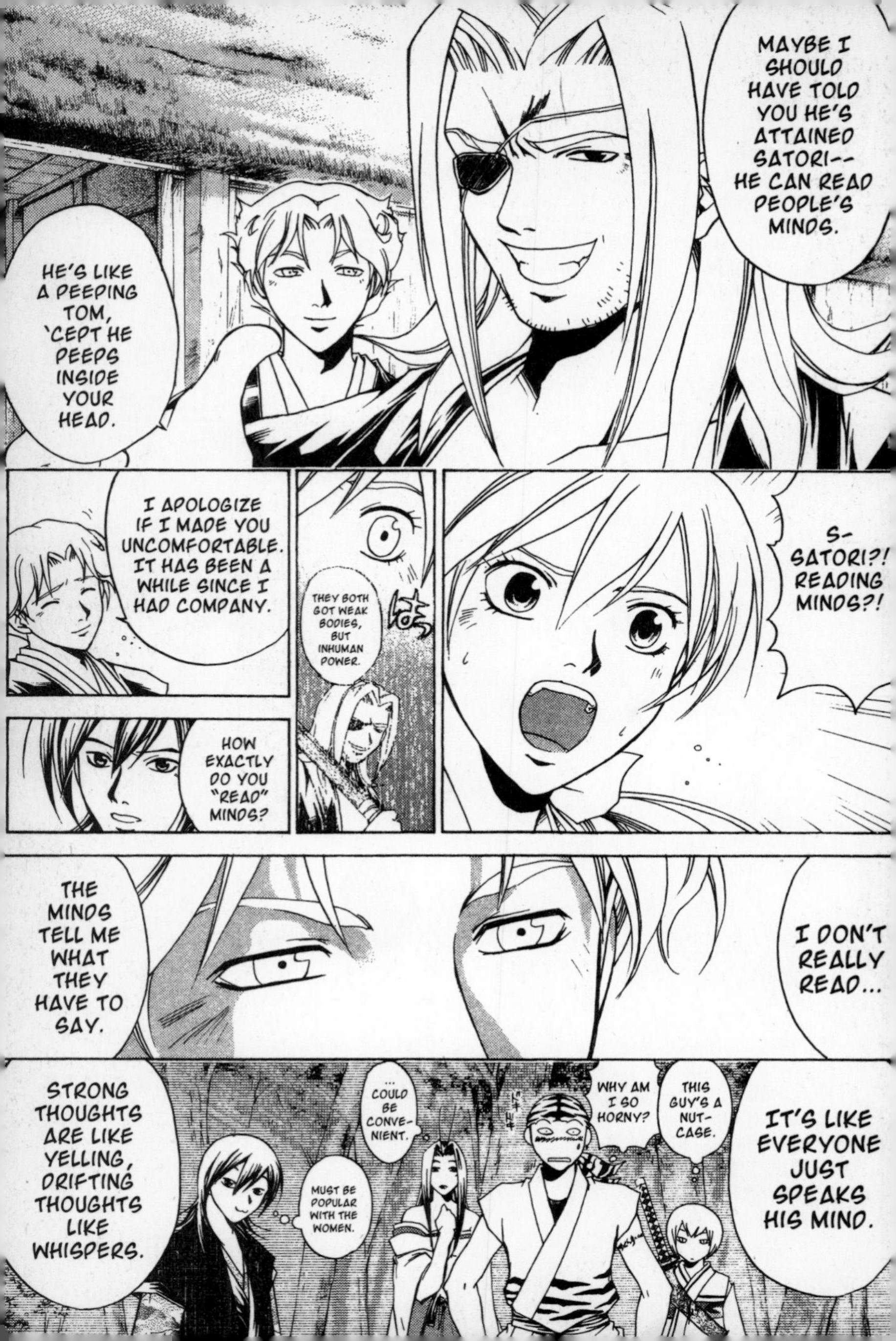
MAYBE I SHOULD HAVE TOLD YOU HE'S ATTAINED SATORI-- HE CAN READ PEOPLE'S MINDS.
HE'S LIKE A PEEPING TOM, 'CEPT HE PEEPS INSIDE YOUR HEAD.
S-SATORI?! READING MINDS?!
THEY BOTH GOT WEAK BODIES, BUT INHUMAN POWER.
I APOLOGIZE IF I MADE YOU UNCOMFORTABLE. IT HAS BEEN A WHILE SINCE I HAD COMPANY.
HOW EXACTLY DO YOU "READ" MINDS?
I DON'T REALLY READ...
THE MINDS TELL ME WHAT THEY HAVE TO SAY.
IT'S LIKE EVERYONE JUST SPEAKS HIS MIND.
THIS GUY'S A NUT-CASE.
WHY AM I SO HORNY?
...COULD BE CONVE-NIENT.
MUST BE POPULAR WITH THE WOMEN.
STRONG THOUGHTS ARE LIKE YELLING, DRIFTING THOUGHTS LIKE WHISPERS.

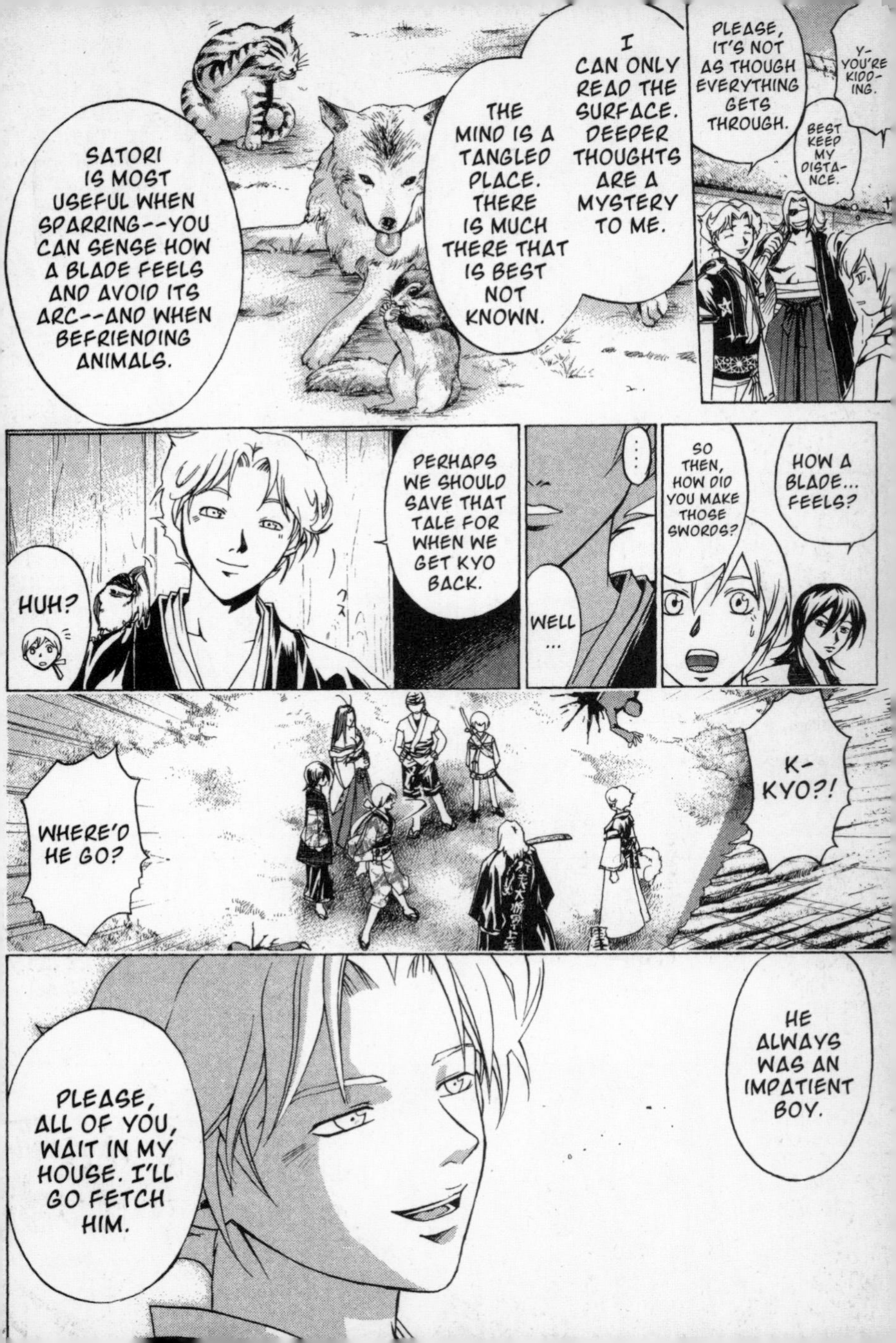
Y-YOU'RE KIDDING.
PLEASE, IT'S NOT AS THOUGH EVERYTHING GETS THROUGH.
BEST KEEP MY DISTANCE.
I CAN ONLY READ THE SURFACE. DEEPER THOUGHTS ARE A MYSTERY TO ME.
THE MIND IS A TANGLED PLACE. THERE IS MUCH THERE THAT IS BEST NOT KNOWN.
SATORI IS MOST USEFUL WHEN SPARRING--YOU CAN SENSE HOW A BLADE FEELS AND AVOID ITS ARC--AND WHEN BEFRIENDING ANIMALS.
HOW A BLADE... FEELS?
SO THEN, HOW DID YOU MAKE THOSE SWORDS?
...
WELL ...
PERHAPS WE SHOULD SAVE THAT TALE FOR WHEN WE GET KYO BACK.
クス
HUH?
K-KYO?!
WHERE'D HE GO?
HE ALWAYS WAS AN IMPATIENT BOY.
PLEASE, ALL OF YOU, WAIT IN MY HOUSE. I'LL GO FETCH HIM.

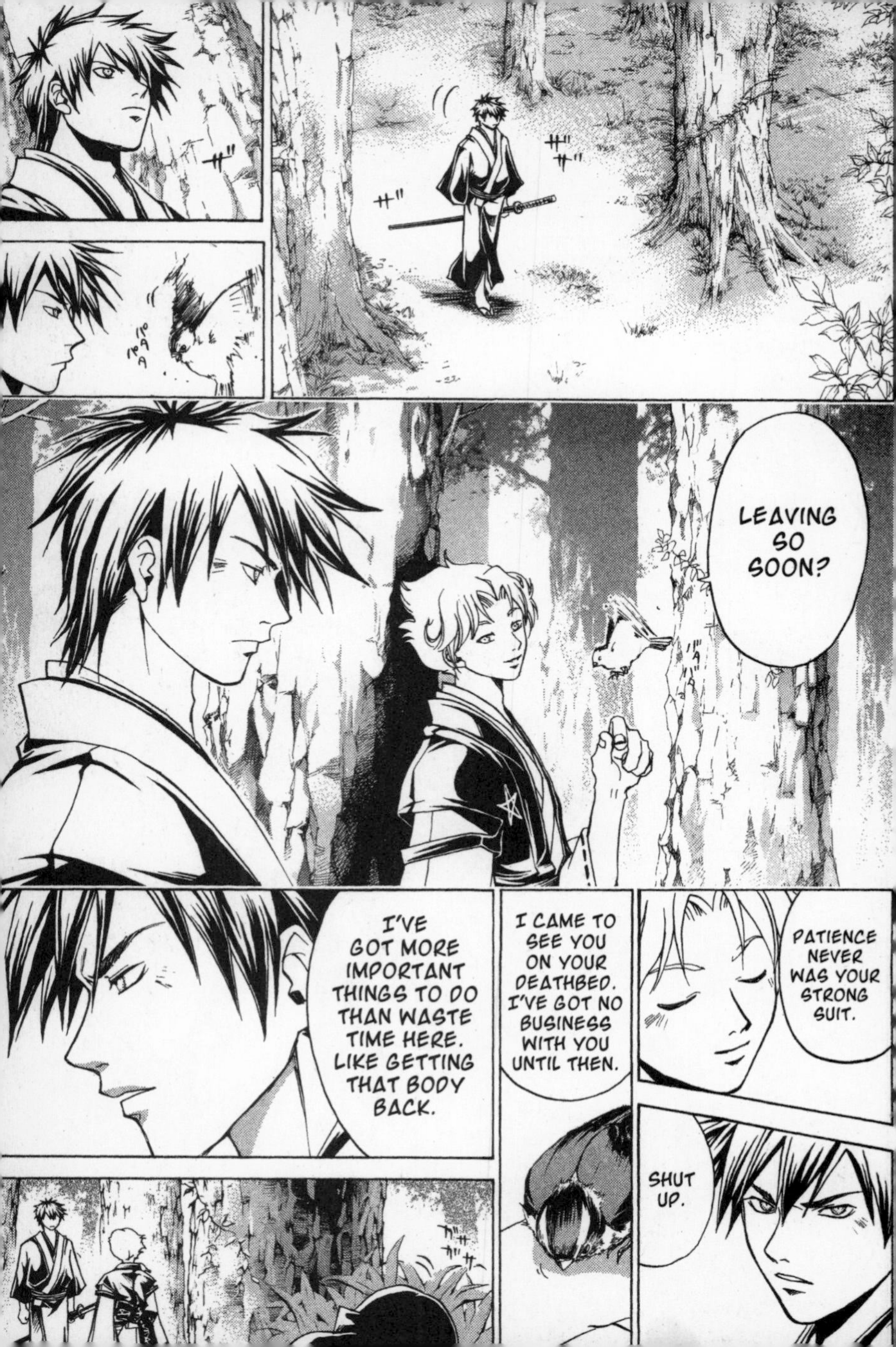
LEAVING SO SOON?
PATIENCE NEVER WAS YOUR STRONG SUIT.
I CAME TO SEE YOU ON YOUR DEATHBED. I'VE GOT NO BUSINESS WITH YOU UNTIL THEN.
I'VE GOT MORE IMPORTANT THINGS TO DO THAN WASTE TIME HERE. LIKE GETTING THAT BODY BACK.
SHUT UP.

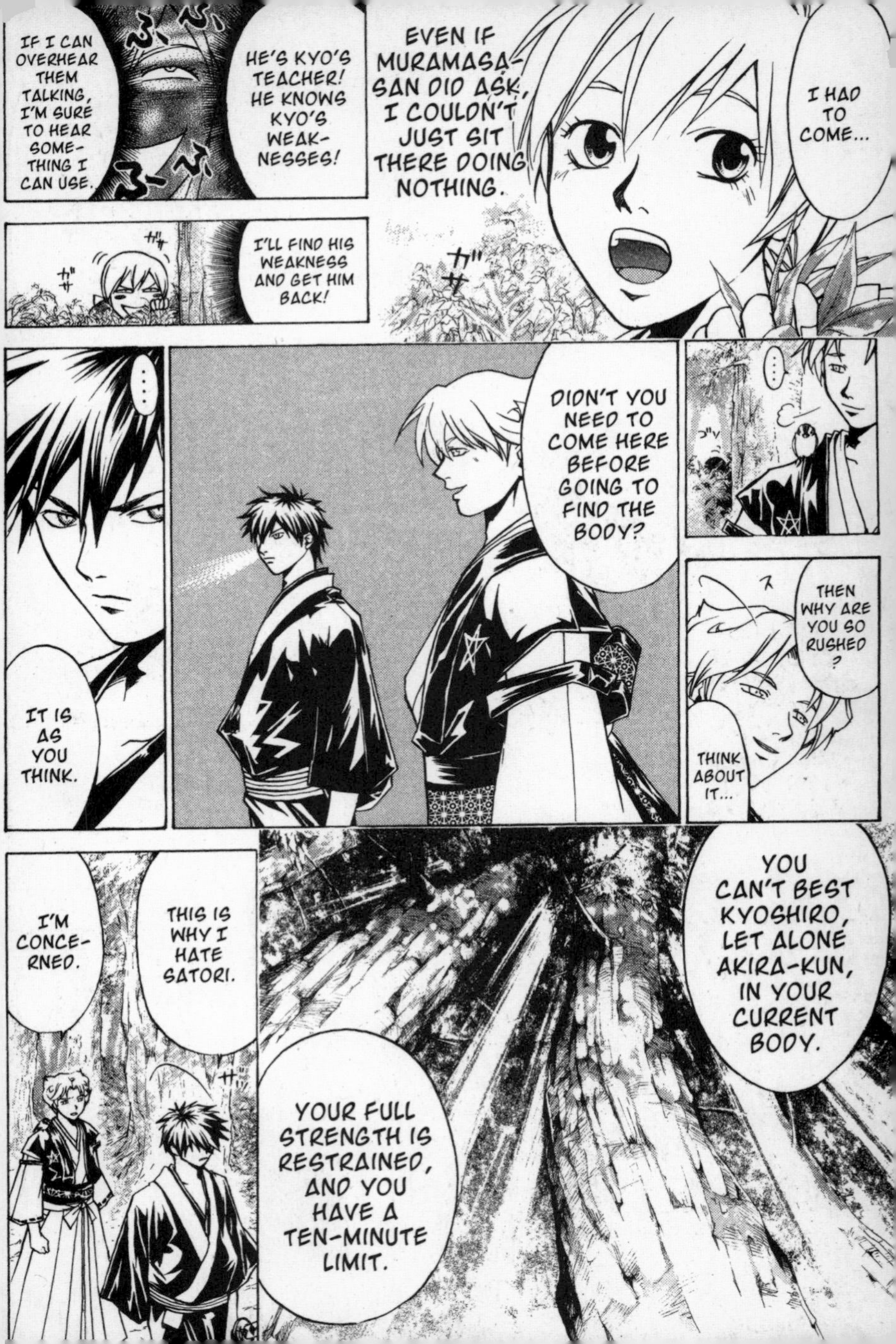
I HAD TO COME...
EVEN IF MURAMASA-SAN DID ASK, I COULDN'T JUST SIT THERE DOING NOTHING.
HE'S KYO'S TEACHER! HE KNOWS KYO'S WEAKNESSES!
IF I CAN OVERHEAR THEM TALKING, I'M SURE TO HEAR SOMETHING I CAN USE.
I'LL FIND HIS WEAKNESS AND GET HIM BACK!
...
THEN WHY ARE YOU SO RUSHED?
THINK ABOUT IT...
DIDN'T YOU NEED TO COME HERE BEFORE GOING TO FIND THE BODY?
...
IT IS AS YOU THINK.
YOU CAN'T BEST KYOSHIRO, LET ALONE AKIRA-KUN, IN YOUR CURRENT BODY.
YOUR FULL STRENGTH IS RESTRAINED, AND YOU HAVE A TEN-MINUTE LIMIT.
THIS IS WHY I HATE SATORI.
I'M CONCERNED.

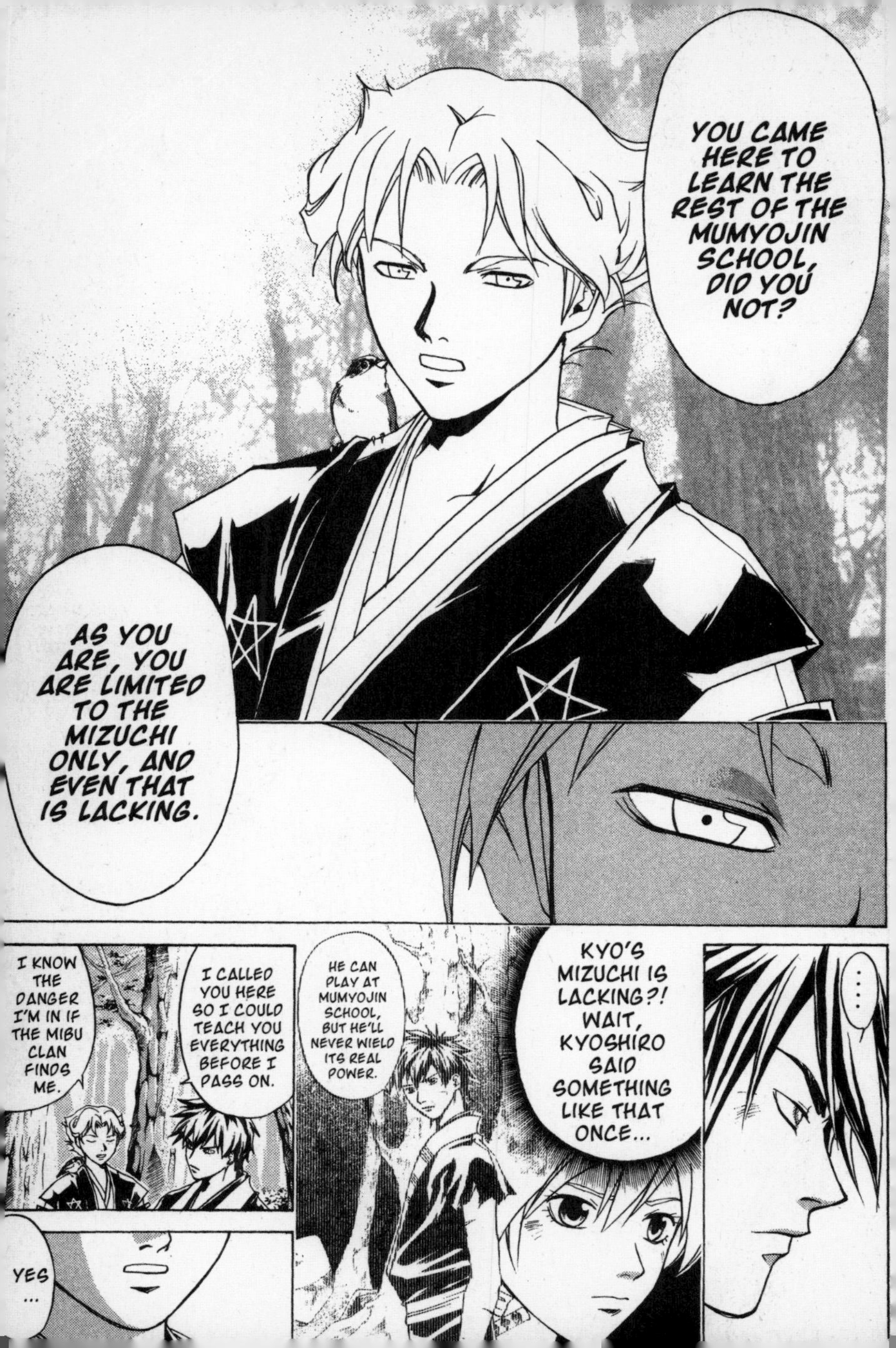

YOU CAME HERE TO LEARN THE REST OF THE MUMYOJIN SCHOOL, DID YOU NOT?
AS YOU ARE, YOU ARE LIMITED TO THE MIZUCHI ONLY, AND EVEN THAT IS LACKING.
...
KYO'S MIZUCHI IS LACKING?! WAIT, KYOSHIRO SAID SOMETHING LIKE THAT ONCE...
HE CAN PLAY AT MUMYOJIN SCHOOL, BUT HE'LL NEVER WIELD ITS REAL POWER.
I CALLED YOU HERE SO I COULD TEACH YOU EVERYTHING BEFORE I PASS ON.
I KNOW THE DANGER I'M IN IF THE MIBU CLAN FINDS ME.
YES ...

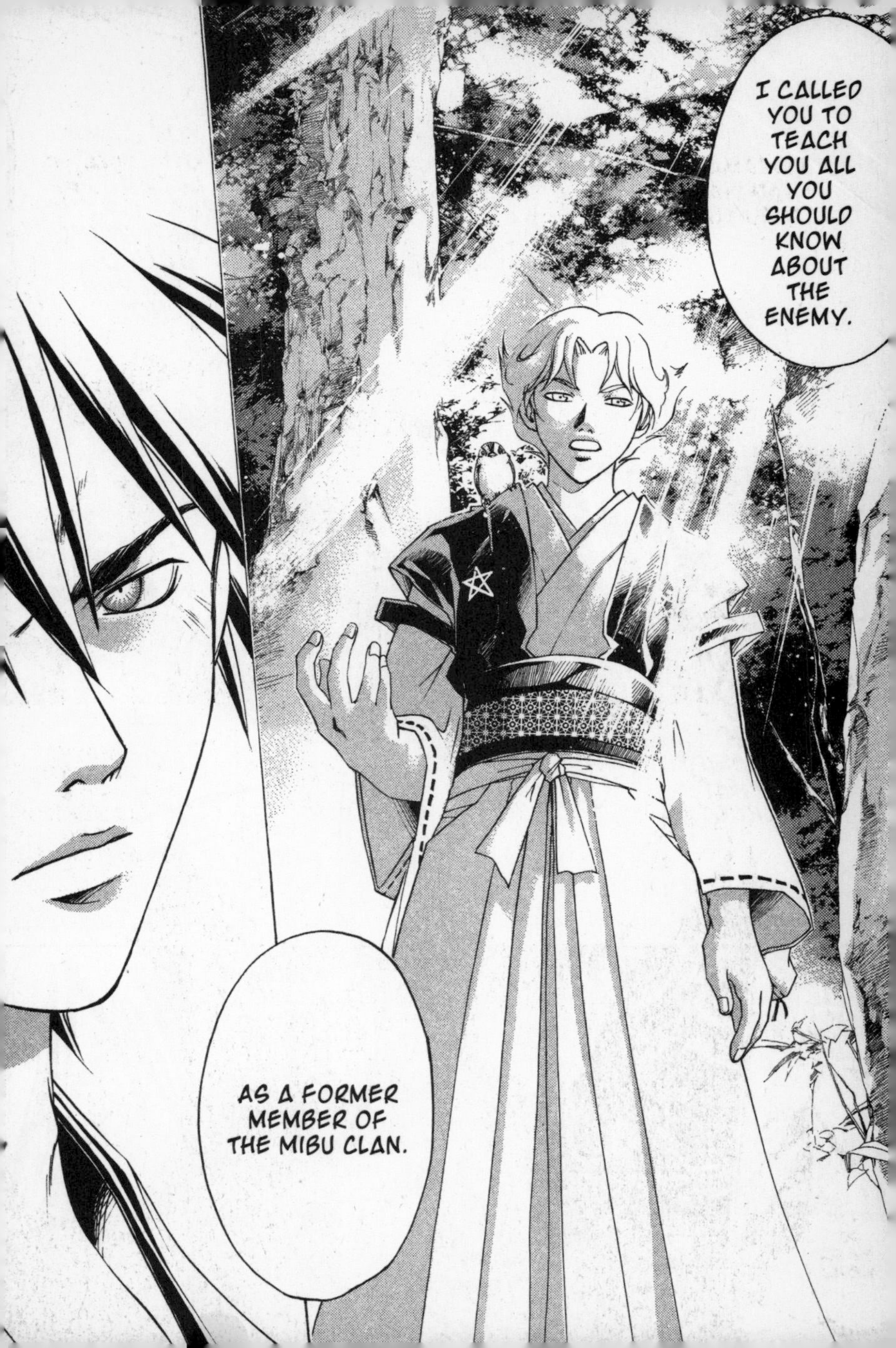
I CALLED YOU TO TEACH YOU ALL YOU SHOULD KNOW ABOUT THE ENEMY.
AS A FORMER MEMBER OF THE MIBU CLAN.

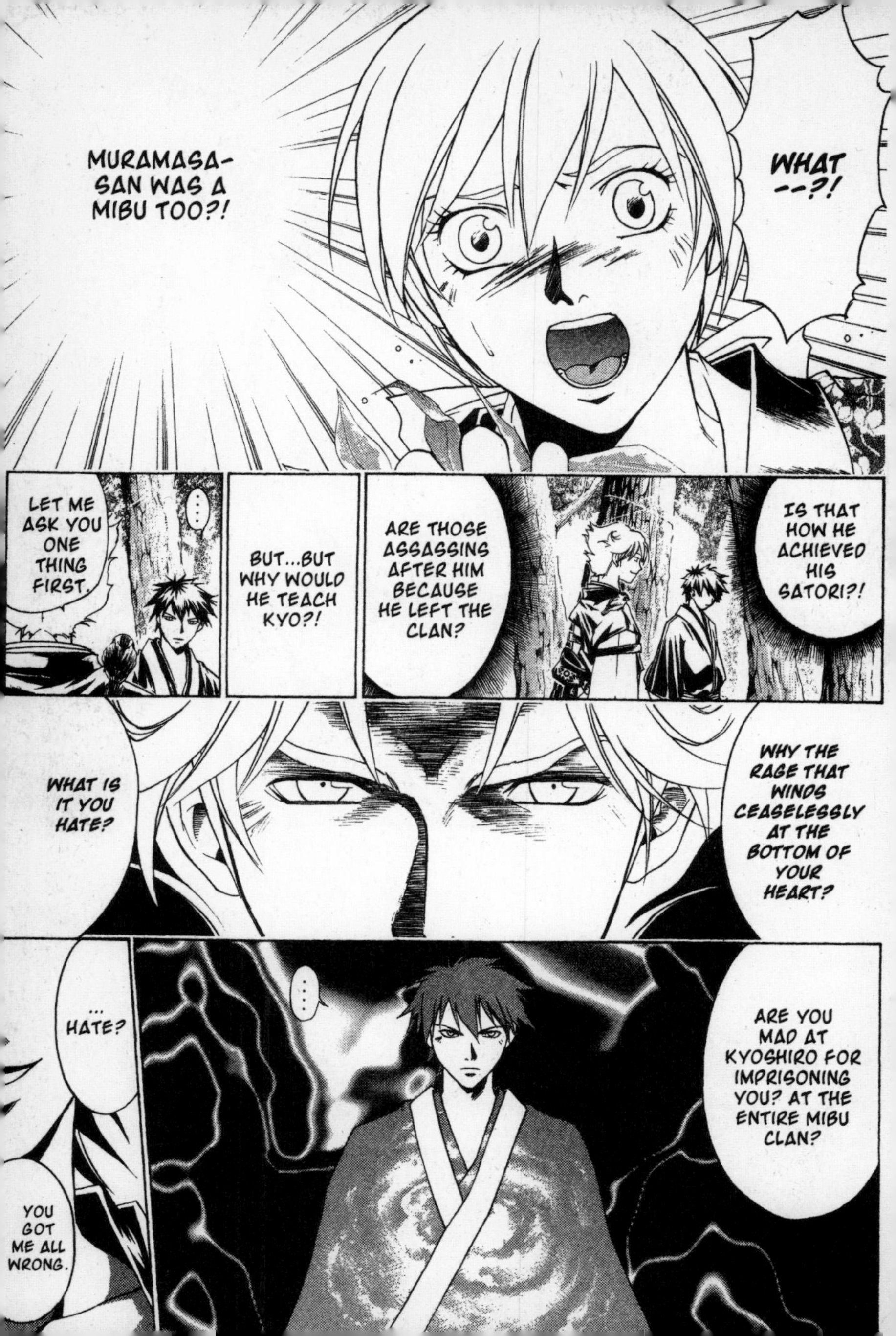
WHAT--?!
MURAMASA-SAN WAS A MIBU TOO?!
IS THAT HOW HE ACHIEVED HIS SATORI?!
ARE THOSE ASSASSINS AFTER HIM BECAUSE HE LEFT THE CLAN?
BUT...BUT WHY WOULD HE TEACH KYO?!
....
LET ME ASK YOU ONE THING FIRST.
WHY THE RAGE THAT WINDS CEASELESSLY AT THE BOTTOM OF YOUR HEART?
WHAT IS IT YOU HATE?
ARE YOU MAD AT KYOSHIRO FOR IMPRISONING YOU? AT THE ENTIRE MIBU CLAN?
....
...HATE?
YOU GOT ME ALL WRONG.

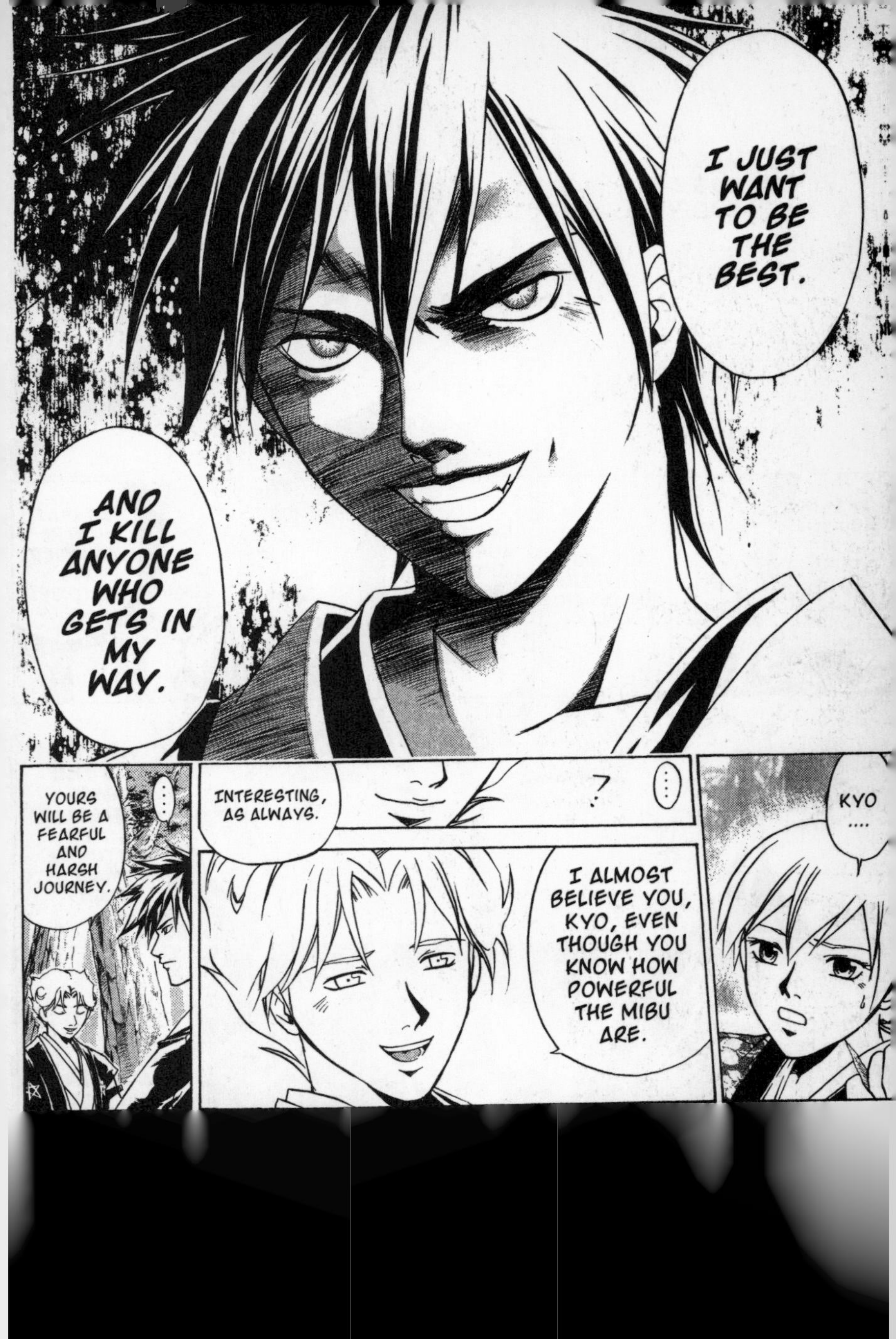
I JUST WANT TO BE THE BEST.
AND I KILL ANYONE WHO GETS IN MY WAY.
KYO ....
...
?
INTERESTING, AS ALWAYS.
I ALMOST BELIEVE YOU, KYO, EVEN THOUGH YOU KNOW HOW POWERFUL THE MIBU ARE.
...
YOURS WILL BE A FEARFUL AND HARSH JOURNEY.

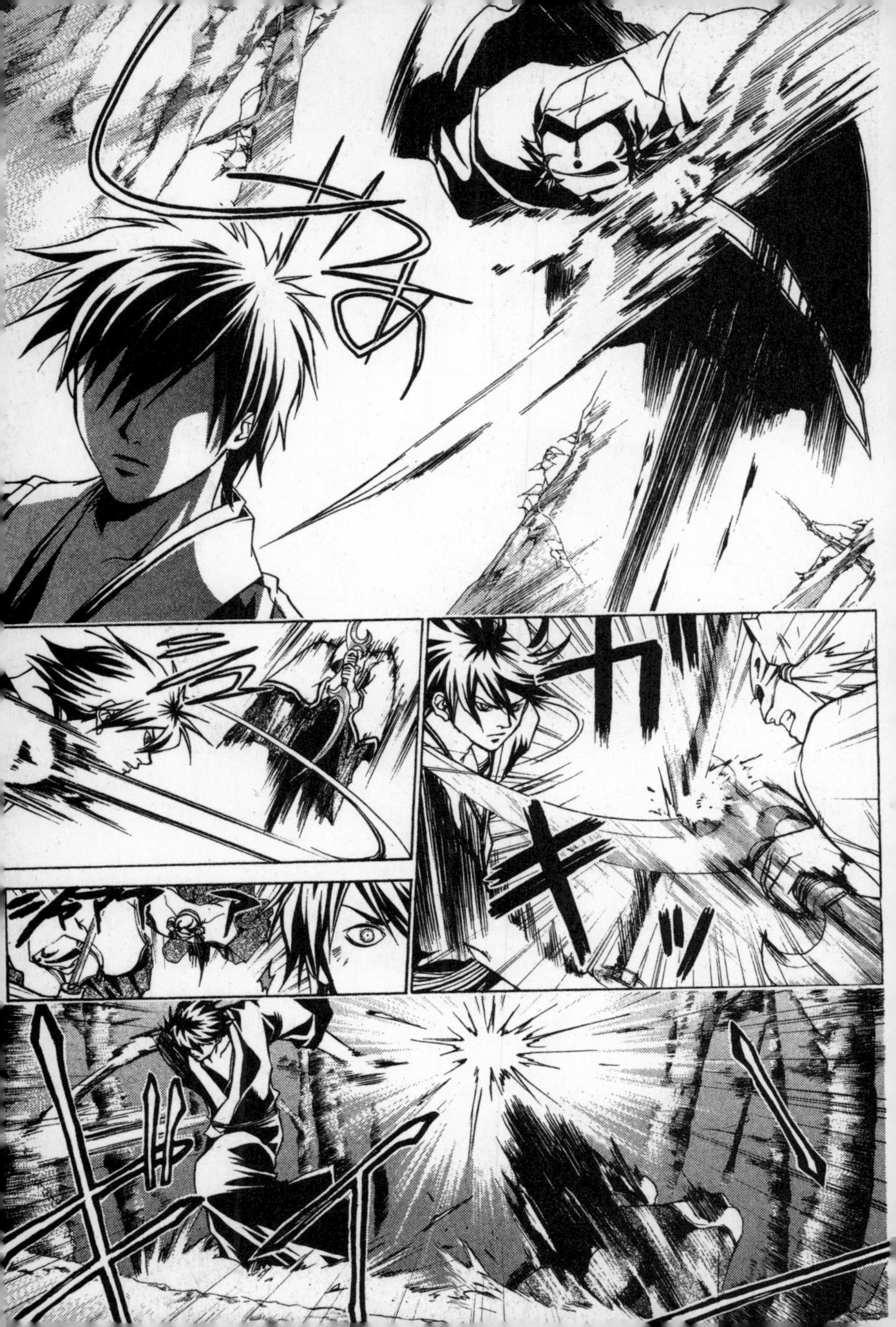

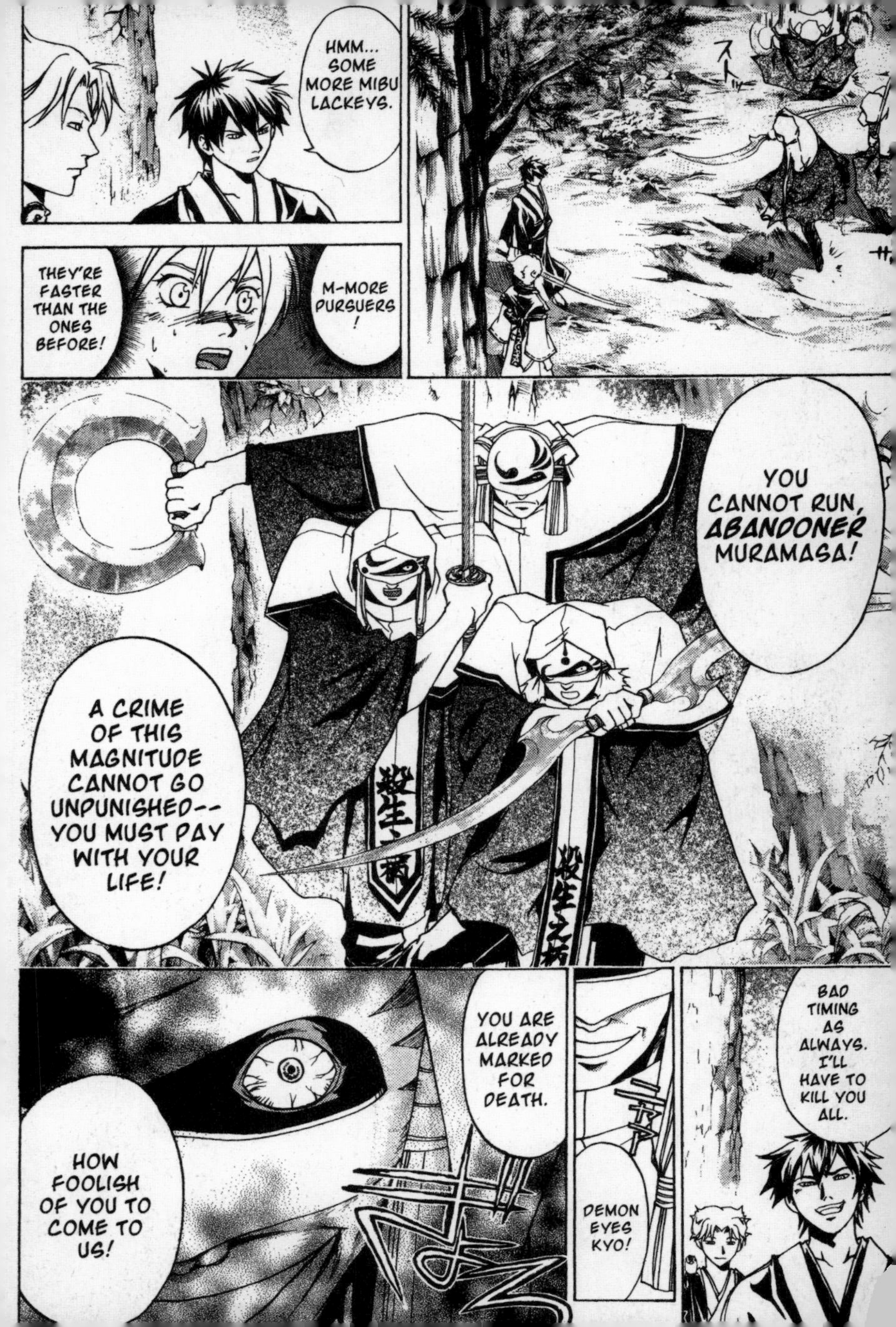
HMM... SOME MORE MIBU LACKEYS.
M-MORE PURSUERS!
THEY'RE FASTER THAN THE ONES BEFORE!
YOU CANNOT RUN, ***ABANDONER*** MURAMASA!
A CRIME OF THIS MAGNITUDE CANNOT GO UNPUNISHED--YOU MUST PAY WITH YOUR LIFE!
BAD TIMING AS ALWAYS. I'LL HAVE TO KILL YOU ALL.
YOU ARE ALREADY MARKED FOR DEATH.
DEMON EYES KYO!
HOW FOOLISH OF YOU TO COME TO US!

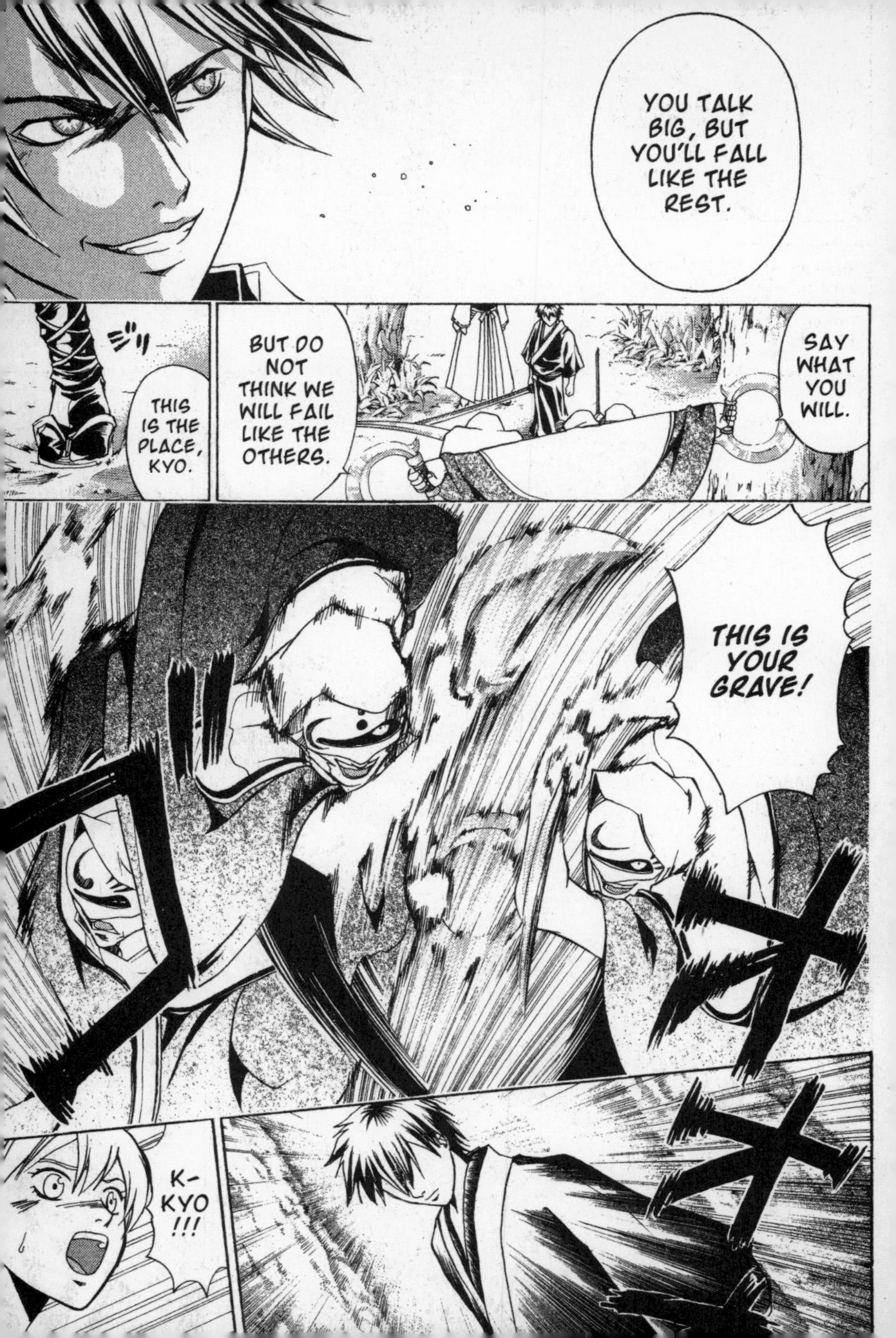
YOU TALK BIG, BUT YOU'LL FALL LIKE THE REST.
SAY WHAT YOU WILL.
BUT DO NOT THINK WE WILL FAIL LIKE THE OTHERS.
ジリ
THIS IS THE PLACE, KYO.
THIS IS YOUR GRAVE!
K-KYO!!!

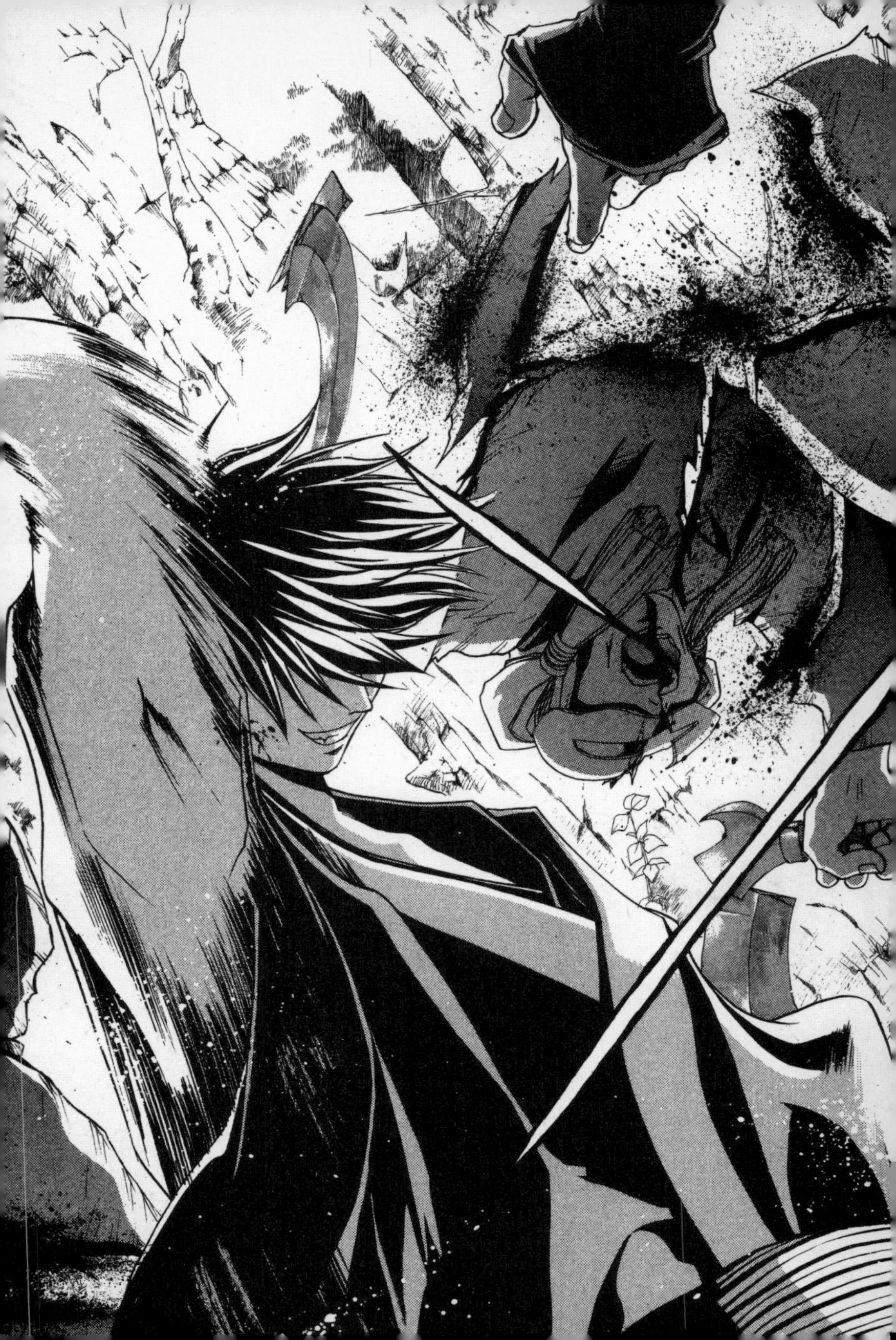

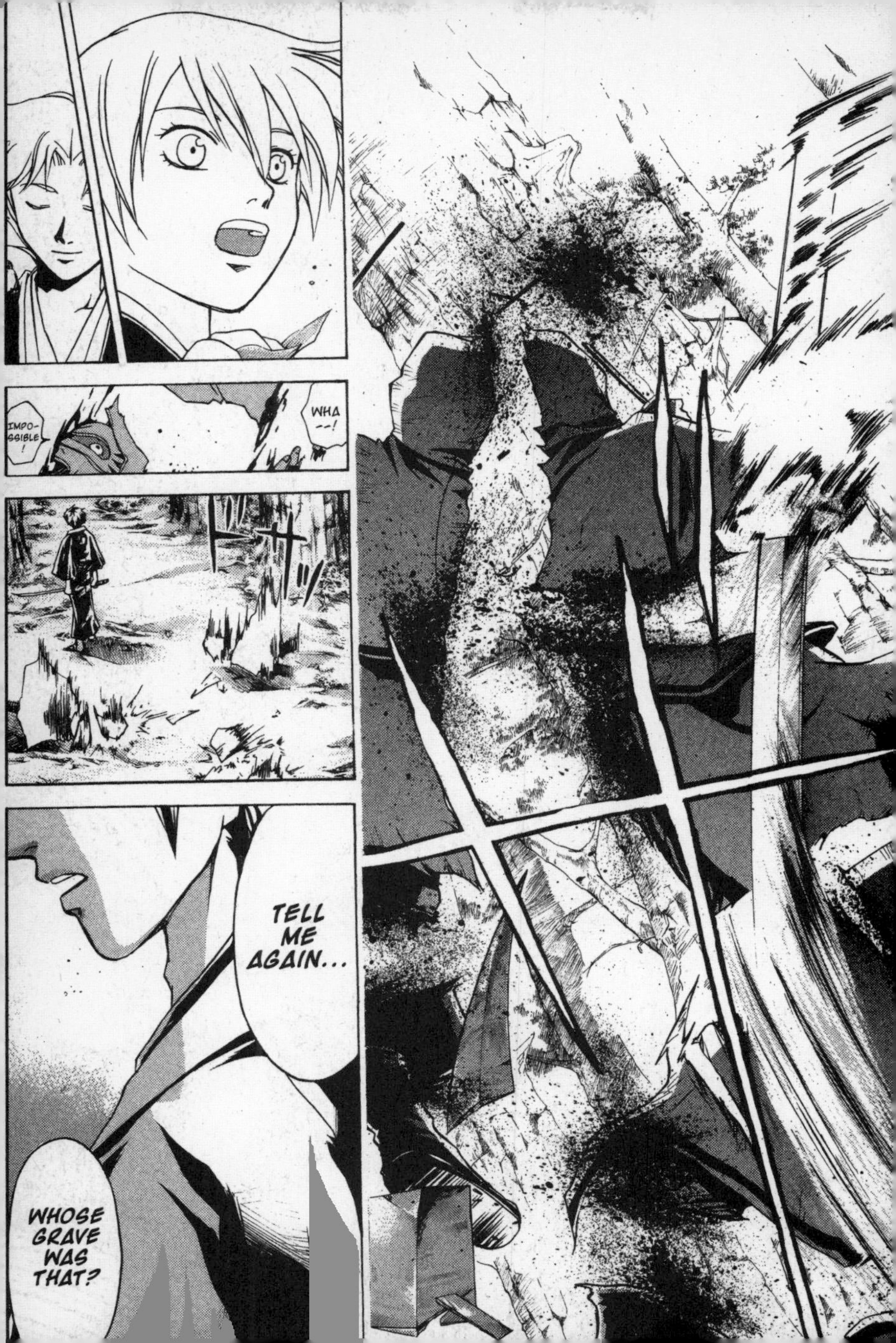
WHA--!
IMPOSSIBLE!
TELL ME AGAIN...
WHOSE GRAVE WAS THAT?

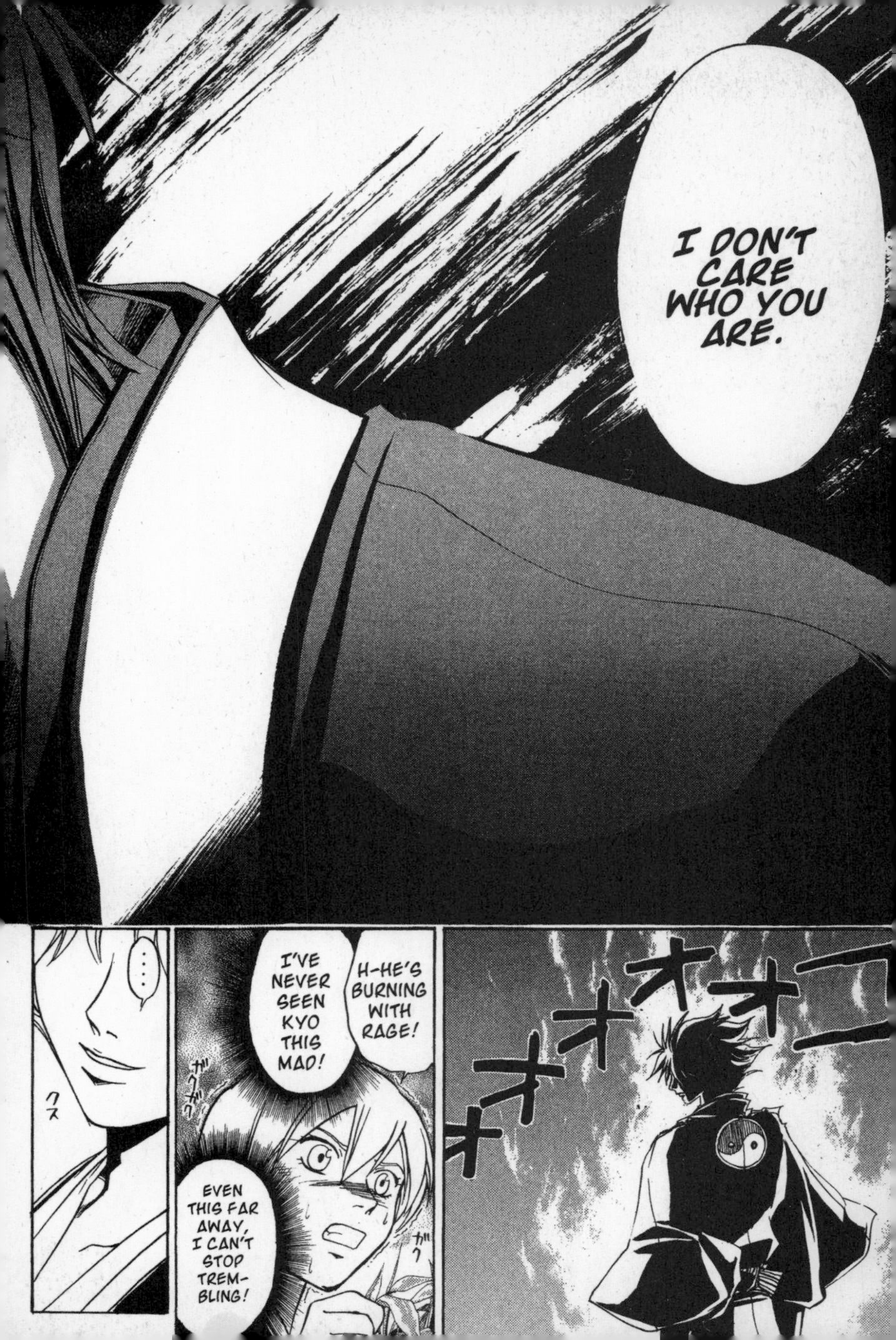

I DON'T CARE WHO YOU ARE.
H-HE'S BURNING WITH RAGE!
I'VE NEVER SEEN KYO THIS MAD!
EVEN THIS FAR AWAY, I CAN'T STOP TREMBLING!
.....

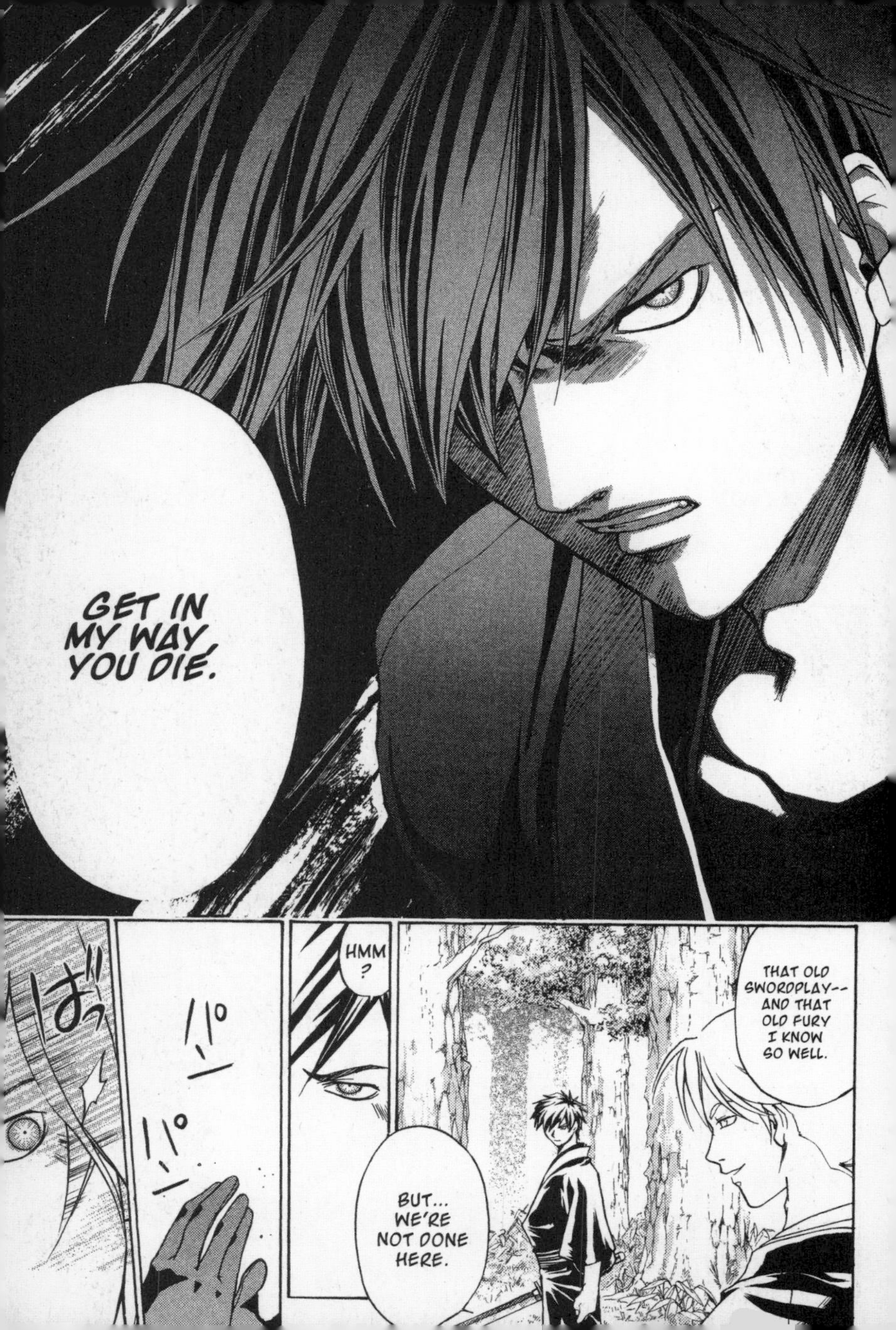
GET IN MY WAY, YOU DIE.
THAT OLD SWORDPLAY-- AND THAT OLD FURY I KNOW SO WELL.
BUT... WE'RE NOT DONE HERE.
HMM ?
パ
パ
はっ

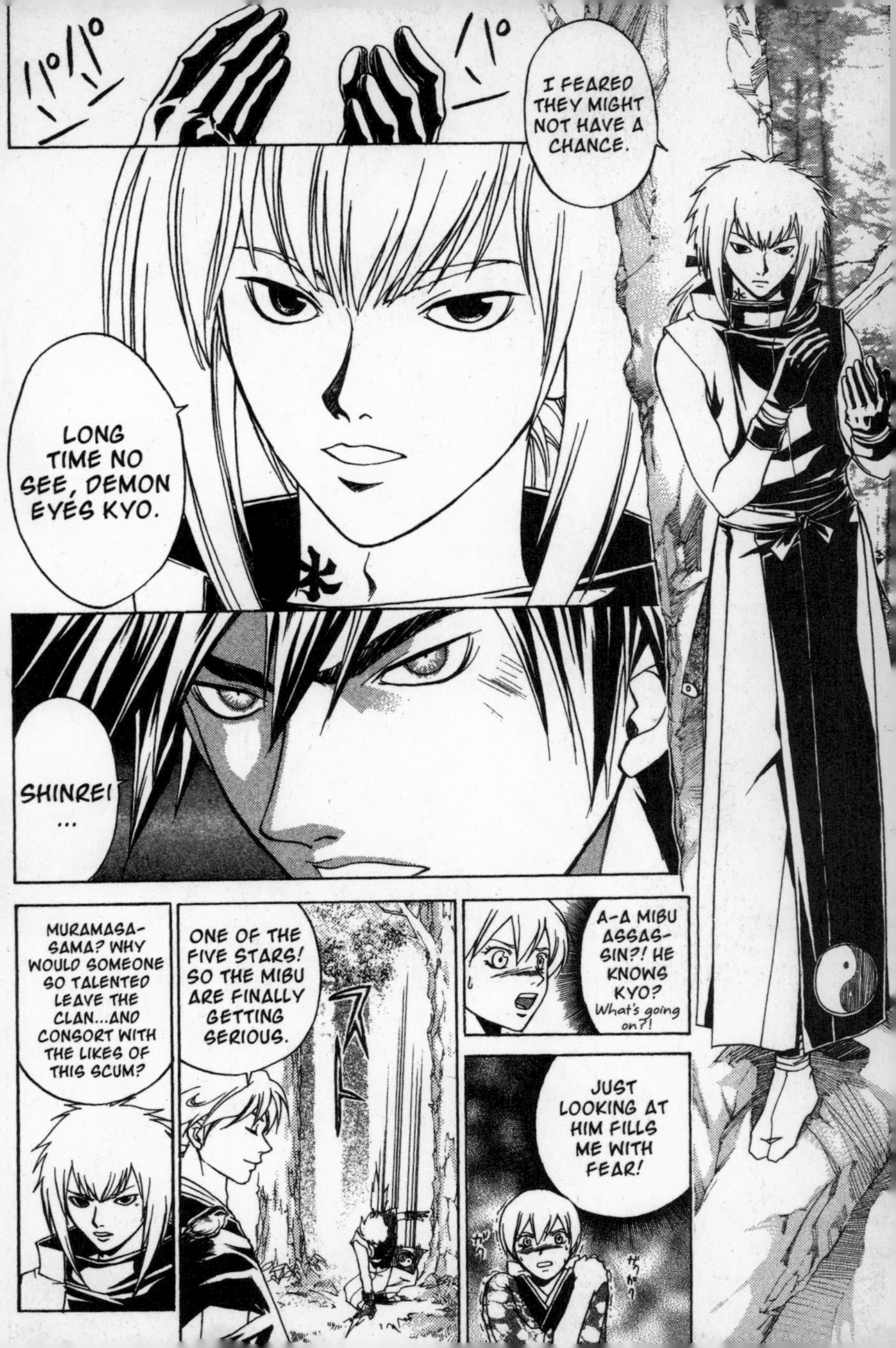
I FEARED THEY MIGHT NOT HAVE A CHANCE.
パパ
パ
LONG TIME NO SEE, DEMON EYES KYO.
SHINREI ...
A-A MIBU ASSASSIN?! HE KNOWS KYO?
What's going on?!
JUST LOOKING AT HIM FILLS ME WITH FEAR!
ONE OF THE FIVE STARS! SO THE MIBU ARE FINALLY GETTING SERIOUS.
MURAMASA-SAMA? WHY WOULD SOMEONE SO TALENTED LEAVE THE CLAN...AND CONSORT WITH THE LIKES OF THIS SCUM?

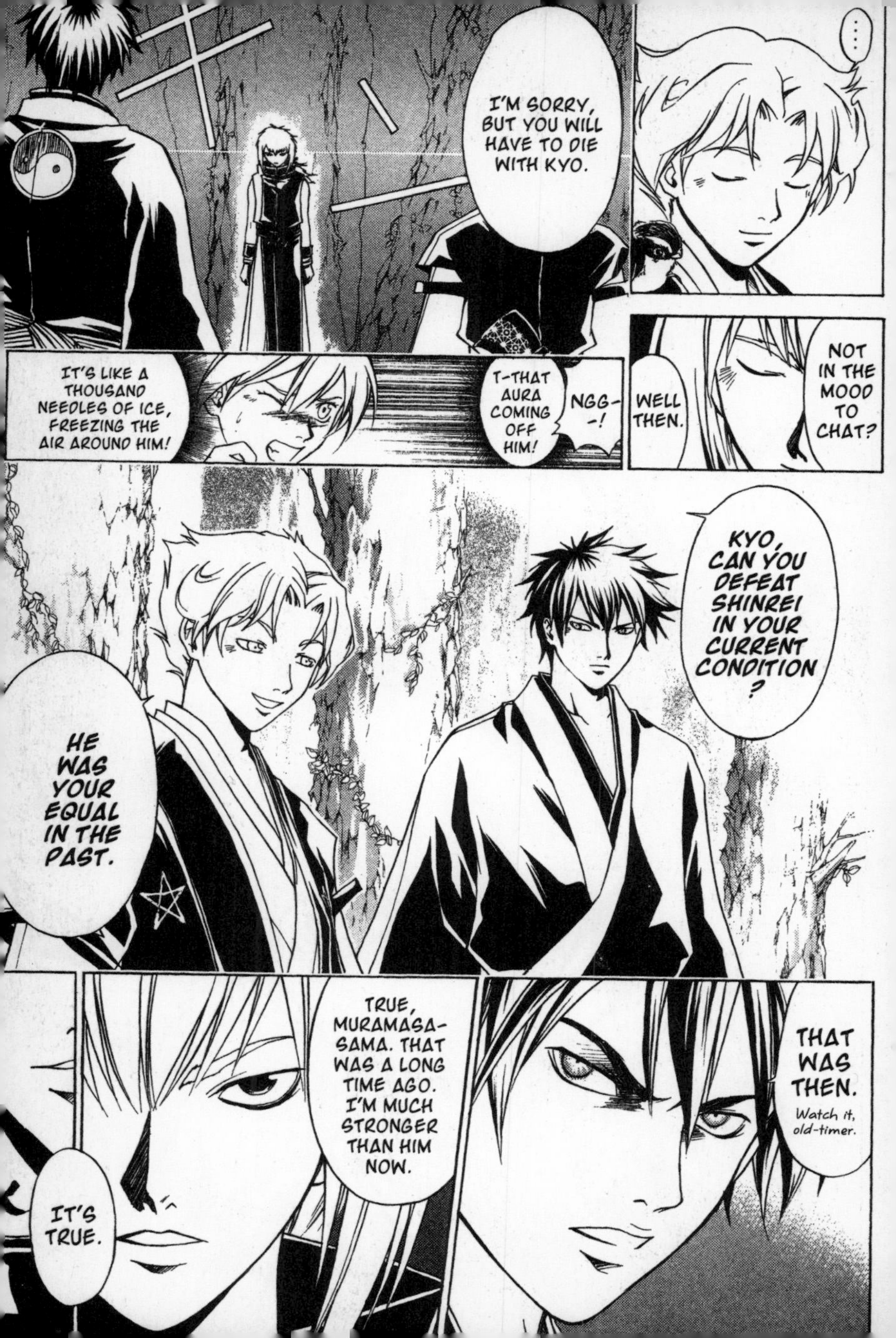
...!
I'M SORRY, BUT YOU WILL HAVE TO DIE WITH KYO.
NOT IN THE MOOD TO CHAT?
WELL THEN.
NGG--!
T-THAT AURA COMING OFF HIM!
IT'S LIKE A THOUSAND NEEDLES OF ICE, FREEZING THE AIR AROUND HIM!
KYO, CAN YOU DEFEAT SHINREI IN YOUR CURRENT CONDITION?
HE WAS YOUR EQUAL IN THE PAST.
THAT WAS THEN.
Watch it, old-timer.
TRUE, MURAMASA-SAMA. THAT WAS A LONG TIME AGO. I'M MUCH STRONGER THAN HIM NOW.
IT'S TRUE.

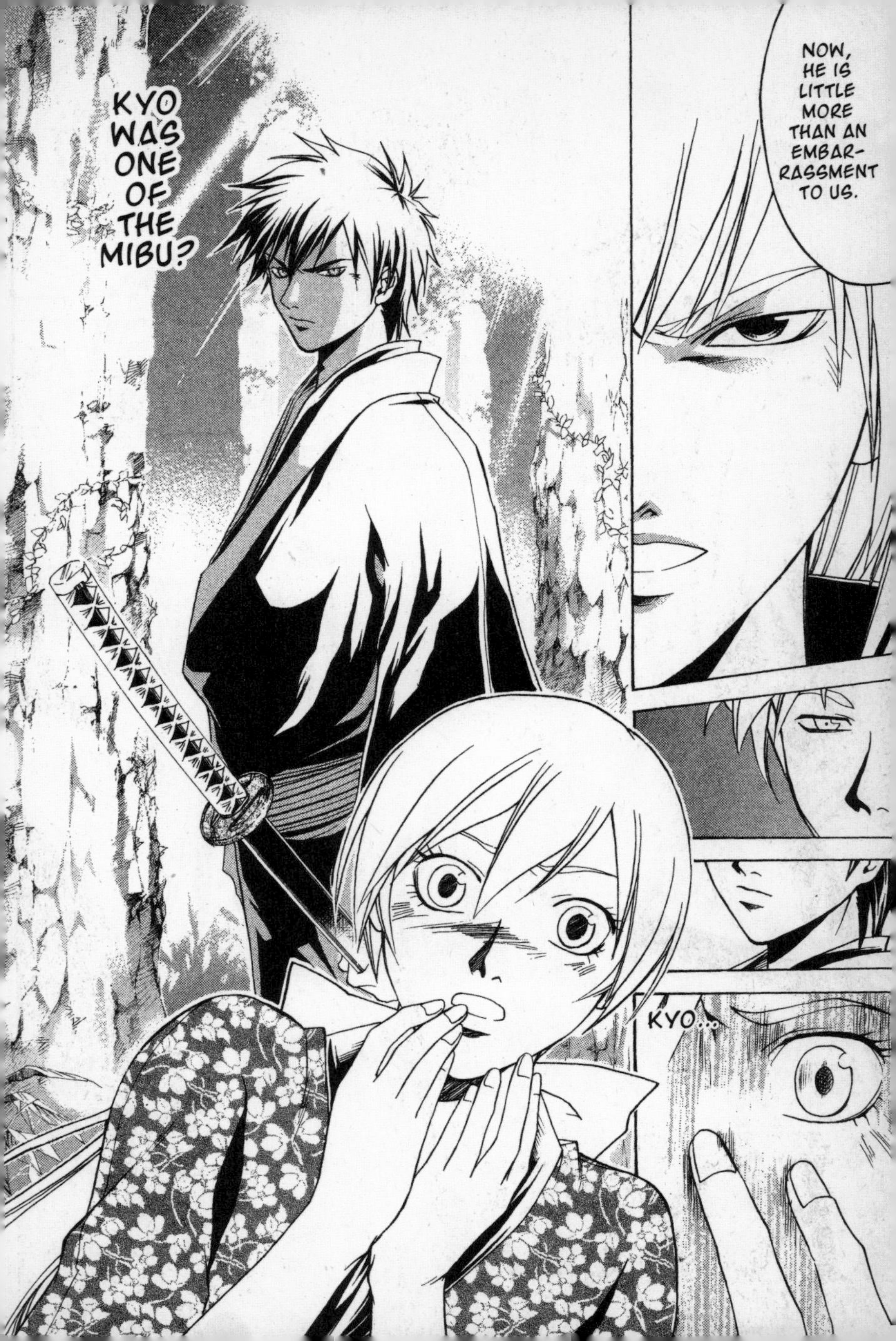
NOW, HE IS LITTLE MORE THAN AN EMBAR-RASSMENT TO US.
KYO...
KYO WAS ONE OF THE MIBU?

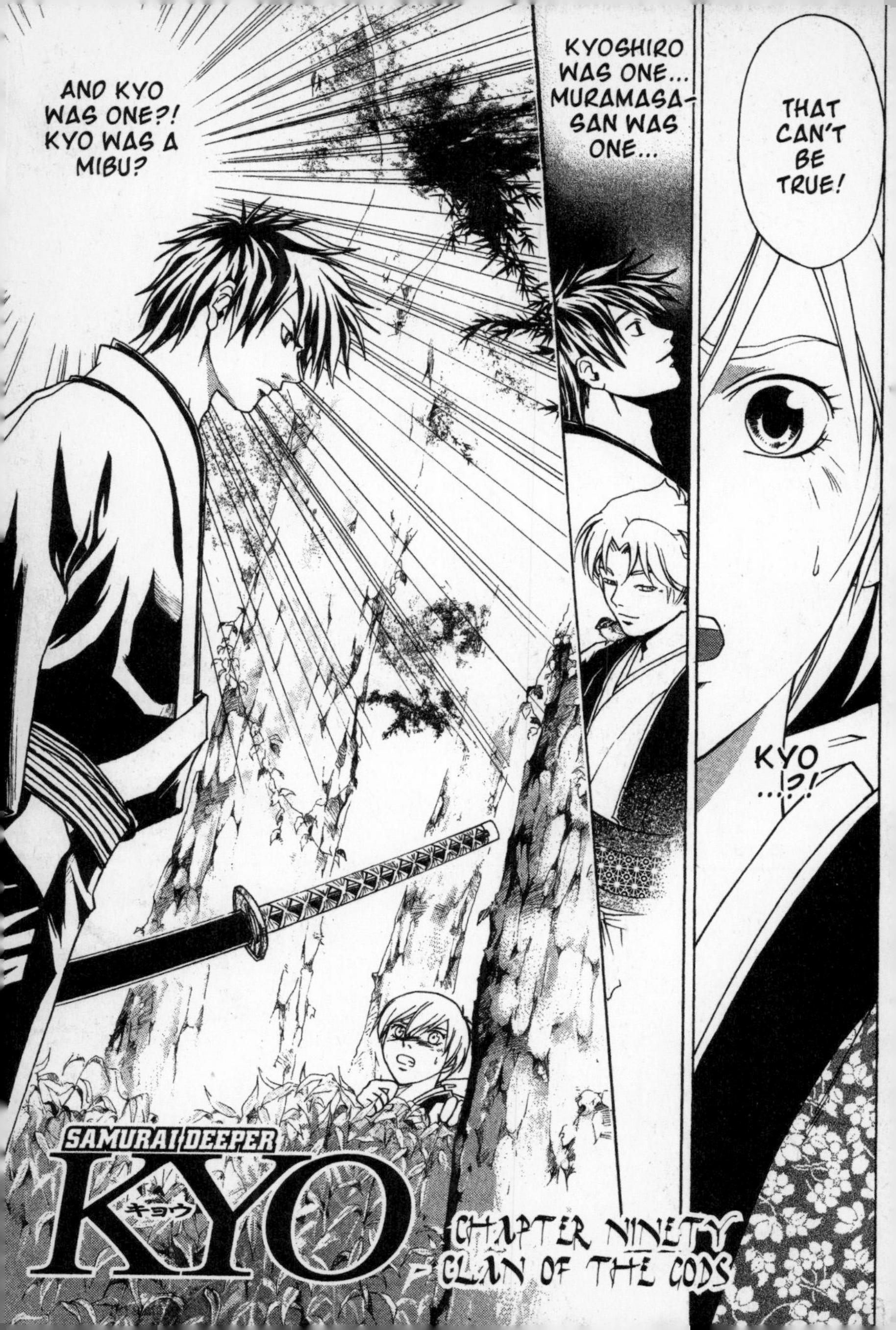
THAT CAN'T BE TRUE!
KYO ...!?!
KYOSHIRO WAS ONE... MURAMASA-SAN WAS ONE...
AND KYO WAS ONE?! KYO WAS A MIBU?
SAMURAI DEEPER KYO
キョウ
CHAPTER NINETY - CLAN OF THE GODS

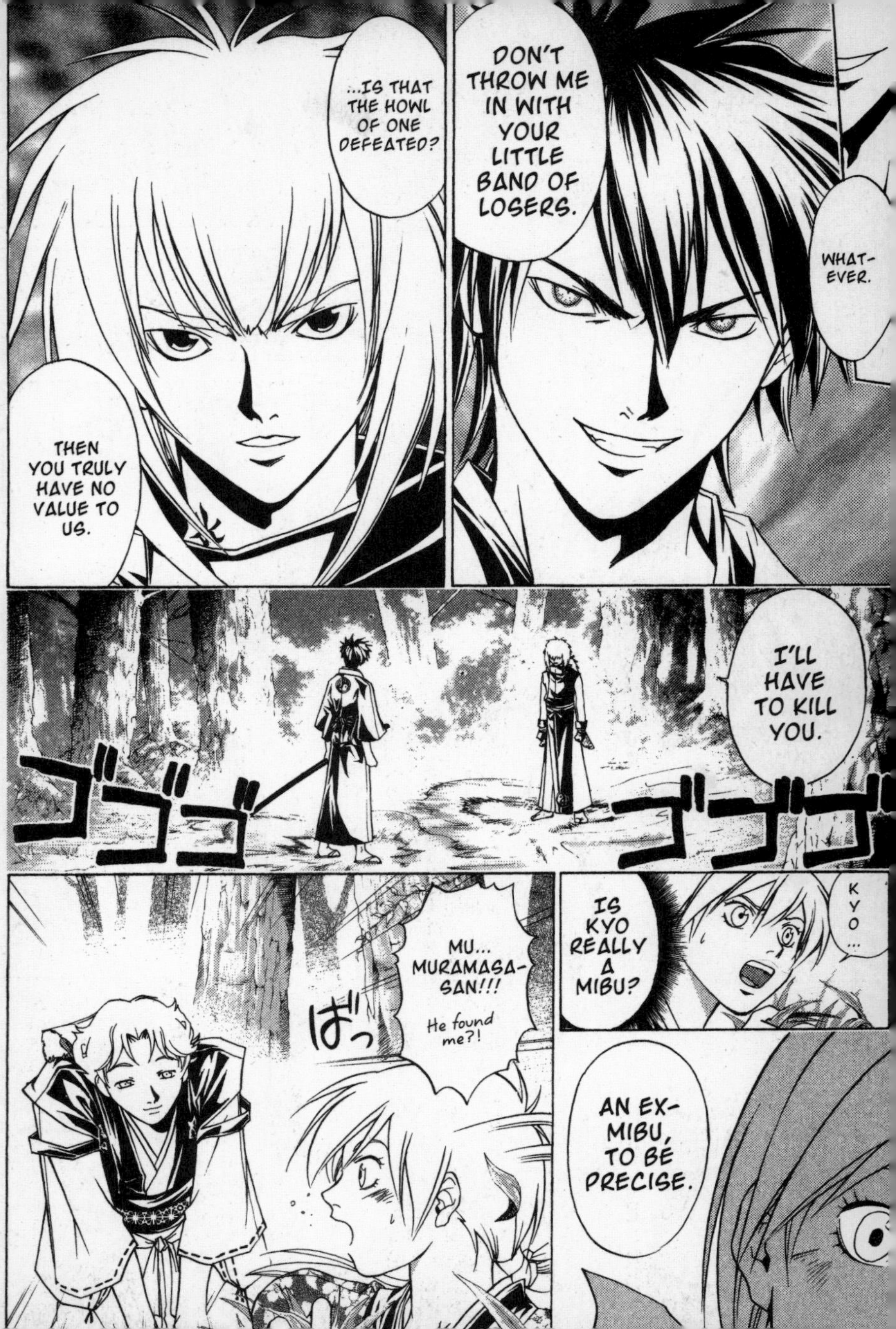
DON'T THROW ME IN WITH YOUR LITTLE BAND OF LOSERS.
WHATEVER.
...IS THAT THE HOWL OF ONE DEFEATED?
THEN YOU TRULY HAVE NO VALUE TO US.
I'LL HAVE TO KILL YOU.
ゴゴゴ
ゴゴゴ
KYO...
IS KYO REALLY A MIBU?
AN EX-MIBU, TO BE PRECISE.
MU... MURAMASA-SAN!!!
He found me?!
ばっ

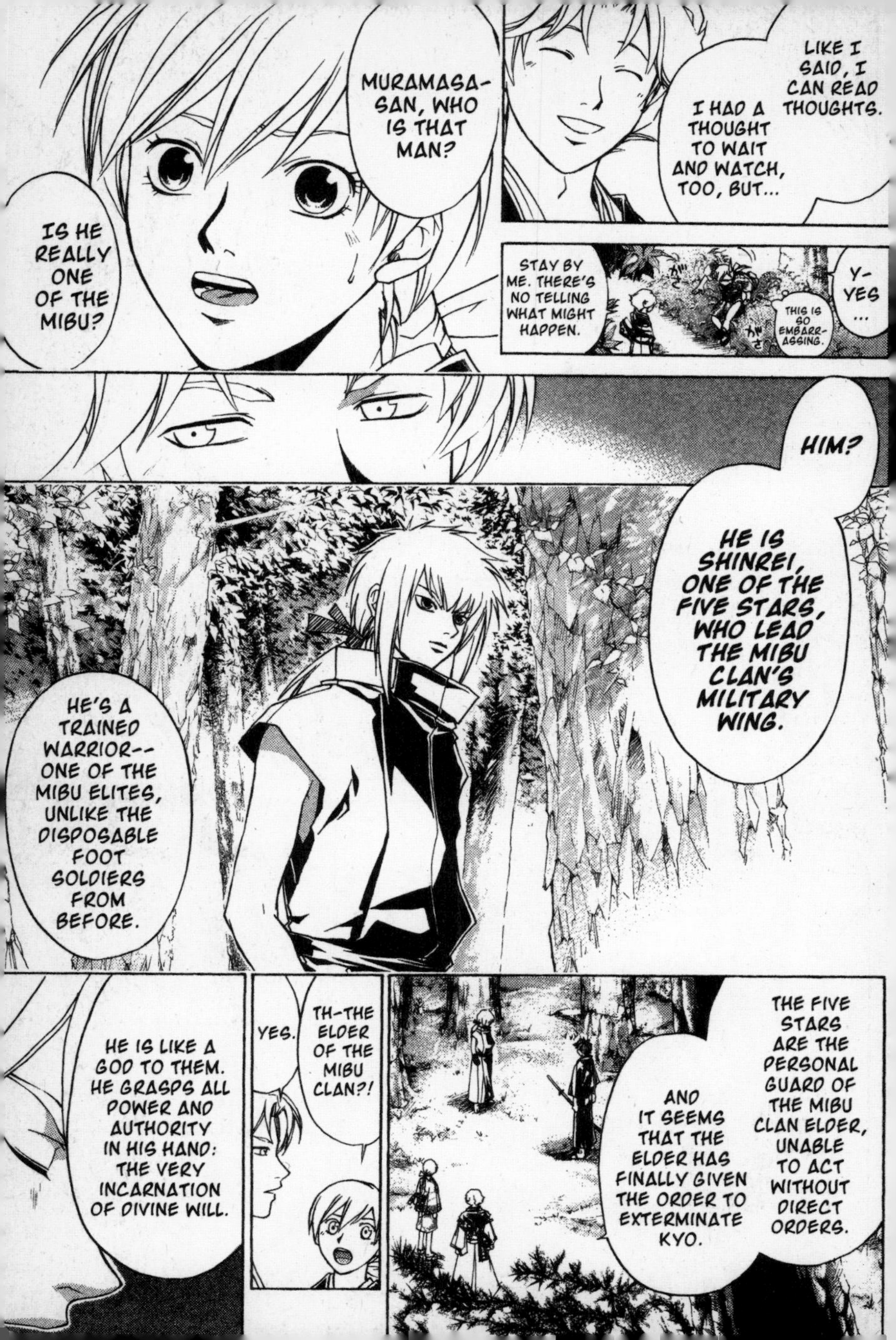
LIKE I SAID, I CAN READ THOUGHTS.
I HAD A THOUGHT TO WAIT AND WATCH, TOO, BUT...
Y-YES...
THIS IS SO EMBARRASSING.
STAY BY ME. THERE'S NO TELLING WHAT MIGHT HAPPEN.
MURAMASA-SAN, WHO IS THAT MAN?
IS HE REALLY ONE OF THE MIBU?
HIM?
HE IS SHINREI, ONE OF THE FIVE STARS, WHO LEAD THE MIBU CLAN'S MILITARY WING.
HE'S A TRAINED WARRIOR--ONE OF THE MIBU ELITES, UNLIKE THE DISPOSABLE FOOT SOLDIERS FROM BEFORE.
THE FIVE STARS ARE THE PERSONAL GUARD OF THE MIBU CLAN ELDER, UNABLE TO ACT WITHOUT DIRECT ORDERS.
AND IT SEEMS THAT THE ELDER HAS FINALLY GIVEN THE ORDER TO EXTERMINATE KYO.
TH-THE ELDER OF THE MIBU CLAN?!
YES.
HE IS LIKE A GOD TO THEM. HE GRASPS ALL POWER AND AUTHORITY IN HIS HAND: THE VERY INCARNATION OF DIVINE WILL.

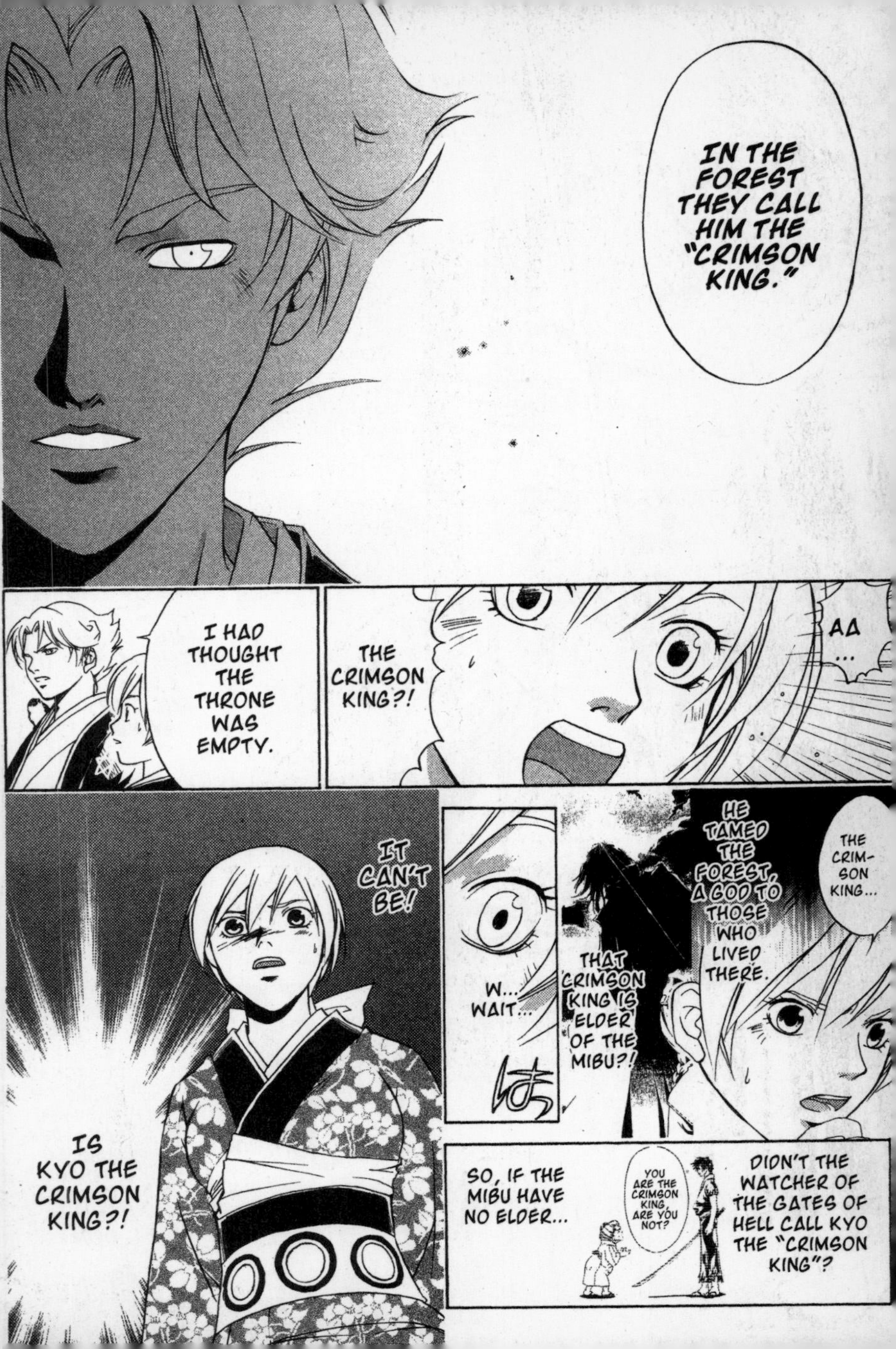
IN THE FOREST THEY CALL HIM THE "CRIMSON KING."
AA ...
THE CRIMSON KING?!
I HAD THOUGHT THE THRONE WAS EMPTY.
THE CRIMSON KING...
HE TAMED THE FOREST, A GOD TO THOSE WHO LIVED THERE.
THAT CRIMSON KING IS ELDER OF THE MIBU?!
W... WAIT...
DIDN'T THE WATCHER OF THE GATES OF HELL CALL KYO THE "CRIMSON KING"?
YOU ARE THE CRIMSON KING, ARE YOU NOT?
SO, IF THE MIBU HAVE NO ELDER...
IT CAN'T BE!
IS KYO THE CRIMSON KING?!

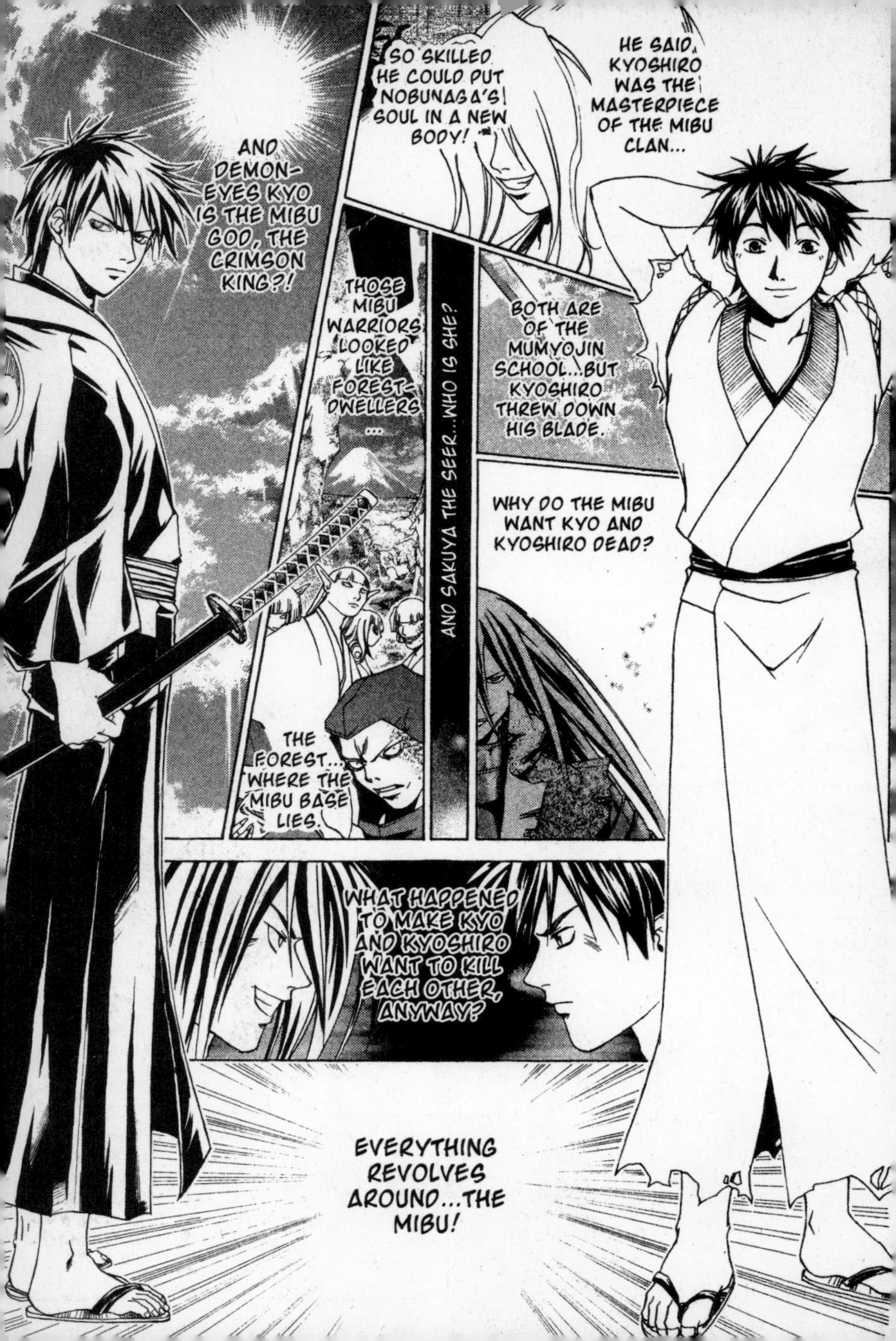
HE SAID, KYOSHIRO WAS THE MASTERPIECE OF THE MIBU CLAN...
SO SKILLED HE COULD PUT NOBUNAGA'S SOUL IN A NEW BODY!
AND DEMON-EYES KYO IS THE MIBU GOD, THE CRIMSON KING?!
BOTH ARE OF THE MUMYOJIN SCHOOL...BUT KYOSHIRO THREW DOWN HIS BLADE.
WHY DO THE MIBU WANT KYO AND KYOSHIRO DEAD?
AND SAKUYA THE SEER...WHO IS SHE?
THOSE MIBU WARRIORS LOOKED LIKE FOREST-DWELLERS ...
THE FOREST... WHERE THE MIBU BASE LIES.
WHAT HAPPENED TO MAKE KYO AND KYOSHIRO WANT TO KILL EACH OTHER, ANYWAY?
EVERYTHING REVOLVES AROUND...THE MIBU!

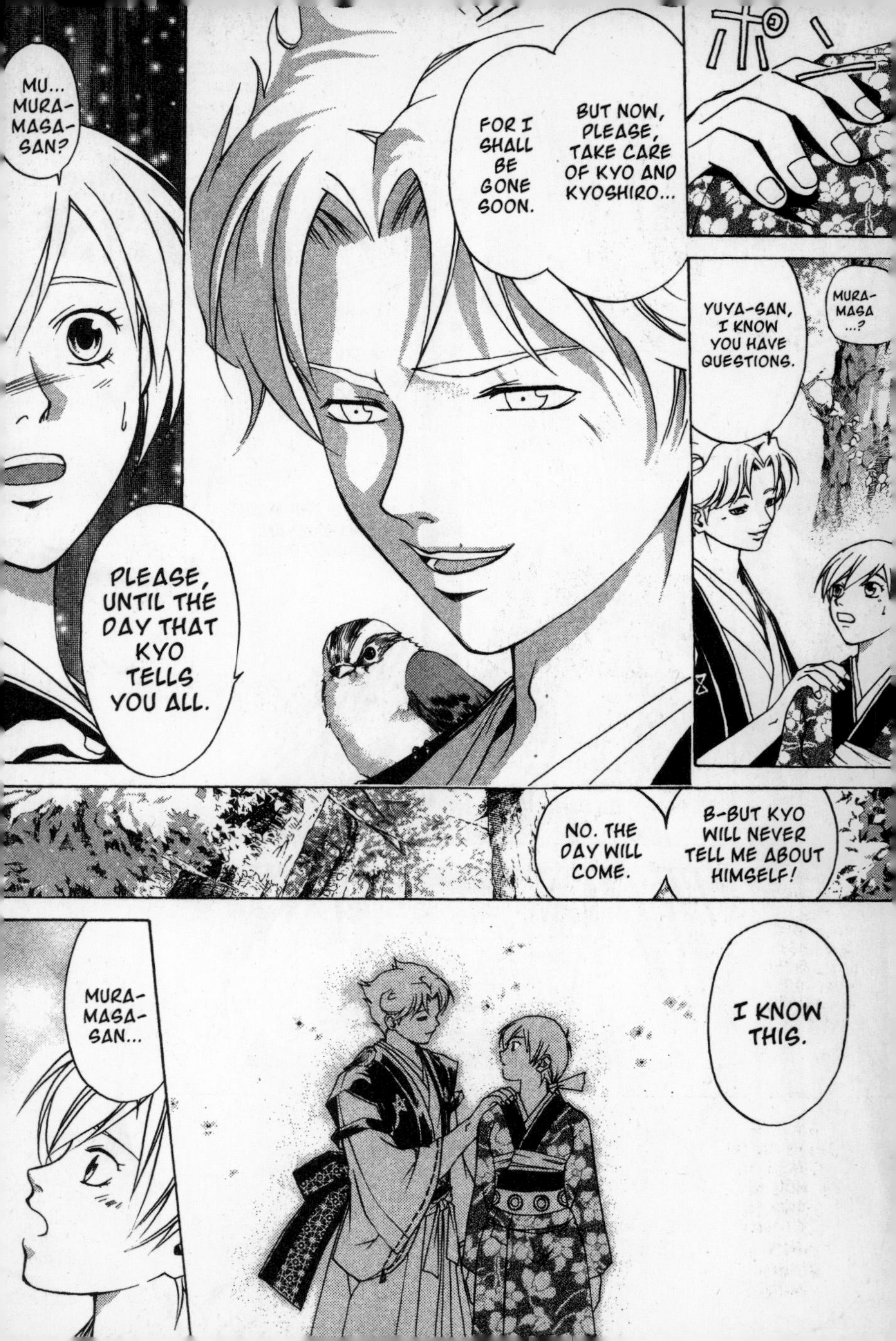
ポン
YUYA-SAN, I KNOW YOU HAVE QUESTIONS.
MURA-MASA ...?
BUT NOW, PLEASE, TAKE CARE OF KYO AND KYOSHIRO...
FOR I SHALL BE GONE SOON.
MU... MURA-MASA-SAN?
PLEASE, UNTIL THE DAY THAT KYO TELLS YOU ALL.
B-BUT KYO WILL NEVER TELL ME ABOUT HIMSELF!
NO. THE DAY WILL COME.
I KNOW THIS.
MURA-MASA-SAN...

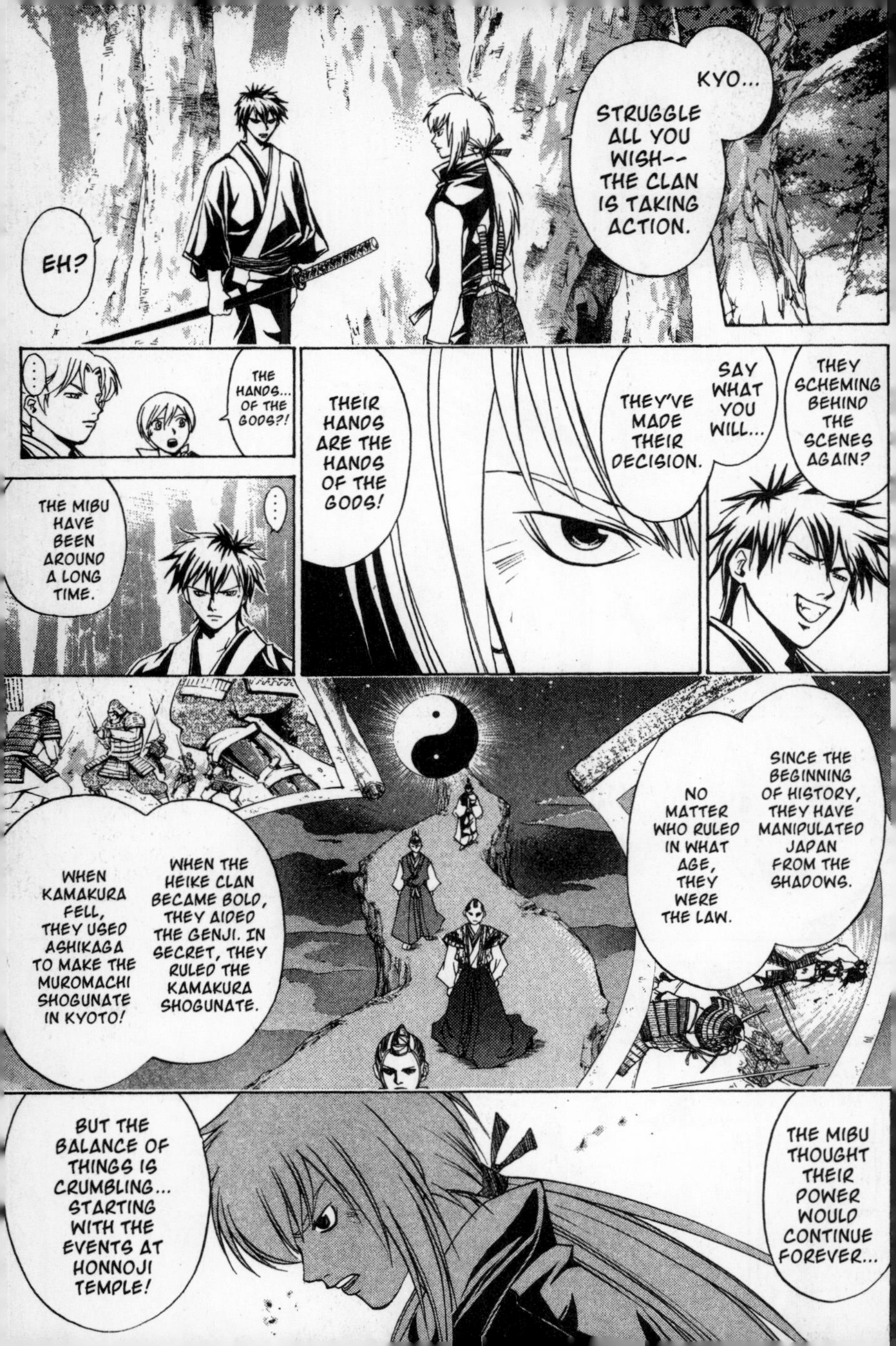
KYO...
STRUGGLE ALL YOU WISH-- THE CLAN IS TAKING ACTION.
EH?
THEY SCHEMING BEHIND THE SCENES AGAIN?
SAY WHAT YOU WILL...
THEY'VE MADE THEIR DECISION.
THEIR HANDS ARE THE HANDS OF THE GODS!
THE HANDS... OF THE GODS?!
...
...
THE MIBU HAVE BEEN AROUND A LONG TIME.
SINCE THE BEGINNING OF HISTORY, THEY HAVE MANIPULATED JAPAN FROM THE SHADOWS.
NO MATTER WHO RULED IN WHAT AGE, THEY WERE THE LAW.
WHEN THE HEIKE CLAN BECAME BOLD, THEY AIDED THE GENJI. IN SECRET, THEY RULED THE KAMAKURA SHOGUNATE.
WHEN KAMAKURA FELL, THEY USED ASHIKAGA TO MAKE THE MUROMACHI SHOGUNATE IN KYOTO!
THE MIBU THOUGHT THEIR POWER WOULD CONTINUE FOREVER...
BUT THE BALANCE OF THINGS IS CRUMBLING... STARTING WITH THE EVENTS AT HONNOJI TEMPLE!

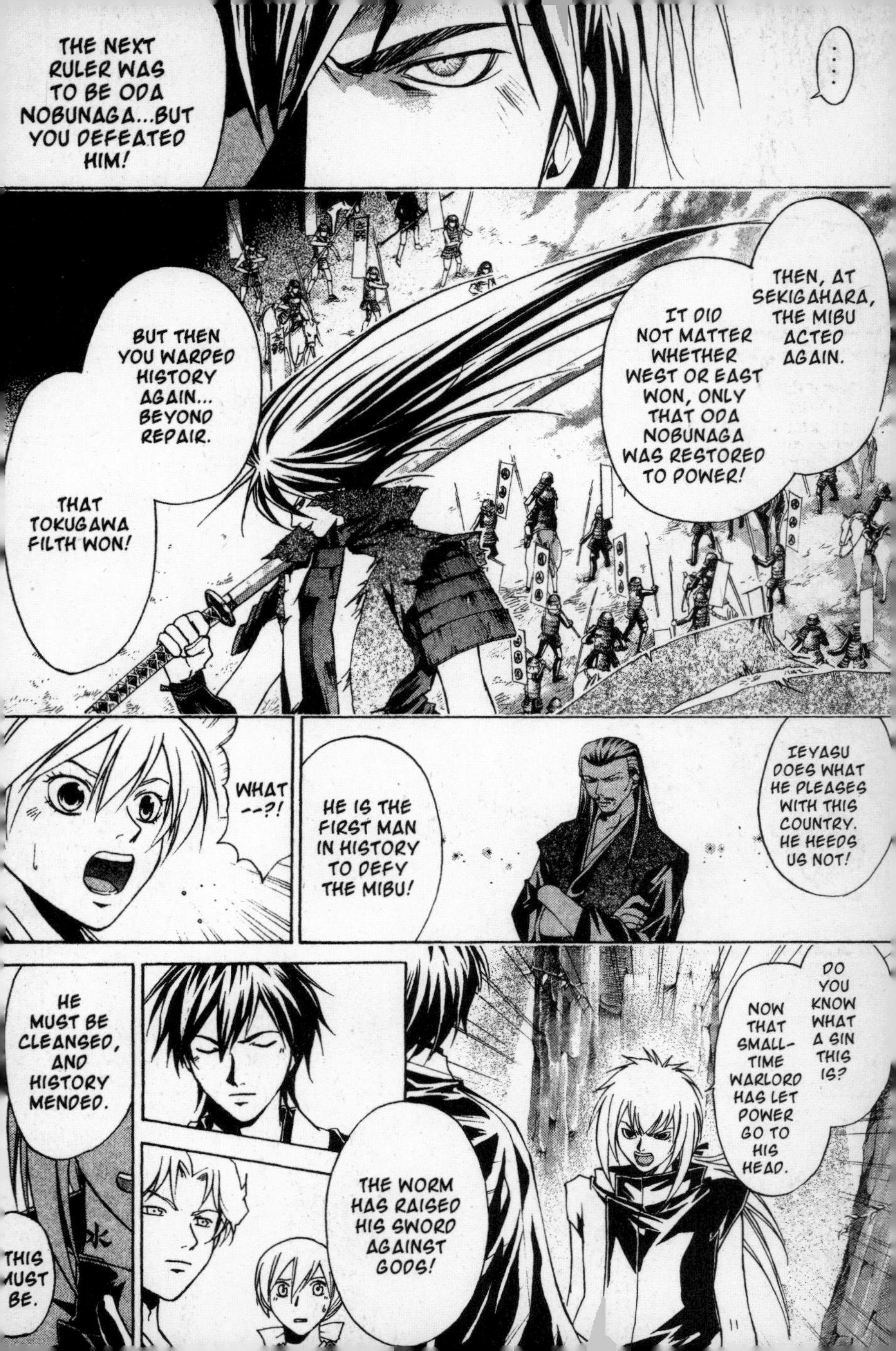
.....
THE NEXT RULER WAS TO BE ODA NOBUNAGA...BUT YOU DEFEATED HIM!
THEN, AT SEKIGAHARA, THE MIBU ACTED AGAIN.
IT DID NOT MATTER WHETHER WEST OR EAST WON, ONLY THAT ODA NOBUNAGA WAS RESTORED TO POWER!
BUT THEN YOU WARPED HISTORY AGAIN... BEYOND REPAIR.
THAT TOKUGAWA FILTH WON!
IEYASU DOES WHAT HE PLEASES WITH THIS COUNTRY. HE HEEDS US NOT!
HE IS THE FIRST MAN IN HISTORY TO DEFY THE MIBU!
WHAT --?!
DO YOU KNOW WHAT A SIN THIS IS?
NOW THAT SMALL-TIME WARLORD HAS LET POWER GO TO HIS HEAD.
THE WORM HAS RAISED HIS SWORD AGAINST GODS!
HE MUST BE CLEANSED, AND HISTORY MENDED.
THIS MUST BE.

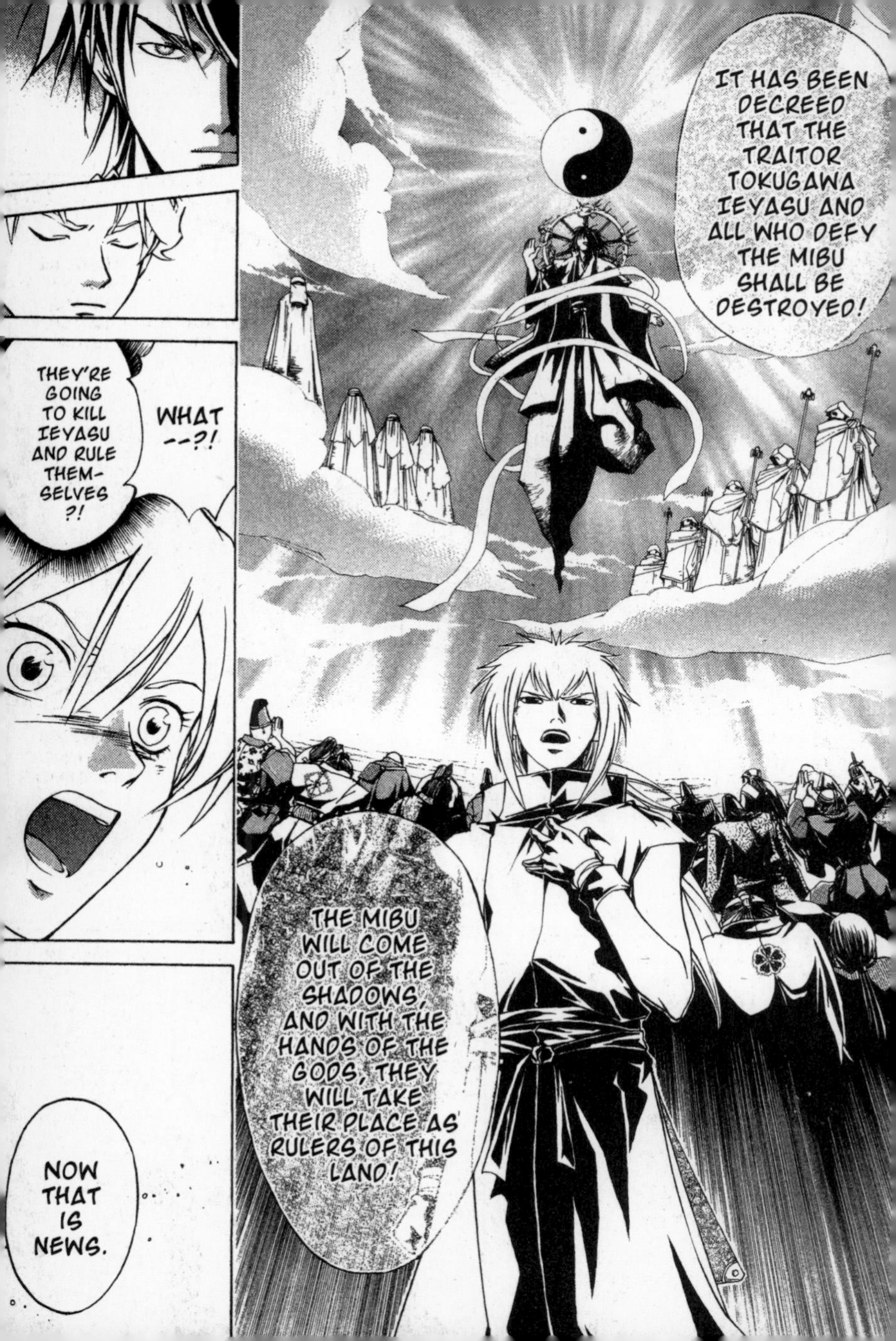
IT HAS BEEN DECREED THAT THE TRAITOR TOKUGAWA IEYASU AND ALL WHO DEFY THE MIBU SHALL BE DESTROYED!
THE MIBU WILL COME OUT OF THE SHADOWS, AND WITH THE HANDS OF THE GODS, THEY WILL TAKE THEIR PLACE AS RULERS OF THIS LAND!
WHAT--?!
THEY'RE GOING TO KILL IEYASU AND RULE THEMSELVES?!
NOW THAT IS NEWS.

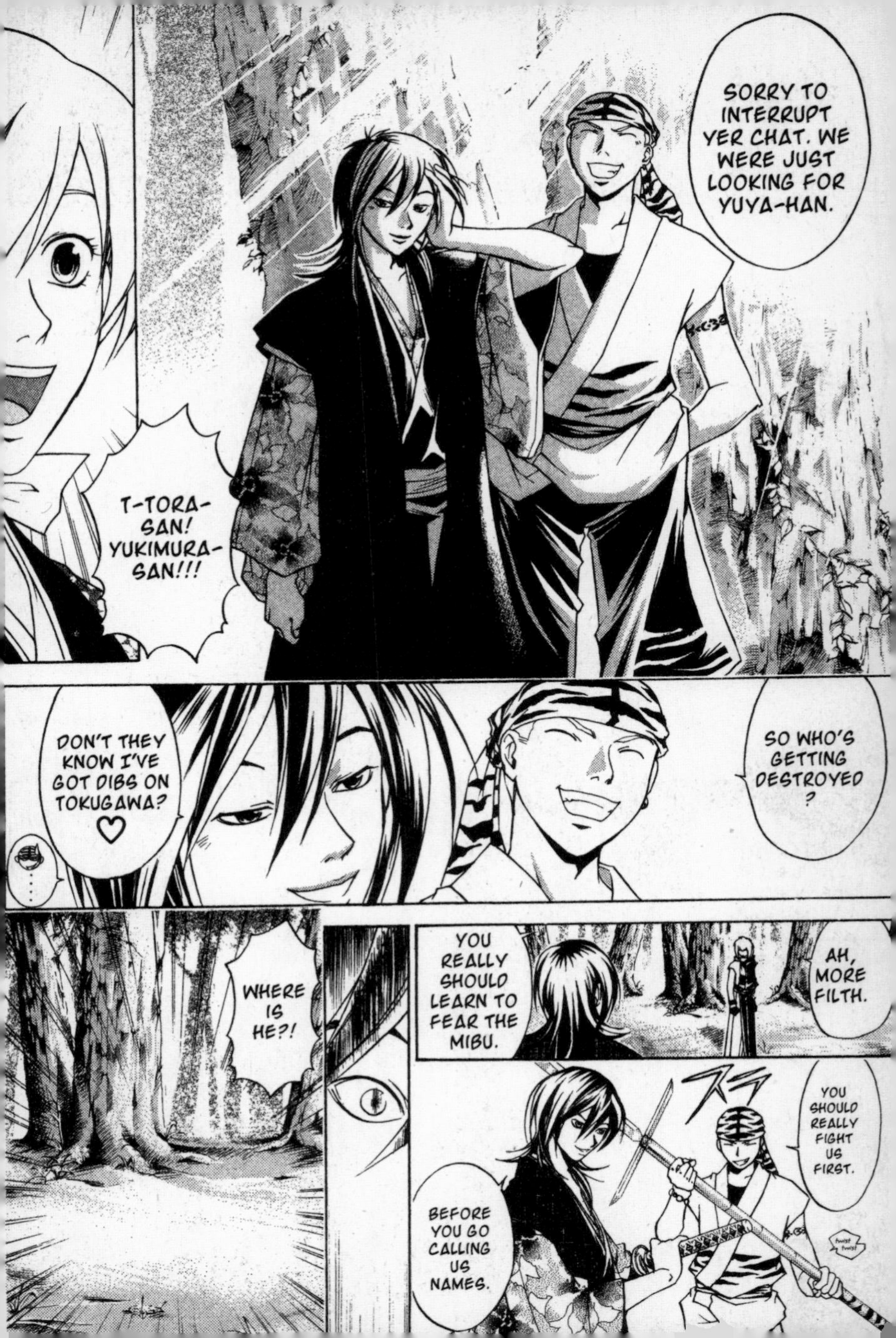
SORRY TO INTERRUPT YER CHAT. WE WERE JUST LOOKING FOR YUYA-HAN.
T-TORA-SAN! YUKIMURA-SAN!!!
SO WHO'S GETTING DESTROYED?
DON'T THEY KNOW I'VE GOT DIBS ON TOKUGAWA? ♡
AH, MORE FILTH.
YOU REALLY SHOULD LEARN TO FEAR THE MIBU.
YOU SHOULD REALLY FIGHT US FIRST.
twist twist
BEFORE YOU GO CALLING US NAMES.
WHERE IS HE?!

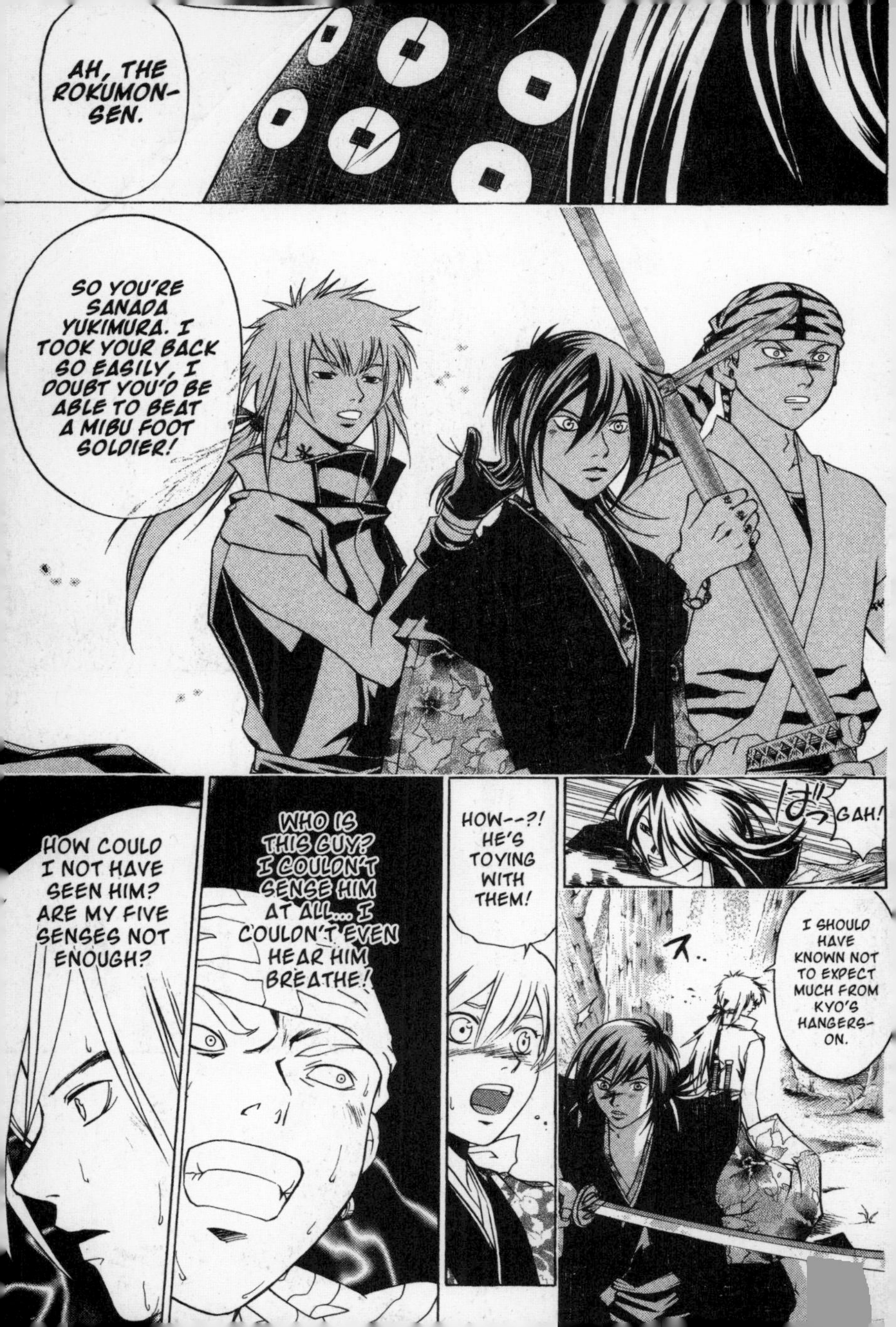
AH, THE ROKUMON-SEN.
SO YOU'RE SANADA YUKIMURA. I TOOK YOUR BACK SO EASILY, I DOUBT YOU'D BE ABLE TO BEAT A MIBU FOOT SOLDIER!
GAH!
I SHOULD HAVE KNOWN NOT TO EXPECT MUCH FROM KYO'S HANGERS-ON.
HOW--?! HE'S TOYING WITH THEM!
WHO IS THIS GUY? I COULDN'T SENSE HIM AT ALL... I COULDN'T EVEN HEAR HIM BREATHE!
HOW COULD I NOT HAVE SEEN HIM? ARE MY FIVE SENSES NOT ENOUGH?

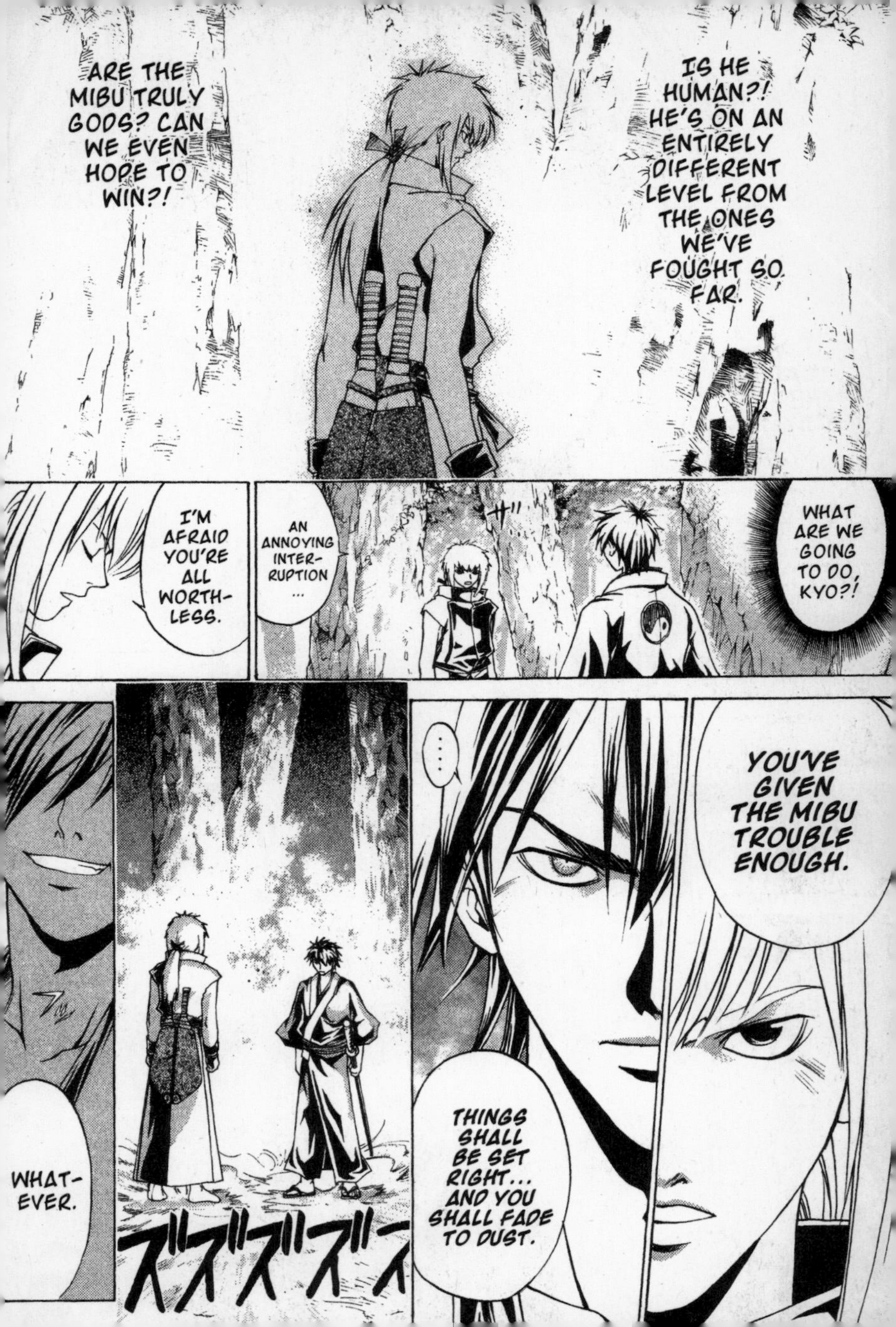

IS HE HUMAN?! HE'S ON AN ENTIRELY DIFFERENT LEVEL FROM THE ONES WE'VE FOUGHT SO FAR.
ARE THE MIBU TRULY GODS? CAN WE EVEN HOPE TO WIN?!
WHAT ARE WE GOING TO DO, KYO?!
AN ANNOYING INTERRUPTION...
I'M AFRAID YOU'RE ALL WORTHLESS.
YOU'VE GIVEN THE MIBU TROUBLE ENOUGH.
....
THINGS SHALL BE SET RIGHT... AND YOU SHALL FADE TO DUST.
ズズズズーィ
WHATEVER.

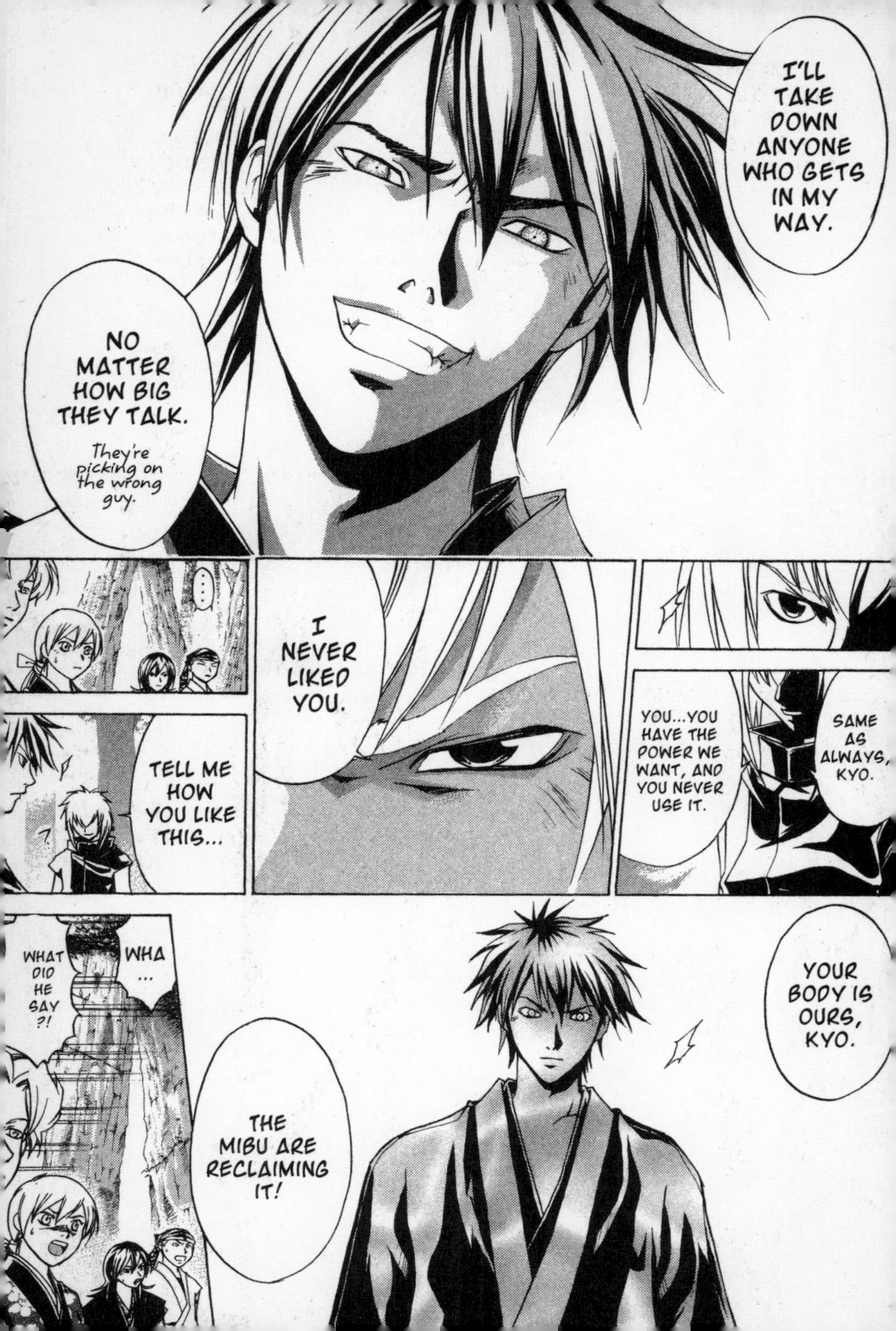
I'LL TAKE DOWN ANYONE WHO GETS IN MY WAY.
NO MATTER HOW BIG THEY TALK.
They're picking on the wrong guy.
SAME AS ALWAYS, KYO.
YOU...YOU HAVE THE POWER WE WANT, AND YOU NEVER USE IT.
I NEVER LIKED YOU.
...
TELL ME HOW YOU LIKE THIS...
?
YOUR BODY IS OURS, KYO.
THE MIBU ARE RECLAIMING IT!
WHA...
WHAT DID HE SAY?!

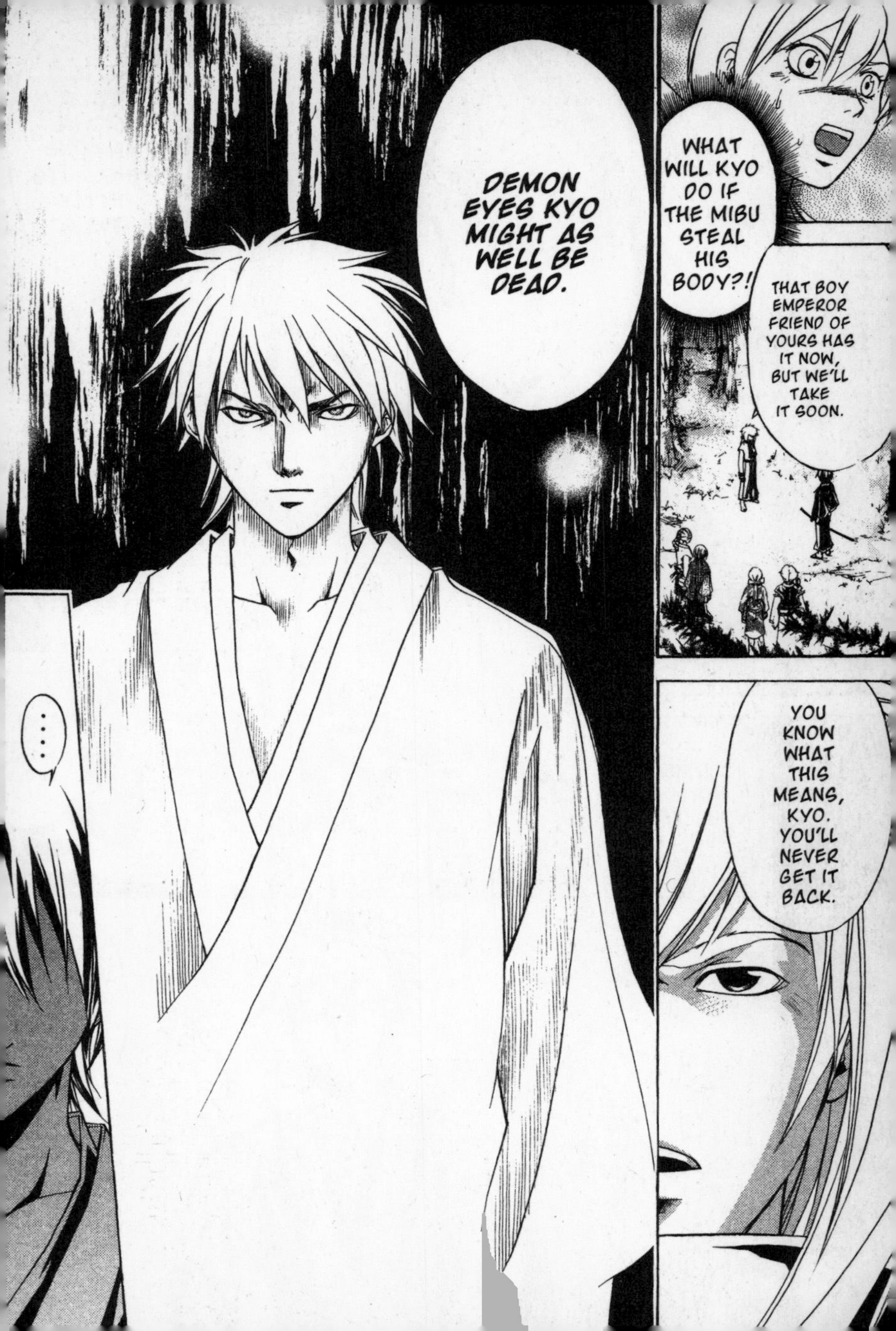
WHAT WILL KYO DO IF THE MIBU STEAL HIS BODY?!
THAT BOY EMPEROR FRIEND OF YOURS HAS IT NOW, BUT WE'LL TAKE IT SOON.
YOU KNOW WHAT THIS MEANS, KYO. YOU'LL NEVER GET IT BACK.
DEMON EYES KYO MIGHT AS WELL BE DEAD.
.....

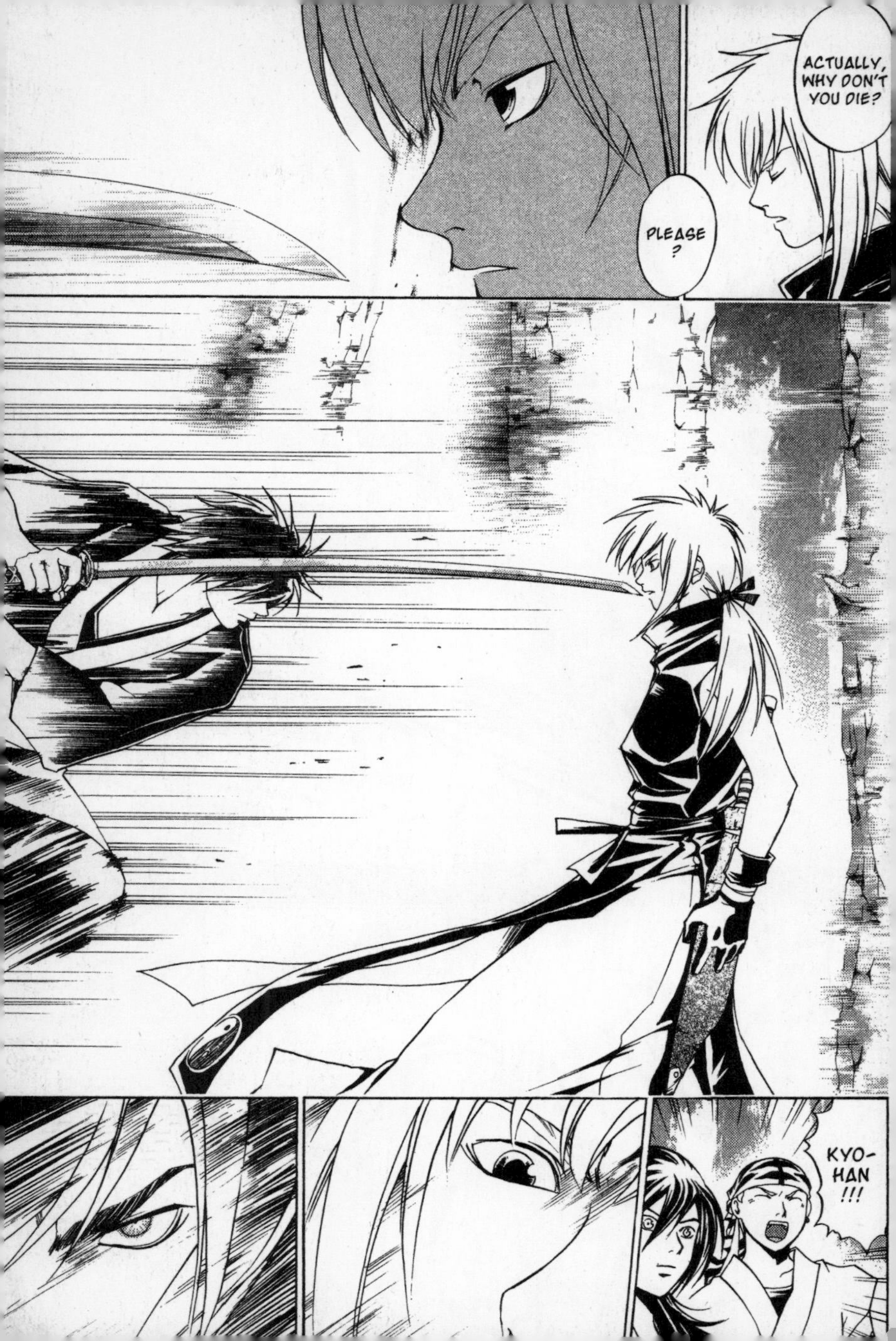
ACTUALLY, WHY DON'T YOU DIE?
PLEASE ?
KYO-HAN !!!

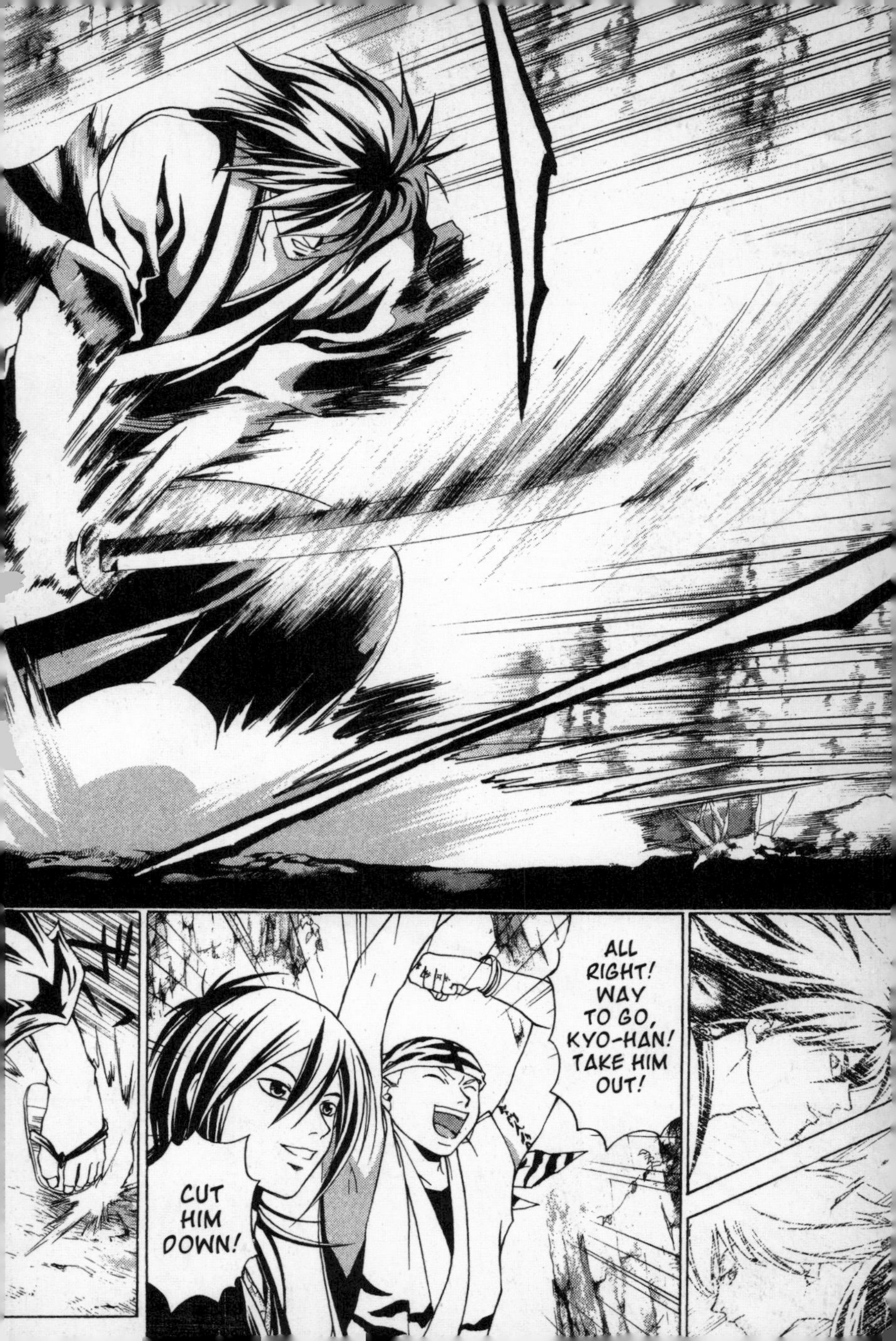
ALL RIGHT! WAY TO GO, KYO-HAN! TAKE HIM OUT!
CUT HIM DOWN!

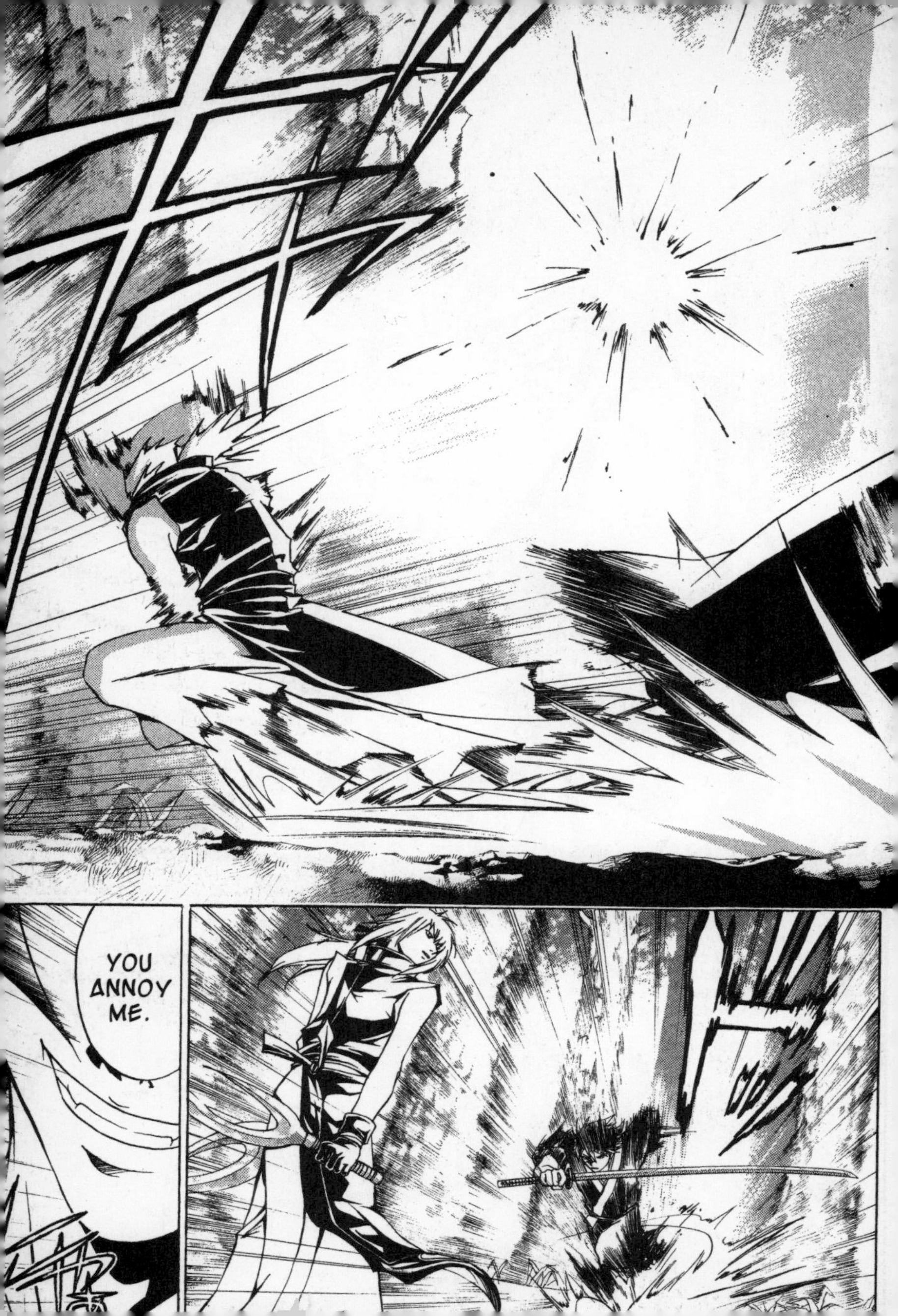
YOU ANNOY ME.

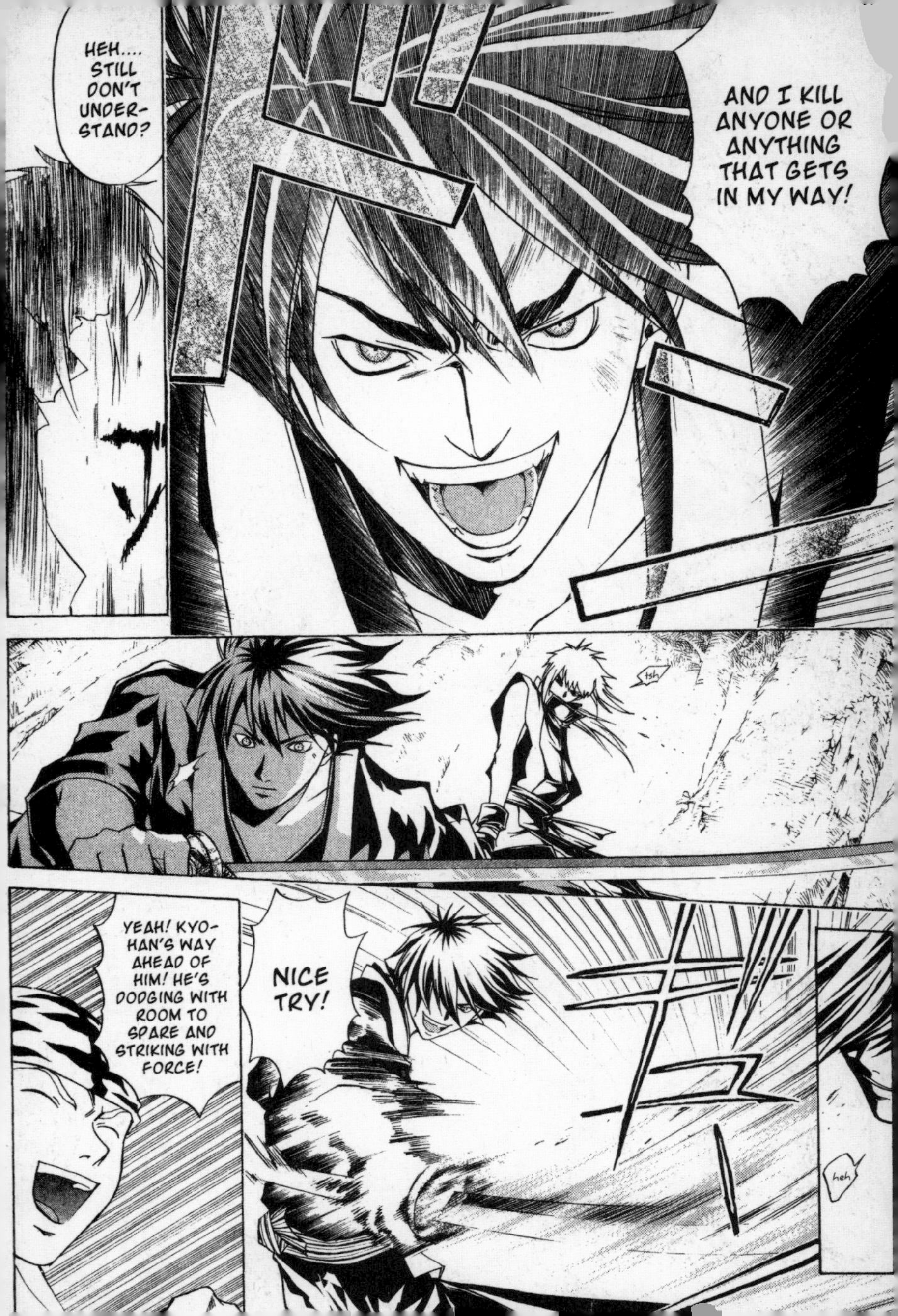
AND I KILL ANYONE OR ANYTHING THAT GETS IN MY WAY!
HEH.... STILL DON'T UNDER-STAND?
tsh
heh
NICE TRY!
YEAH! KYO-HAN'S WAY AHEAD OF HIM! HE'S DODGING WITH ROOM TO SPARE AND STRIKING WITH FORCE!

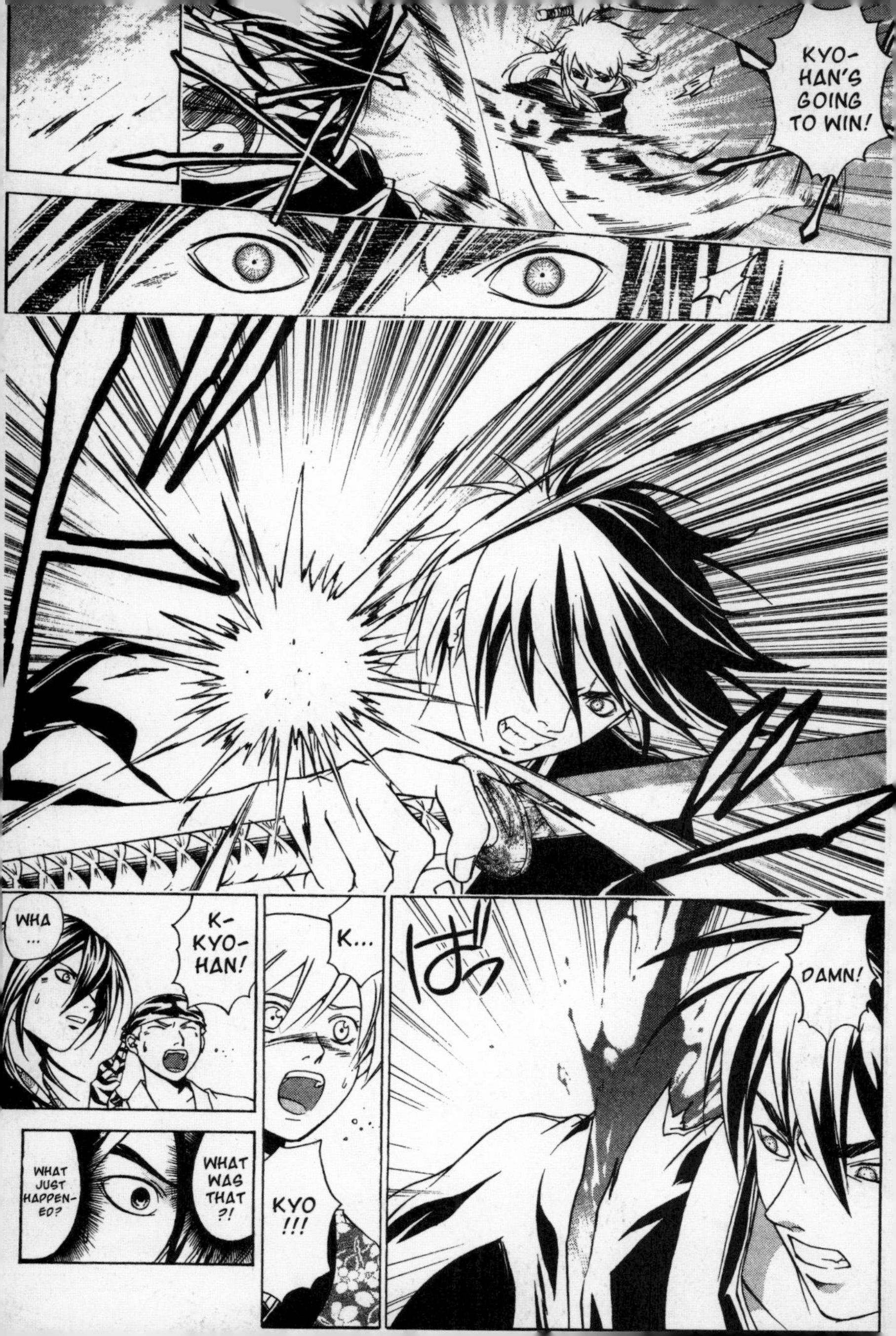
KYO-HAN'S GOING TO WIN!
ばっ
DAMN!
K...
KYO!!!
K-KYO-HAN!
WHA...
WHAT WAS THAT?!
WHAT JUST HAPPENED?

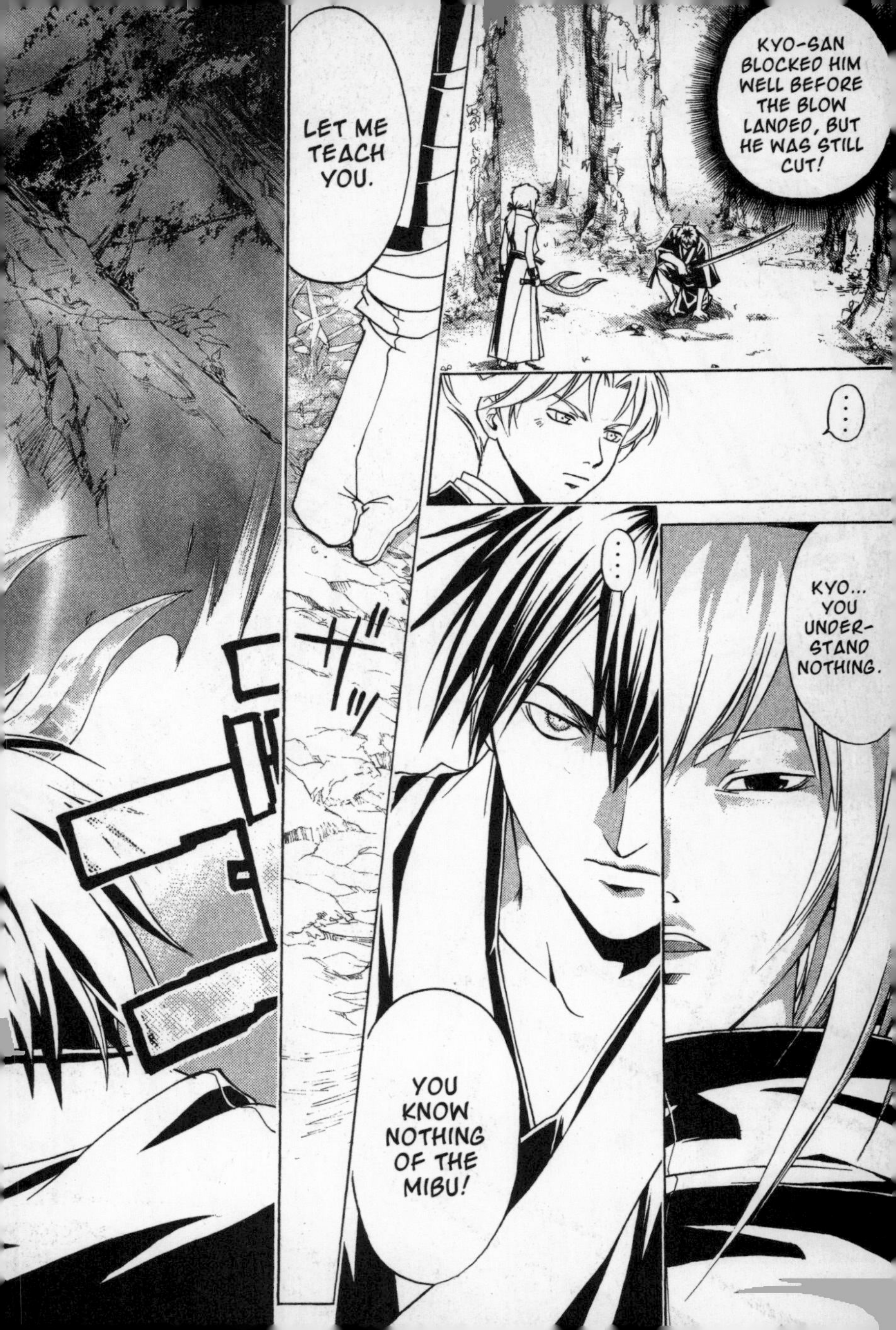

KYO-SAN BLOCKED HIM WELL BEFORE THE BLOW LANDED, BUT HE WAS STILL CUT!
...
...
KYO... YOU UNDER-STAND NOTHING.
YOU KNOW NOTHING OF THE MIBU!
LET ME TEACH YOU.
ザッ

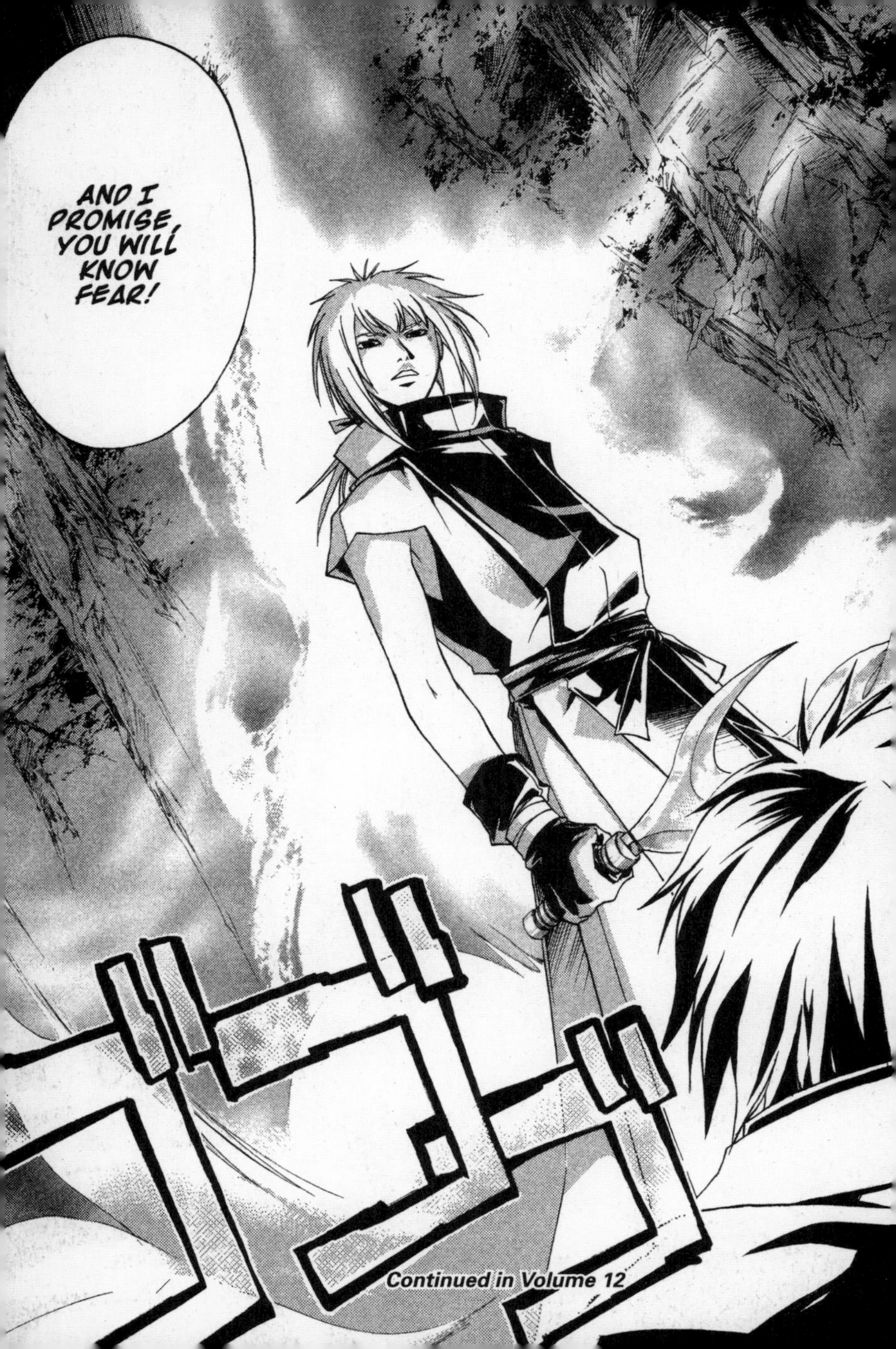
AND I PROMISE, YOU WILL KNOW FEAR!

Continued in Volume 12

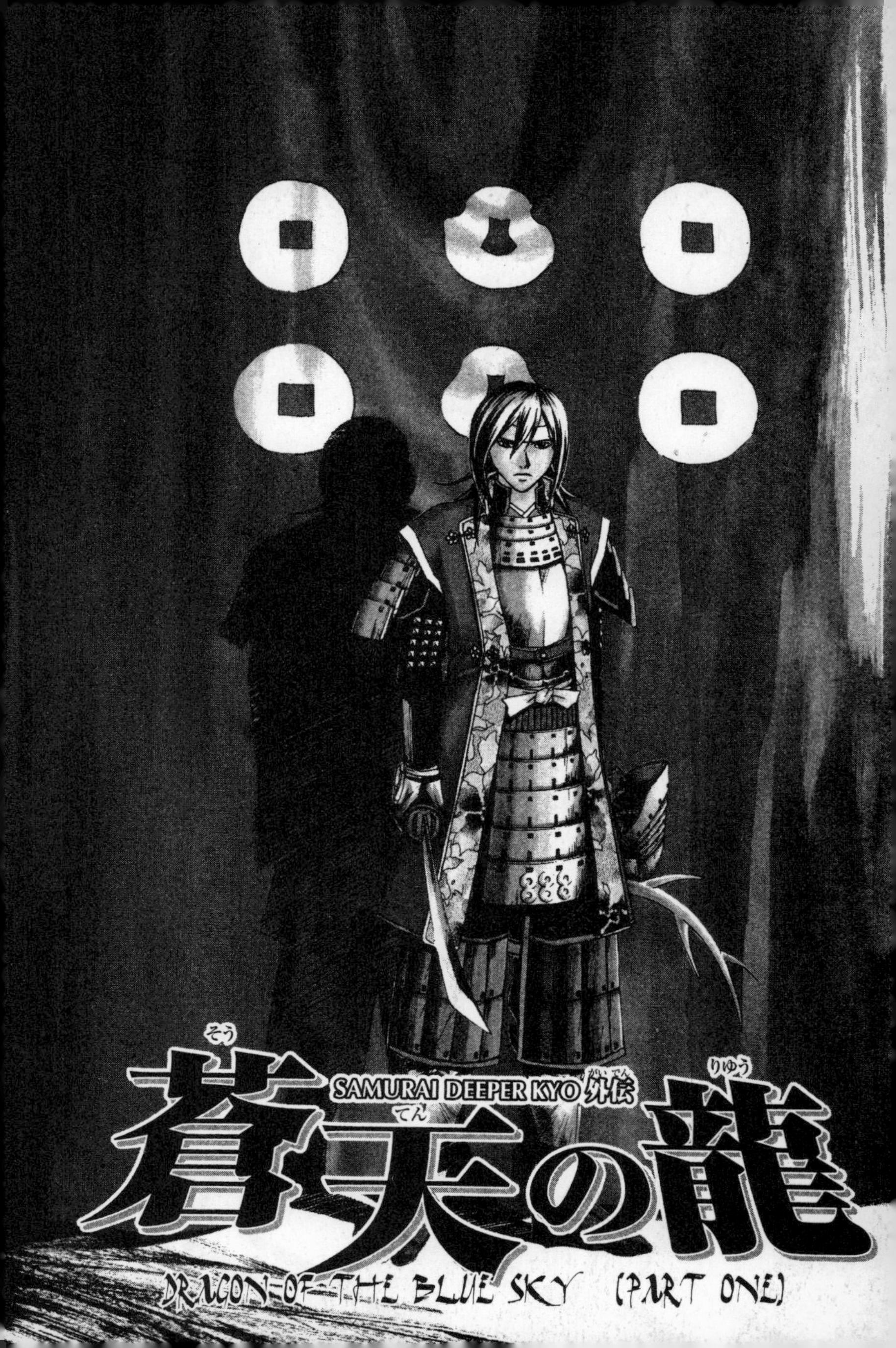
SAMURAI DEEPER KYO 外伝
蒼天の龍
DRAGON OF THE BLUE SKY (PART ONE)

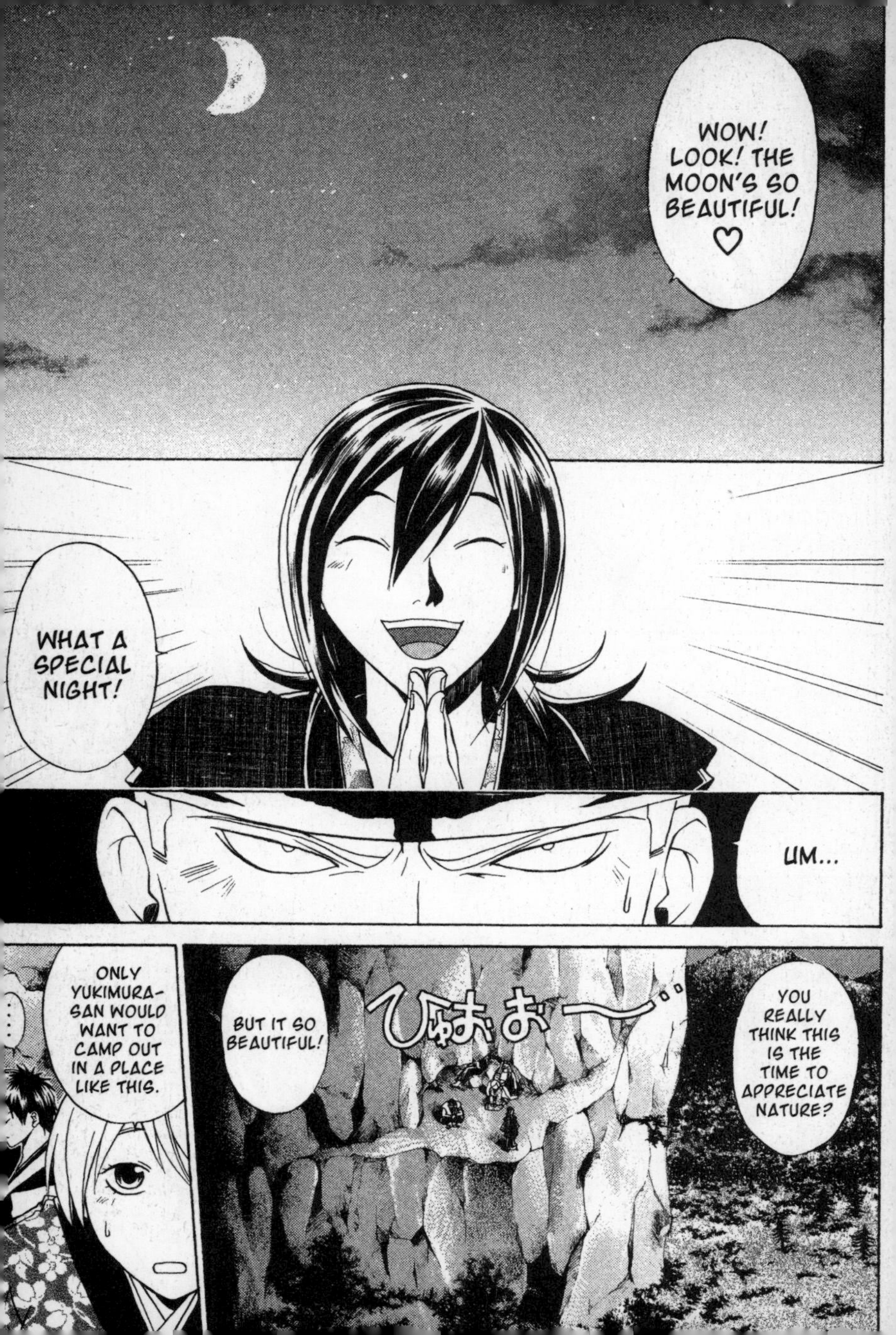
WOW! LOOK! THE MOON'S SO BEAUTIFUL! ♡
WHAT A SPECIAL NIGHT!
UM...
YOU REALLY THINK THIS IS THE TIME TO APPRECIATE NATURE?
ひゅおぉー
BUT IT SO BEAUTIFUL!
ONLY YUKIMURA-SAN WOULD WANT TO CAMP OUT IN A PLACE LIKE THIS.
......

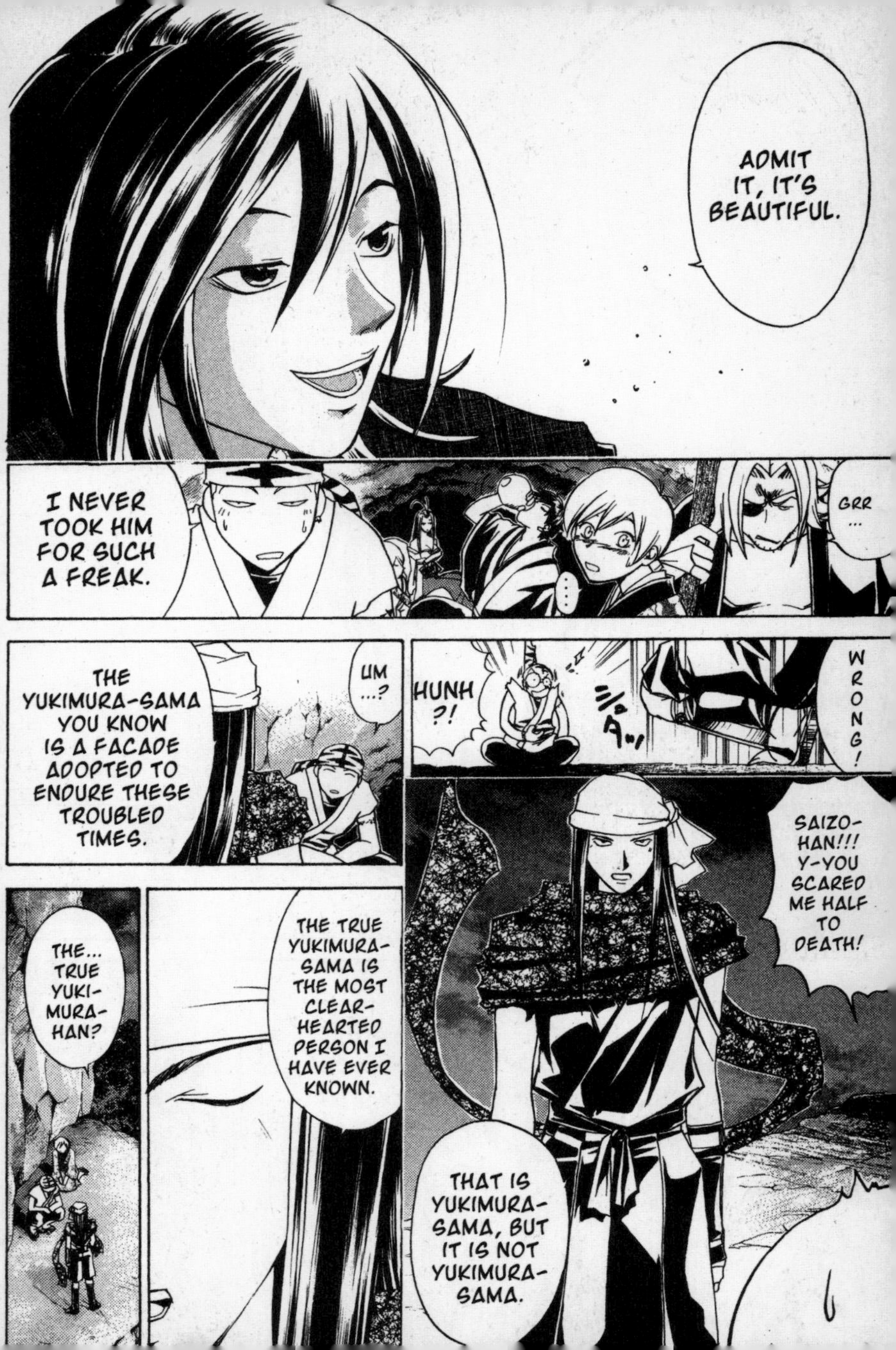
ADMIT IT, IT'S BEAUTIFUL.
GRR ...
...
I NEVER TOOK HIM FOR SUCH A FREAK.
WRONG!
HUNH ?!
SAIZO-HAN!!! Y-YOU SCARED ME HALF TO DEATH!
UM ...?
THE YUKIMURA-SAMA YOU KNOW IS A FACADE ADOPTED TO ENDURE THESE TROUBLED TIMES.
THAT IS YUKIMURA-SAMA, BUT IT IS NOT YUKIMURA-SAMA.
THE TRUE YUKIMURA-SAMA IS THE MOST CLEAR-HEARTED PERSON I HAVE EVER KNOWN.
THE... TRUE YUKIMURA-HAN?

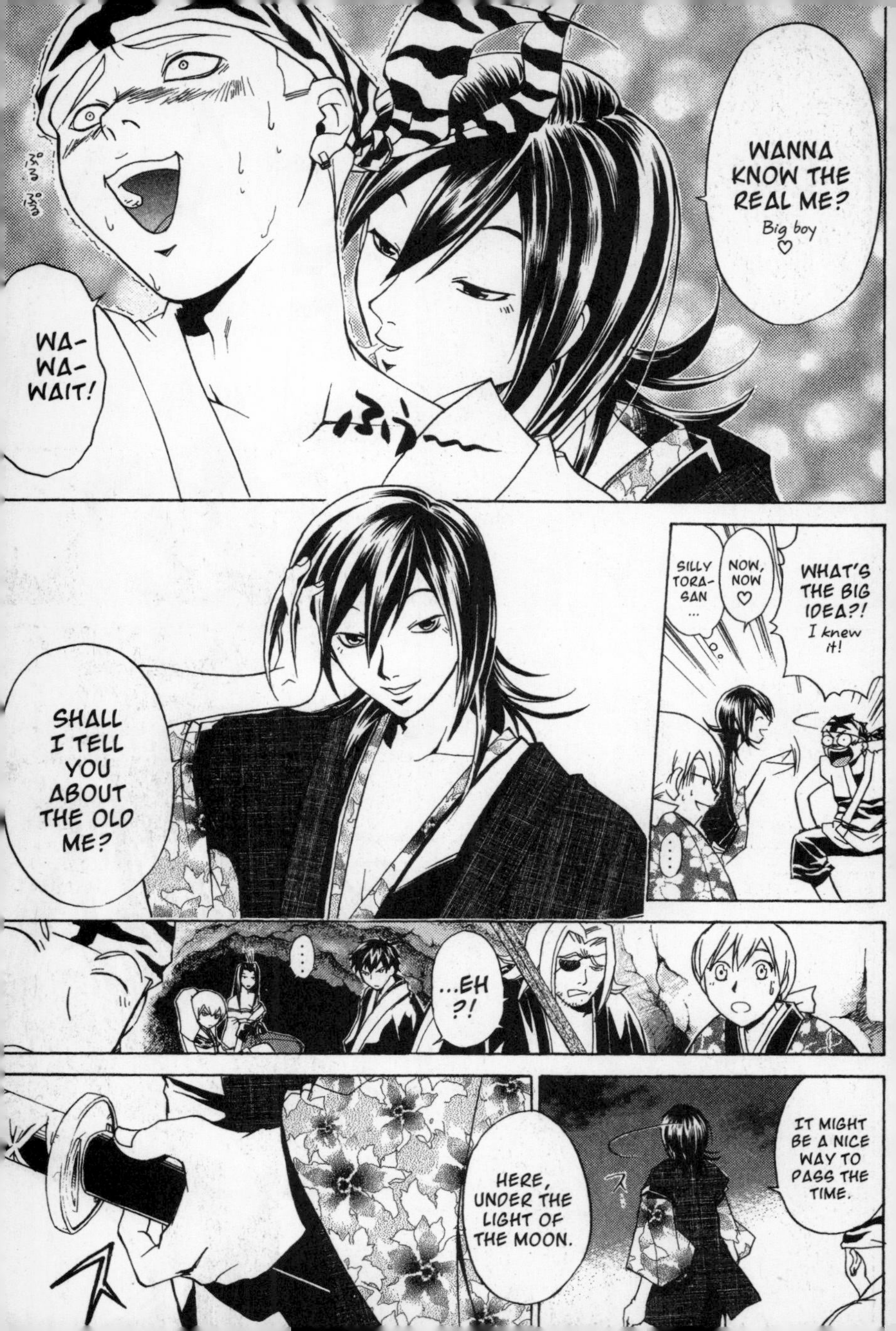
WANNA KNOW THE REAL ME?
Big boy ♡
WA-WA-WAIT!
ふぅ〜
WHAT'S THE BIG IDEA?!
I knew it!
NOW, NOW ♡
SILLY TORA-SAN ...
...
SHALL I TELL YOU ABOUT THE OLD ME?
...EH ?!
...
IT MIGHT BE A NICE WAY TO PASS THE TIME.
HERE, UNDER THE LIGHT OF THE MOON.

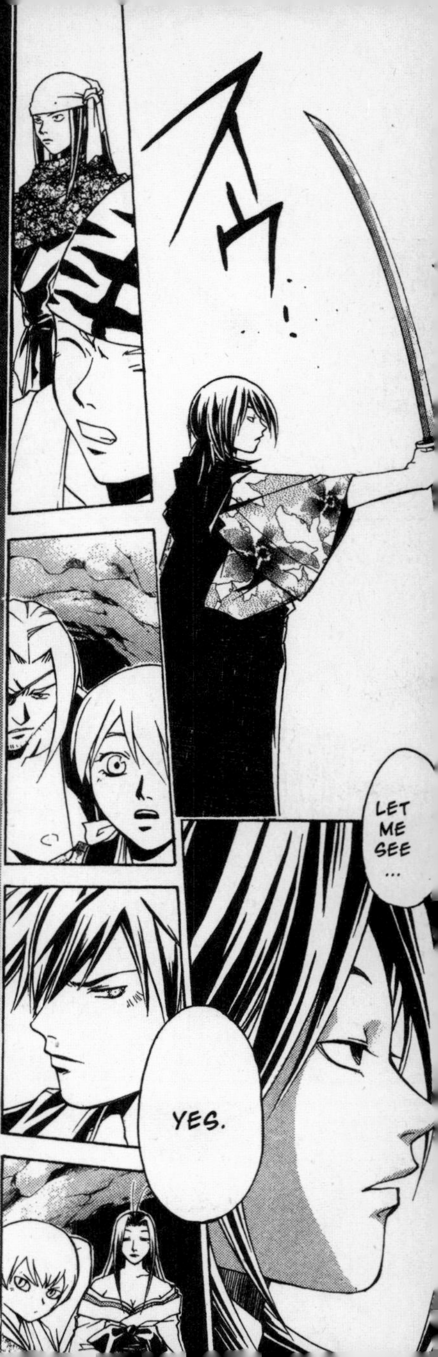
LET ME SEE ...
YES.
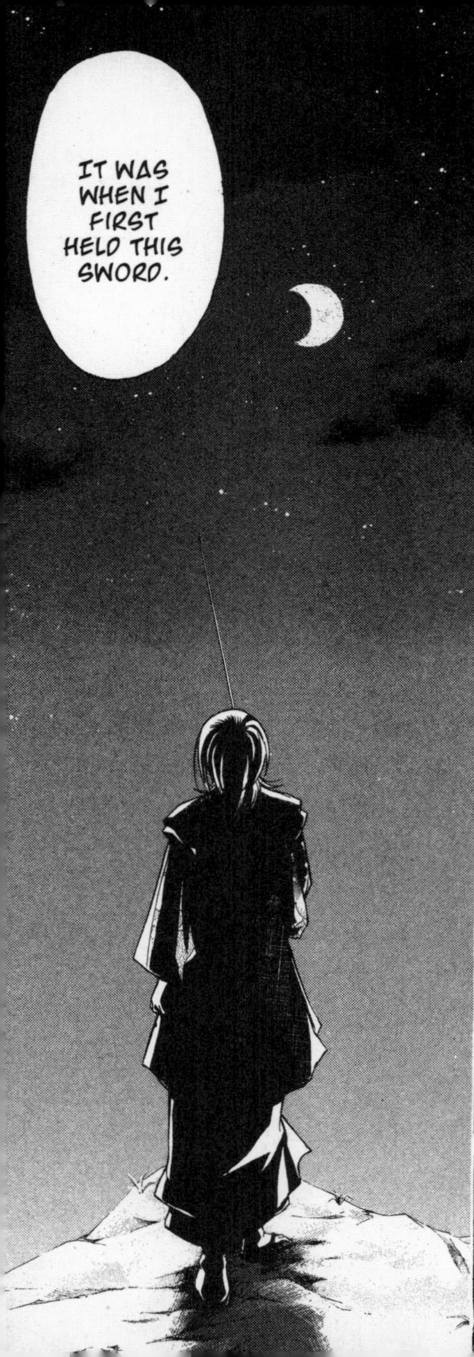
IT WAS WHEN I FIRST HELD THIS SWORD.

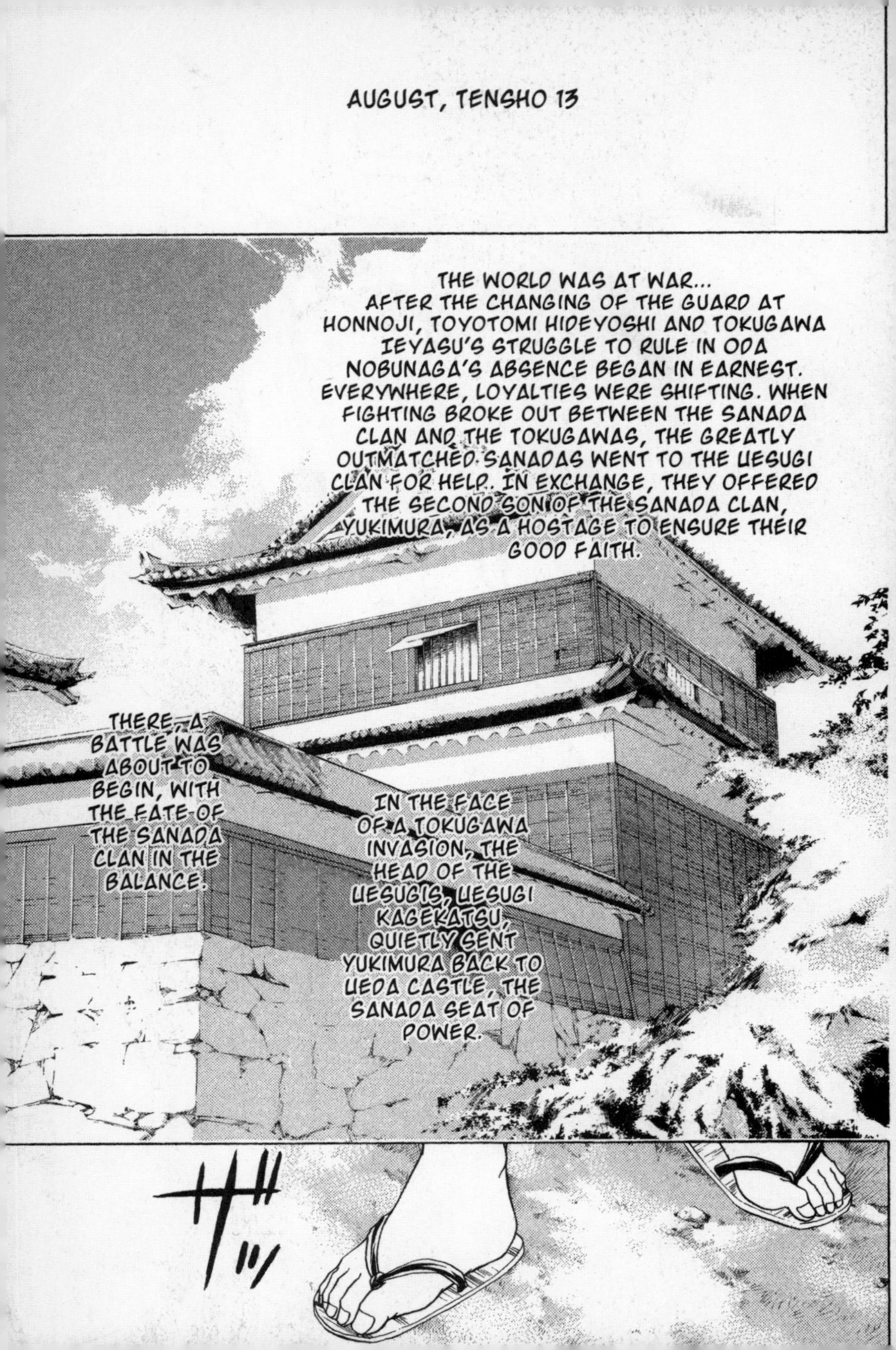
AUGUST, TENSHO 13
THE WORLD WAS AT WAR... AFTER THE CHANGING OF THE GUARD AT HONNOJI, TOYOTOMI HIDEYOSHI AND TOKUGAWA IEYASU'S STRUGGLE TO RULE IN ODA NOBUNAGA'S ABSENCE BEGAN IN EARNEST. EVERYWHERE, LOYALTIES WERE SHIFTING. WHEN FIGHTING BROKE OUT BETWEEN THE SANADA CLAN AND THE TOKUGAWAS, THE GREATLY OUTMATCHED SANADAS WENT TO THE UESUGI CLAN FOR HELP. IN EXCHANGE, THEY OFFERED THE SECOND SON OF THE SANADA CLAN, YUKIMURA, AS A HOSTAGE TO ENSURE THEIR GOOD FAITH.
IN THE FACE OF A TOKUGAWA INVASION, THE HEAD OF THE UESUGIS, UESUGI KAGEKATSU, QUIETLY SENT YUKIMURA BACK TO UEDA CASTLE, THE SANADA SEAT OF POWER.
THERE, A BATTLE WAS ABOUT TO BEGIN, WITH THE FATE OF THE SANADA CLAN IN THE BALANCE.
ザッ

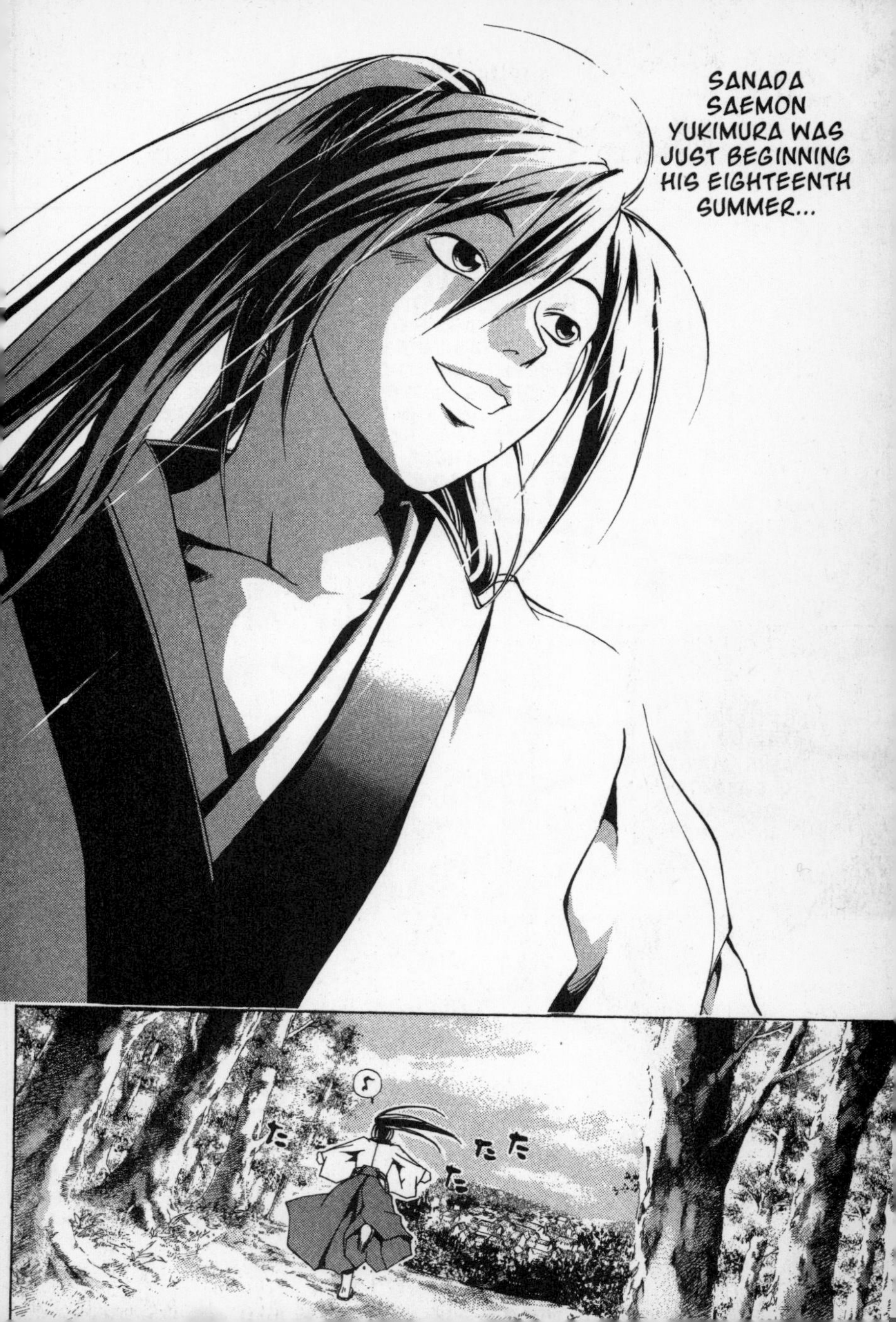
SANADA SAEMON YUKIMURA WAS JUST BEGINNING HIS EIGHTEENTH SUMMER...
たた
た
た

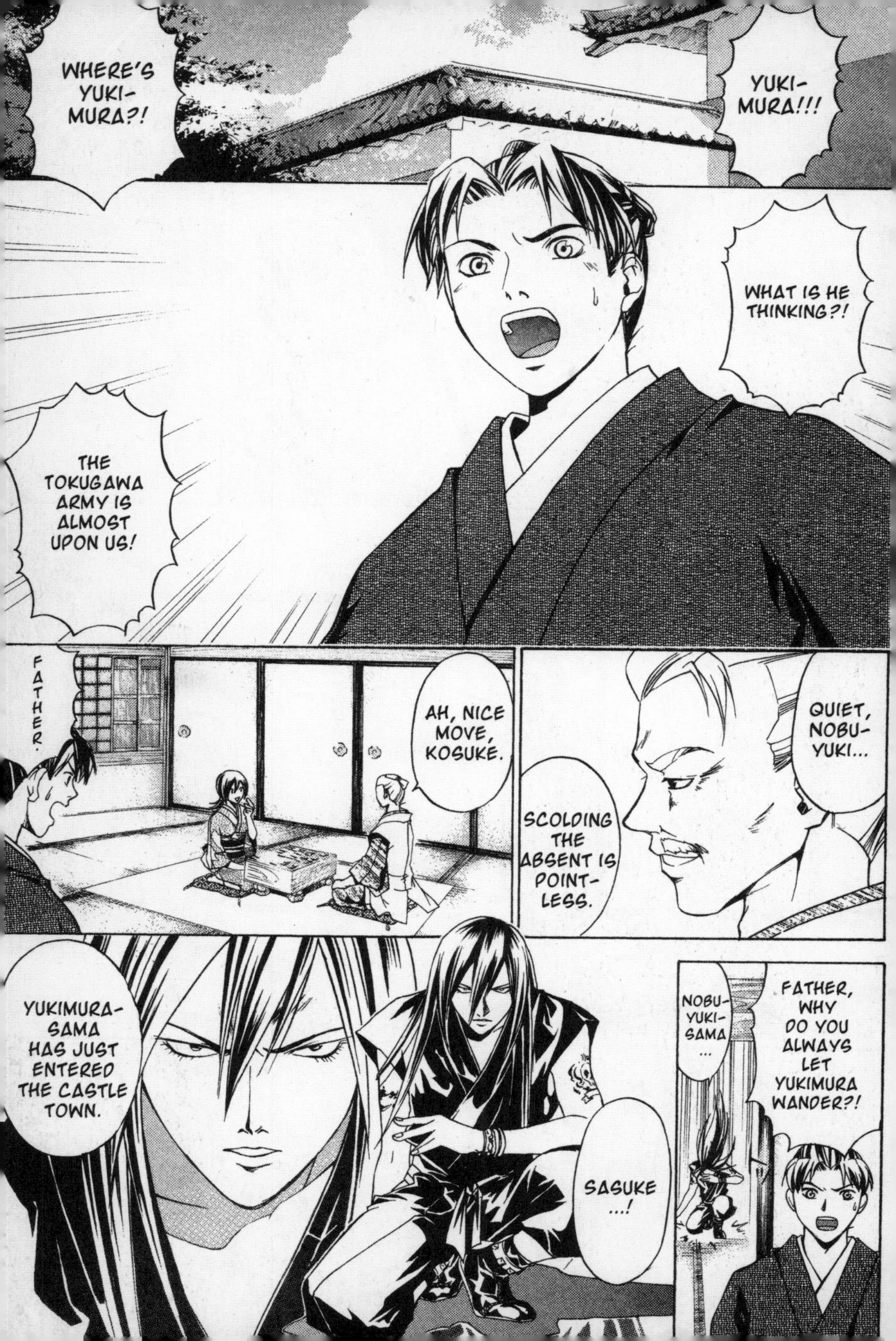
YUKI-MURA!!!
WHERE'S YUKI-MURA?!
WHAT IS HE THINKING?!
THE TOKUGAWA ARMY IS ALMOST UPON US!
QUIET, NOBU-YUKI...
SCOLDING THE ABSENT IS POINT-LESS.
AH, NICE MOVE, KOSUKE.
FATHER.
FATHER, WHY DO YOU ALWAYS LET YUKIMURA WANDER?!
NOBU-YUKI-SAMA ...
SASUKE ...!
YUKIMURA-SAMA HAS JUST ENTERED THE CASTLE TOWN.

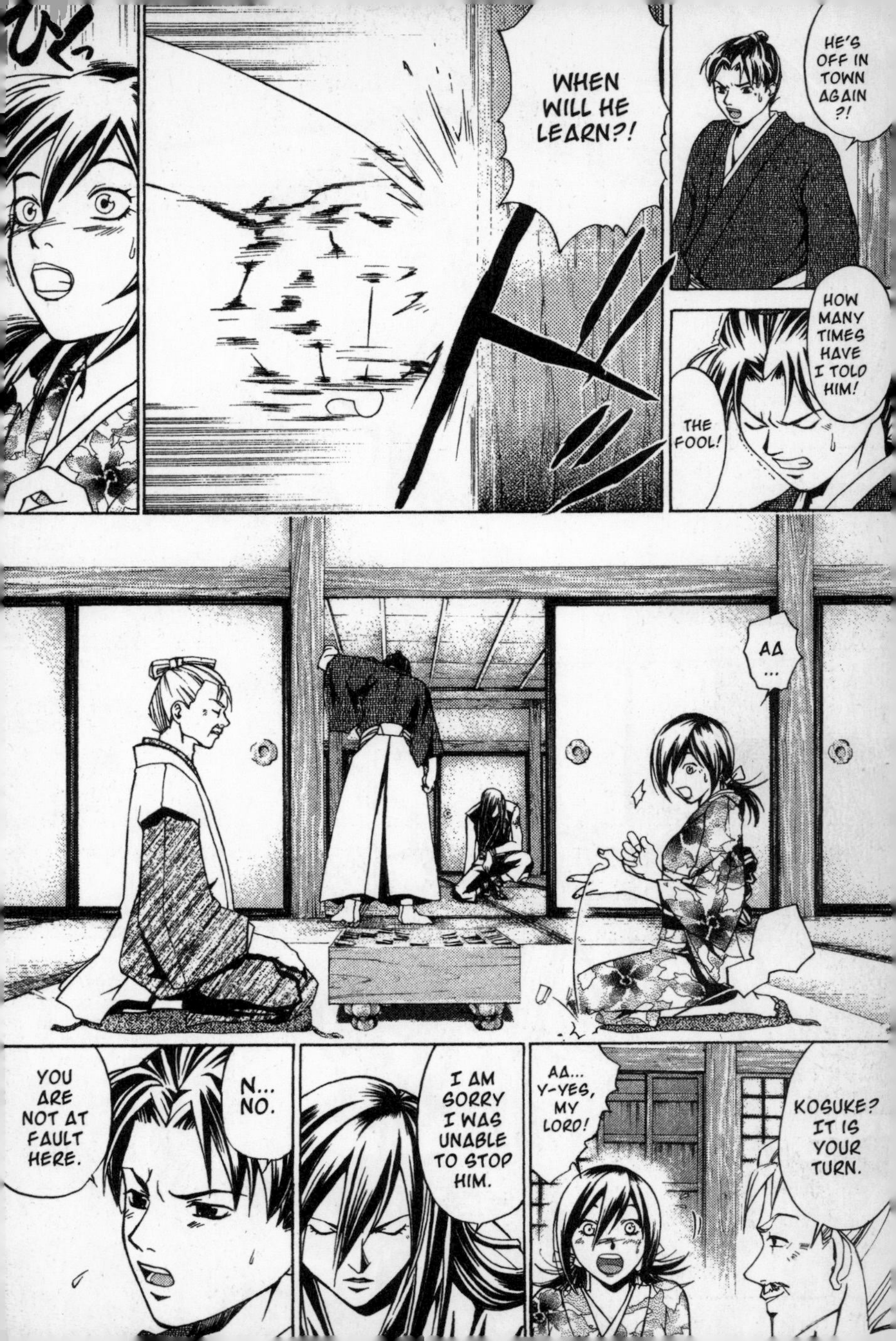
HE'S OFF IN TOWN AGAIN ?!
HOW MANY TIMES HAVE I TOLD HIM!
THE FOOL!
WHEN WILL HE LEARN?!
ひくっ
AA ...
KOSUKE? IT IS YOUR TURN.
AA... Y-YES, MY LORD!
I AM SORRY I WAS UNABLE TO STOP HIM.
N... NO.
YOU ARE NOT AT FAULT HERE.

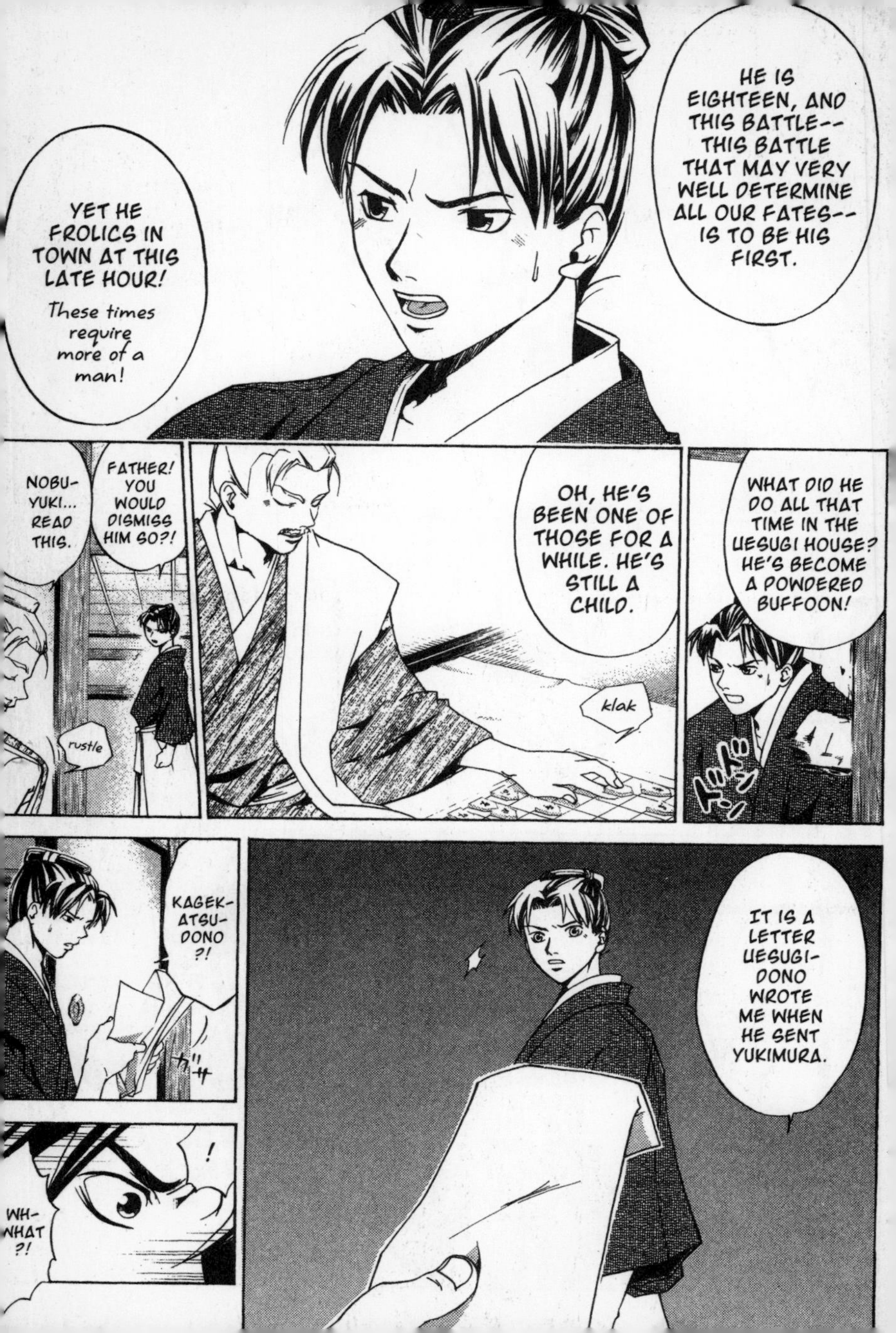
HE IS EIGHTEEN, AND THIS BATTLE-- THIS BATTLE THAT MAY VERY WELL DETERMINE ALL OUR FATES-- IS TO BE HIS FIRST.
YET HE FROLICS IN TOWN AT THIS LATE HOUR!
These times require more of a man!
WHAT DID HE DO ALL THAT TIME IN THE UESUGI HOUSE? HE'S BECOME A POWDERED BUFFOON!
OH, HE'S BEEN ONE OF THOSE FOR A WHILE. HE'S STILL A CHILD.
klak
FATHER! YOU WOULD DISMISS HIM SO?!
NOBU-YUKI... READ THIS.
rustle
IT IS A LETTER UESUGI-DONO WROTE ME WHEN HE SENT YUKIMURA.
KAGEK-ATSU-DONO ?!
!
WH-WHAT ?!

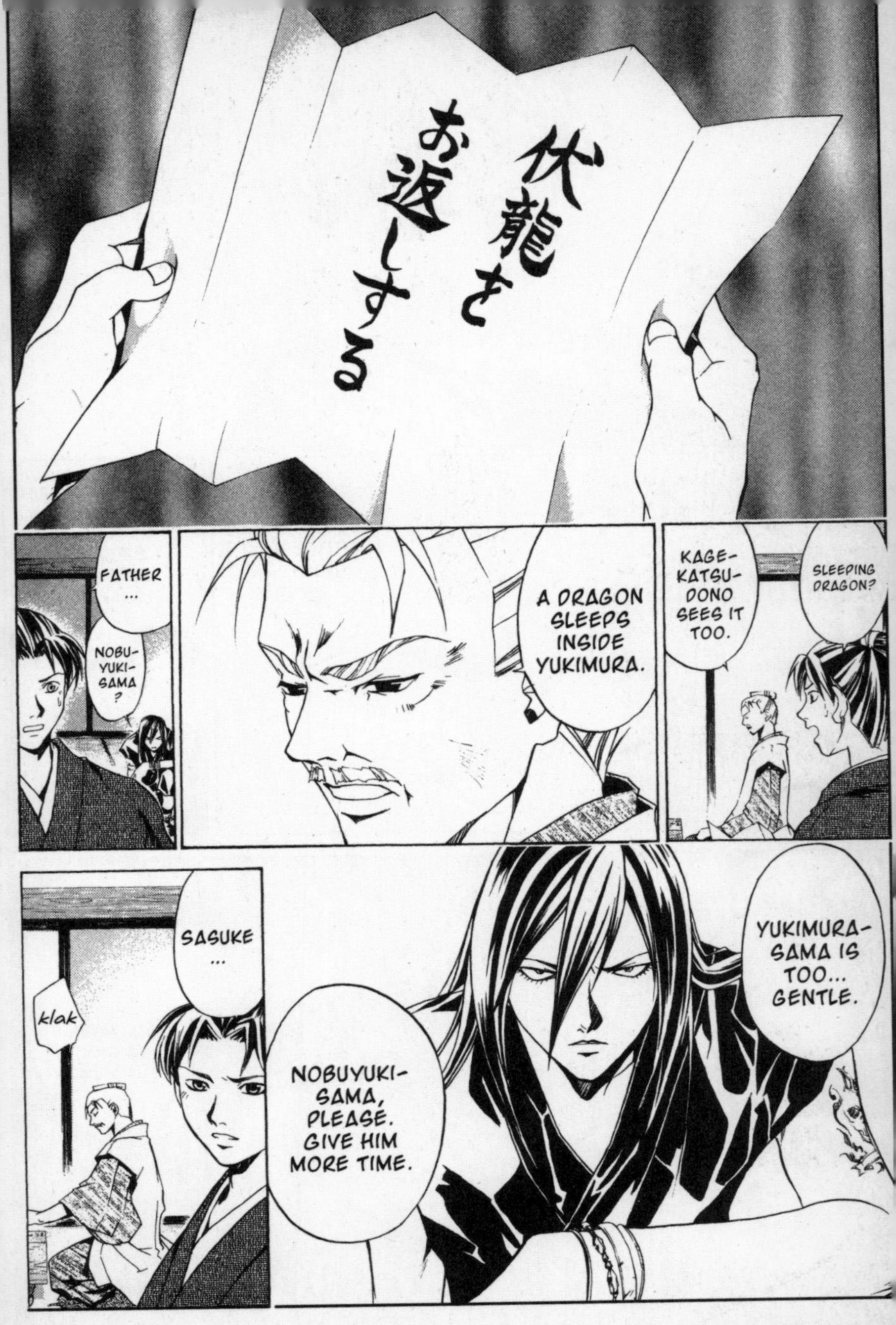
伏龍をお返しする
SLEEPING DRAGON?
KAGE-KATSU-DONO SEES IT TOO.
A DRAGON SLEEPS INSIDE YUKIMURA.
FATHER ...
NOBU-YUKI-SAMA ?
YUKIMURA-SAMA IS TOO... GENTLE.
NOBUYUKI-SAMA, PLEASE. GIVE HIM MORE TIME.
SASUKE ...
klak

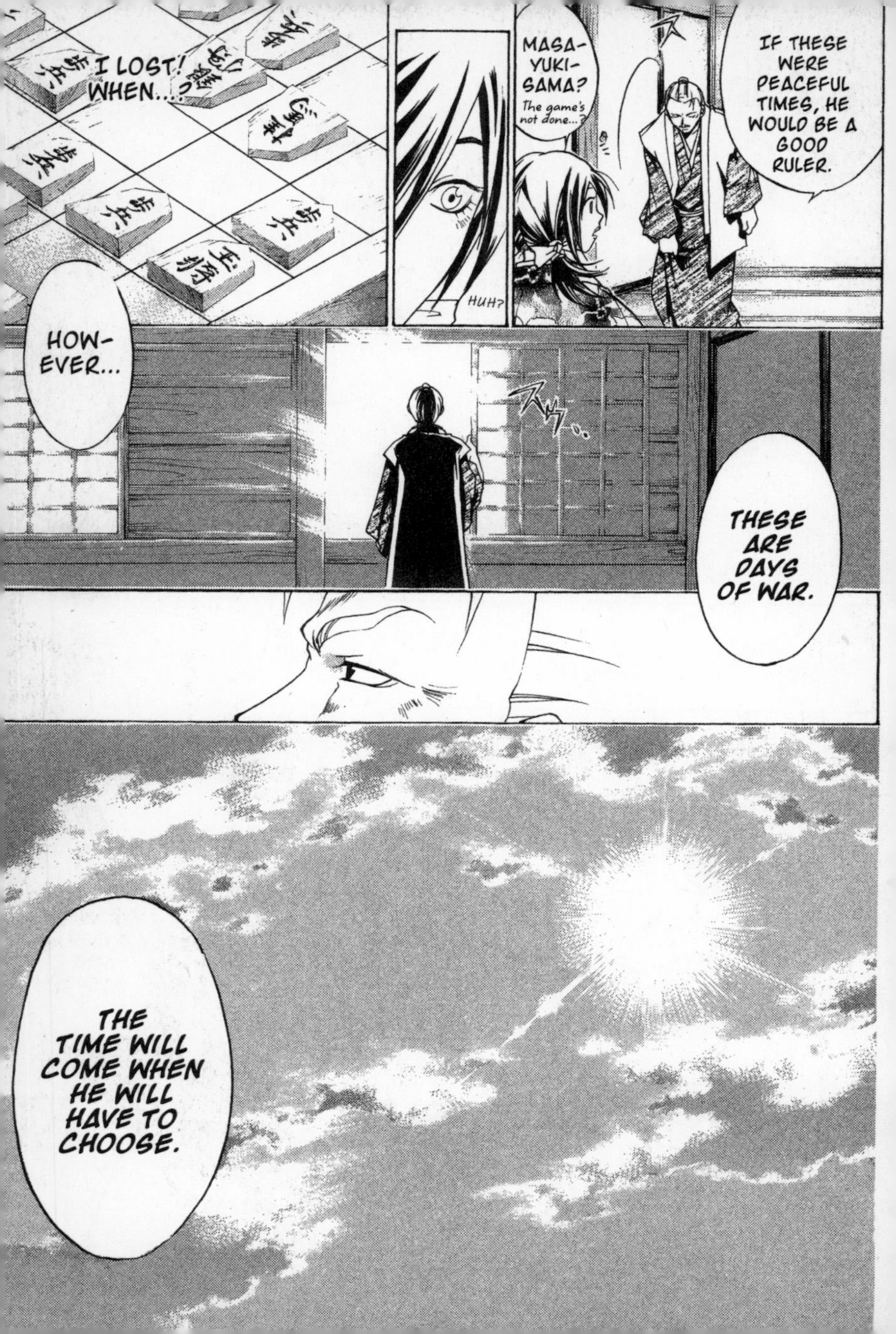

IF THESE WERE PEACEFUL TIMES, HE WOULD BE A GOOD RULER.
MASA-YUKI-SAMA?
The game's not done...?
HUH?
I LOST! WHEN...?
HOW-EVER...
THESE ARE DAYS OF WAR.
THE TIME WILL COME WHEN HE WILL HAVE TO CHOOSE.

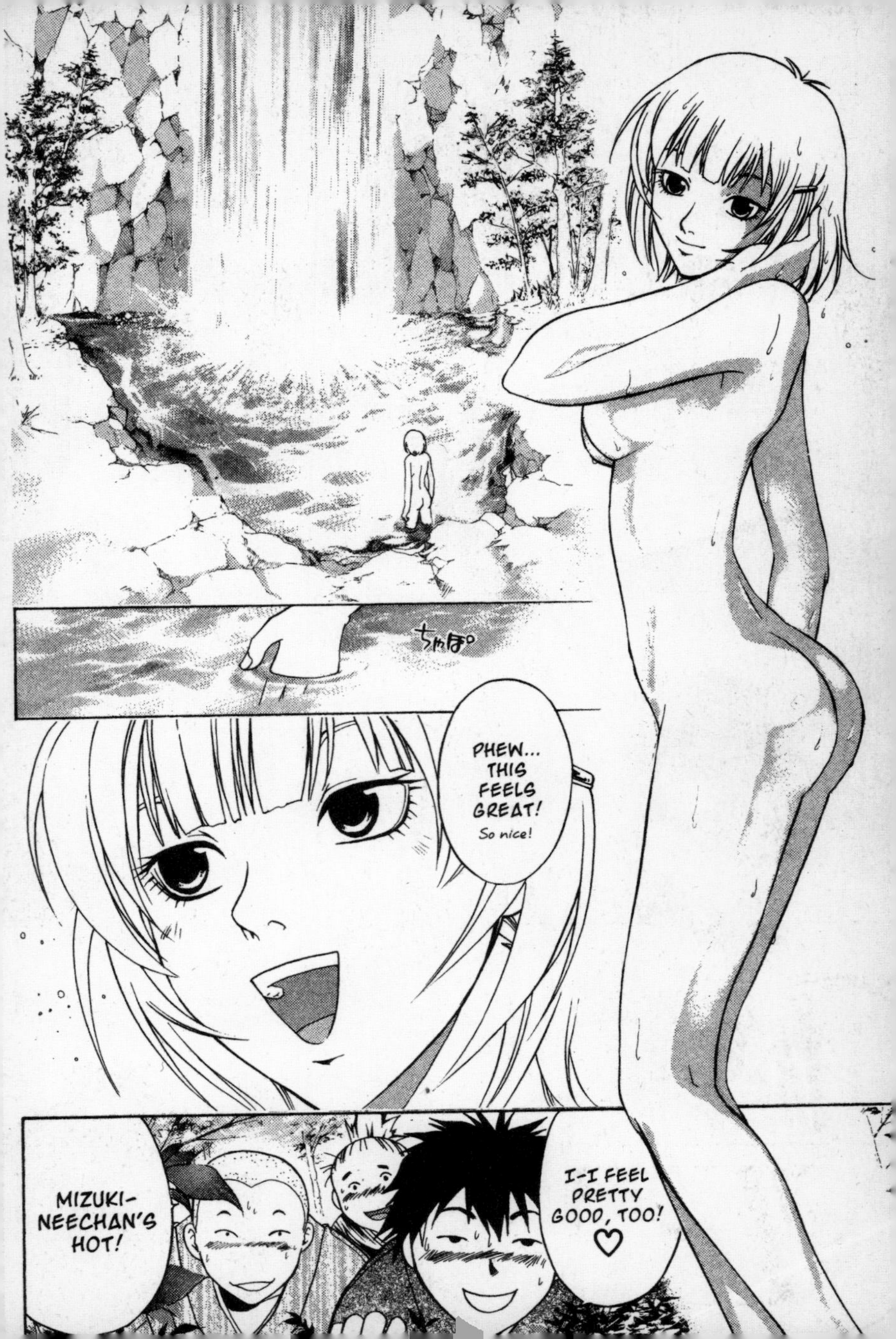
ちゃぽ
PHEW... THIS FEELS GREAT!
So nice!
I-I FEEL PRETTY GOOD, TOO! ♡
MIZUKI-NEECHAN'S HOT!

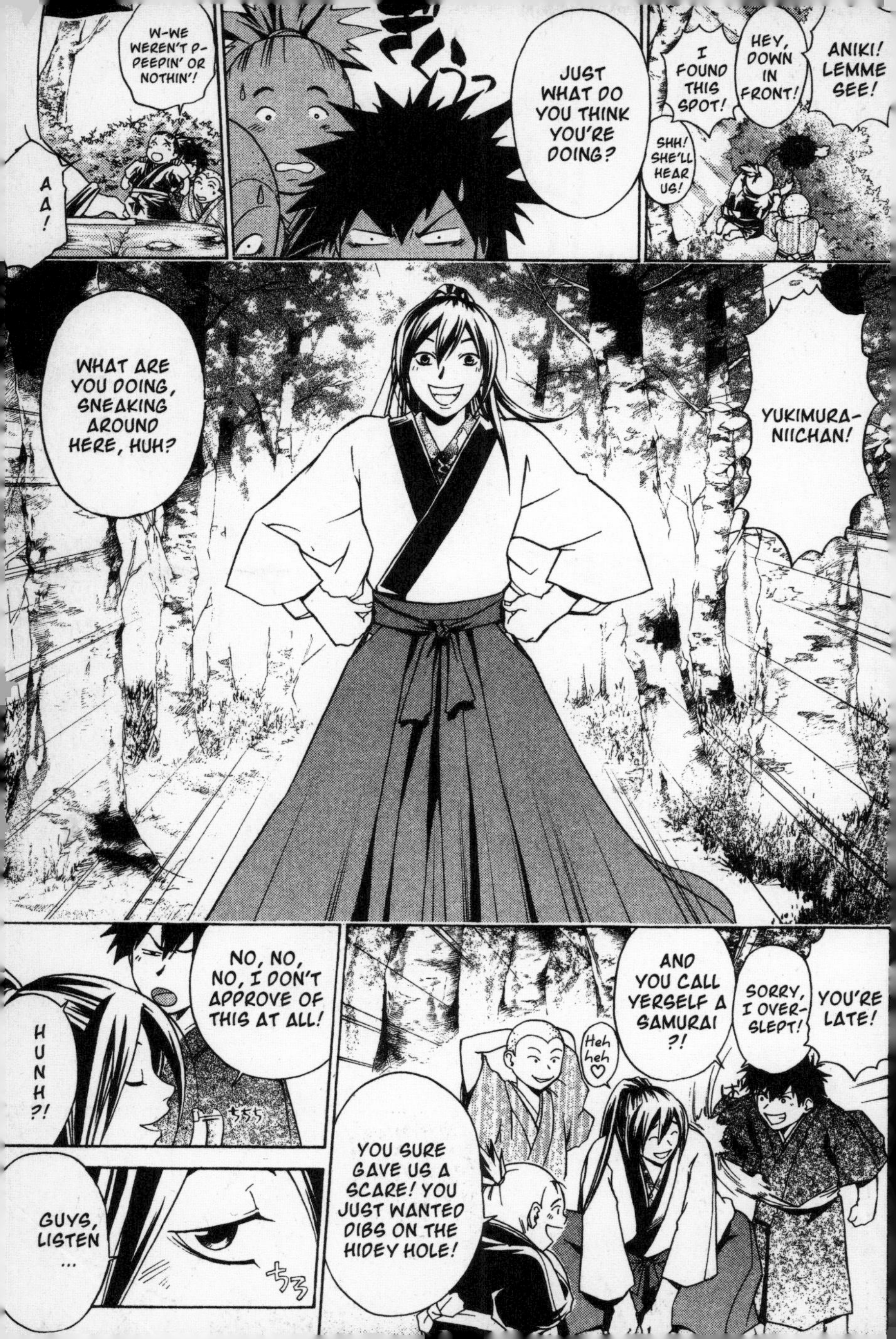
ANIKI! LEMME SEE!
HEY, DOWN IN FRONT!
I FOUND THIS SPOT!
SHH! SHE'LL HEAR US!
JUST WHAT DO YOU THINK YOU'RE DOING?
W-WE WEREN'T P-PEEPIN' OR NOTHIN'!
A A!
YUKIMURA-NIICHAN!
WHAT ARE YOU DOING, SNEAKING AROUND HERE, HUH?
YOU'RE LATE!
SORRY, I OVER-SLEPT!
AND YOU CALL YERSELF A SAMURAI ?!
Heh heh ♡
YOU SURE GAVE US A SCARE! YOU JUST WANTED DIBS ON THE HIDEY HOLE!
NO, NO, NO, I DON'T APPROVE OF THIS AT ALL!
HUNH?!
GUYS, LISTEN ...

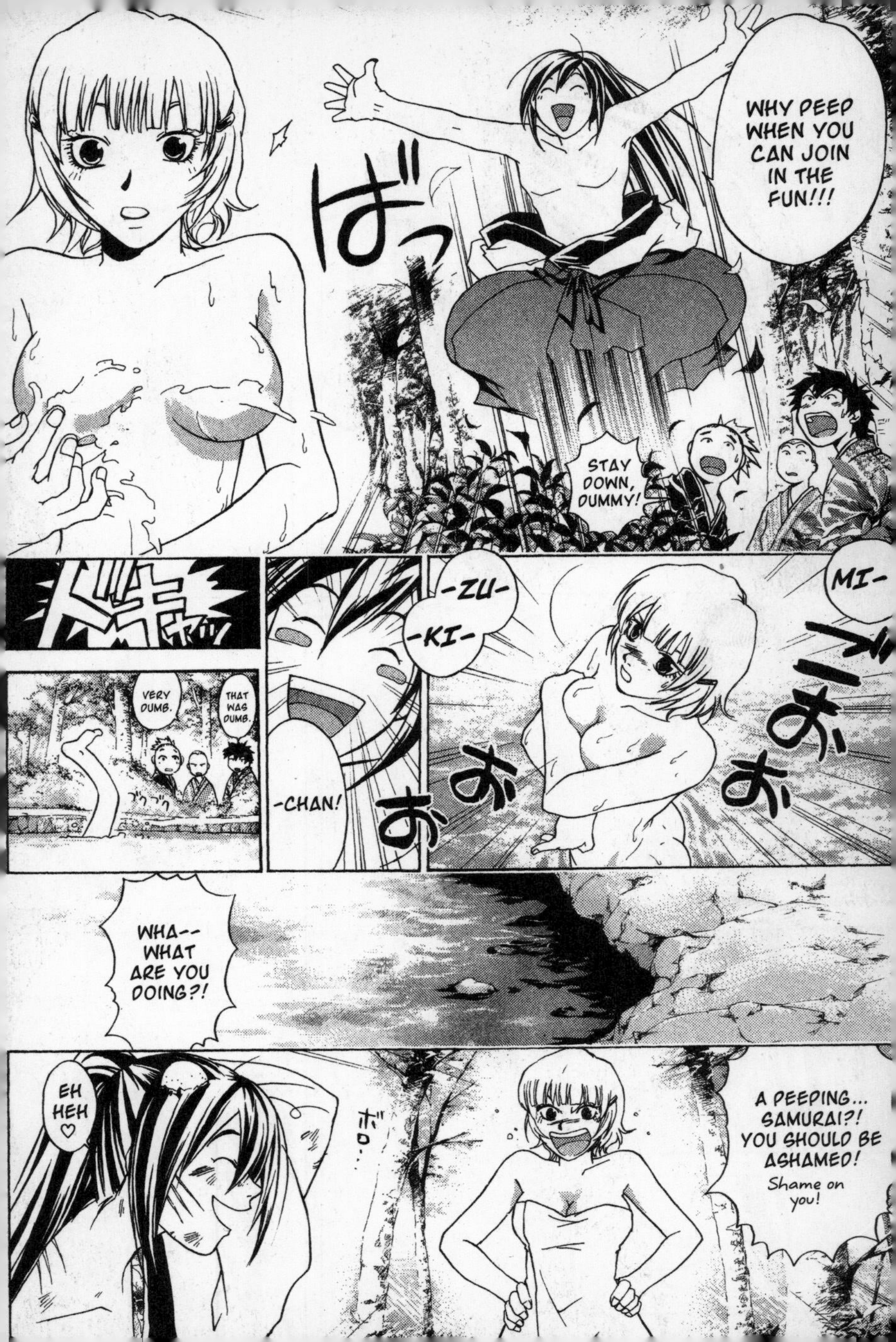
WHY PEEP WHEN YOU CAN JOIN IN THE FUN!!!
ばっ
STAY DOWN, DUMMY!
MI-
-ZU-
-KI-
-CHAN!
THAT WAS DUMB.
VERY DUMB.
WHA-- WHAT ARE YOU DOING?!
A PEEPING... SAMURAI?! YOU SHOULD BE ASHAMED!
Shame on you!
EH HEH ♡

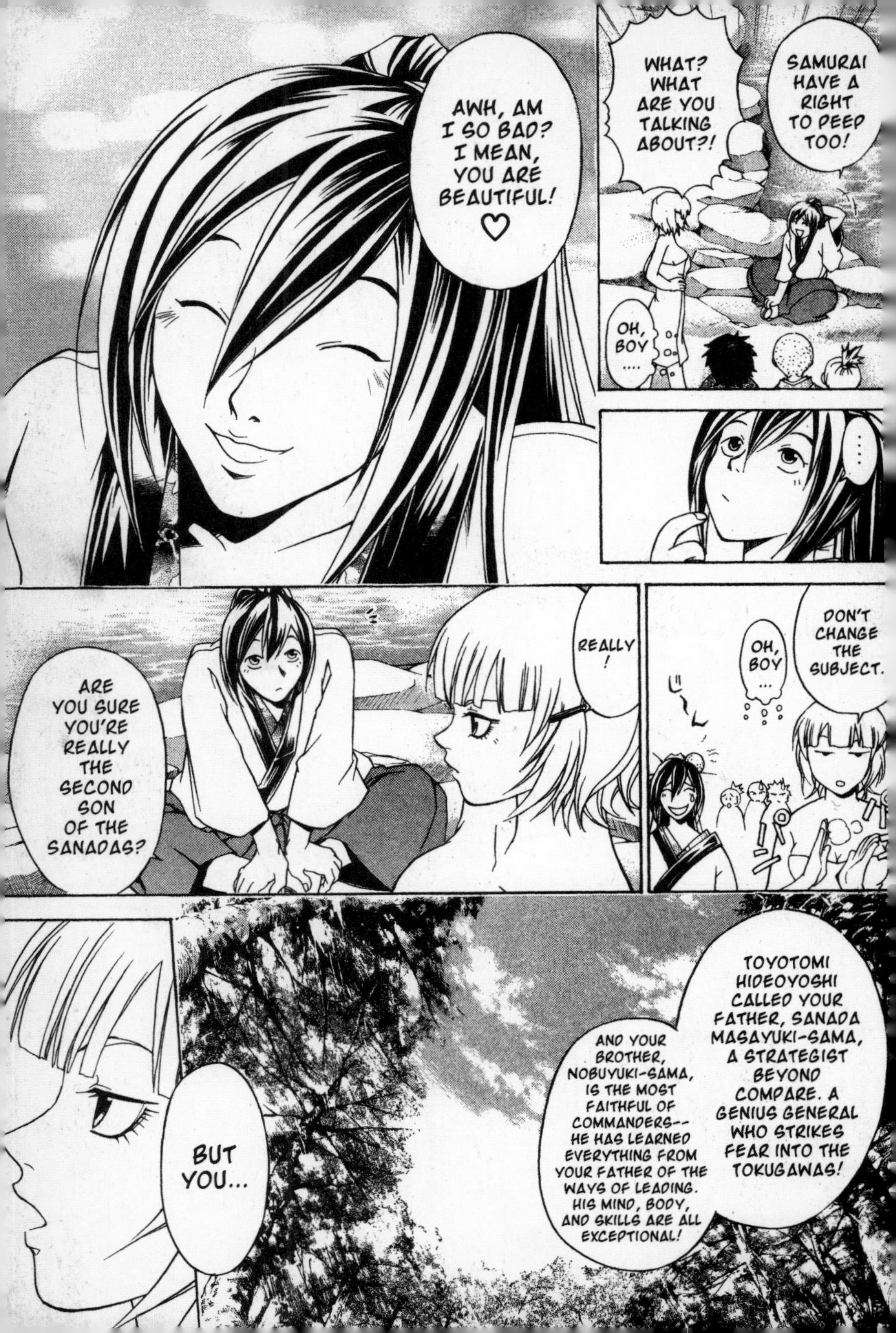
SAMURAI HAVE A RIGHT TO PEEP TOO!
WHAT? WHAT ARE YOU TALKING ABOUT?!
OH, BOY ....
...
AWH, AM I SO BAD? I MEAN, YOU ARE BEAUTIFUL! ♡
DON'T CHANGE THE SUBJECT.
OH, BOY ...
REALLY!
ARE YOU SURE YOU'RE REALLY THE SECOND SON OF THE SANADAS?
TOYOTOMI HIDEOYOSHI CALLED YOUR FATHER, SANADA MASAYUKI-SAMA, A STRATEGIST BEYOND COMPARE. A GENIUS GENERAL WHO STRIKES FEAR INTO THE TOKUGAWAS!
AND YOUR BROTHER, NOBUYUKI-SAMA, IS THE MOST FAITHFUL OF COMMANDERS-- HE HAS LEARNED EVERYTHING FROM YOUR FATHER OF THE WAYS OF LEADING. HIS MIND, BODY, AND SKILLS ARE ALL EXCEPTIONAL!
BUT YOU...

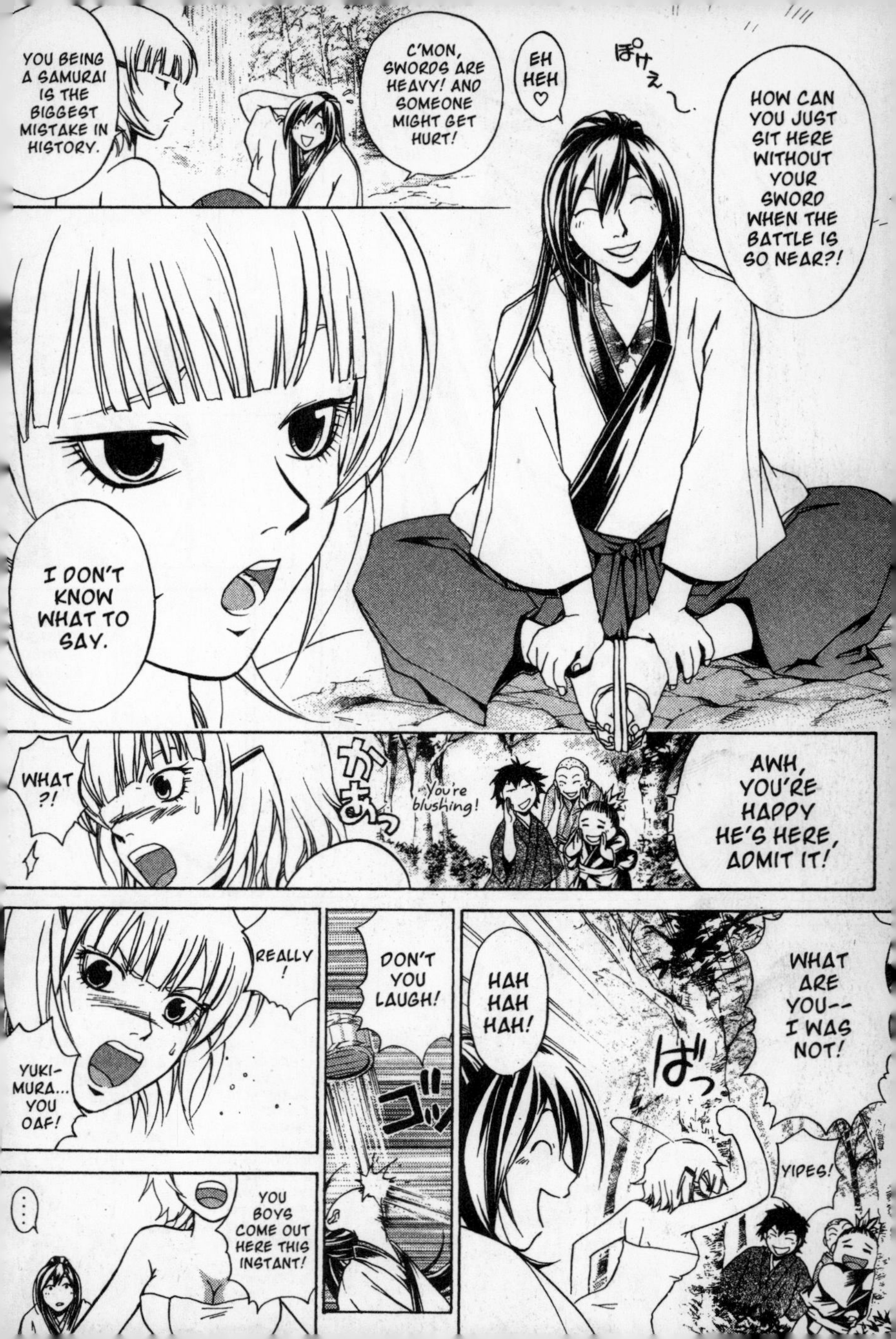
HOW CAN YOU JUST SIT HERE WITHOUT YOUR SWORD WHEN THE BATTLE IS SO NEAR?!
ぽけぇ~
EH HEH ♡
C'MON, SWORDS ARE HEAVY! AND SOMEONE MIGHT GET HURT!
YOU BEING A SAMURAI IS THE BIGGEST MISTAKE IN HISTORY.
I DON'T KNOW WHAT TO SAY.
AWH, YOU'RE HAPPY HE'S HERE, ADMIT IT!
You're blushing!
かぁっ
WHAT?!
WHAT ARE YOU-- I WAS NOT!
ばっ
HAH HAH HAH!
YIPES!
DON'T YOU LAUGH!
ゴッ
REALLY!
YUKI-MURA... YOU OAF!
YOU BOYS COME OUT HERE THIS INSTANT!
...

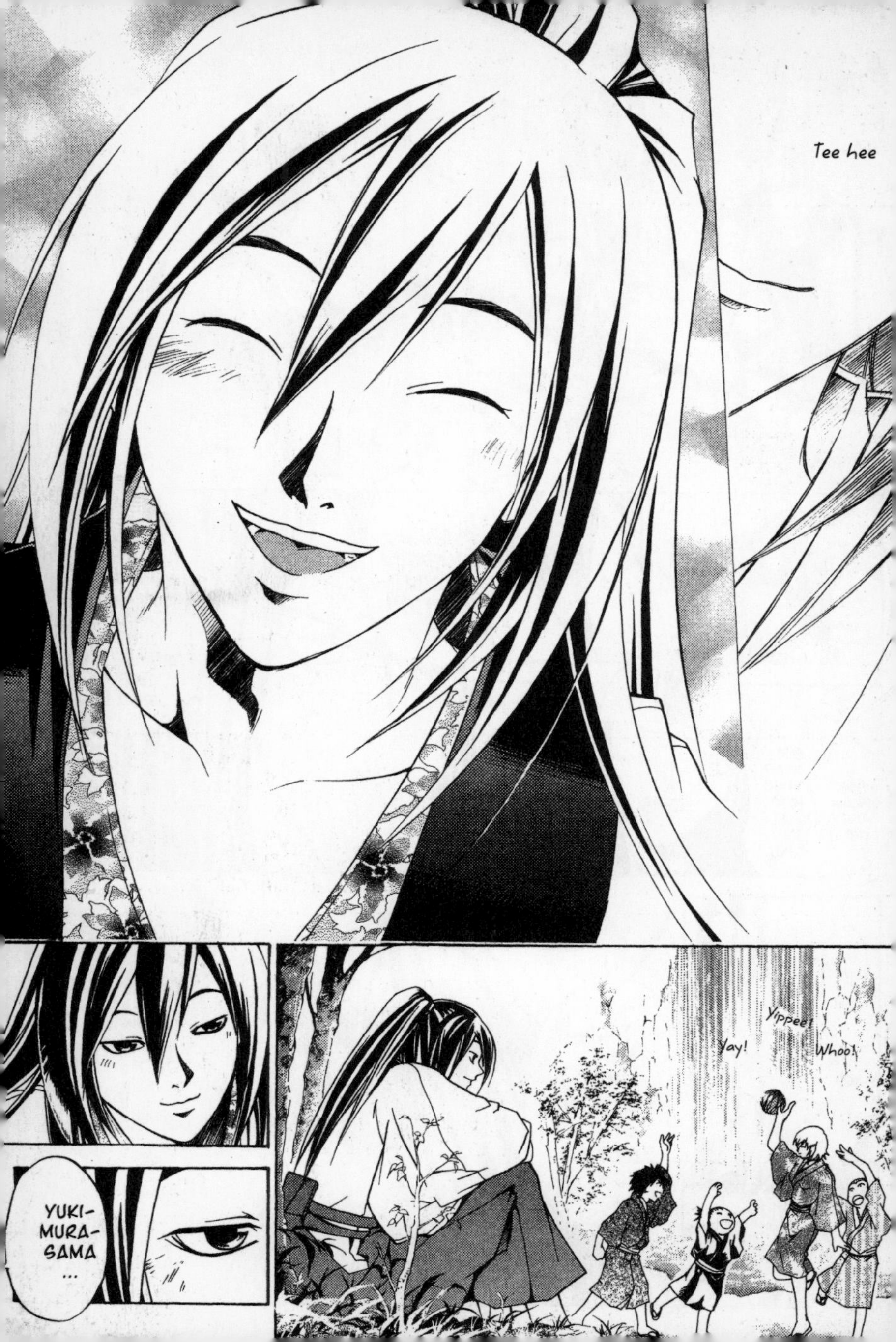
Tee hee
Yippee!
Whoo!
Yay!
YUKI-MURA-SAMA ...

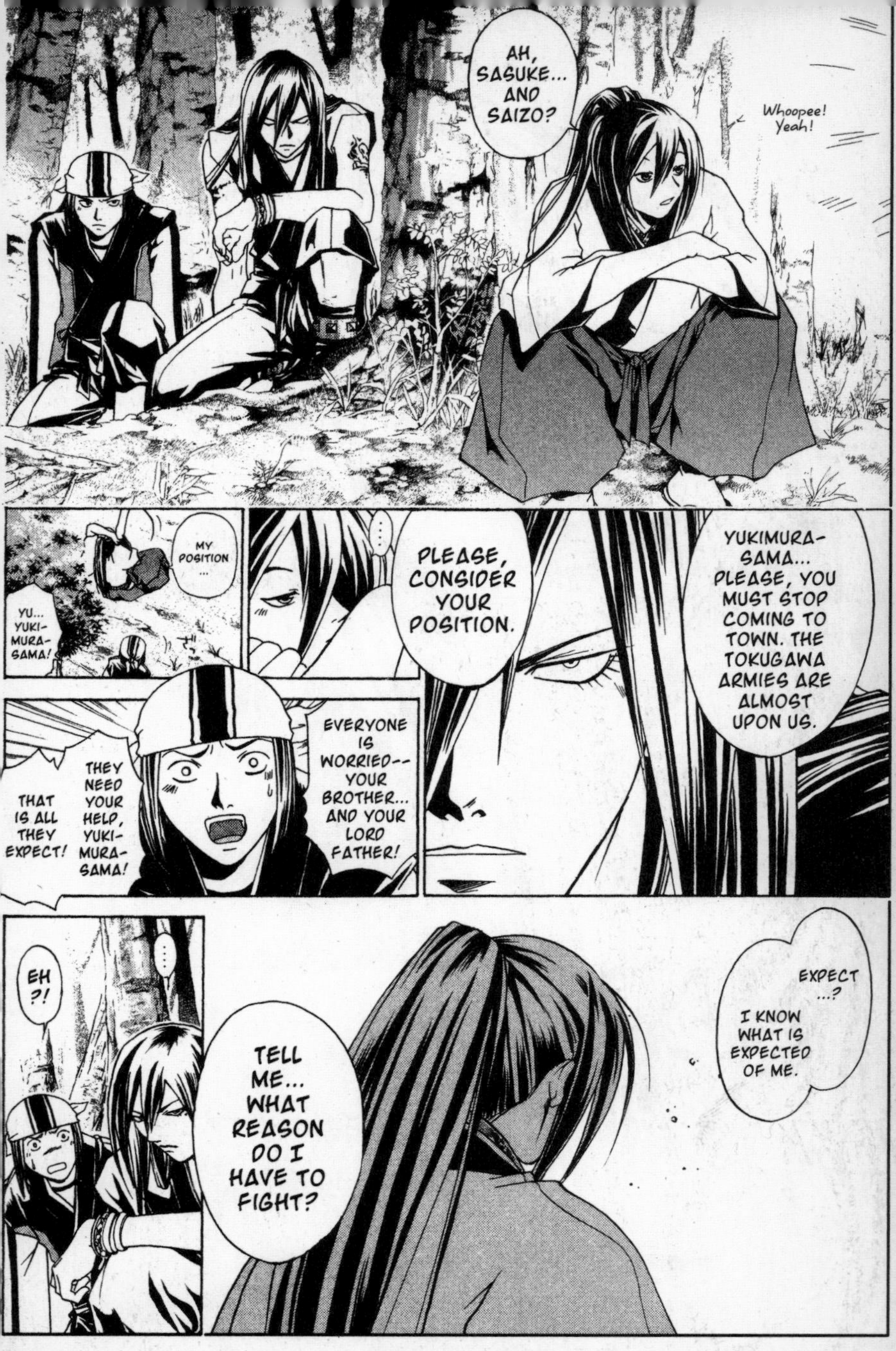
AH, SASUKE... AND SAIZO?
Whoopee! Yeah!
YUKIMURA-SAMA... PLEASE, YOU MUST STOP COMING TO TOWN. THE TOKUGAWA ARMIES ARE ALMOST UPON US.
PLEASE, CONSIDER YOUR POSITION.
...
MY POSITION ...
YU... YUKI-MURA-SAMA!
EVERYONE IS WORRIED-- YOUR BROTHER... AND YOUR LORD FATHER!
THEY NEED YOUR HELP, YUKI-MURA-SAMA!
THAT IS ALL THEY EXPECT!
EXPECT ...?
I KNOW WHAT IS EXPECTED OF ME.
TELL ME... WHAT REASON DO I HAVE TO FIGHT?
...
EH ?!

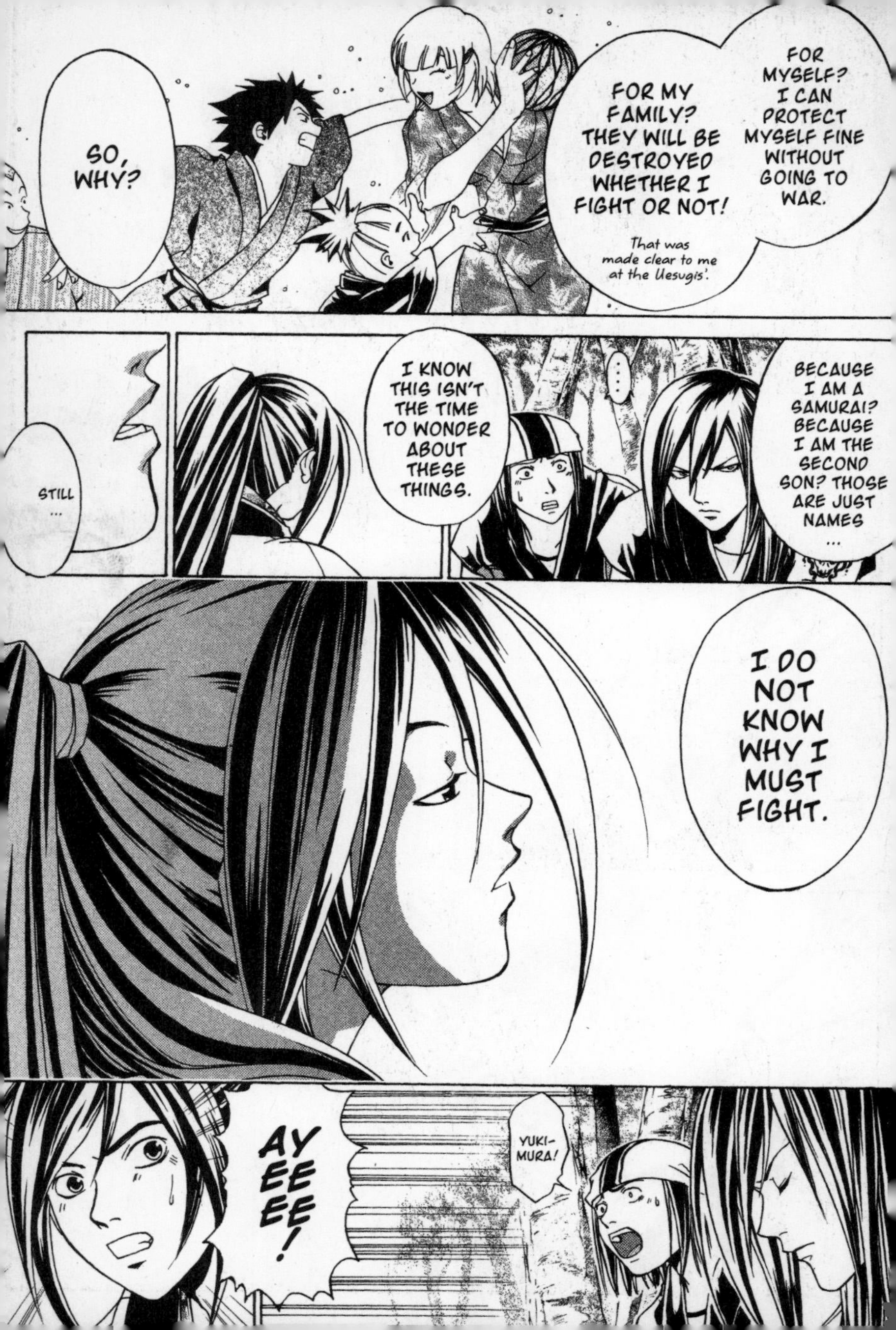
FOR MYSELF? I CAN PROTECT MYSELF FINE WITHOUT GOING TO WAR.
FOR MY FAMILY? THEY WILL BE DESTROYED WHETHER I FIGHT OR NOT!
That was made clear to me at the Uesugis'.
SO, WHY?
BECAUSE I AM A SAMURAI? BECAUSE I AM THE SECOND SON? THOSE ARE JUST NAMES ...
...
I KNOW THIS ISN'T THE TIME TO WONDER ABOUT THESE THINGS.
STILL ...
I DO NOT KNOW WHY I MUST FIGHT.
YUKI-MURA!
AYEEEEE!

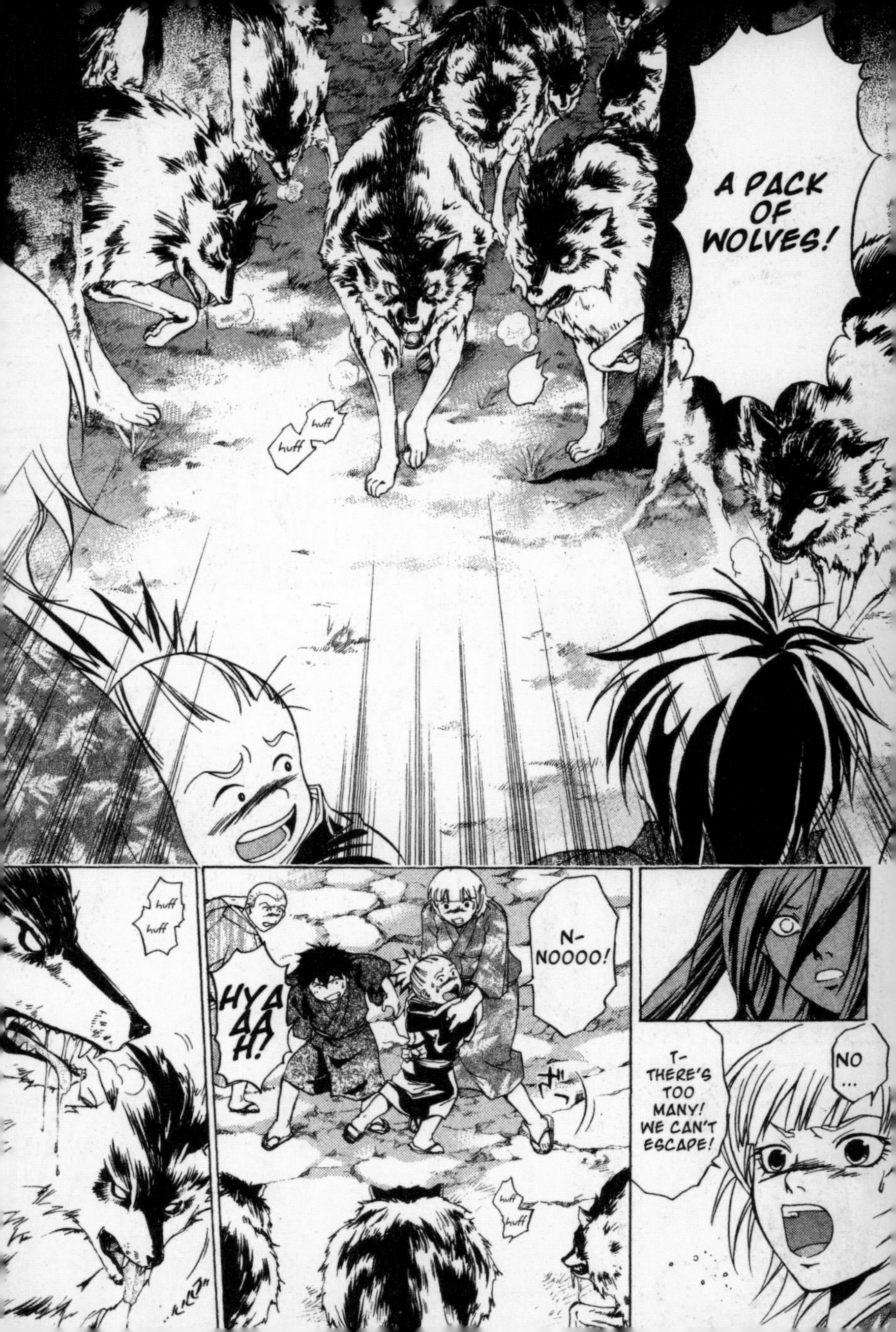
A PACK OF WOLVES!
huff huff
NO ...
T-THERE'S TOO MANY! WE CAN'T ESCAPE!
N-NOOOO!
HYAAAH!
huff huff
huff huff

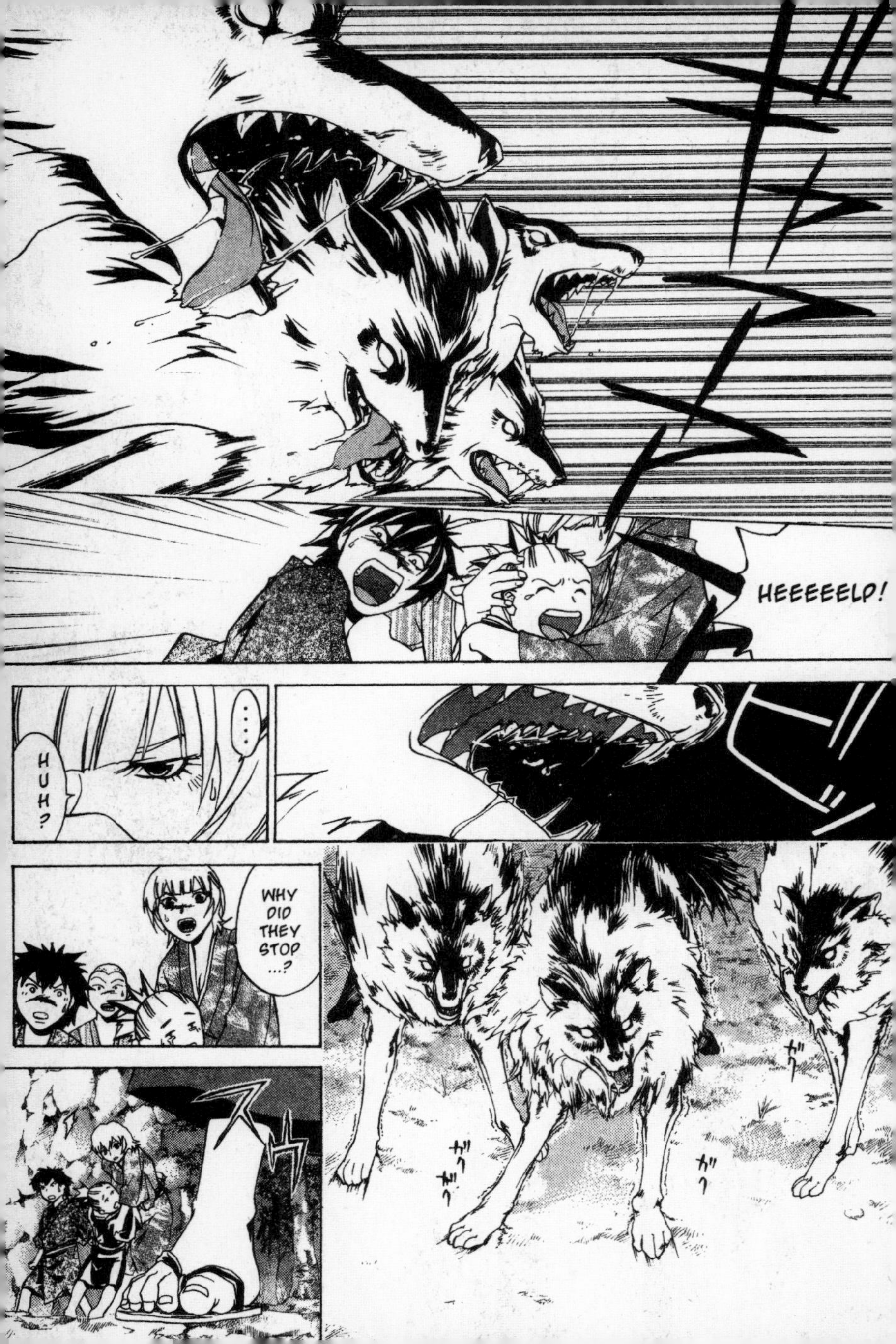
HEEEEELP!
....
HUH?
WHY DID THEY STOP ...?

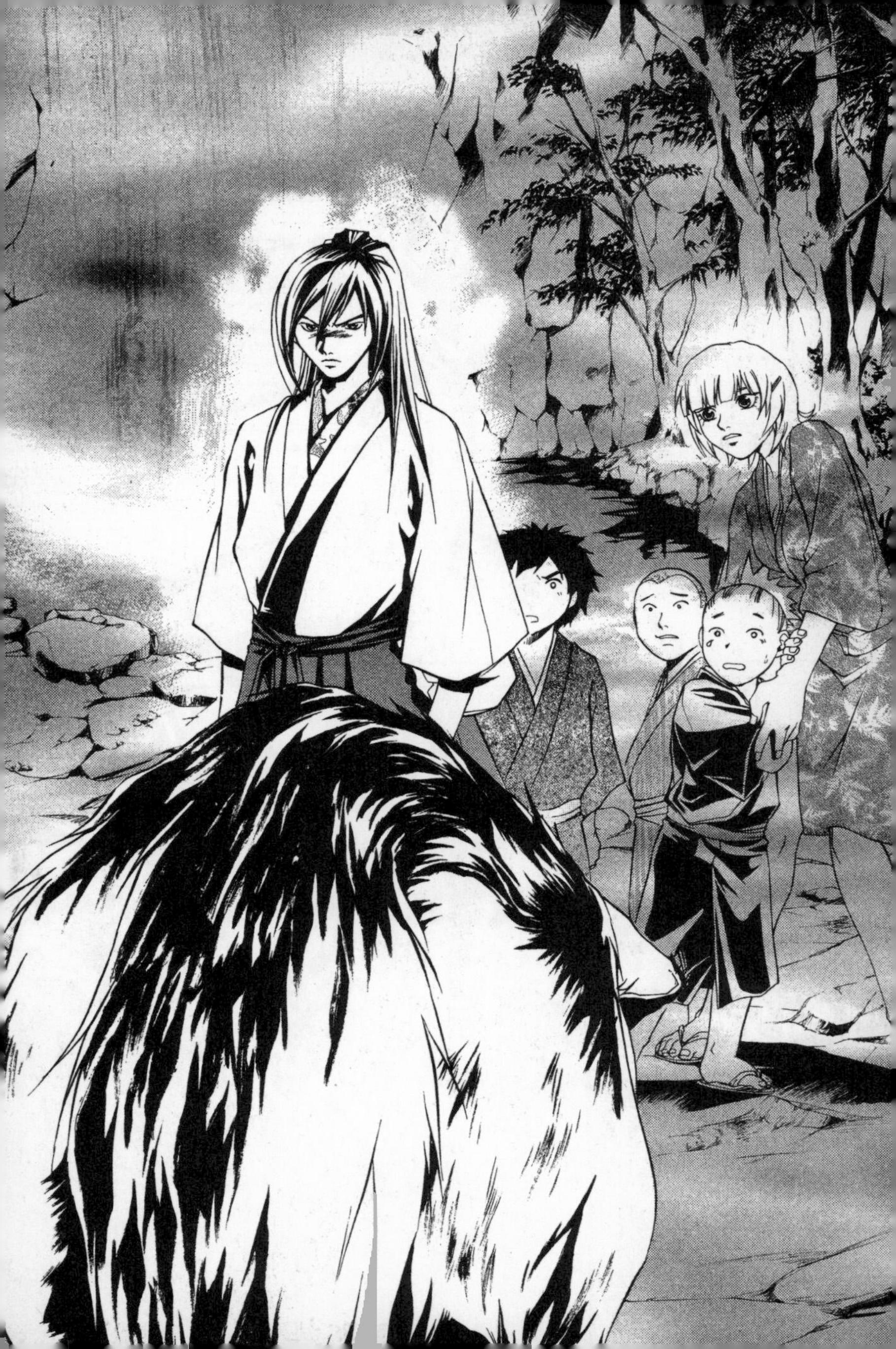

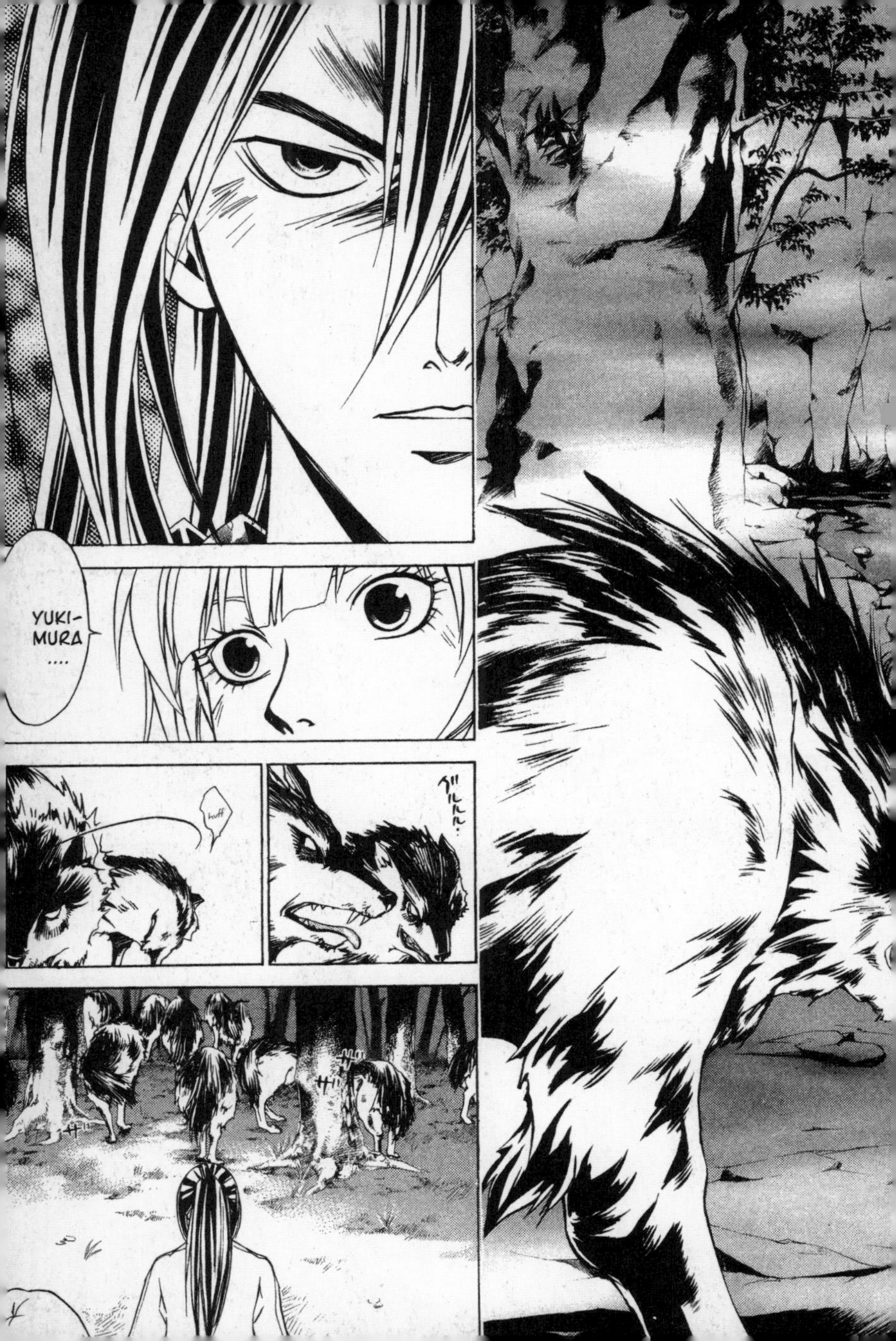
YUKI-MURA ....
ヴルルル‥
huff

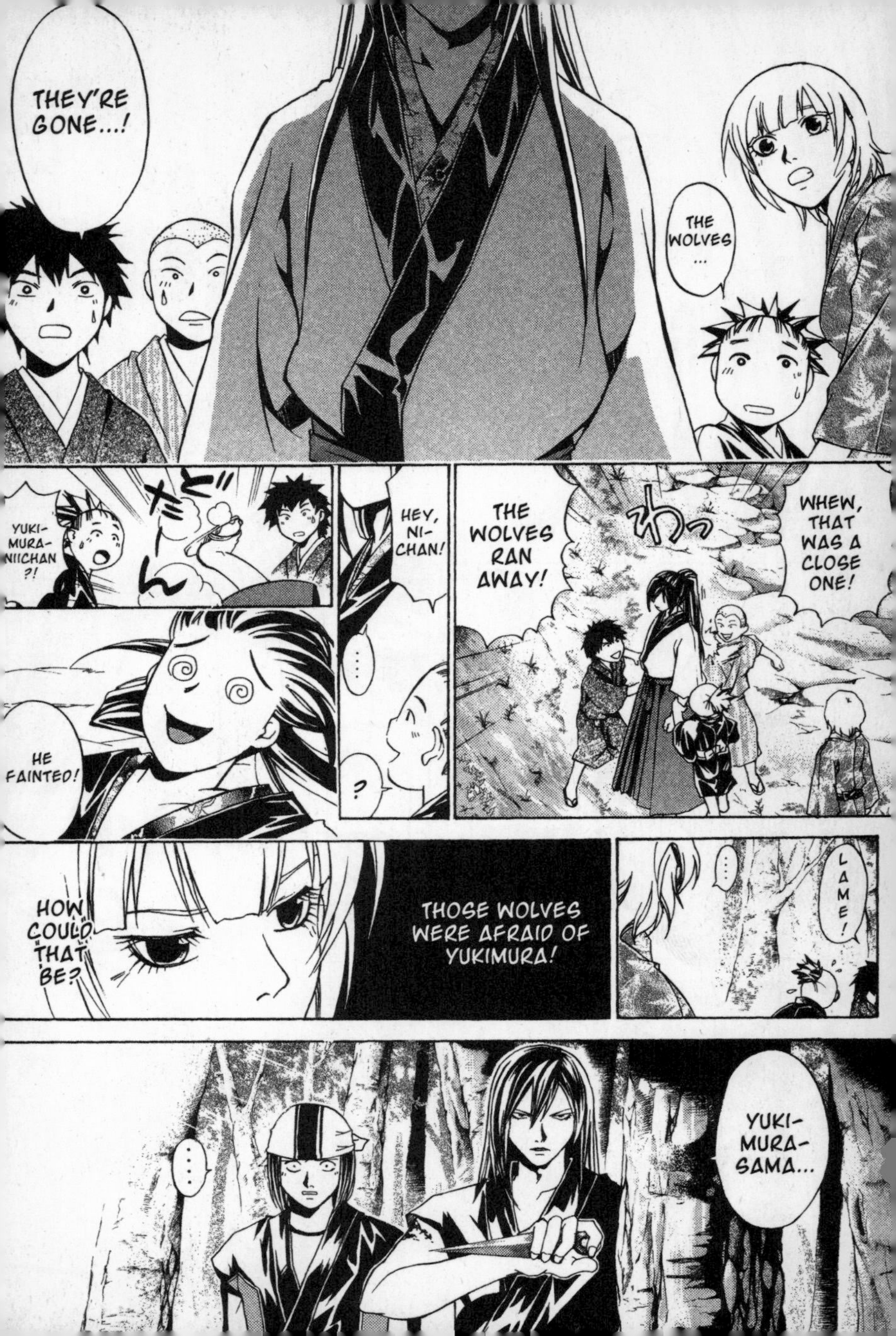
THE WOLVES ...
THEY'RE GONE...!
WHEW, THAT WAS A CLOSE ONE!
わっ
THE WOLVES RAN AWAY!
HEY, NI-CHAN!
....
?
YUKI-MURA-NIICHAN?!
HE FAINTED!
LAME!
....
THOSE WOLVES WERE AFRAID OF YUKIMURA!
HOW COULD THAT BE?
YUKI-MURA-SAMA...
....

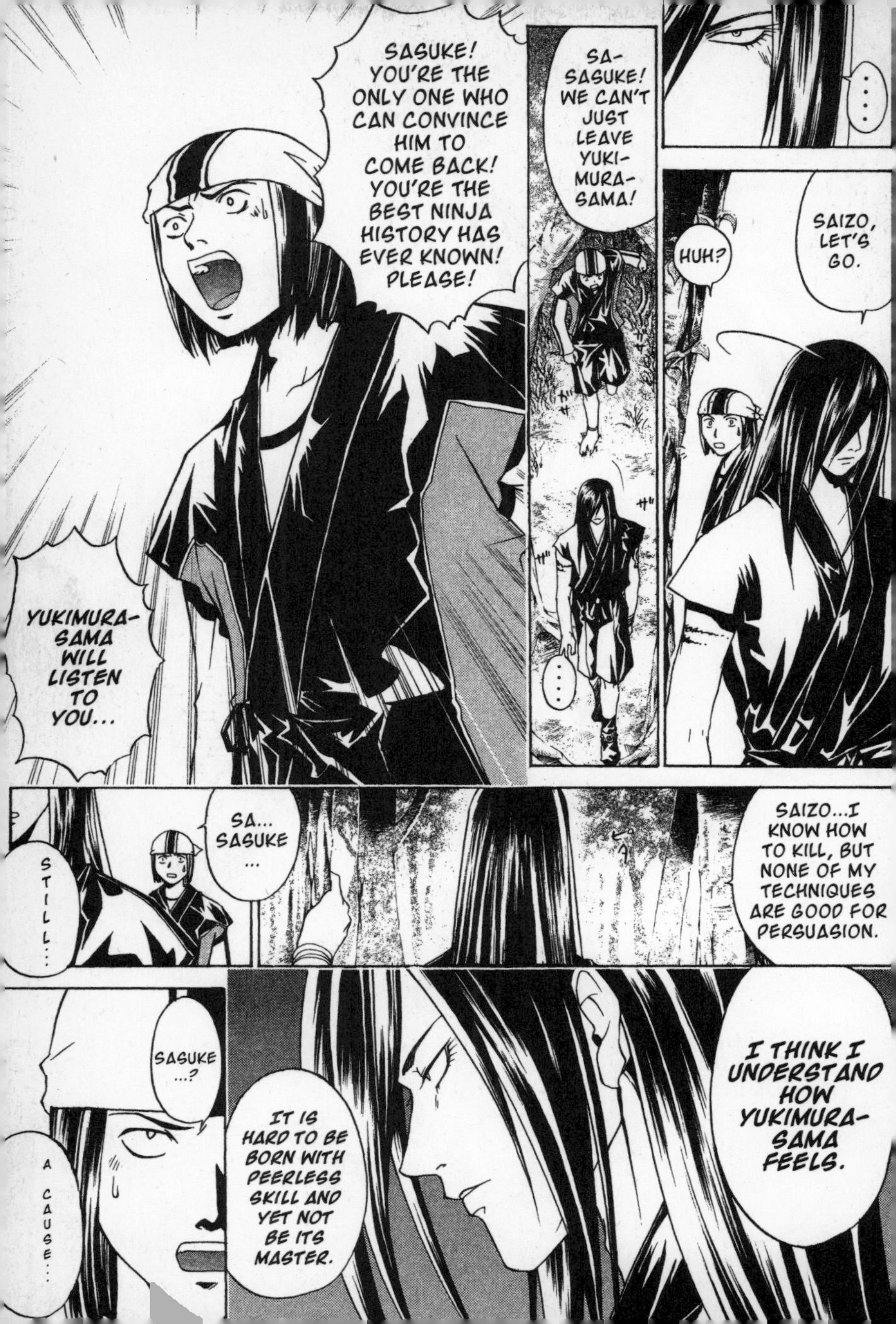
...
SAIZO, LET'S GO.
HUH?
SA-SASUKE! WE CAN'T JUST LEAVE YUKIMURA-SAMA!
...
SASUKE! YOU'RE THE ONLY ONE WHO CAN CONVINCE HIM TO COME BACK! YOU'RE THE BEST NINJA HISTORY HAS EVER KNOWN! PLEASE!
YUKIMURA-SAMA WILL LISTEN TO YOU...
SAIZO...I KNOW HOW TO KILL, BUT NONE OF MY TECHNIQUES ARE GOOD FOR PERSUASION.
SA... SASUKE ...
STILL...
I THINK I UNDERSTAND HOW YUKIMURA-SAMA FEELS.
IT IS HARD TO BE BORN WITH PEERLESS SKILL AND YET NOT BE ITS MASTER.
SASUKE ...?
A CAUSE...

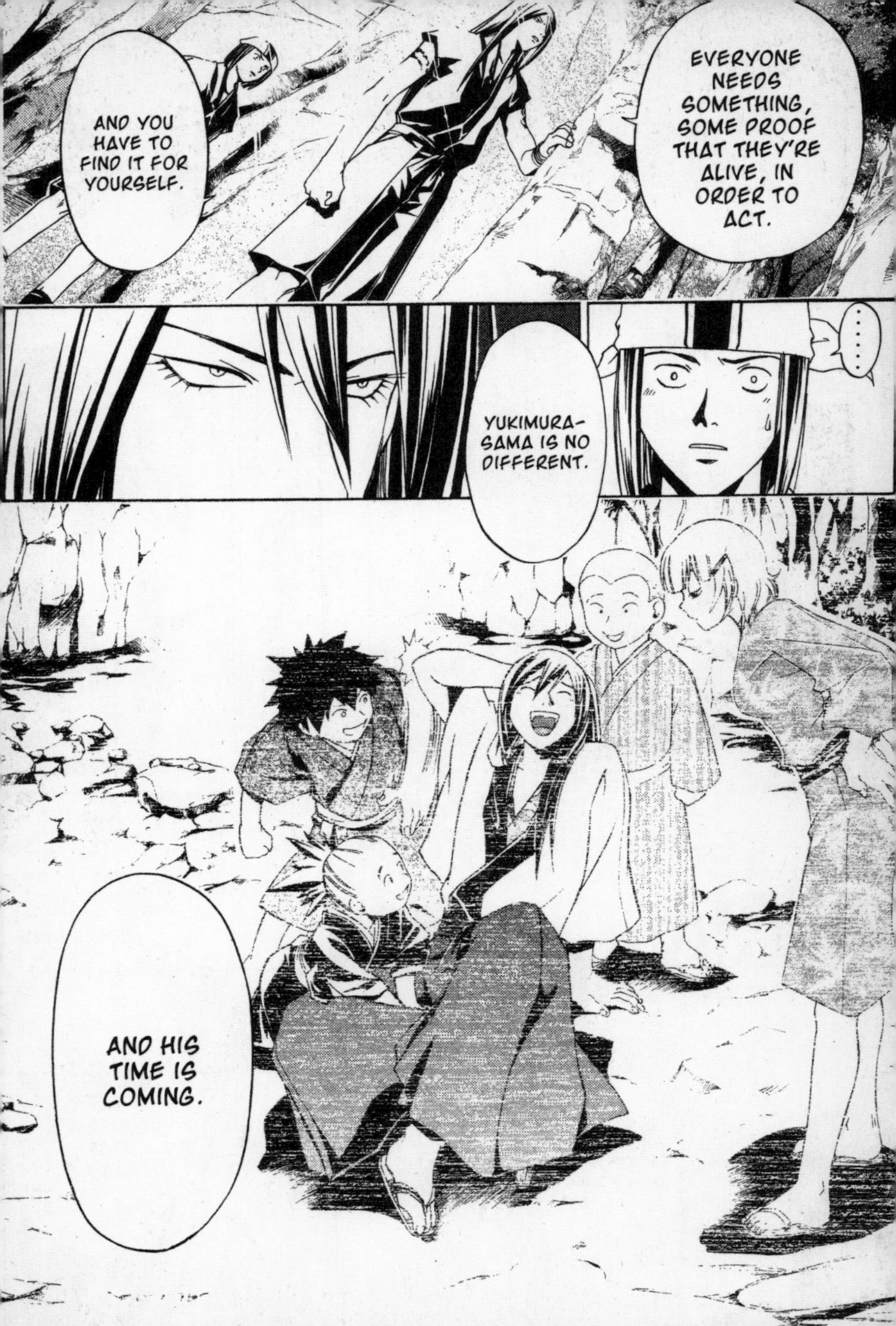
EVERYONE NEEDS SOMETHING, SOME PROOF THAT THEY'RE ALIVE, IN ORDER TO ACT.
AND YOU HAVE TO FIND IT FOR YOURSELF.
......
YUKIMURA-SAMA IS NO DIFFERENT.
AND HIS TIME IS COMING.

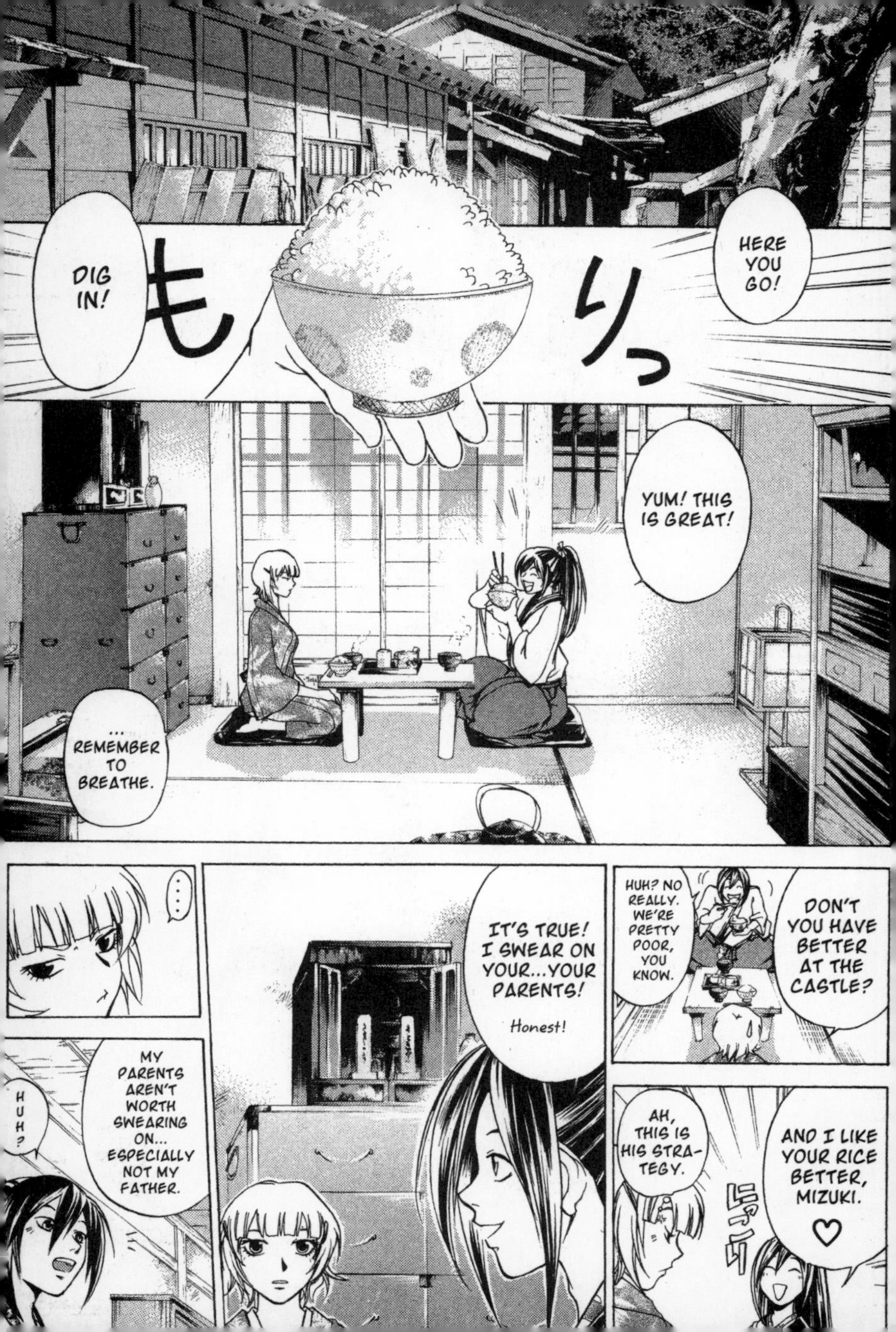
HERE YOU GO!
もりっ
DIG IN!
YUM! THIS IS GREAT!
... REMEMBER TO BREATHE.
DON'T YOU HAVE BETTER AT THE CASTLE?
HUH? NO REALLY. WE'RE PRETTY POOR, YOU KNOW.
AND I LIKE YOUR RICE BETTER, MIZUKI. ♥
AH, THIS IS HIS STRATEGY.
IT'S TRUE! I SWEAR ON YOUR...YOUR PARENTS!
Honest!
...
MY PARENTS AREN'T WORTH SWEARING ON... ESPECIALLY NOT MY FATHER.
HUH?

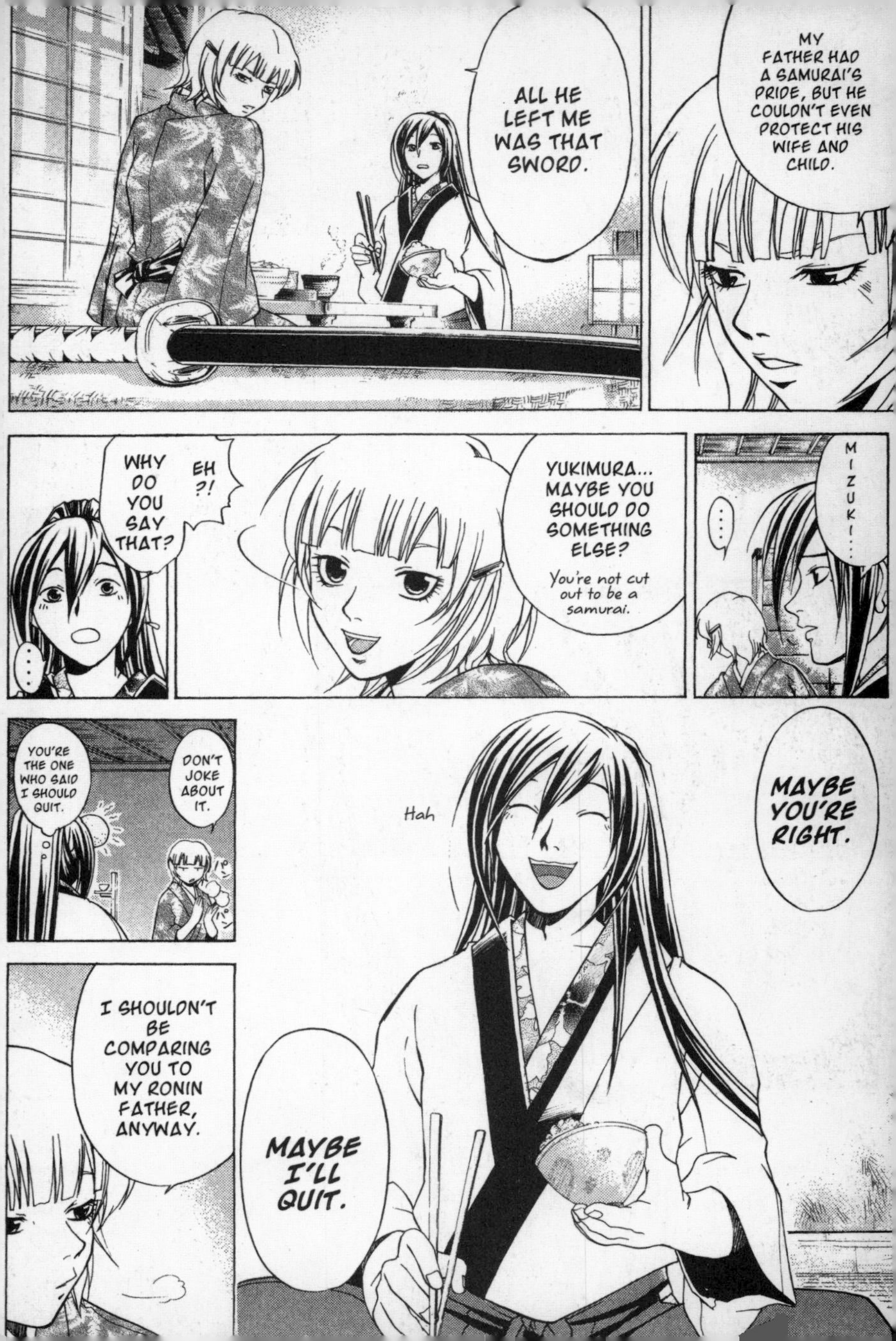
MY FATHER HAD A SAMURAI'S PRIDE, BUT HE COULDN'T EVEN PROTECT HIS WIFE AND CHILD.
ALL HE LEFT ME WAS THAT SWORD.
MIZUKI...
...
YUKIMURA... MAYBE YOU SHOULD DO SOMETHING ELSE?
You're not cut out to be a samurai.
EH ?!
WHY DO YOU SAY THAT?
...
MAYBE YOU'RE RIGHT.
Hah
MAYBE I'LL QUIT.
DON'T JOKE ABOUT IT.
YOU'RE THE ONE WHO SAID I SHOULD QUIT.
I SHOULDN'T BE COMPARING YOU TO MY RONIN FATHER, ANYWAY.

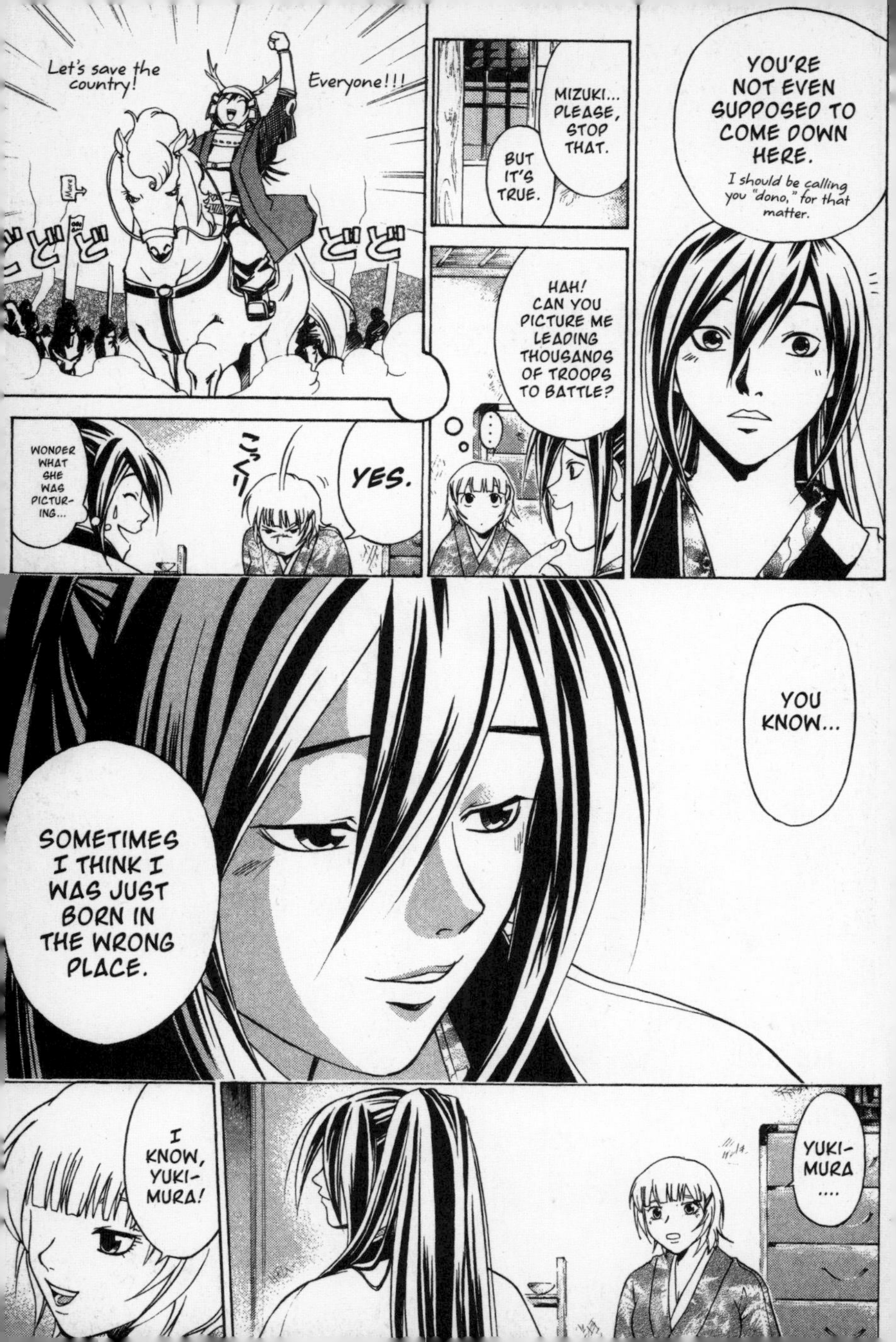
YOU'RE NOT EVEN SUPPOSED TO COME DOWN HERE.
I should be calling you "dono," for that matter.
MIZUKI... PLEASE, STOP THAT.
BUT IT'S TRUE.
HAH! CAN YOU PICTURE ME LEADING THOUSANDS OF TROOPS TO BATTLE?
...
Everyone!!!
Let's save the country!
どどど
どど
YES.
WONDER WHAT SHE WAS PICTUR-ING...
YOU KNOW...
SOMETIMES I THINK I WAS JUST BORN IN THE WRONG PLACE.
YUKI-MURA....
I KNOW, YUKI-MURA!

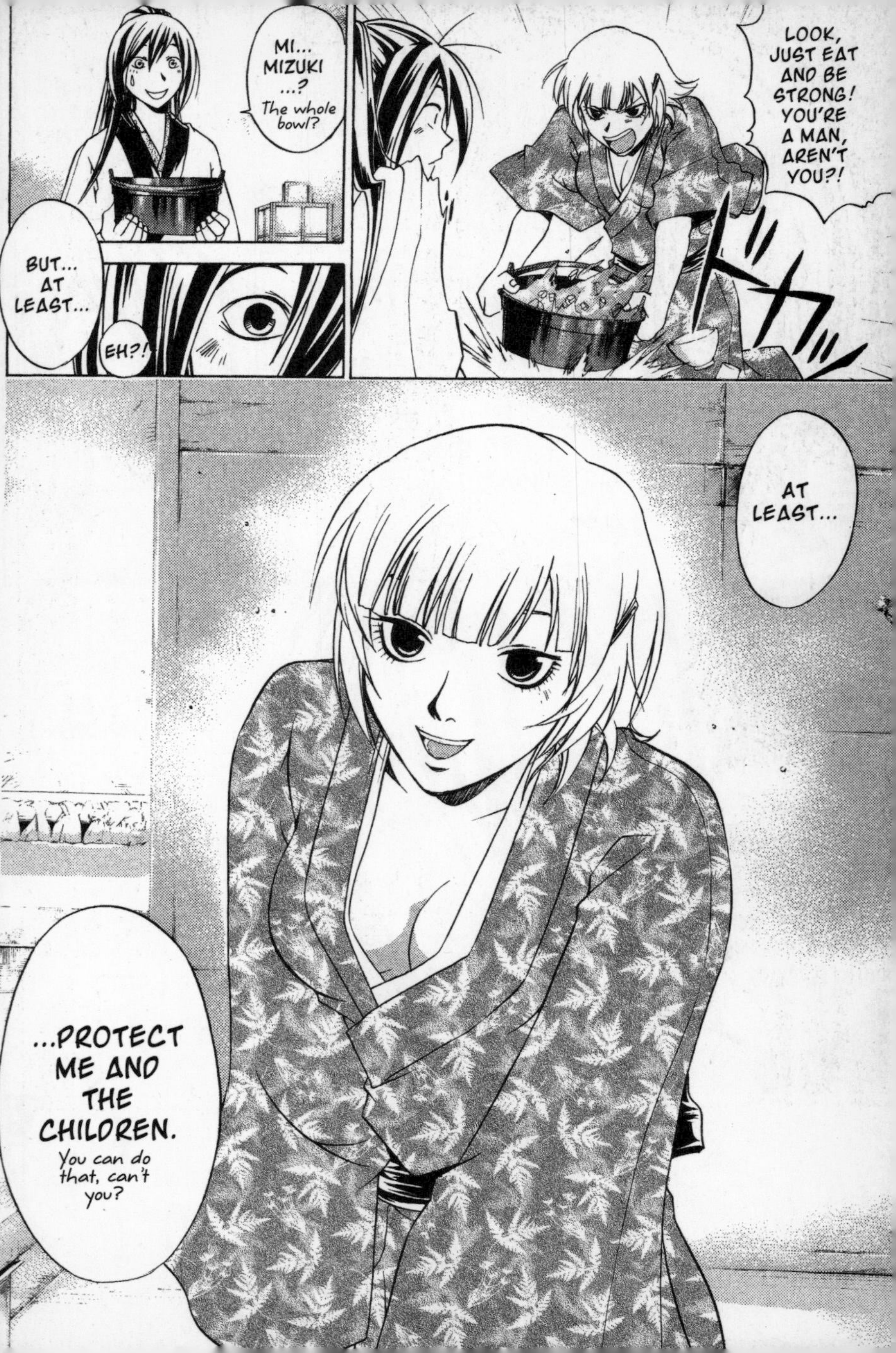
LOOK, JUST EAT AND BE STRONG! YOU'RE A MAN, AREN'T YOU?!
MI... MIZUKI ...? The whole bowl?
BUT... AT LEAST...
EH?!
AT LEAST...
...PROTECT ME AND THE CHILDREN. You can do that, can't you?

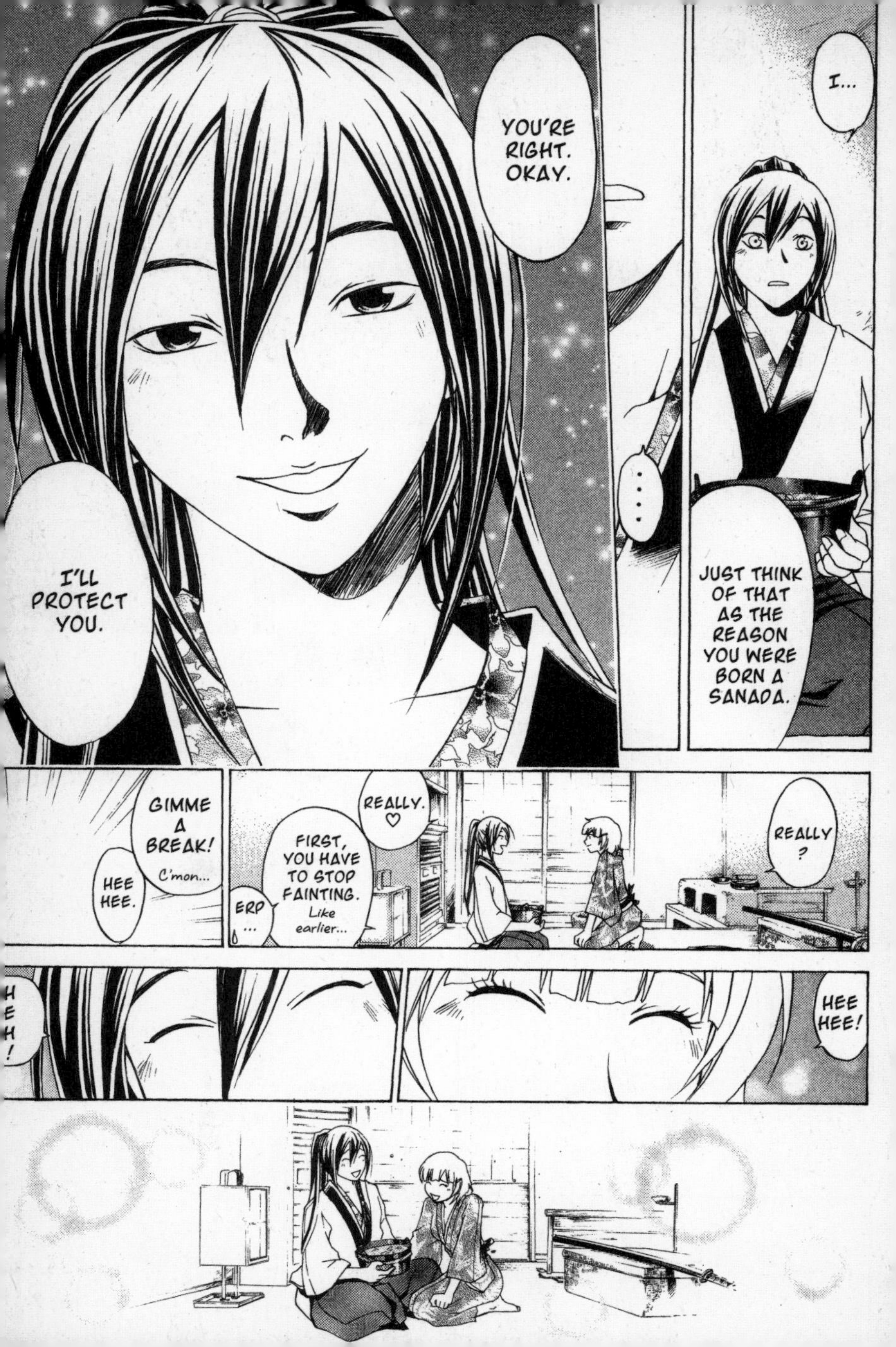
I...
JUST THINK OF THAT AS THE REASON YOU WERE BORN A SANADA.
....
YOU'RE RIGHT. OKAY.
I'LL PROTECT YOU.
REALLY?
REALLY. ♡
FIRST, YOU HAVE TO STOP FAINTING.
Like earlier...
ERP...
GIMME A BREAK!
C'mon...
HEE HEE.
HEE HEE!
HEH!

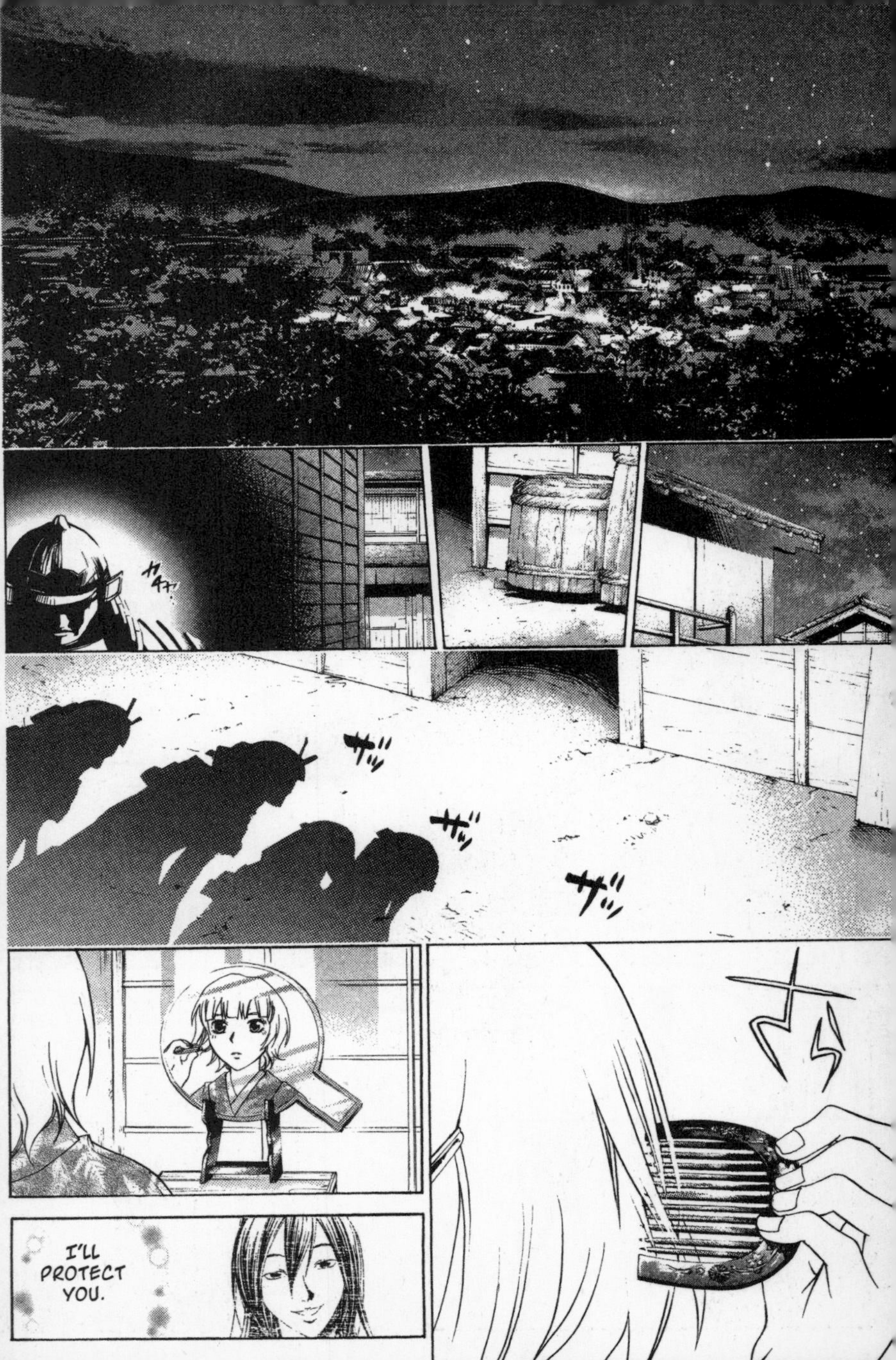
ザッ
ザッ
ザッ
I'LL PROTECT YOU.

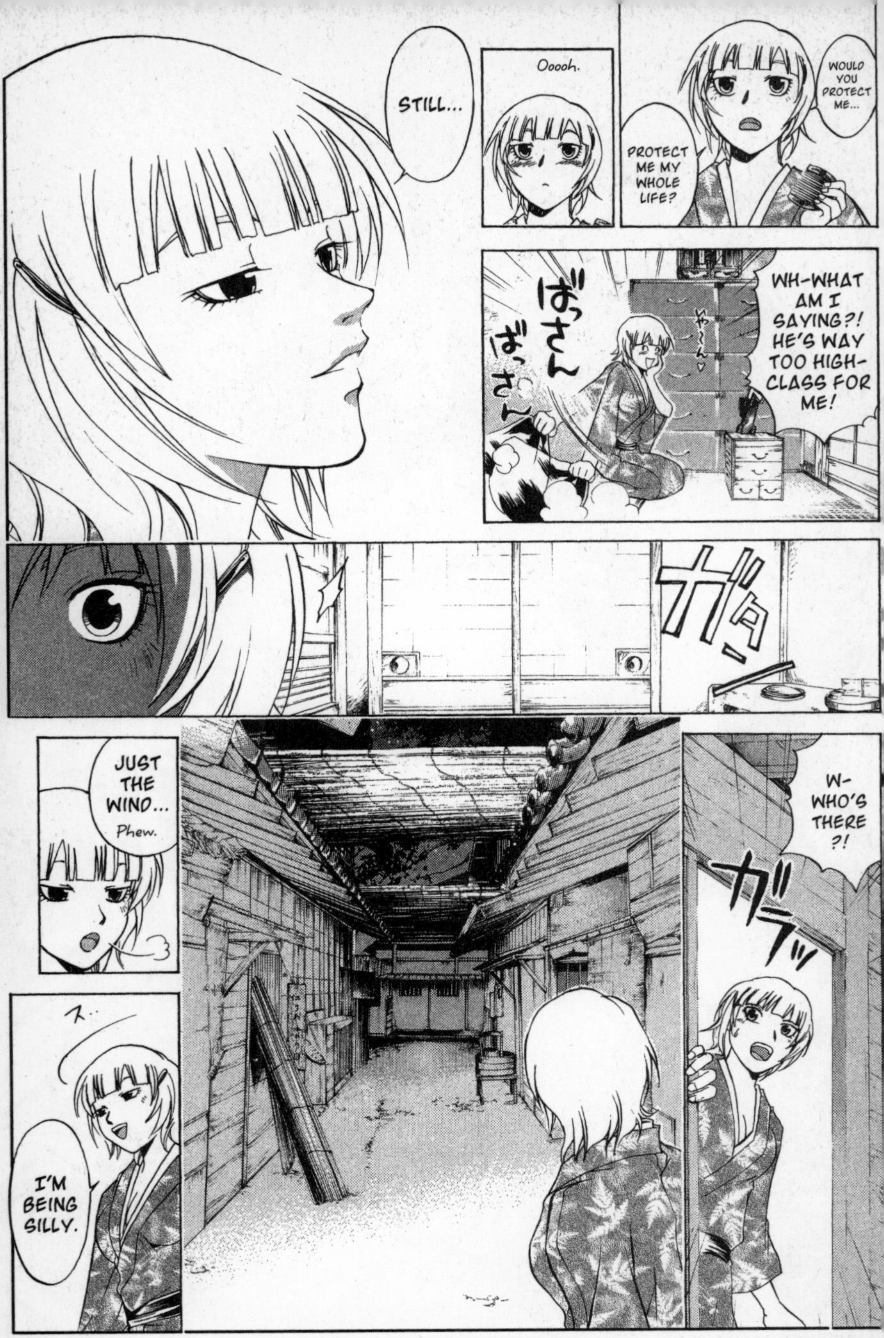
WOULD YOU PROTECT ME...
PROTECT ME MY WHOLE LIFE?
Ooooh.
WH-WHAT AM I SAYING?! HE'S WAY TOO HIGH-CLASS FOR ME!
ばっさん
ばっさん
いや〜ん♥
STILL...
ガタ
W-WHO'S THERE?!
ガラッ
JUST THE WIND...
Phew.
ス..
I'M BEING SILLY.

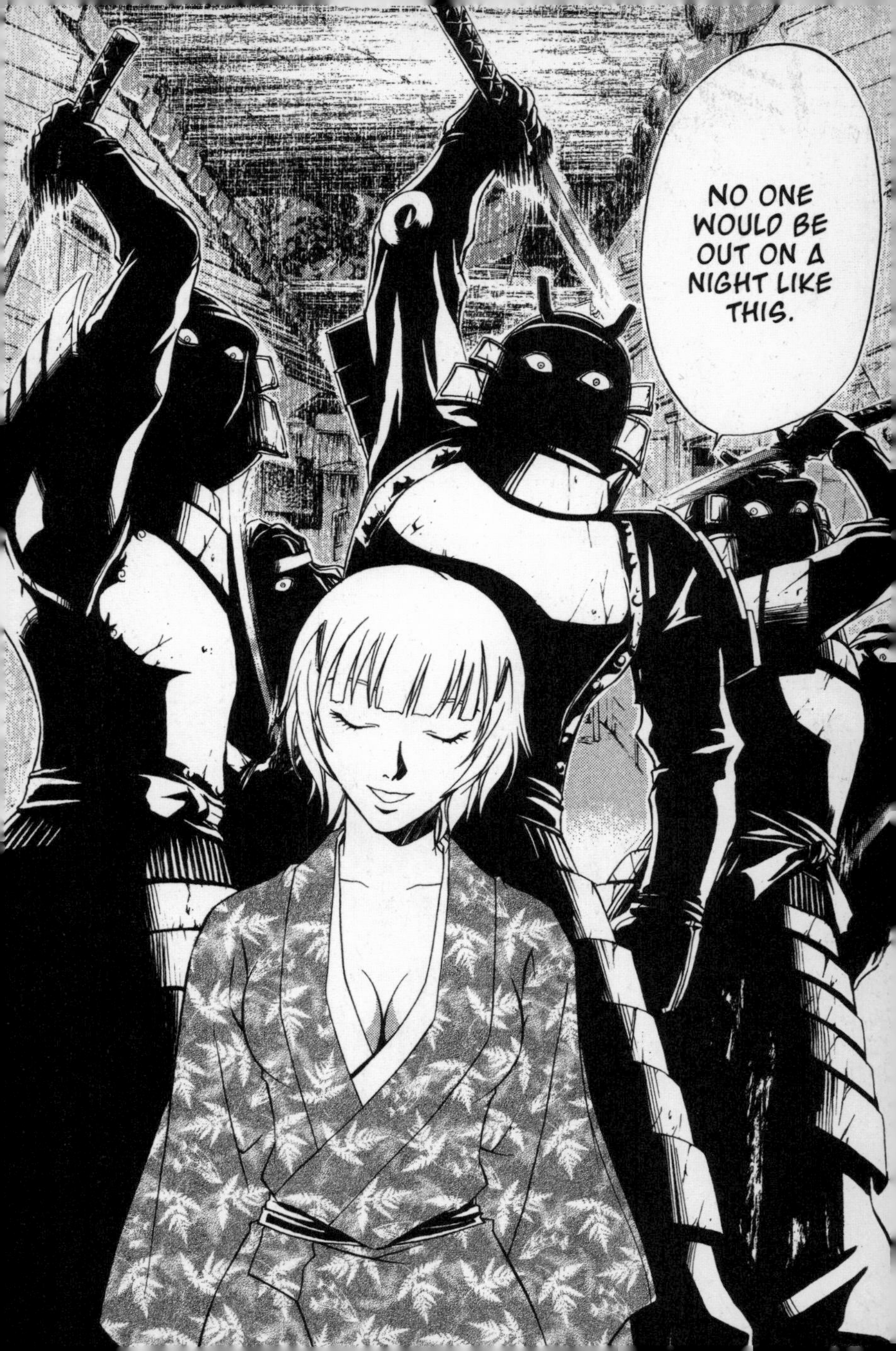
NO ONE WOULD BE OUT ON A NIGHT LIKE THIS.

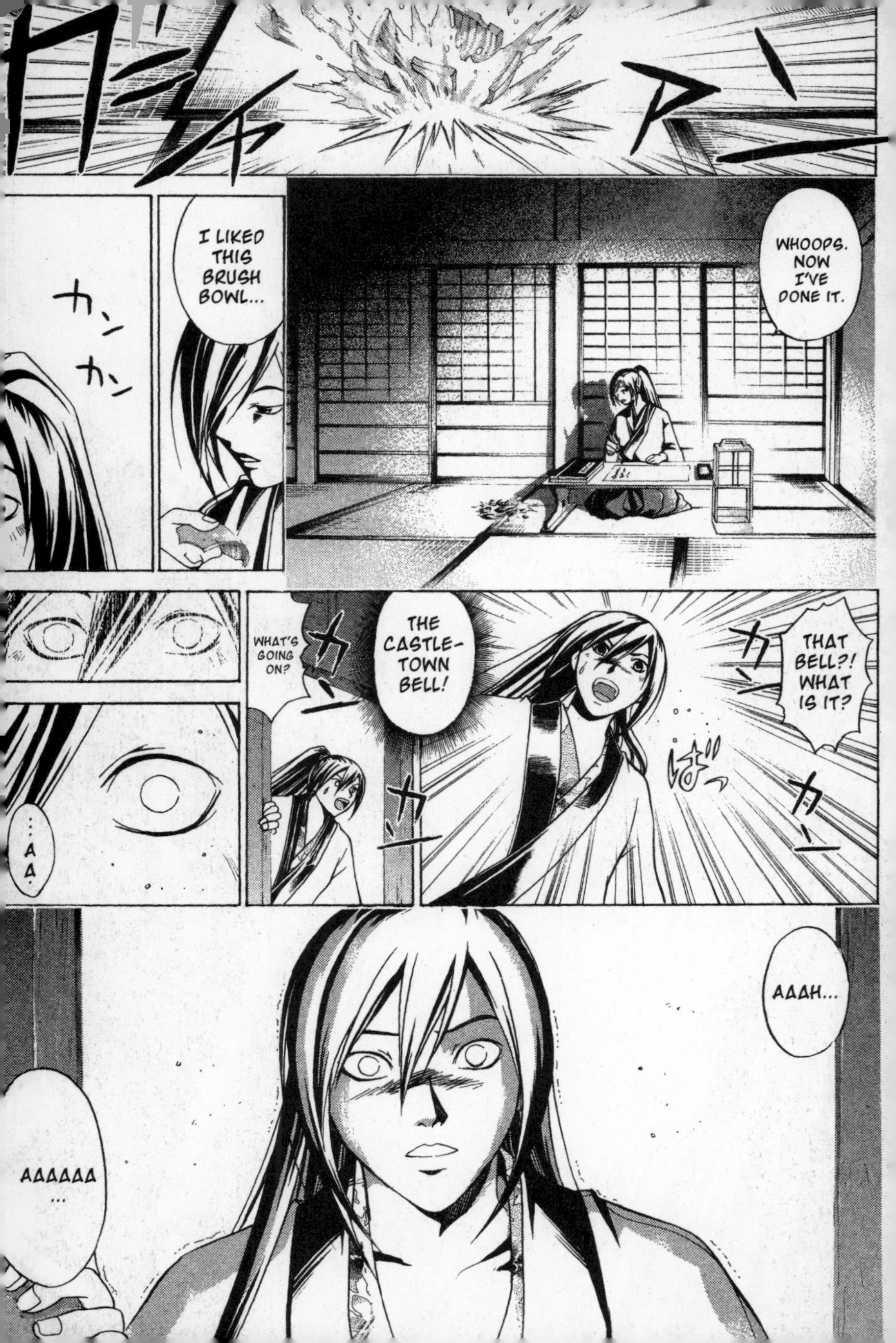
ガシャアン
WHOOPS. NOW I'VE DONE IT.
I LIKED THIS BRUSH BOWL...
カンカン
THAT BELL?! WHAT IS IT?
カーン
ばっ
カーン
THE CASTLE-TOWN BELL!
WHAT'S GOING ON?
カーン
カーン
...AA.
AAAH...
AAAAAA ...

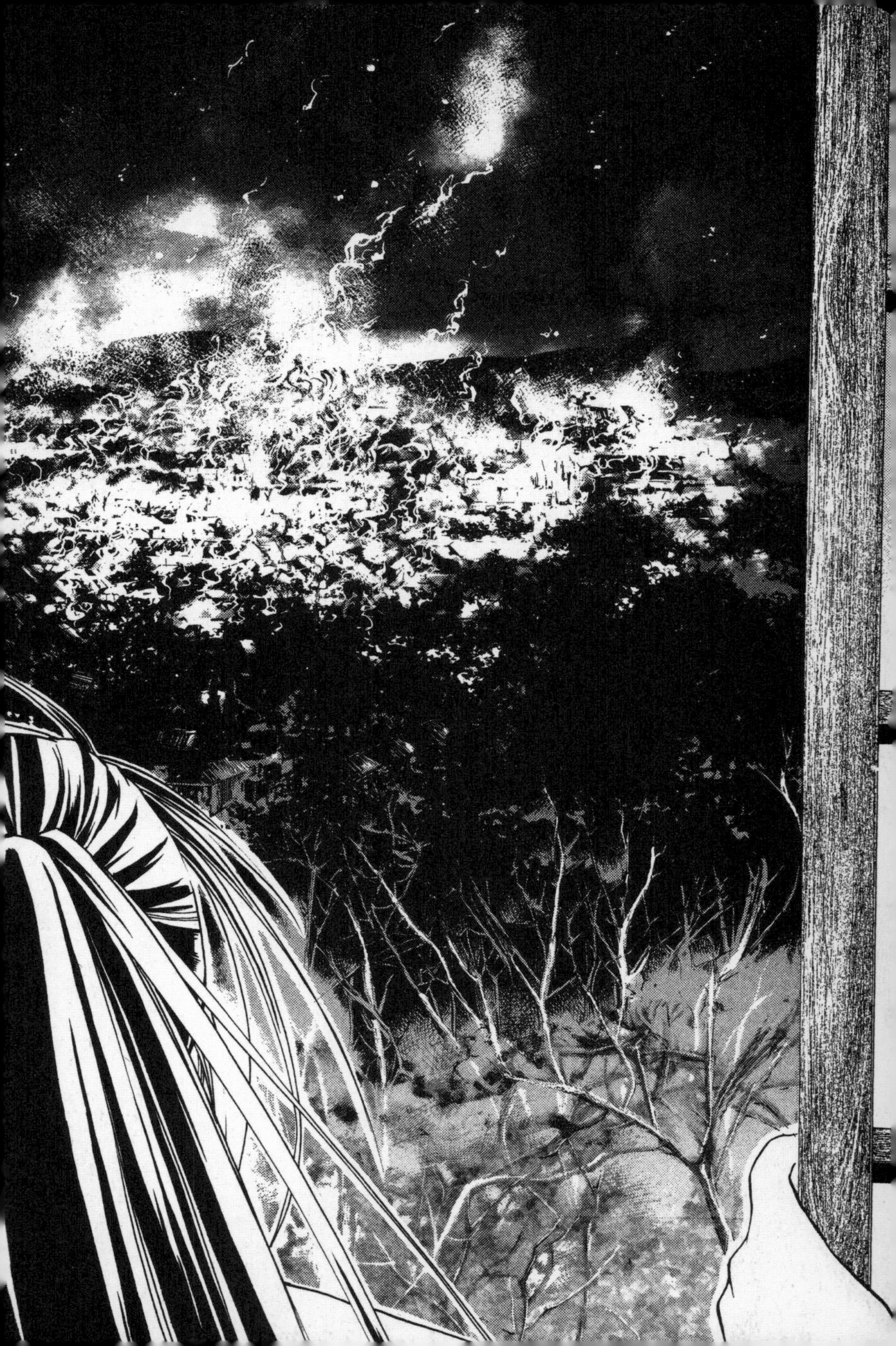

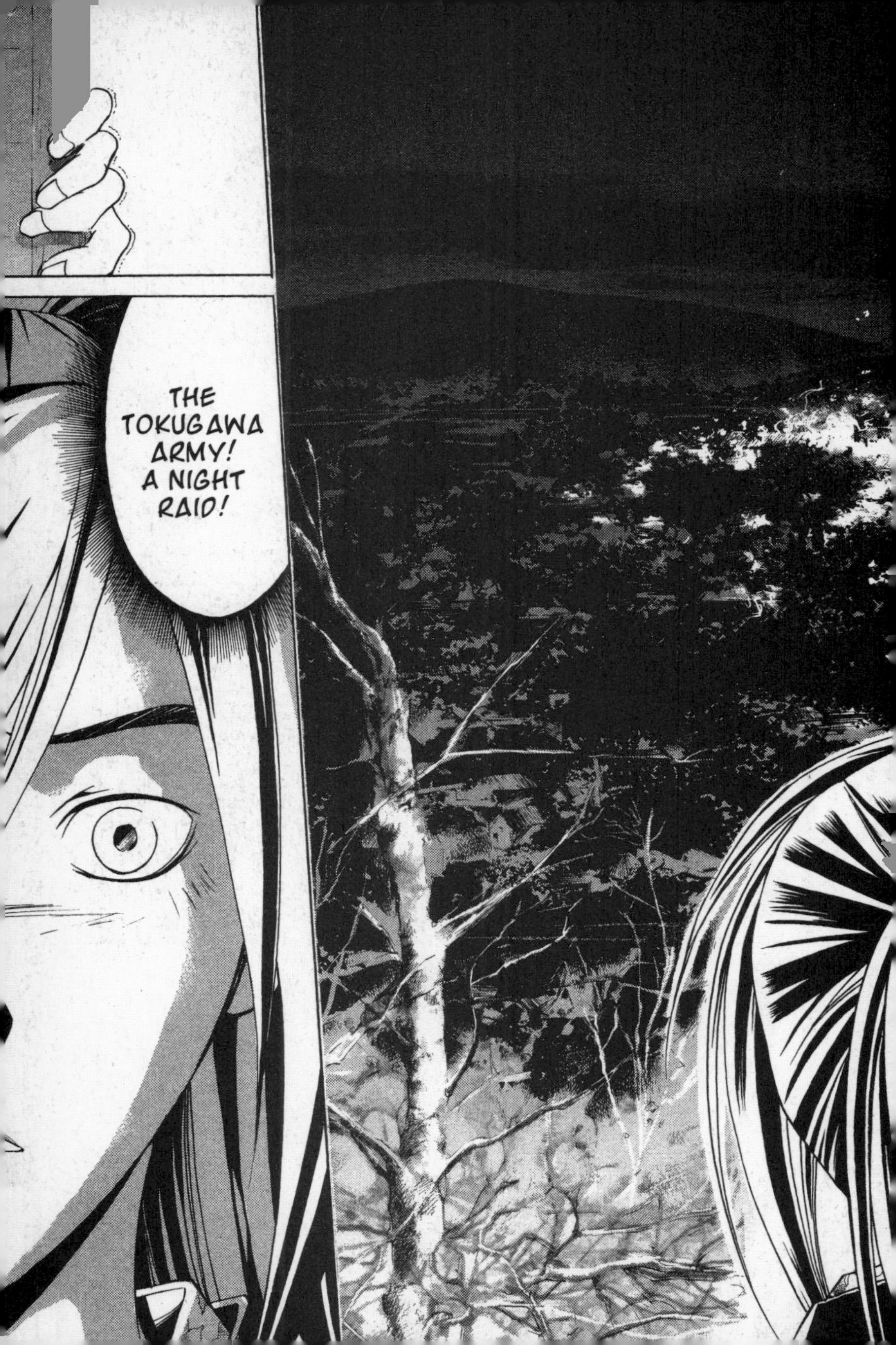
THE TOKUGAWA ARMY! A NIGHT RAID!

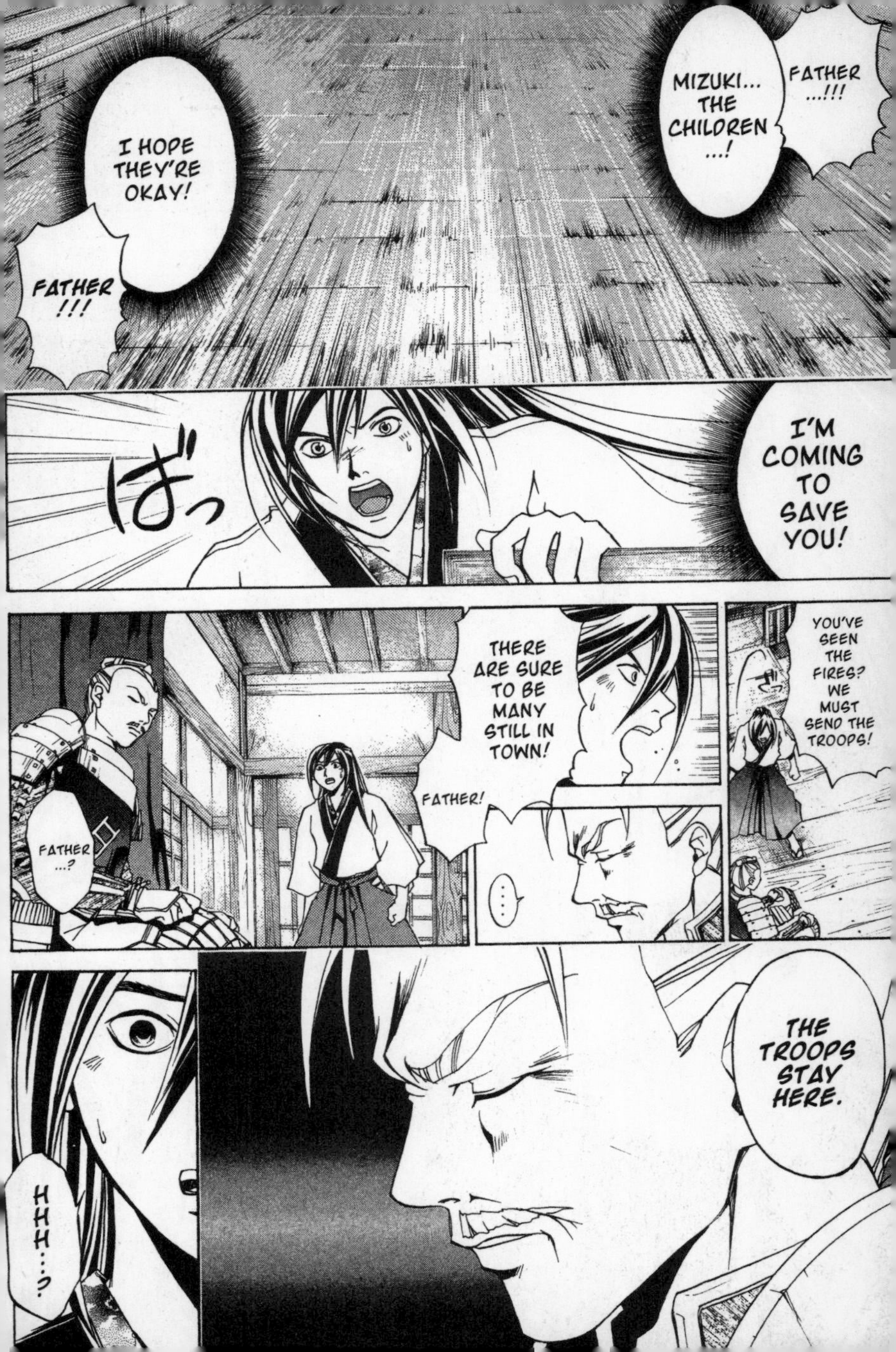
FATHER ...!!!
MIZUKI... THE CHILDREN ...!
I HOPE THEY'RE OKAY!
FATHER !!!
I'M COMING TO SAVE YOU!
ばっ
YOU'VE SEEN THE FIRES? WE MUST SEND THE TROOPS!
THERE ARE SURE TO BE MANY STILL IN TOWN!
....
FATHER!
FATHER ...?
THE TROOPS STAY HERE.
HHH...?

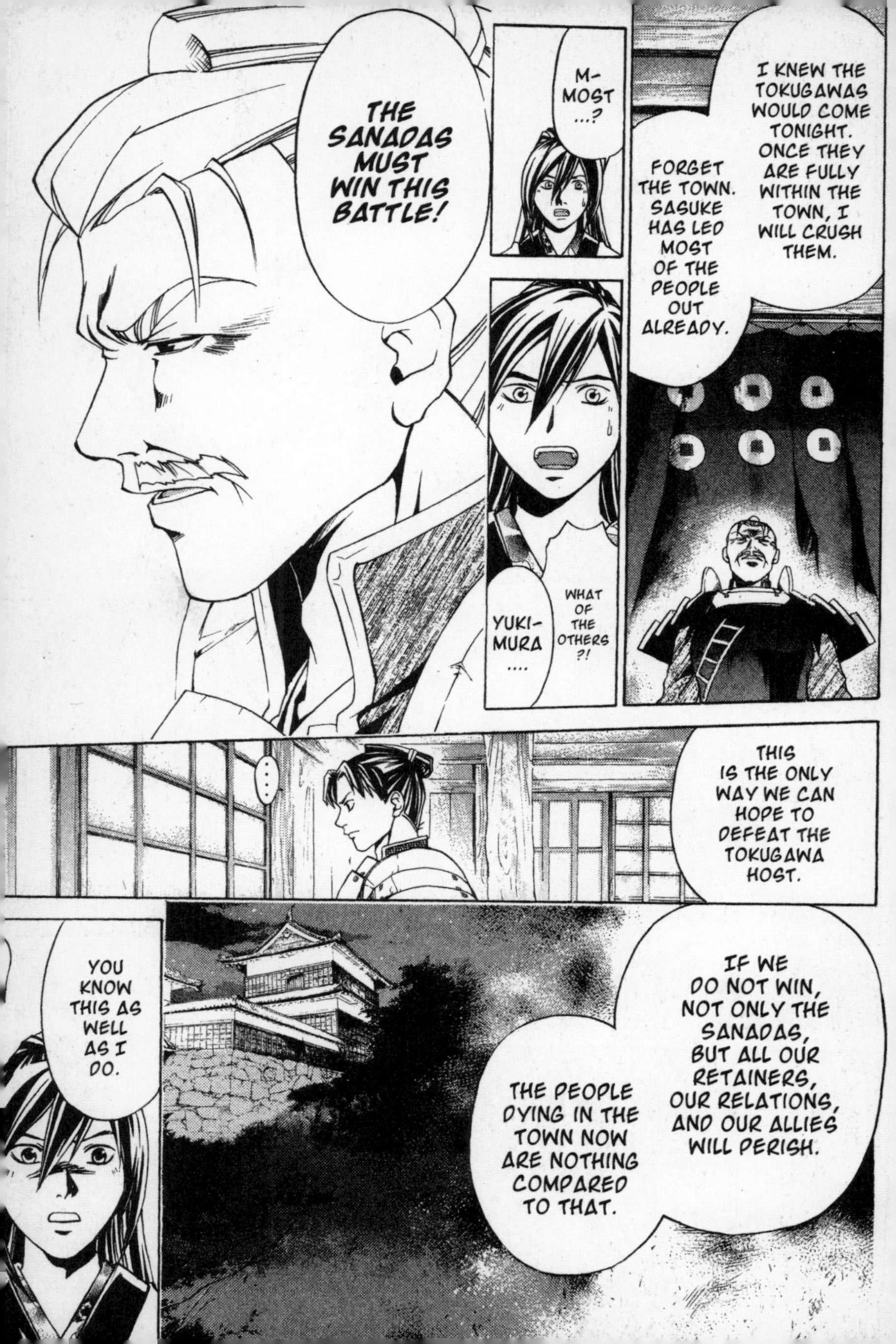
I KNEW THE TOKUGAWAS WOULD COME TONIGHT. ONCE THEY ARE FULLY WITHIN THE TOWN, I WILL CRUSH THEM.
FORGET THE TOWN. SASUKE HAS LED MOST OF THE PEOPLE OUT ALREADY.
M-MOST ...?
WHAT OF THE OTHERS ?!
YUKI-MURA ....
THE SANADAS MUST WIN THIS BATTLE!
THIS IS THE ONLY WAY WE CAN HOPE TO DEFEAT THE TOKUGAWA HOST.
...
IF WE DO NOT WIN, NOT ONLY THE SANADAS, BUT ALL OUR RETAINERS, OUR RELATIONS, AND OUR ALLIES WILL PERISH.
THE PEOPLE DYING IN THE TOWN NOW ARE NOTHING COMPARED TO THAT.
YOU KNOW THIS AS WELL AS I DO.

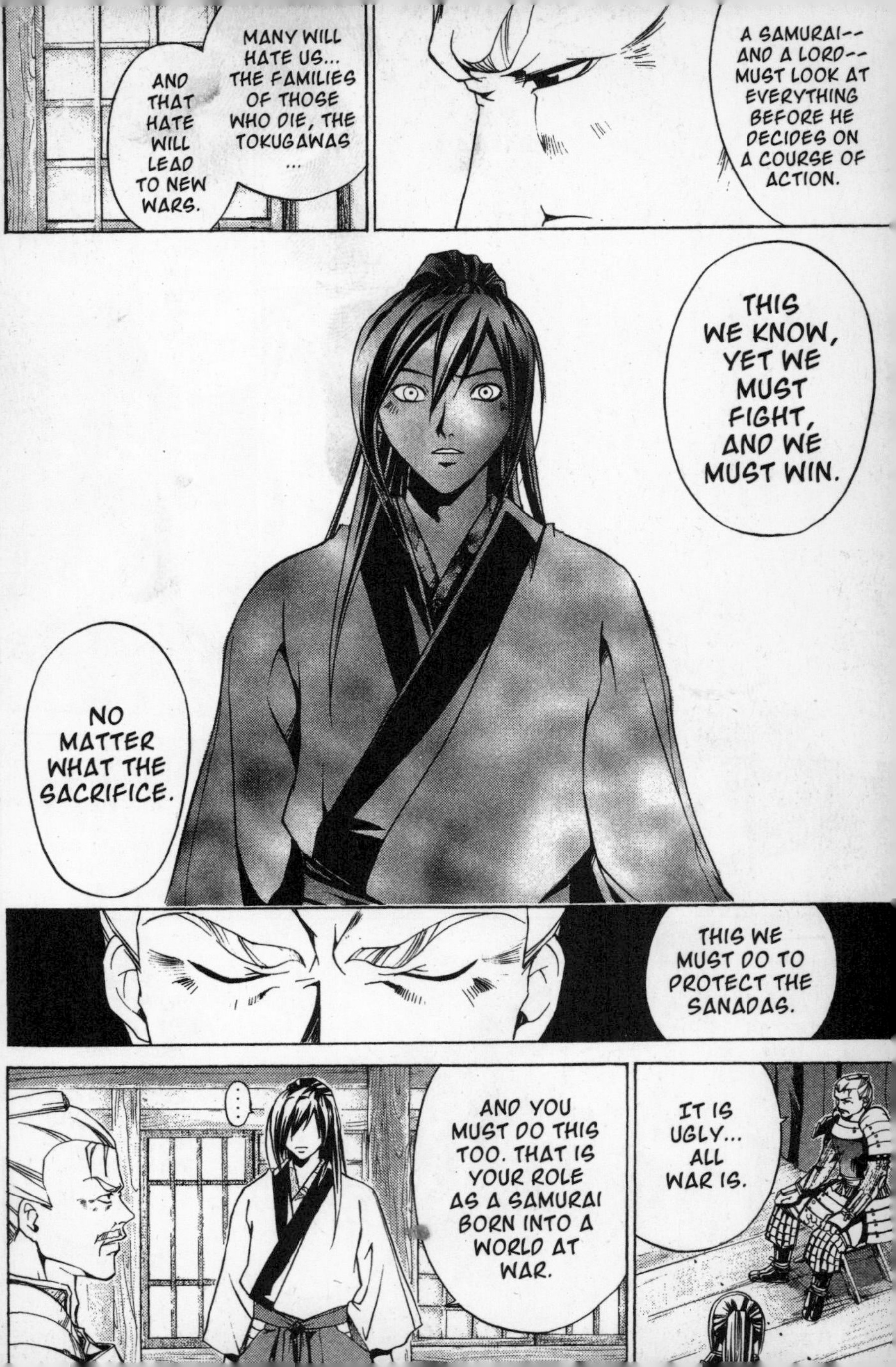
A SAMURAI--AND A LORD--MUST LOOK AT EVERYTHING BEFORE HE DECIDES ON A COURSE OF ACTION.
MANY WILL HATE US... THE FAMILIES OF THOSE WHO DIE, THE TOKUGAWAS ...
AND THAT HATE WILL LEAD TO NEW WARS.
THIS WE KNOW, YET WE MUST FIGHT, AND WE MUST WIN.
NO MATTER WHAT THE SACRIFICE.
THIS WE MUST DO TO PROTECT THE SANADAS.
IT IS UGLY... ALL WAR IS.
AND YOU MUST DO THIS TOO. THAT IS YOUR ROLE AS A SAMURAI BORN INTO A WORLD AT WAR.
...

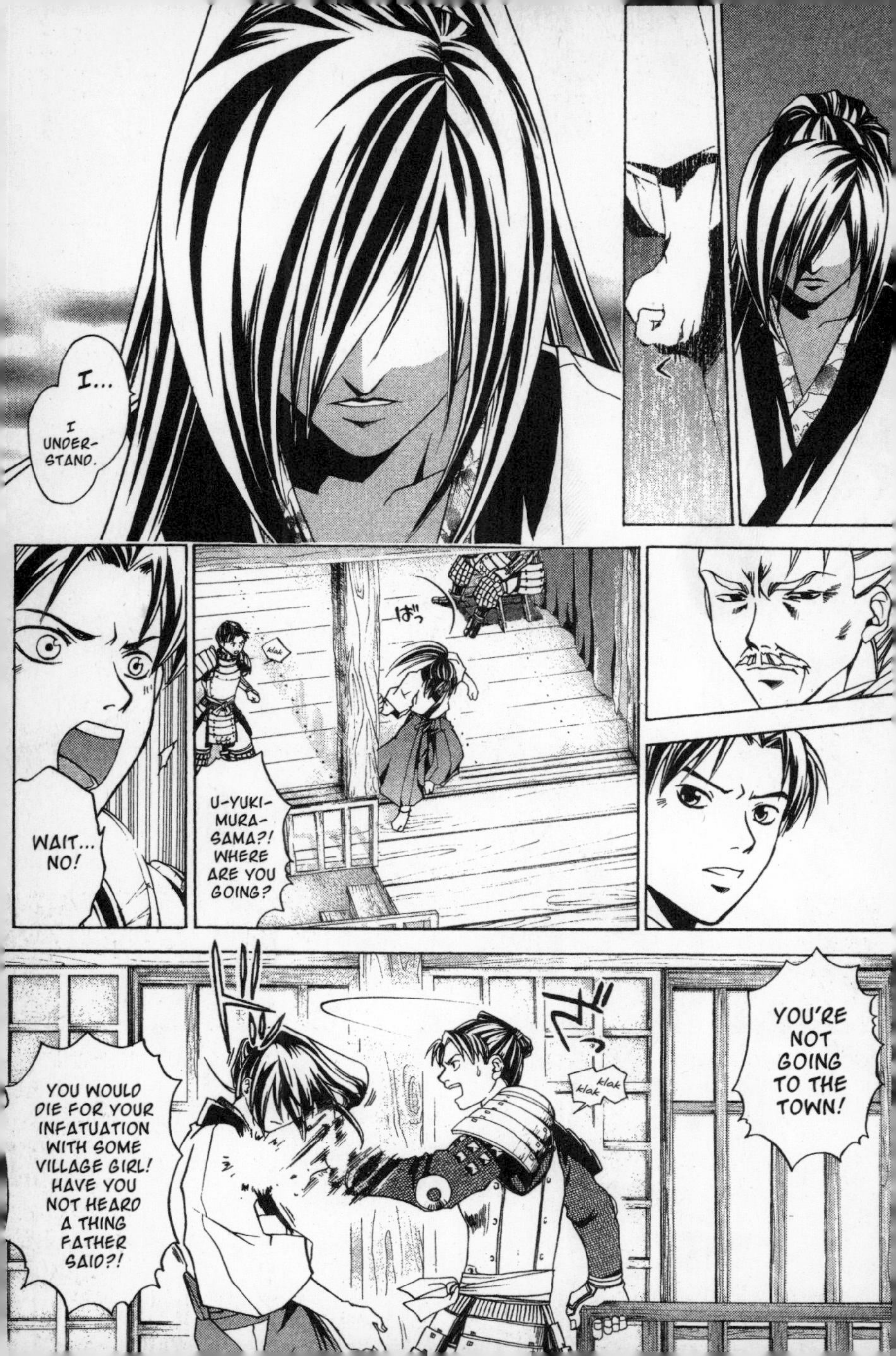

I...
I UNDER-STAND.
ぱっ
klak
U-YUKI-MURA-SAMA?! WHERE ARE YOU GOING?
WAIT... NO!
YOU'RE NOT GOING TO THE TOWN!
klak klak
YOU WOULD DIE FOR YOUR INFATUATION WITH SOME VILLAGE GIRL! HAVE YOU NOT HEARD A THING FATHER SAID?!

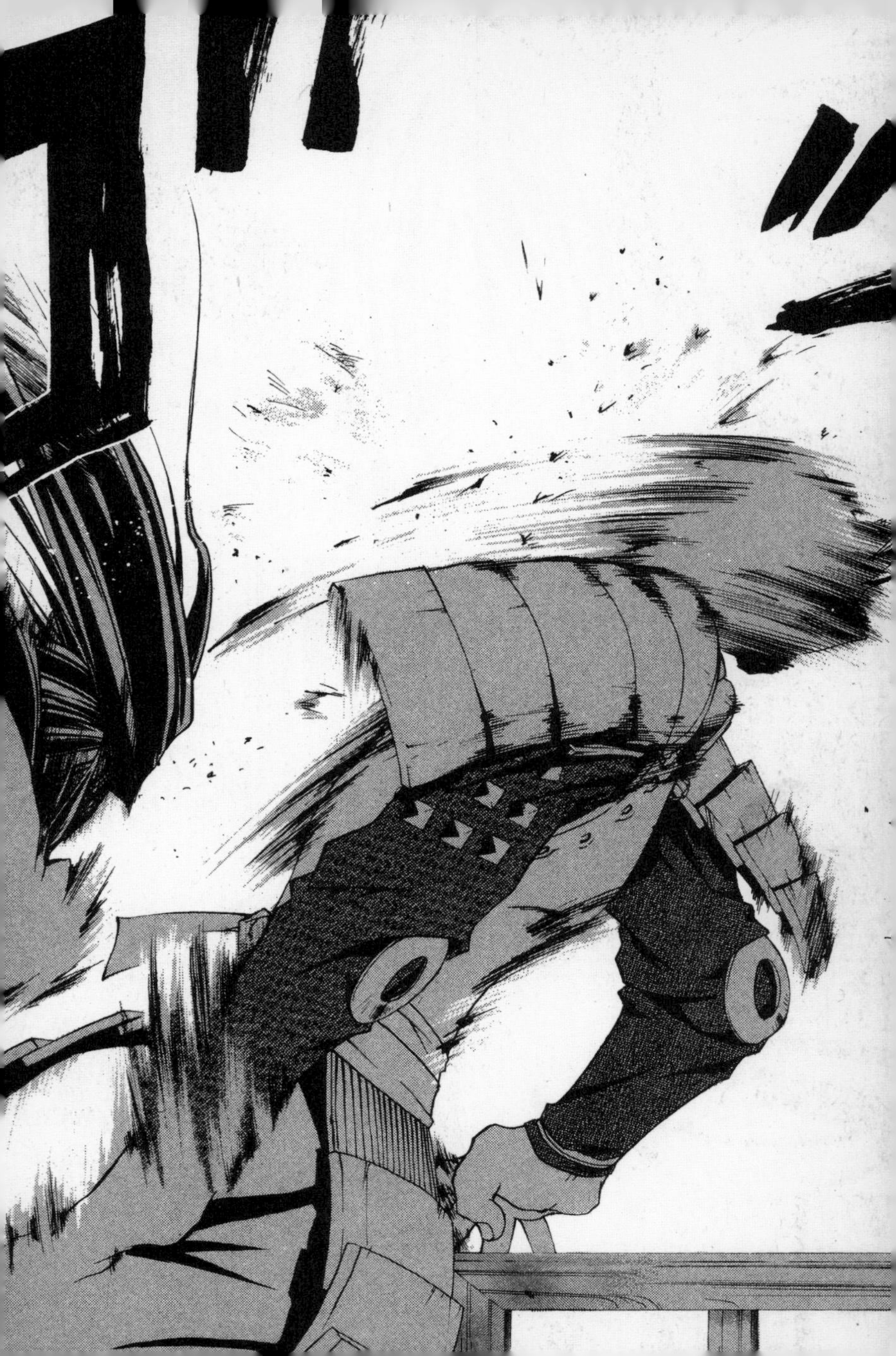

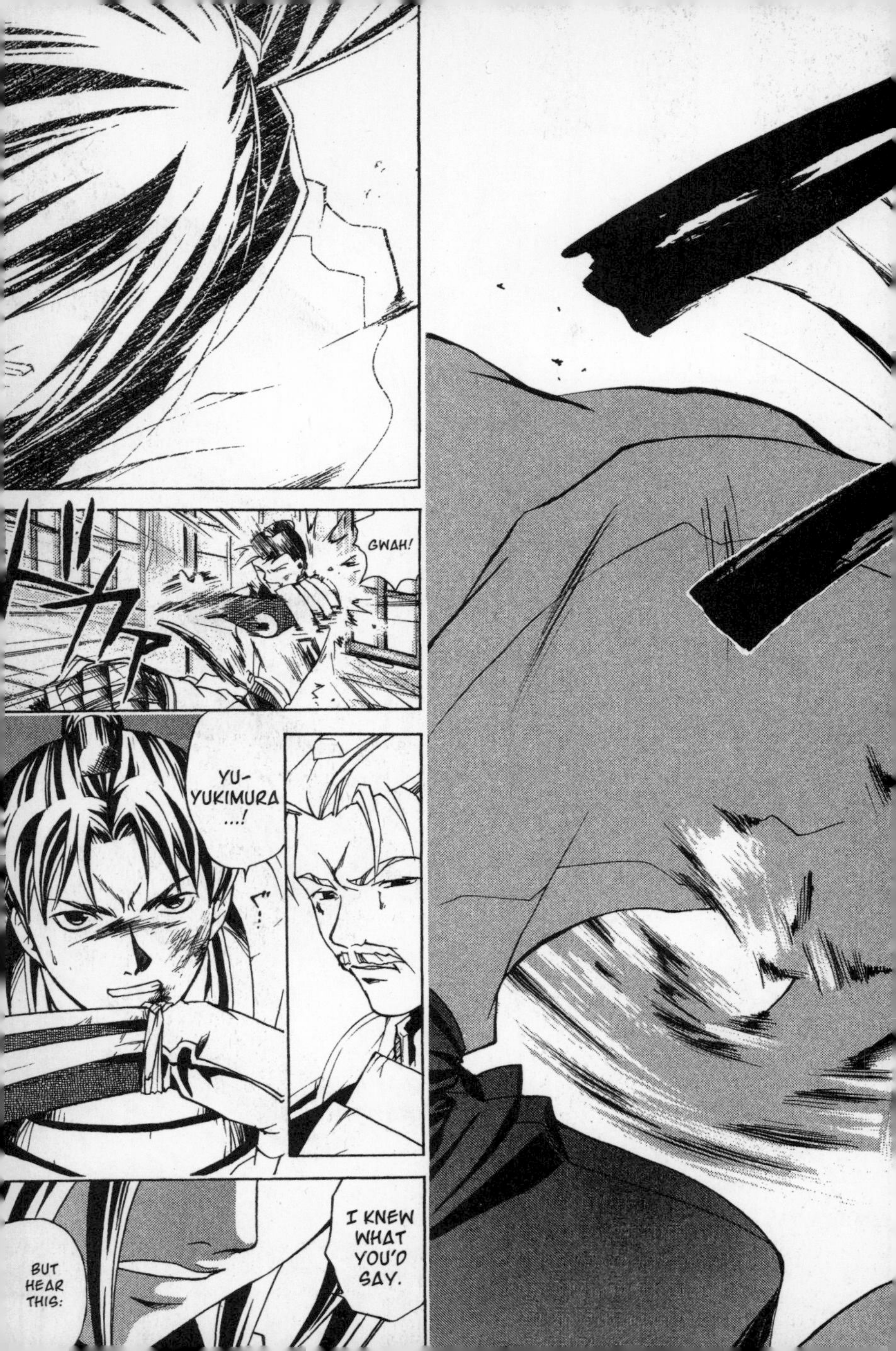
GWAH!
YU-YUKIMURA...!
I KNEW WHAT YOU'D SAY.
BUT HEAR THIS:

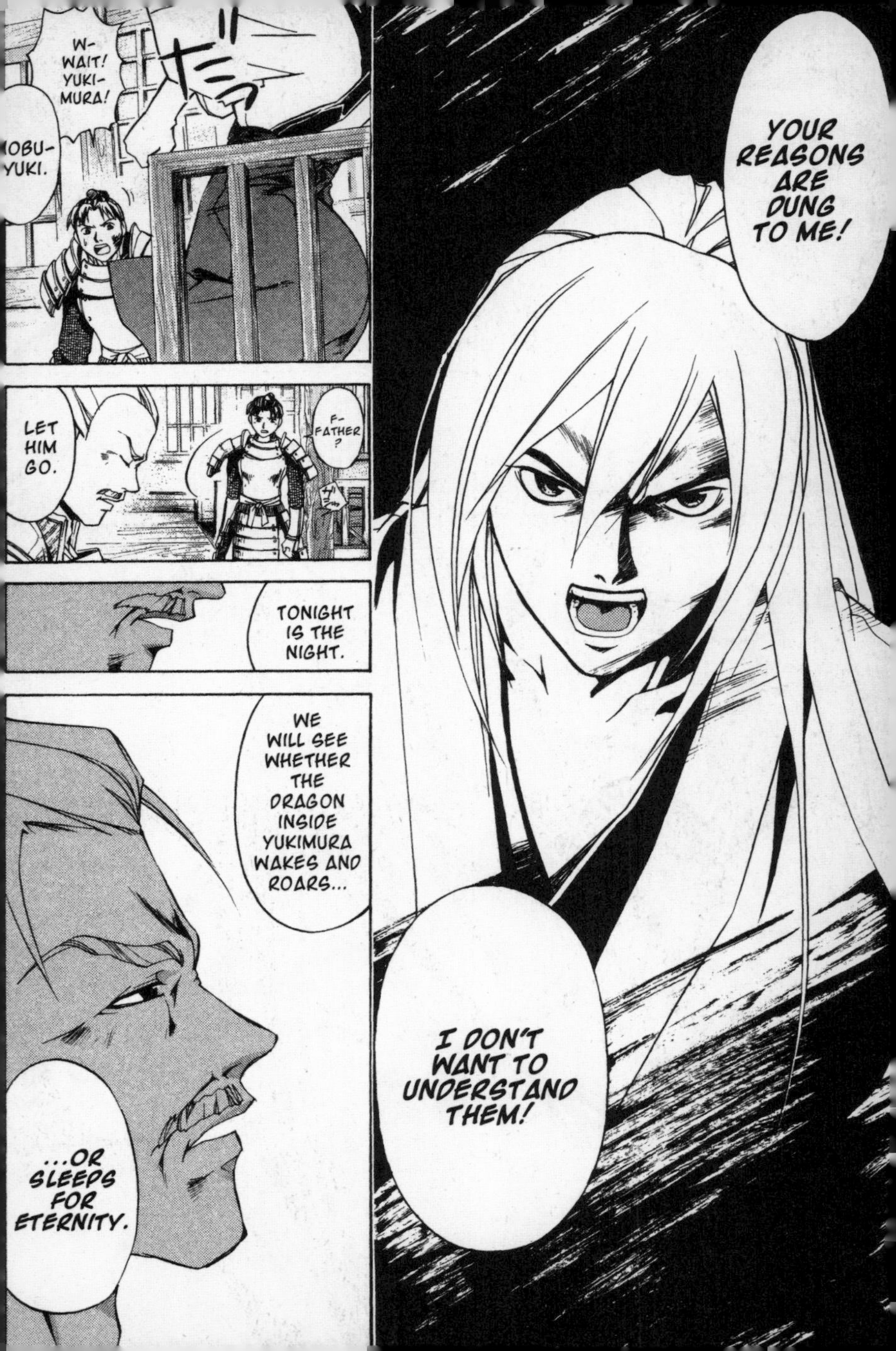
YOUR REASONS ARE DUNG TO ME!
I DON'T WANT TO UNDERSTAND THEM!
W-WAIT! YUKIMURA!
OBU-YUKI.
F-FATHER?
LET HIM GO.
TONIGHT IS THE NIGHT.
WE WILL SEE WHETHER THE DRAGON INSIDE YUKIMURA WAKES AND ROARS...
...OR SLEEPS FOR ETERNITY.

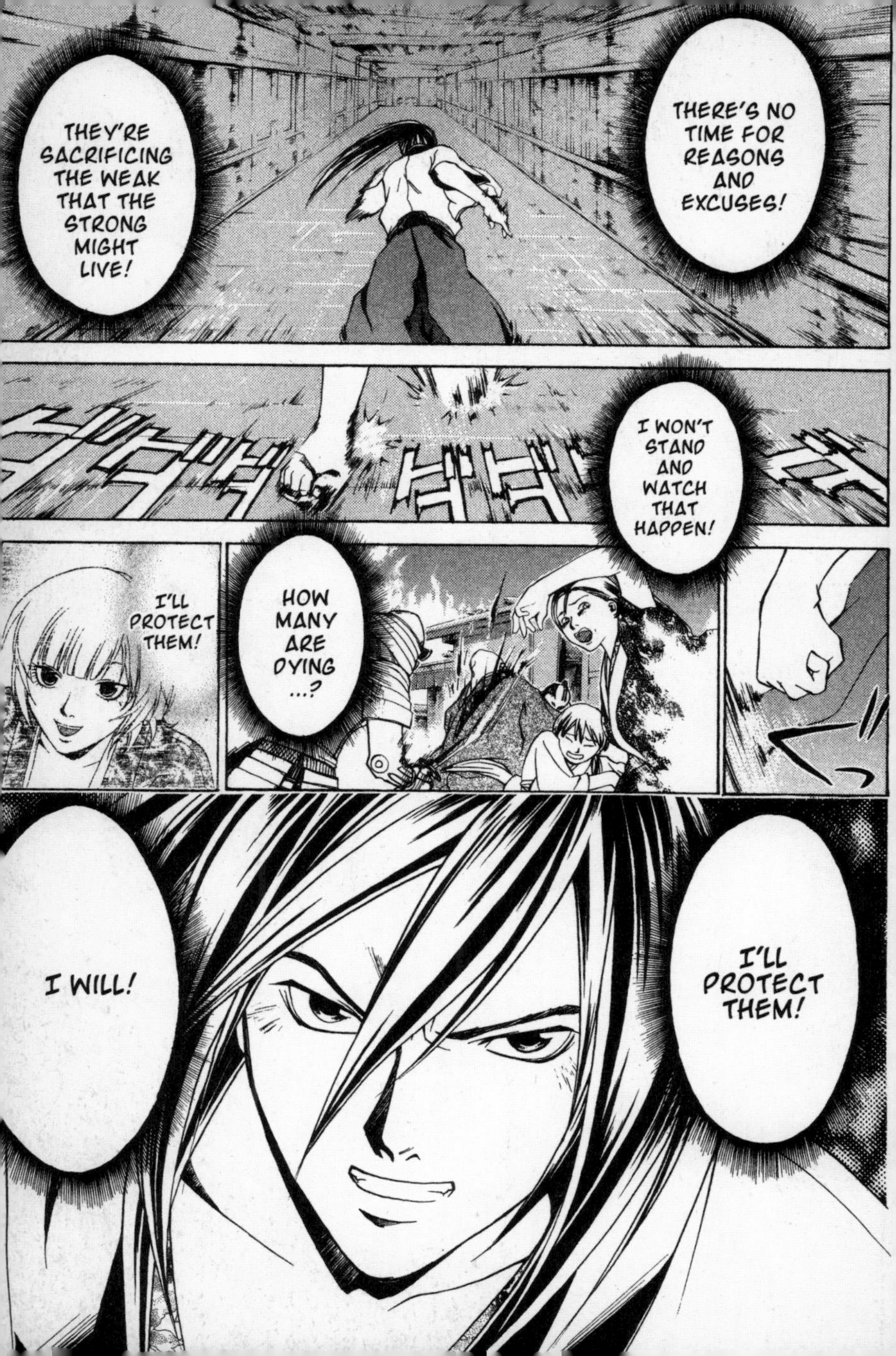
THERE'S NO TIME FOR REASONS AND EXCUSES!
THEY'RE SACRIFICING THE WEAK THAT THE STRONG MIGHT LIVE!
I WON'T STAND AND WATCH THAT HAPPEN!
HOW MANY ARE DYING ...?
I'LL PROTECT THEM!
I'LL PROTECT THEM!
I WILL!

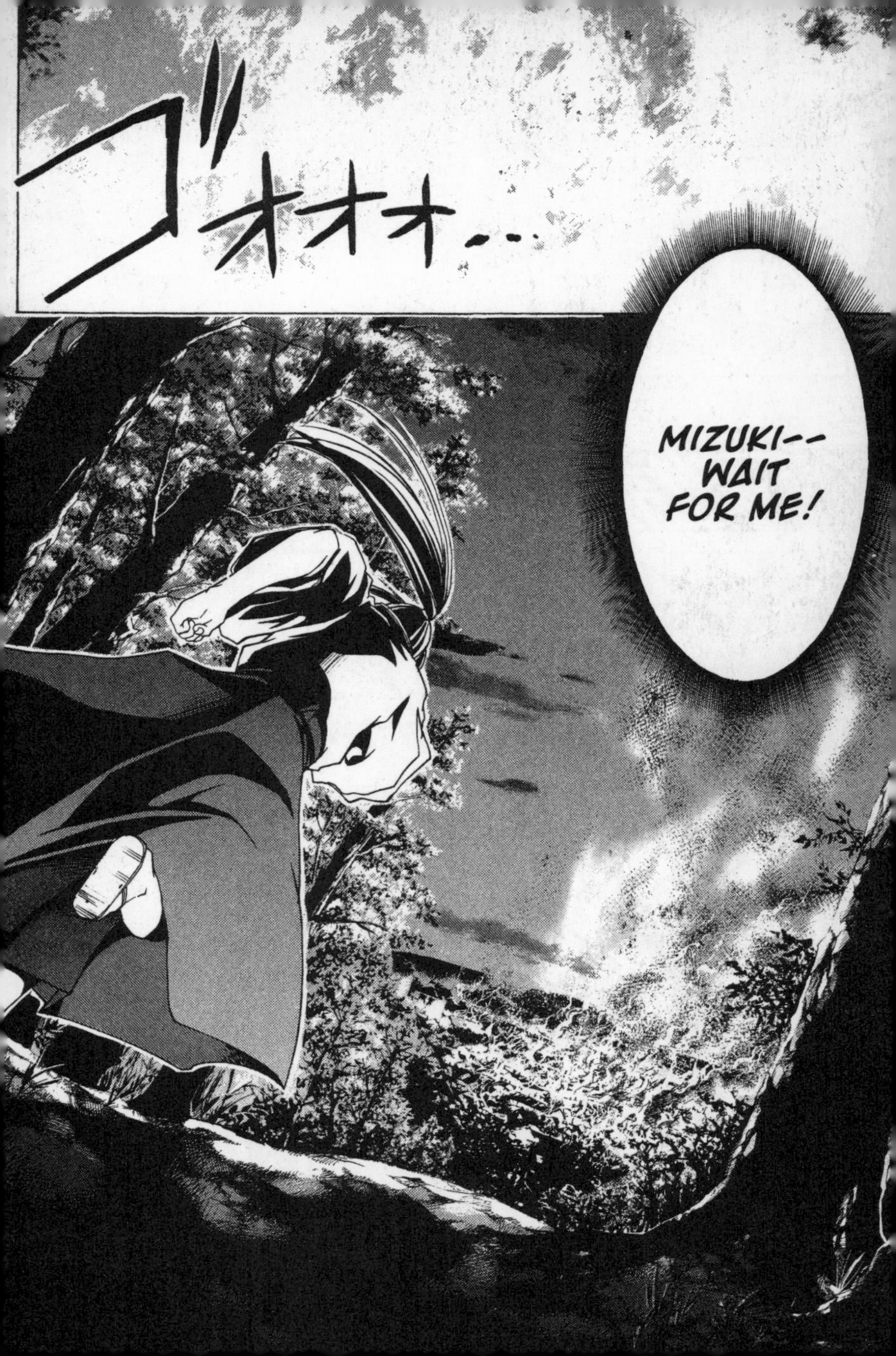
ゴオオオ…
MIZUKI--
WAIT
FOR ME!

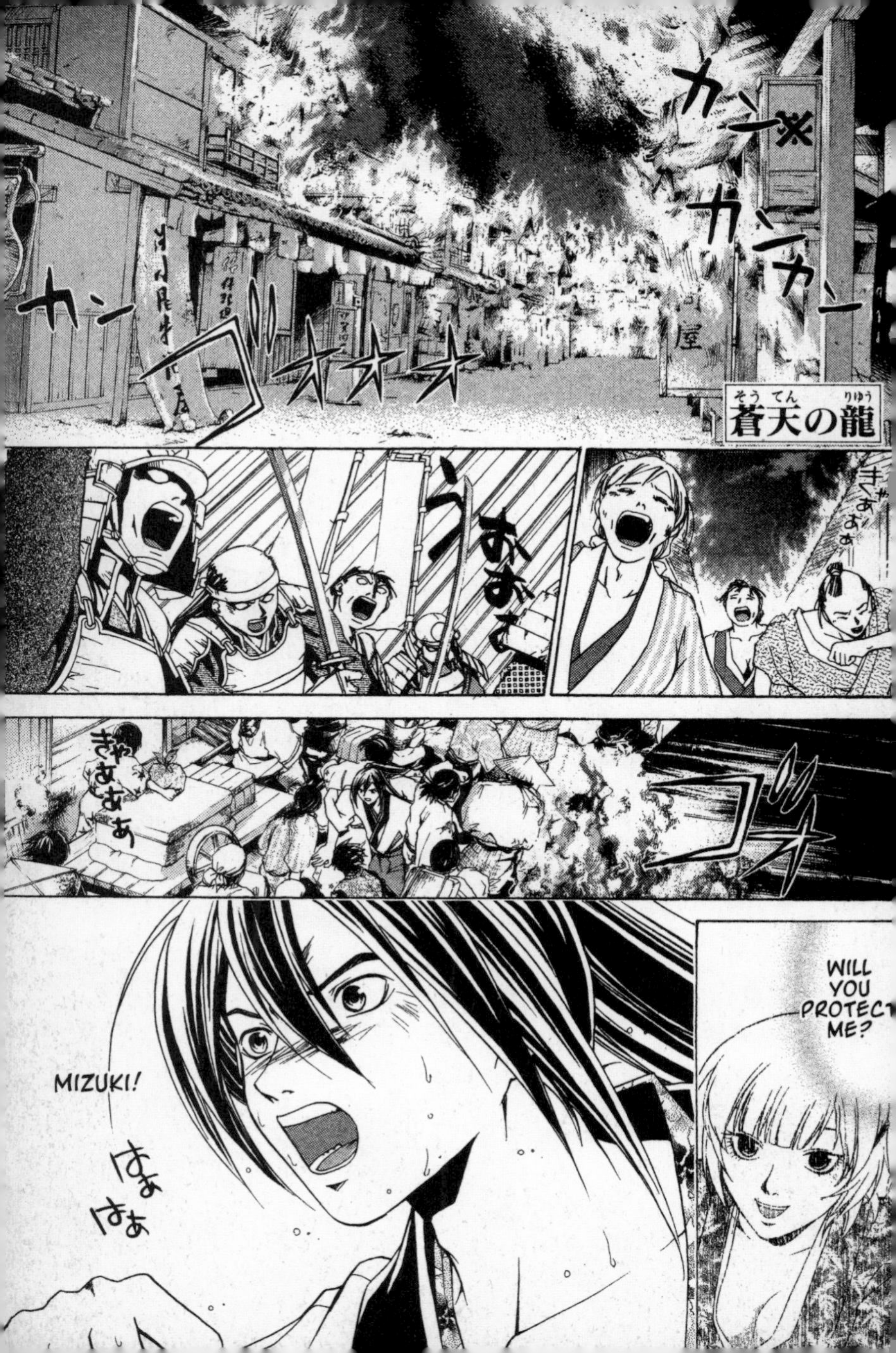

カン※
カンカン
ゴォォォ
カン
蒼天の龍
きゃあぁぁ
うあぁぁ
ゴォ
きゃあぁぁ
WILL YOU PROTECT ME?
MIZUKI!
はぁはぁ

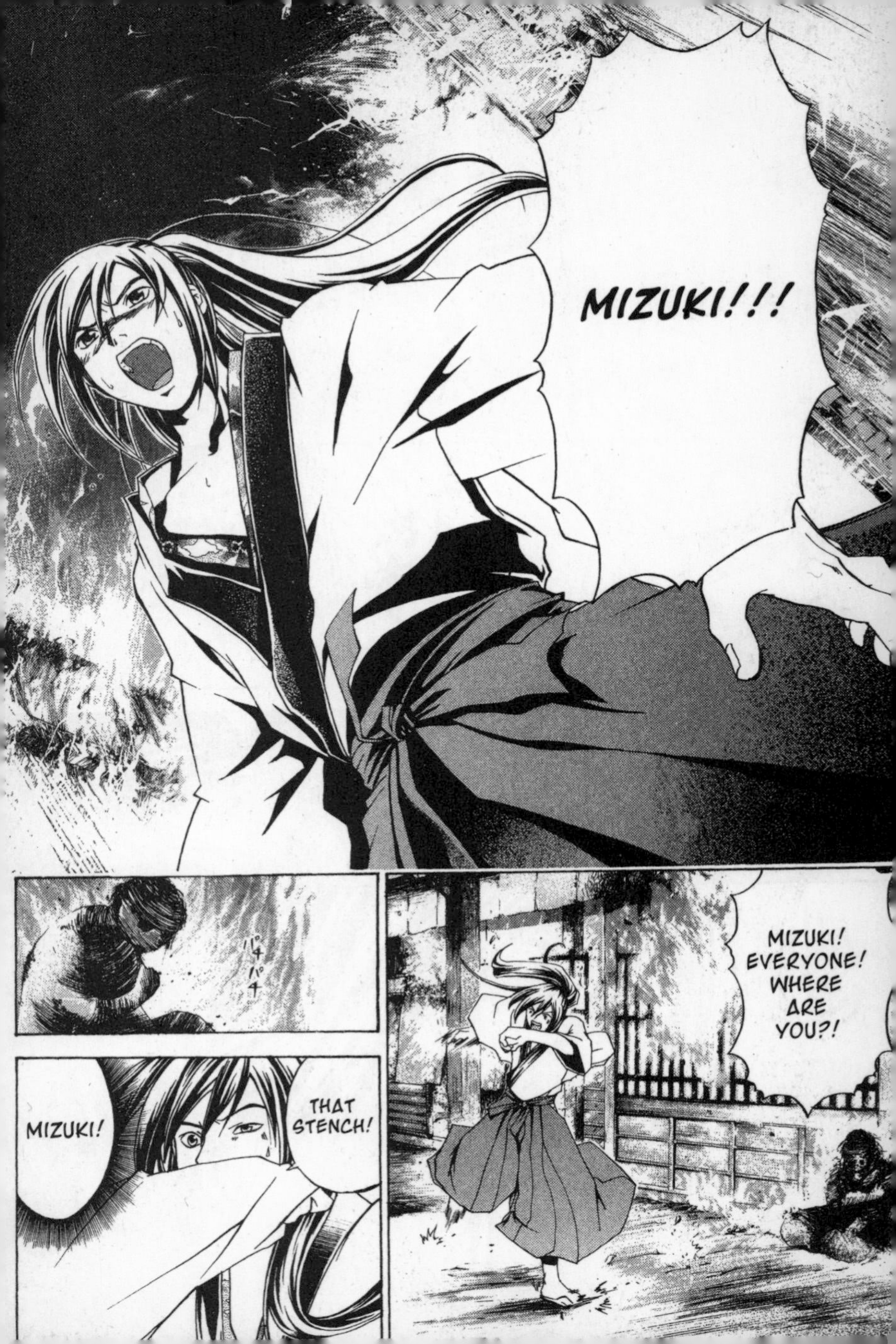
MIZUKI!!!
MIZUKI! EVERYONE! WHERE ARE YOU?!
パチパチ
THAT STENCH!
MIZUKI!

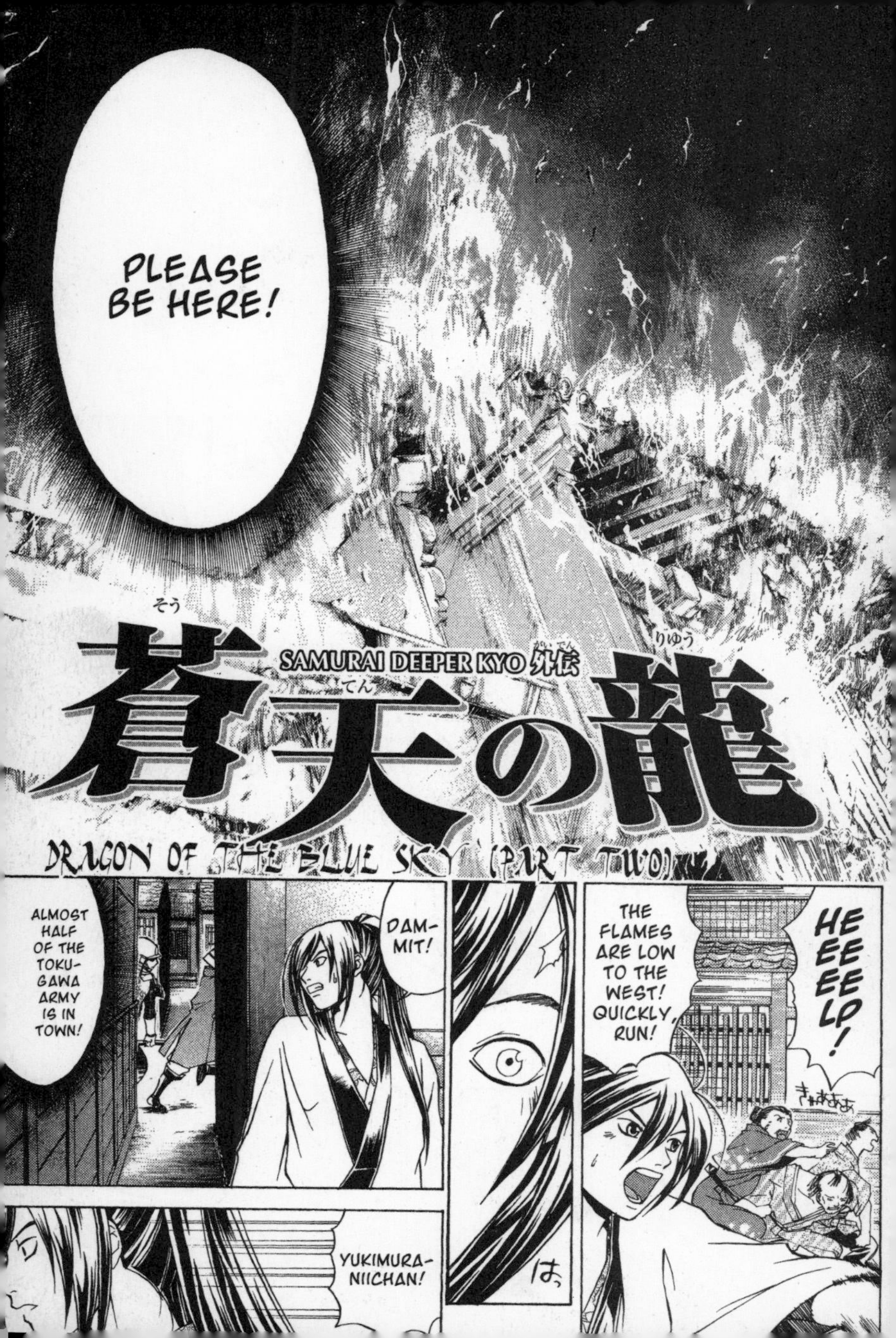
PLEASE BE HERE!
SAMURAI DEEPER KYO 外伝
蒼天の龍
DRAGON OF THE BLUE SKY (PART TWO)
THE FLAMES ARE LOW TO THE WEST! QUICKLY, RUN!
HEEEELP!
きゃあああ
は
DAM-MIT!
ALMOST HALF OF THE TOKU-GAWA ARMY IS IN TOWN!
YUKIMURA-NIICHAN!

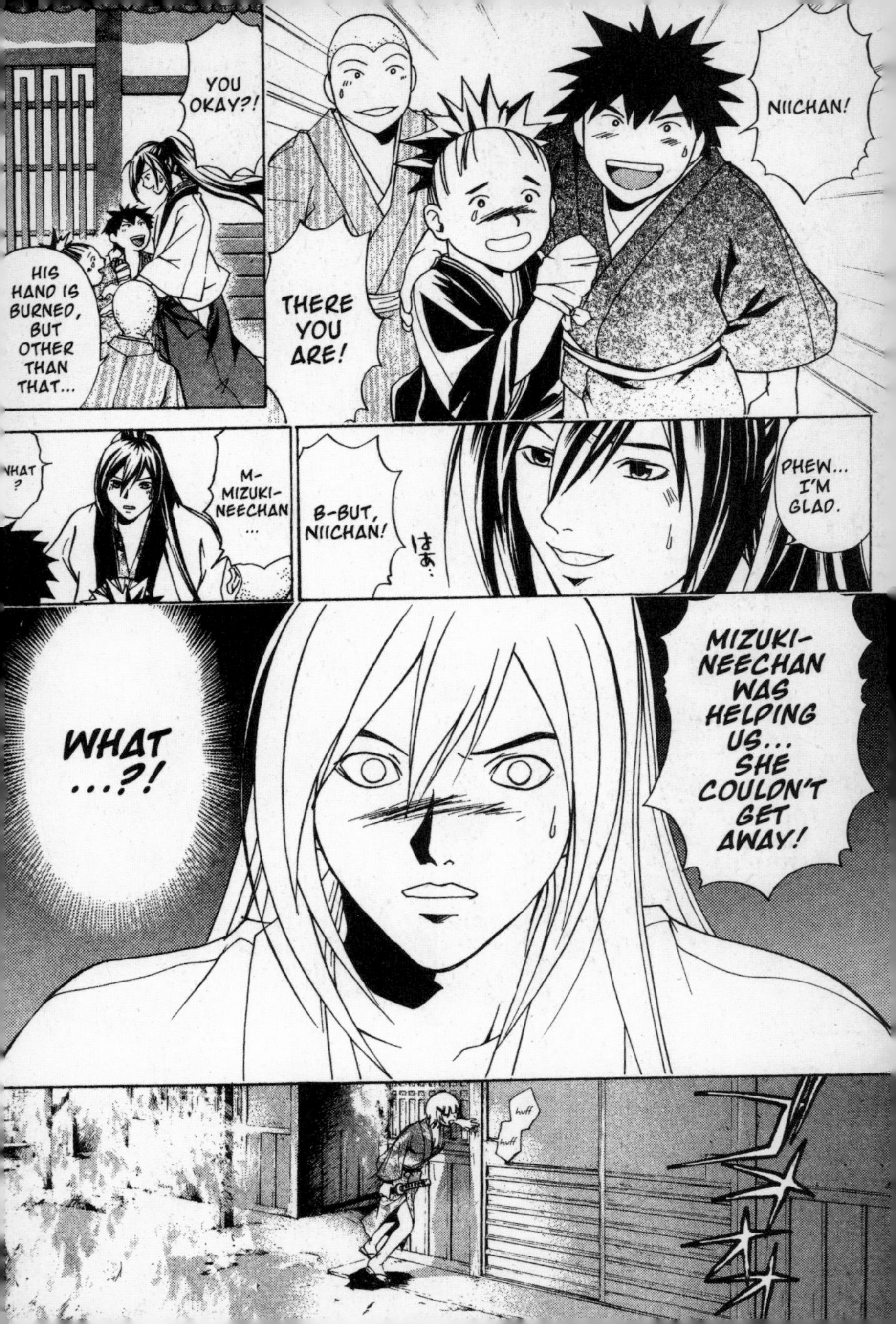
NIICHAN!
THERE YOU ARE!
YOU OKAY?!
HIS HAND IS BURNED, BUT OTHER THAN THAT...
PHEW... I'M GLAD.
はぁ…
B-BUT, NIICHAN!
M-MIZUKI-NEECHAN...
WHAT?
MIZUKI-NEECHAN WAS HELPING US... SHE COULDN'T GET AWAY!
WHAT...?!
huff
huff

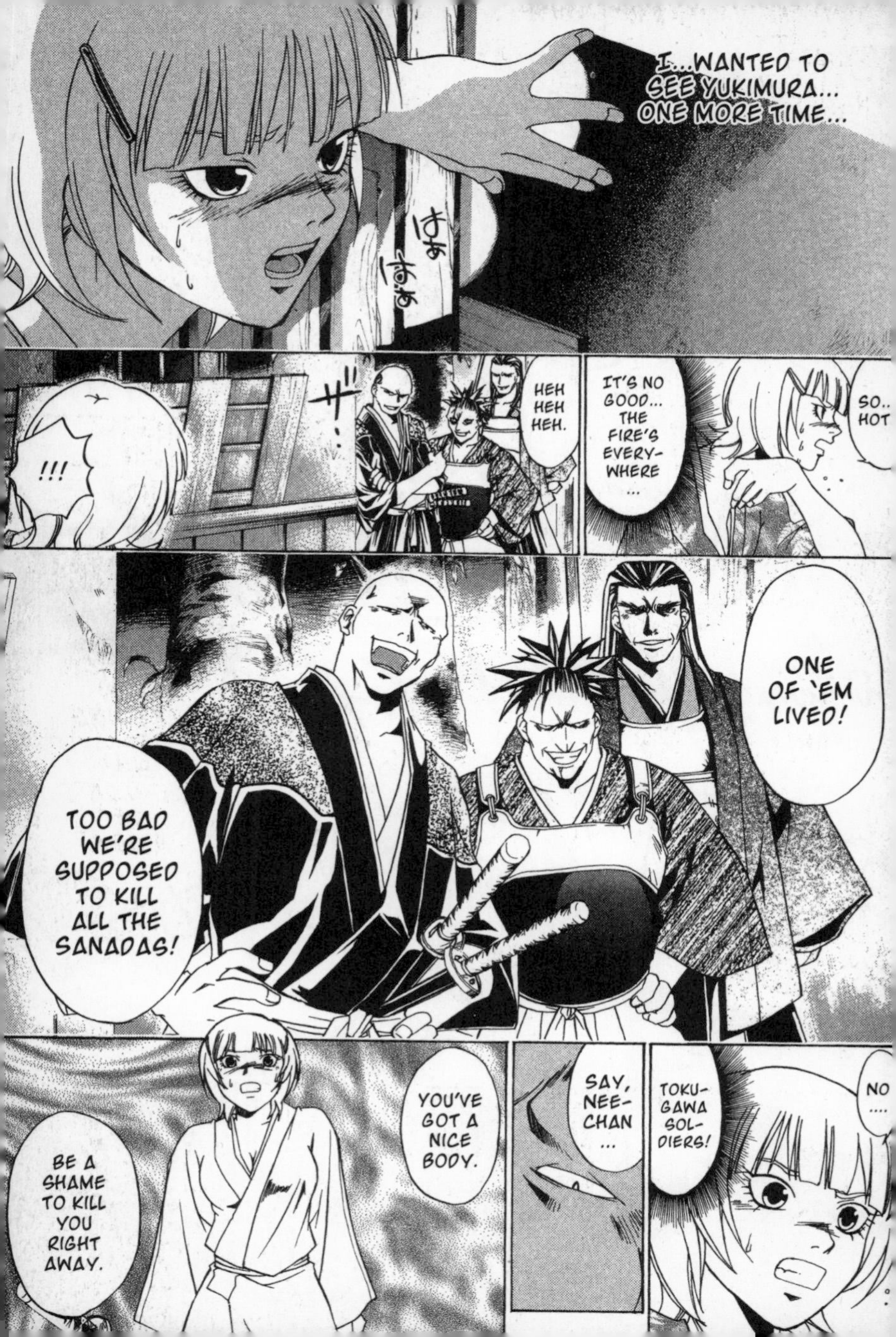
I...WANTED TO SEE YUKIMURA... ONE MORE TIME...
はぁ
はぁ
SO.. HOT
IT'S NO GOOD... THE FIRE'S EVERY-WHERE ...
HEH HEH HEH.
ザ!
!!!
ONE OF 'EM LIVED!
TOO BAD WE'RE SUPPOSED TO KILL ALL THE SANADAS!
NO ....
TOKU-GAWA SOL-DIERS!
SAY, NEE-CHAN ...
YOU'VE GOT A NICE BODY.
BE A SHAME TO KILL YOU RIGHT AWAY.

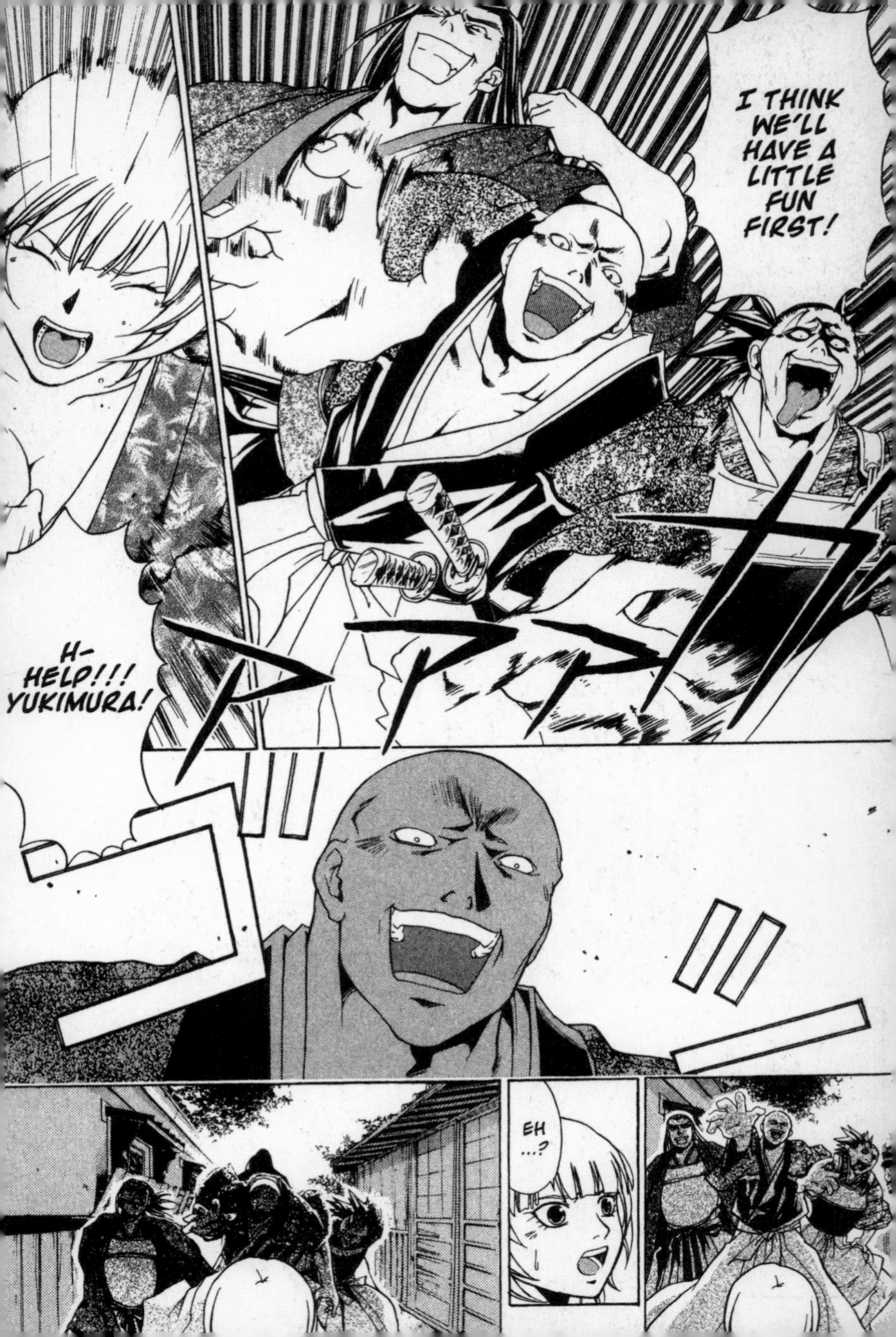
I THINK WE'LL HAVE A LITTLE FUN FIRST!
H-HELP!!! YUKIMURA!
EH ...?

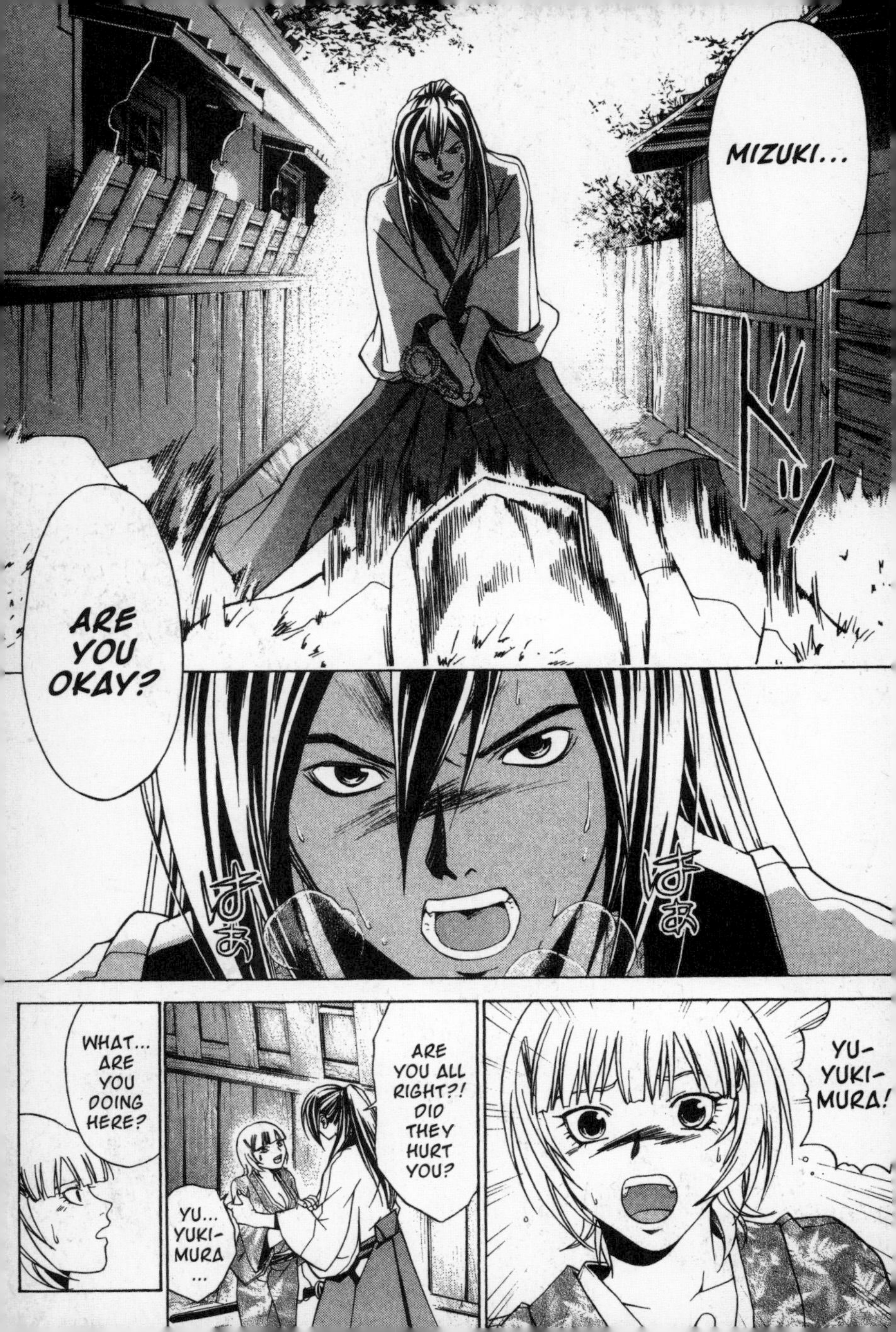
MIZUKI...
ドドッ
ARE YOU OKAY?
はあ
はあ
YU-YUKI-MURA!
ARE YOU ALL RIGHT?! DID THEY HURT YOU?
YU... YUKI-MURA ...
WHAT... ARE YOU DOING HERE?

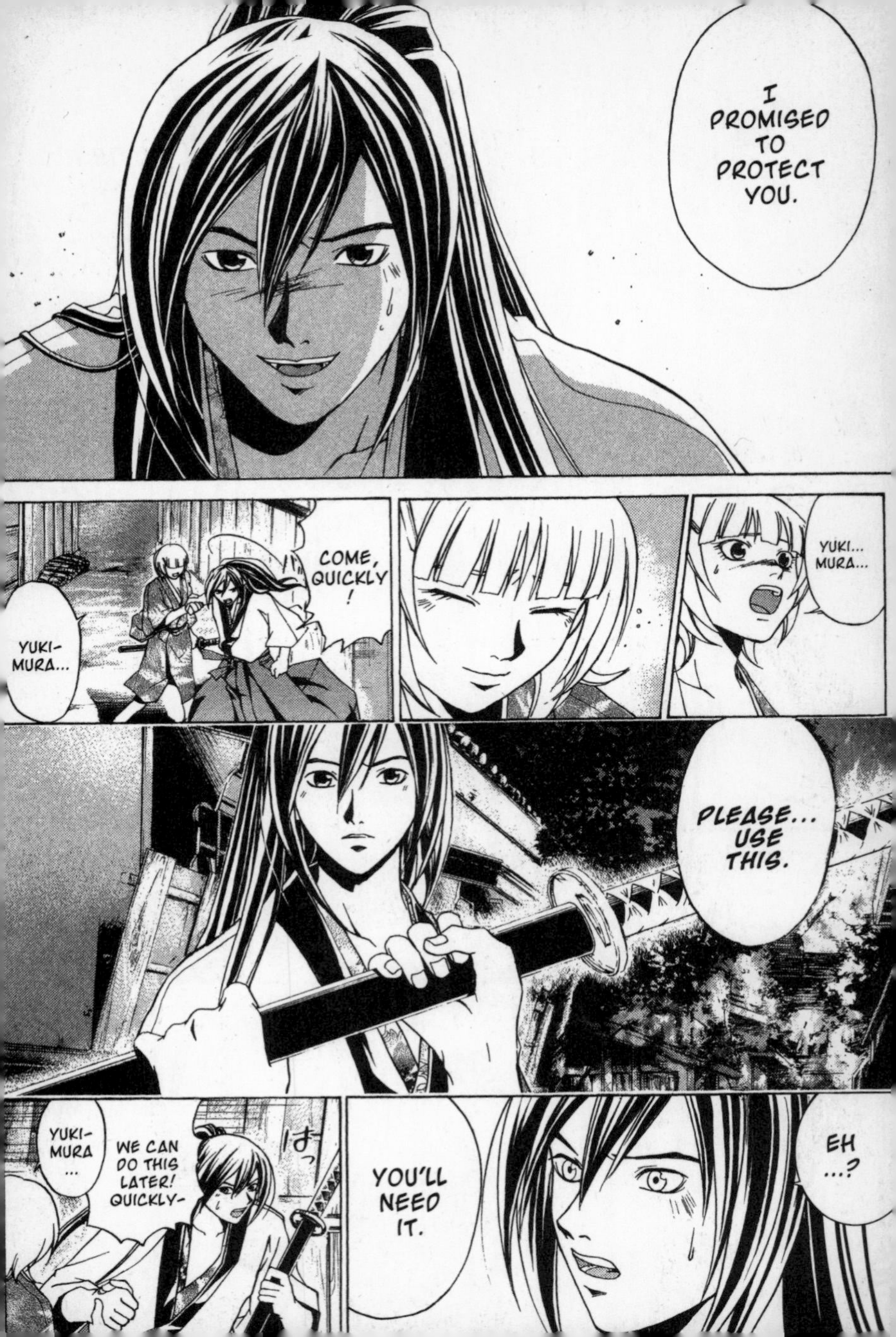
I PROMISED TO PROTECT YOU.
YUKI... MURA...
COME, QUICKLY!
YUKI-MURA...
PLEASE... USE THIS.
EH ...?
YOU'LL NEED IT.
はっ
WE CAN DO THIS LATER! QUICKLY-
YUKI-MURA ...

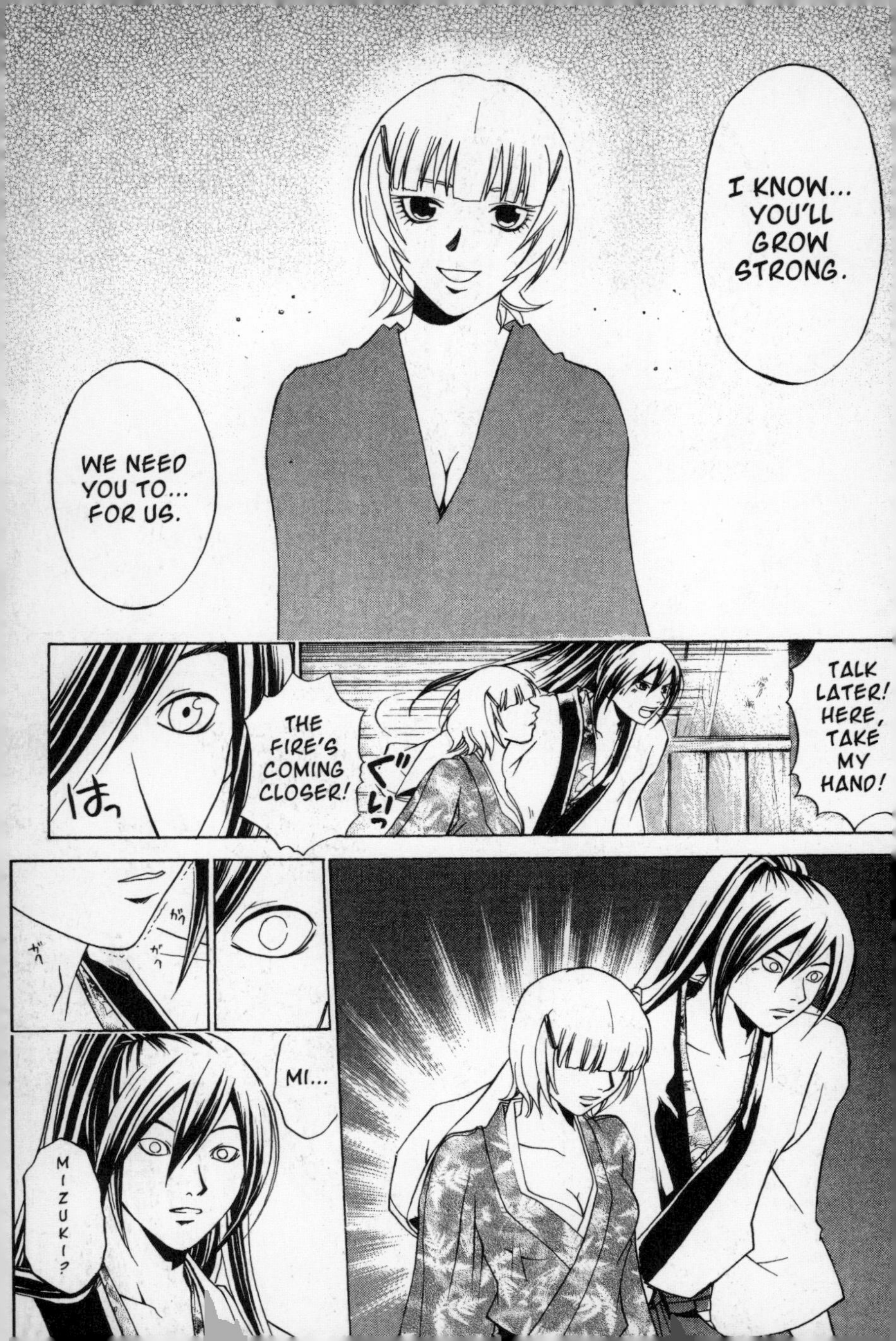
I KNOW... YOU'LL GROW STRONG.
WE NEED YOU TO... FOR US.
TALK LATER! HERE, TAKE MY HAND!
THE FIRE'S COMING CLOSER!
ぐいっ
はっ
MI...
MIZUKI?

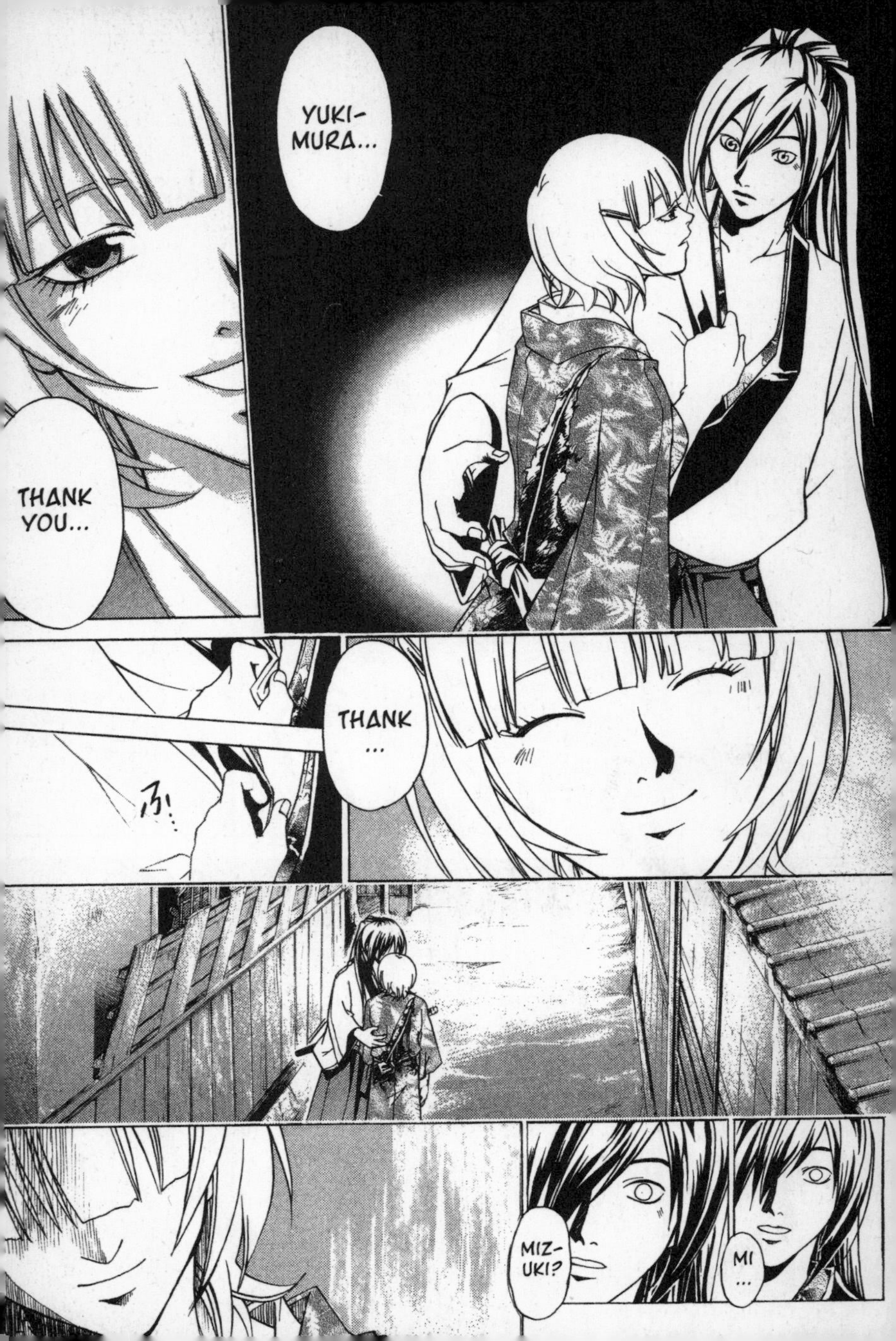
YUKI-MURA...
THANK YOU...
THANK ...
MI ...
MIZ-UKI?

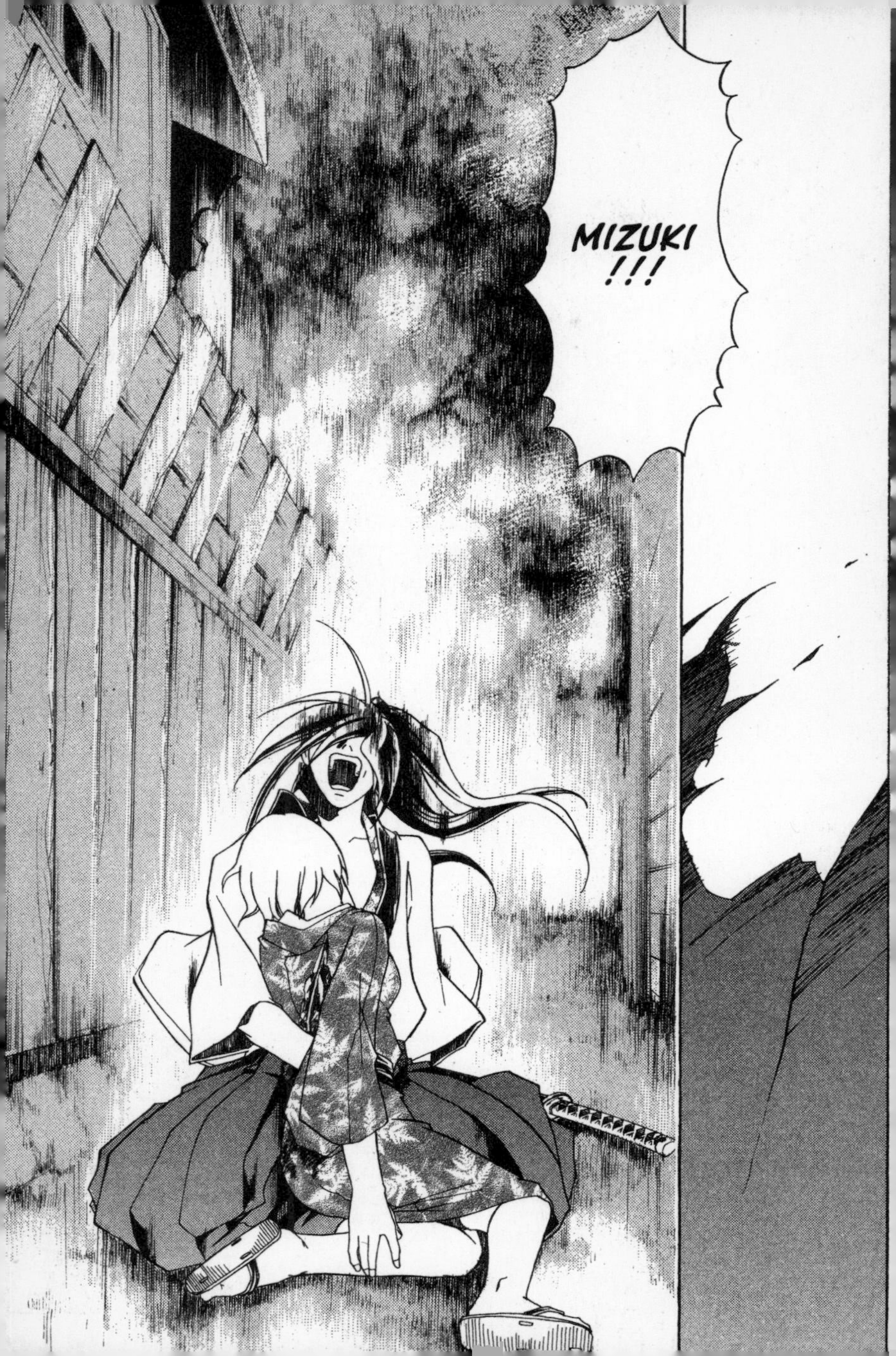
MIZUKI
!!!

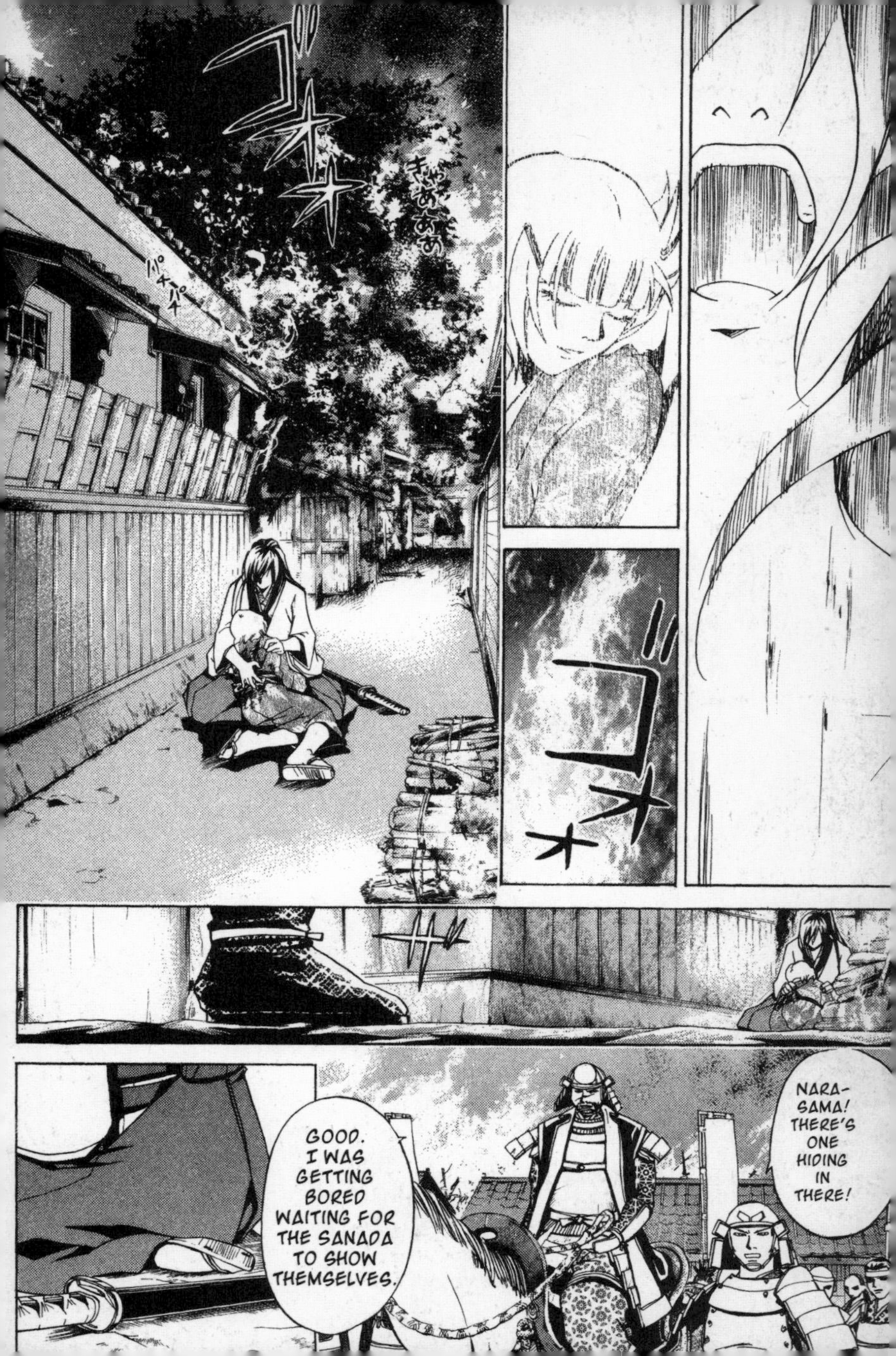
NARA-SAMA! THERE'S ONE HIDING IN THERE!
GOOD. I WAS GETTING BORED WAITING FOR THE SANADA TO SHOW THEMSELVES.

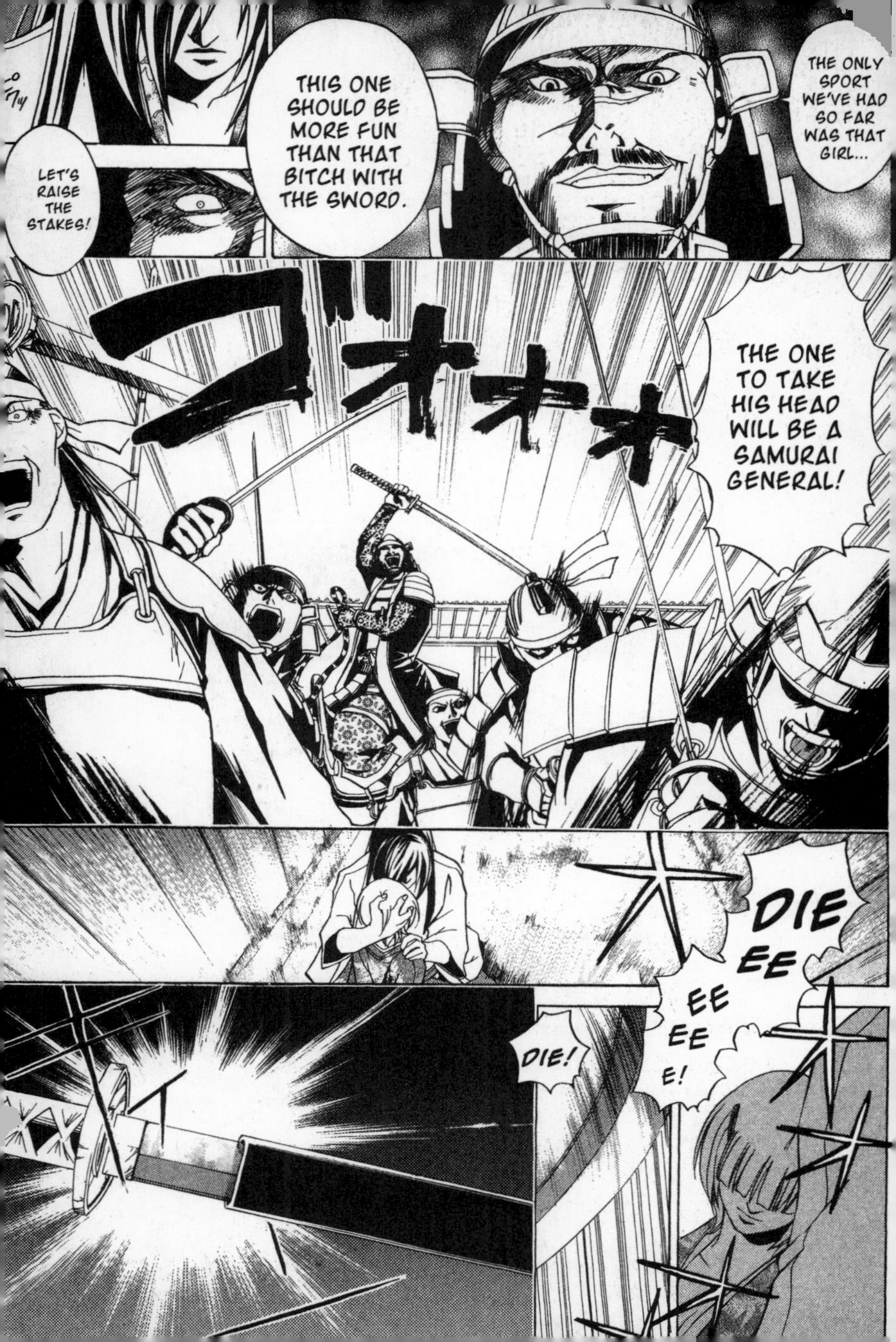
THE ONLY SPORT WE'VE HAD SO FAR WAS THAT GIRL...
THIS ONE SHOULD BE MORE FUN THAN THAT BITCH WITH THE SWORD.
LET'S RAISE THE STAKES!
THE ONE TO TAKE HIS HEAD WILL BE A SAMURAI GENERAL!
ゴオォォ
DIE EE EE EE E!
DIE!

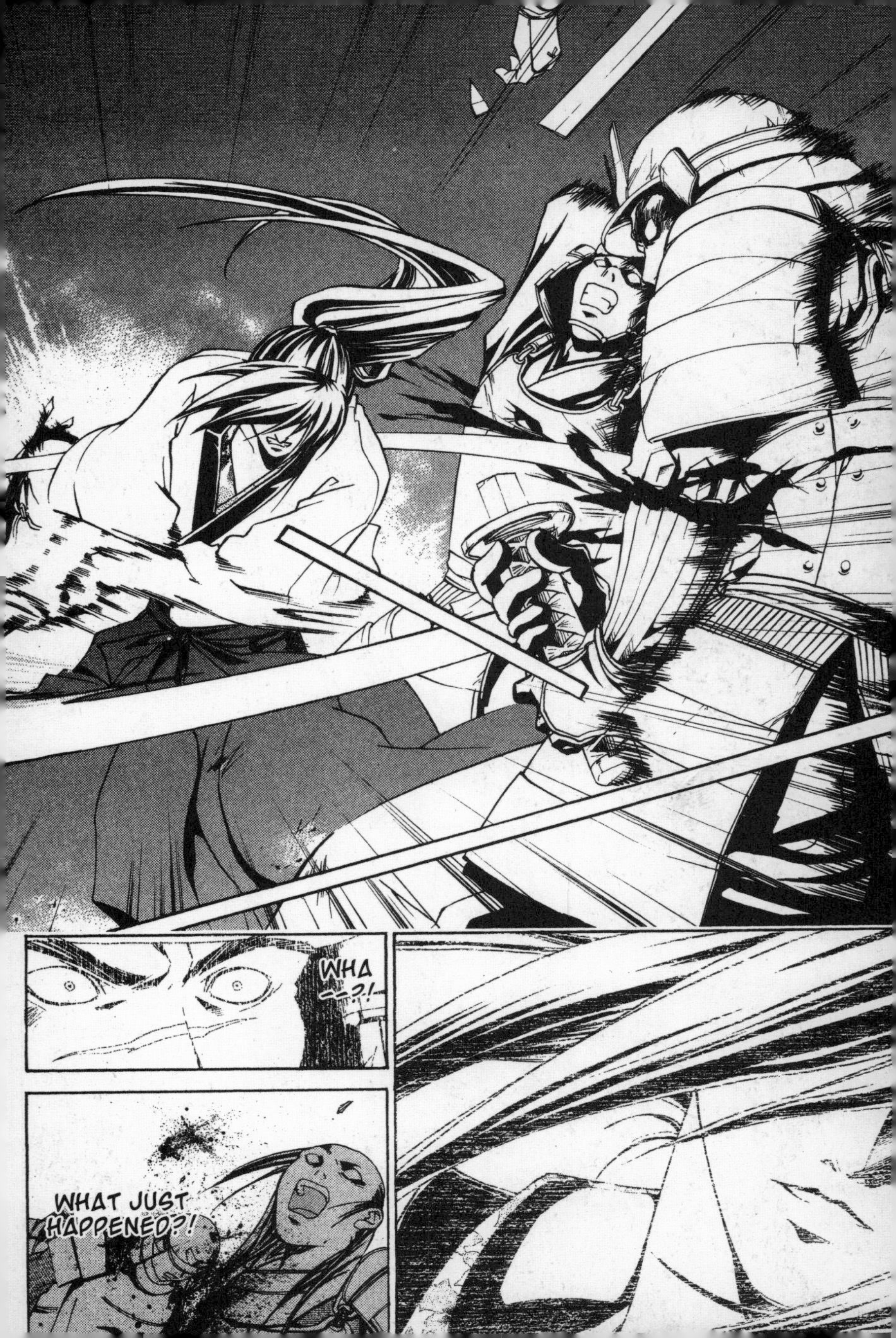
WHA --?!
WHAT JUST HAPPENED?!

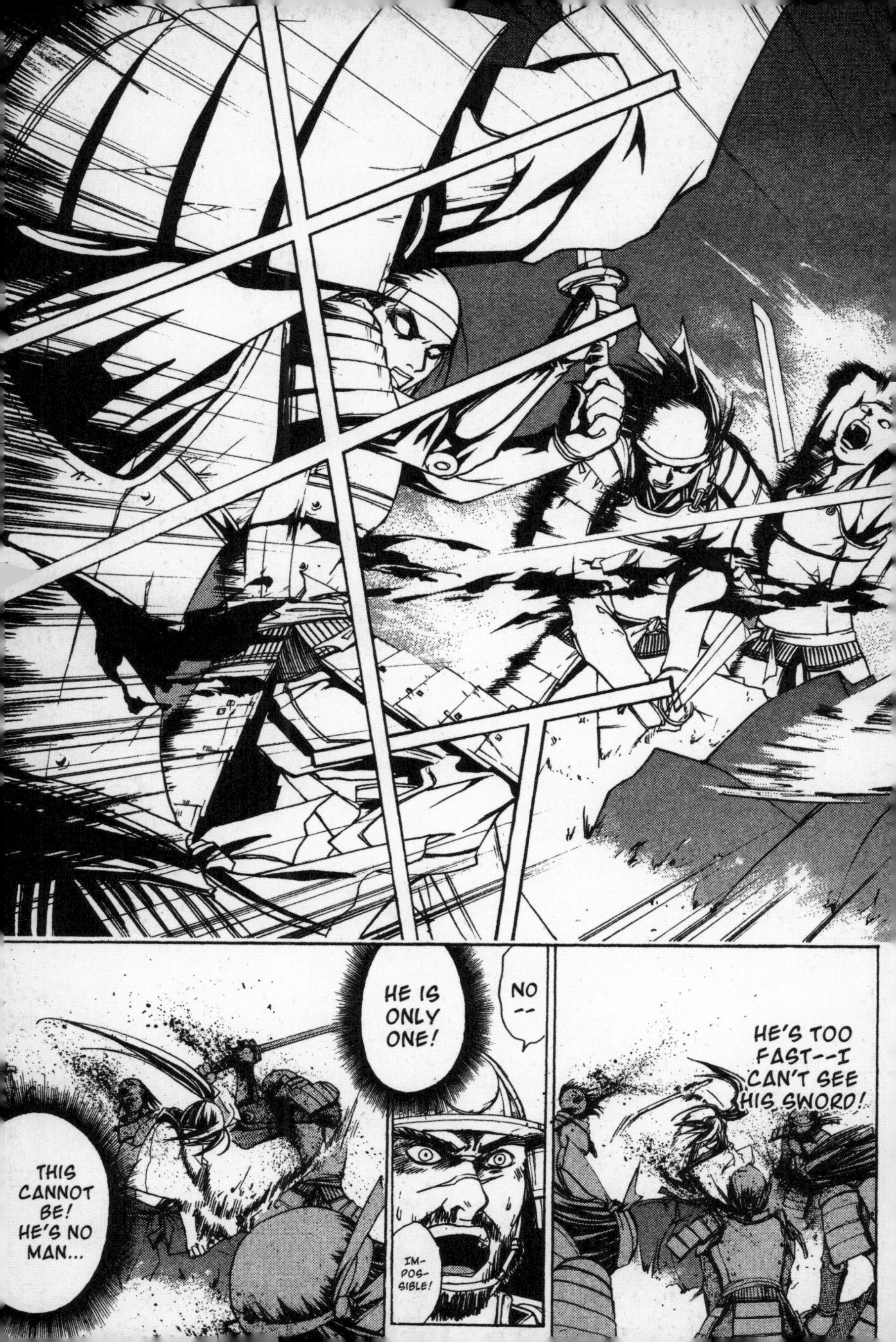
HE'S TOO FAST--I CAN'T SEE HIS SWORD!
NO --
IM-POS-SIBLE!
HE IS ONLY ONE!
THIS CANNOT BE! HE'S NO MAN...

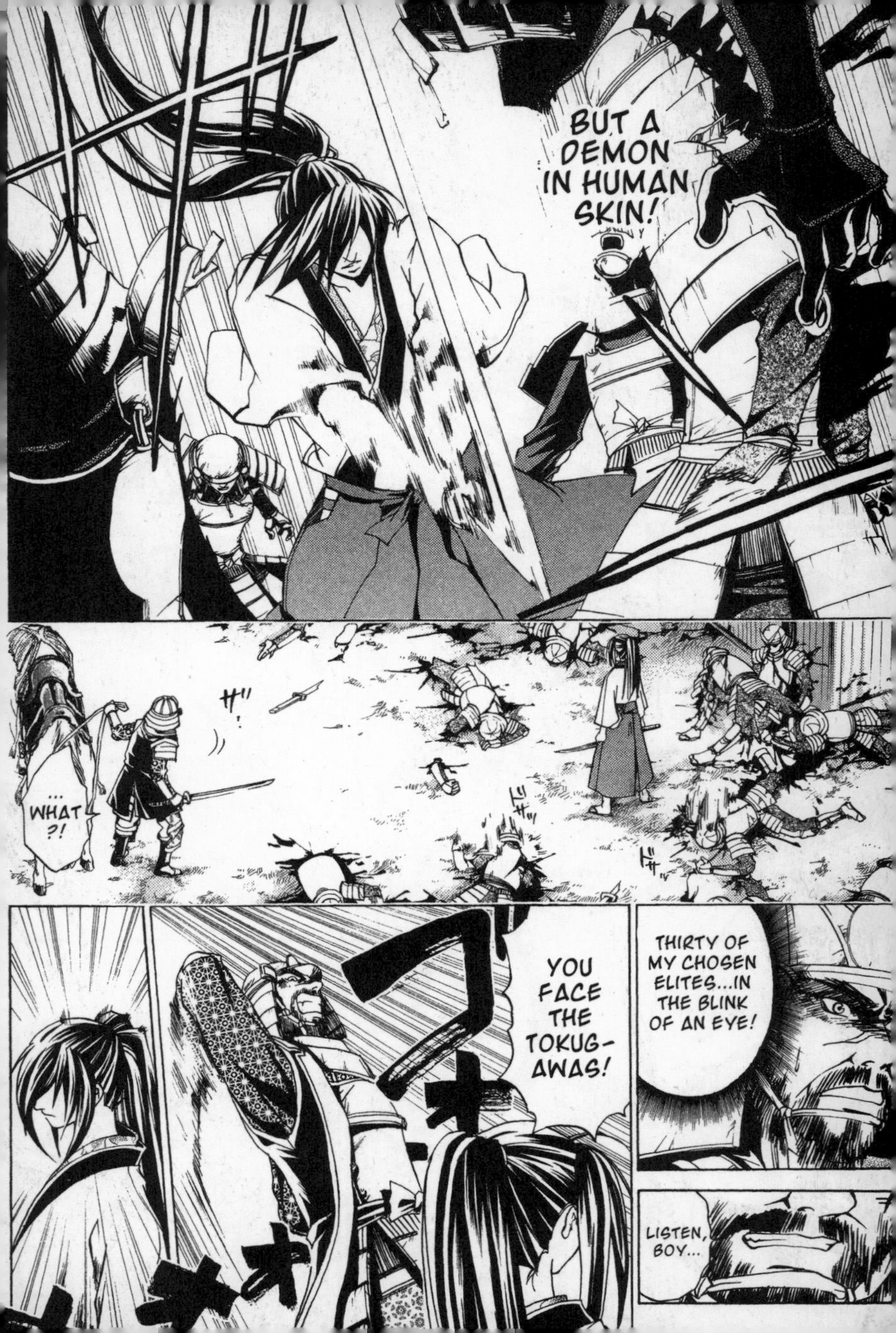
BUT A DEMON IN HUMAN SKIN!
... WHAT ?!
THIRTY OF MY CHOSEN ELITES...IN THE BLINK OF AN EYE!
LISTEN, BOY...
YOU FACE THE TOKUG-AWAS!

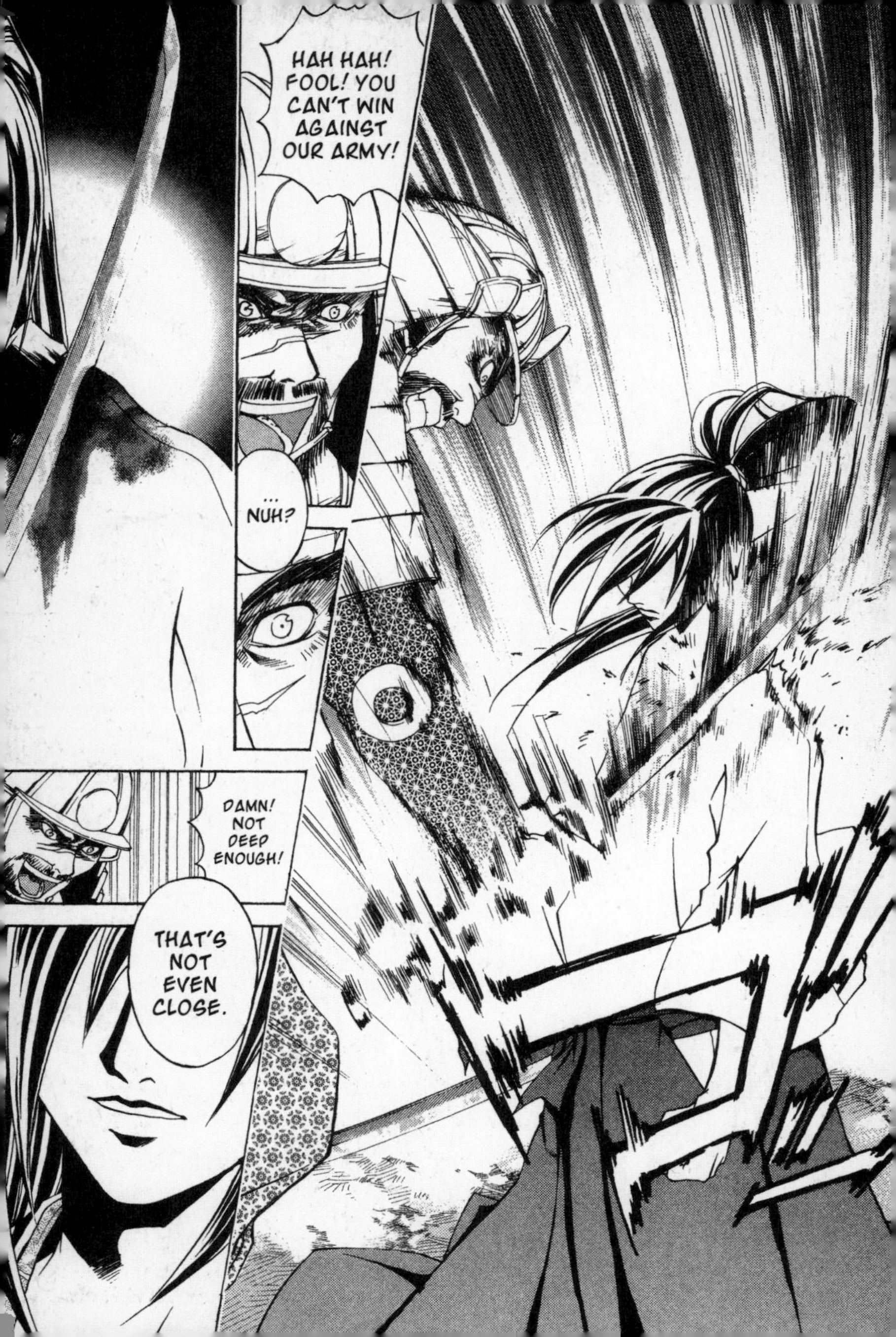
HAH HAH! FOOL! YOU CAN'T WIN AGAINST OUR ARMY!
... NUH?
DAMN! NOT DEEP ENOUGH!
THAT'S NOT EVEN CLOSE.

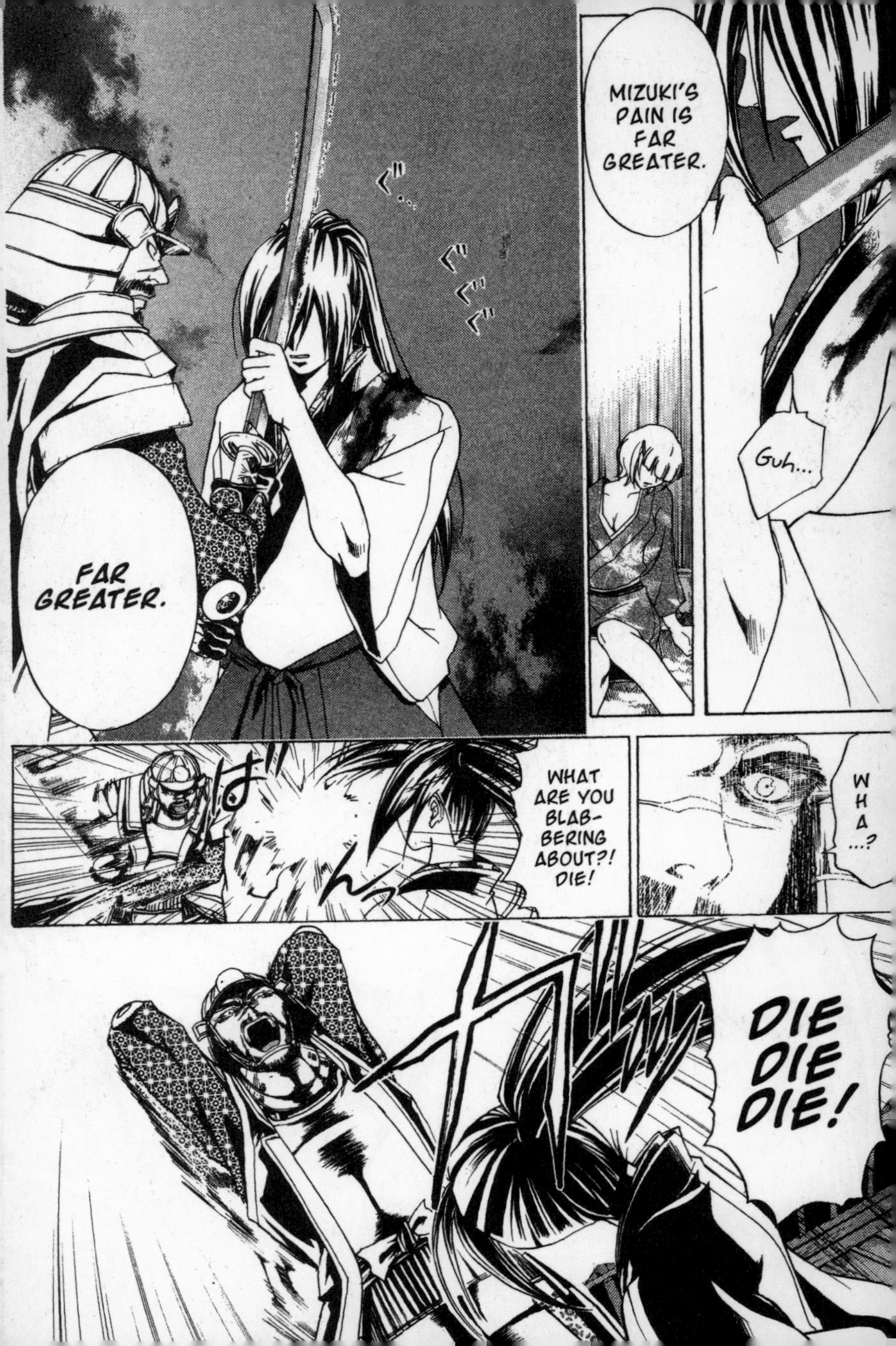
Guh...
MIZUKI'S PAIN IS FAR GREATER.
ぐ…
ぐぐぐ
FAR GREATER.
WHA...?
WHAT ARE YOU BLABBERING ABOUT?! DIE!
DIE DIE DIE!

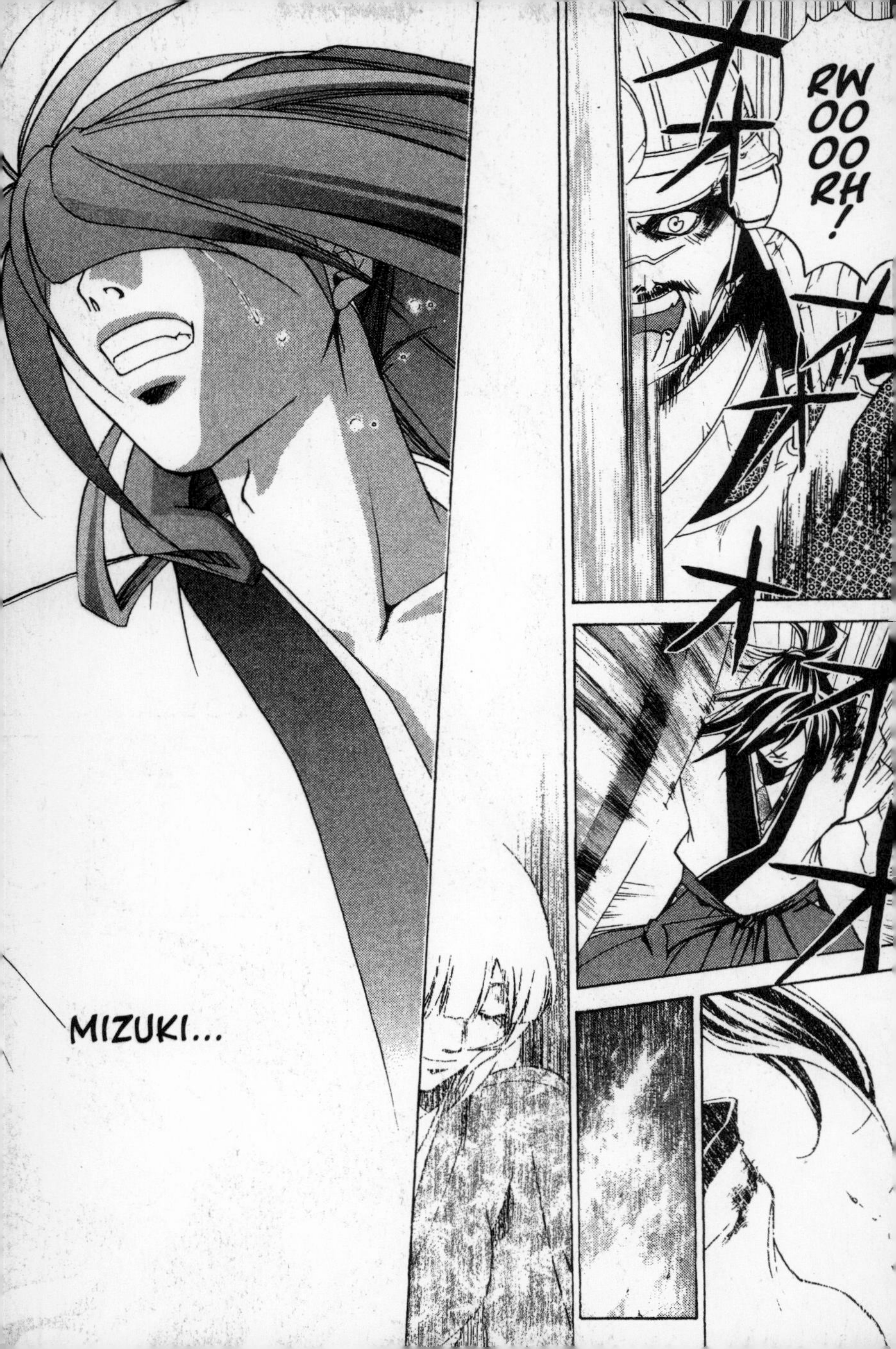
RWOOOOOORH!
MIZUKI...

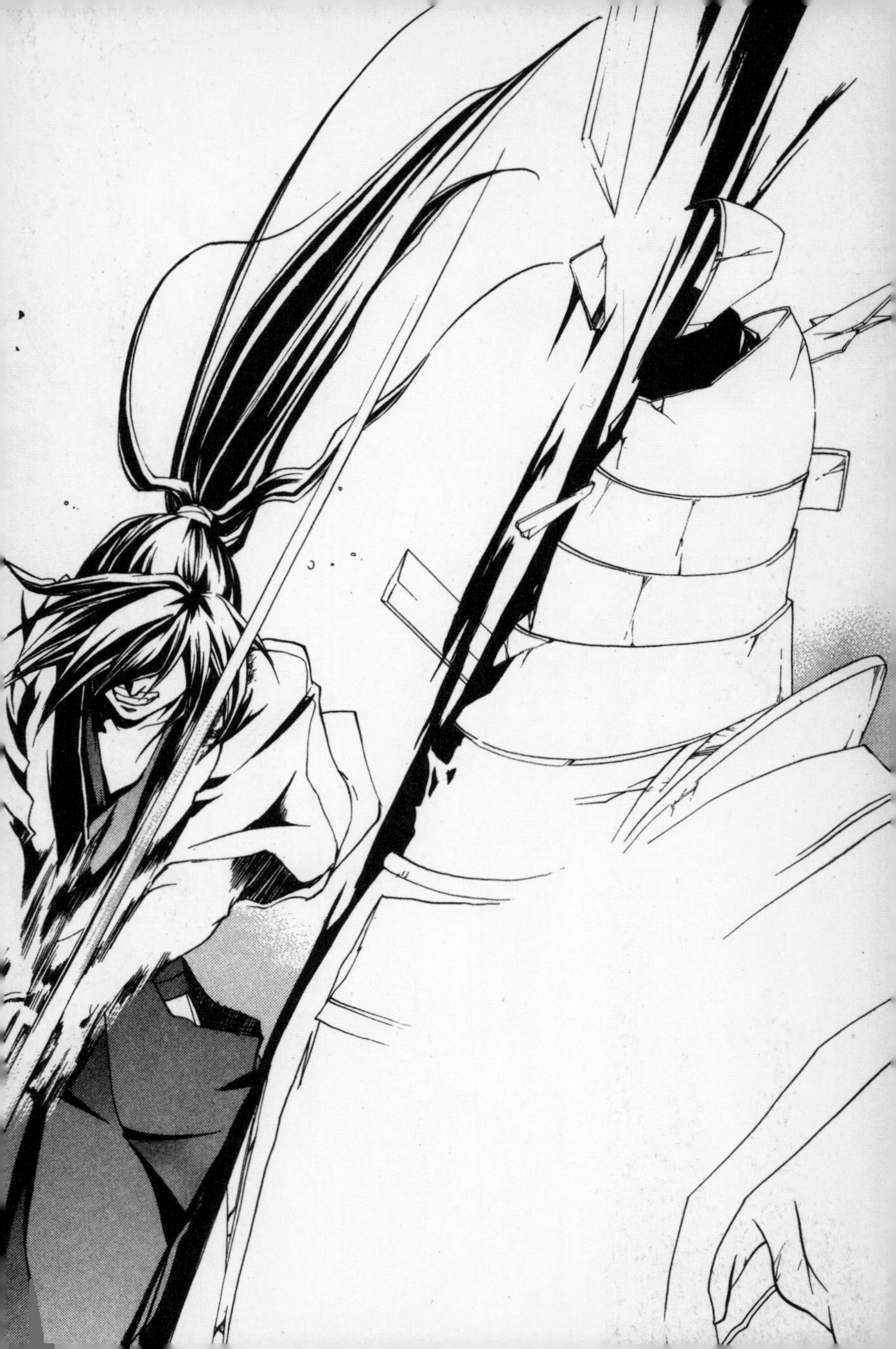

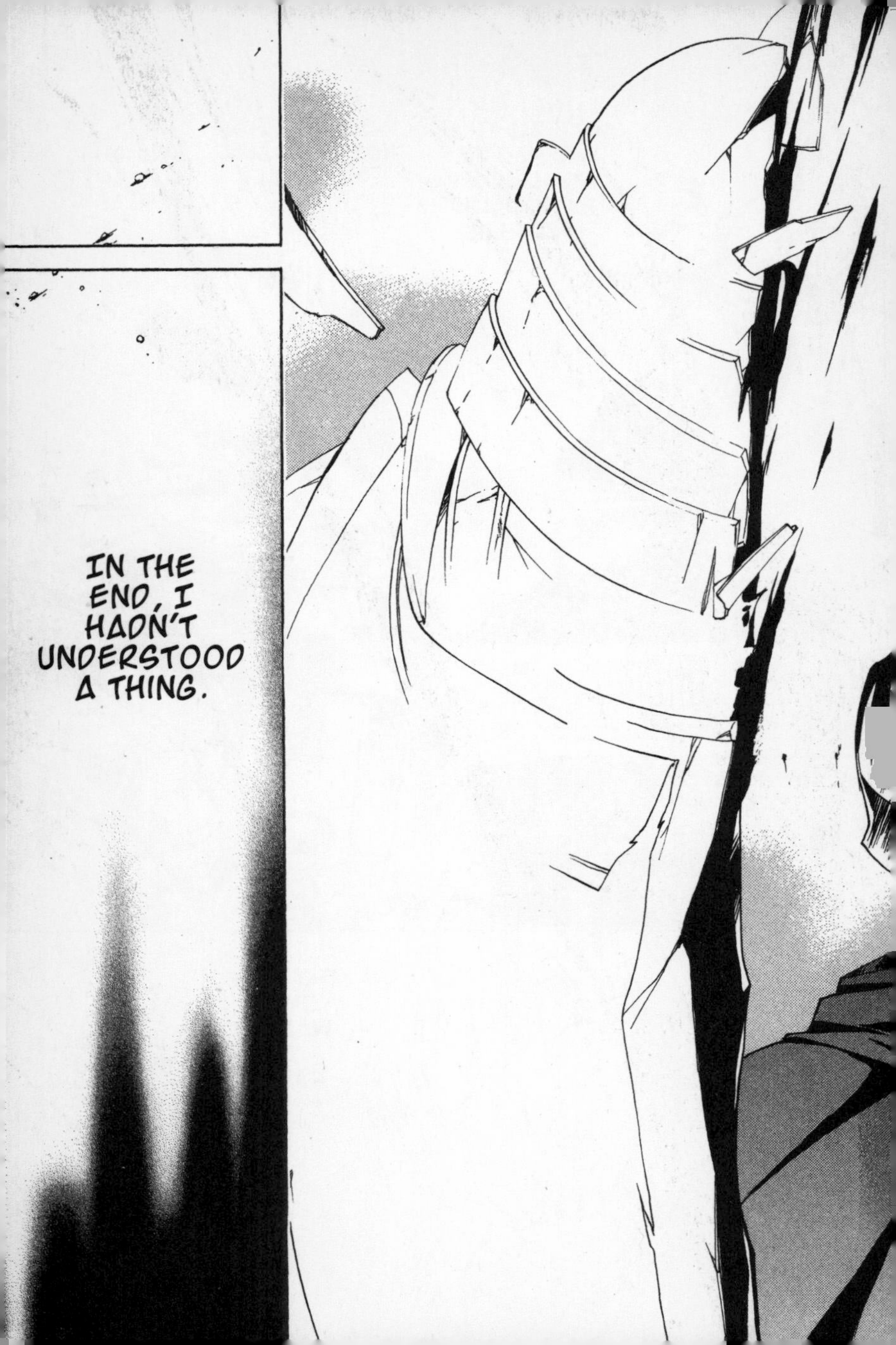
IN THE END, I HADN'T UNDERSTOOD A THING.

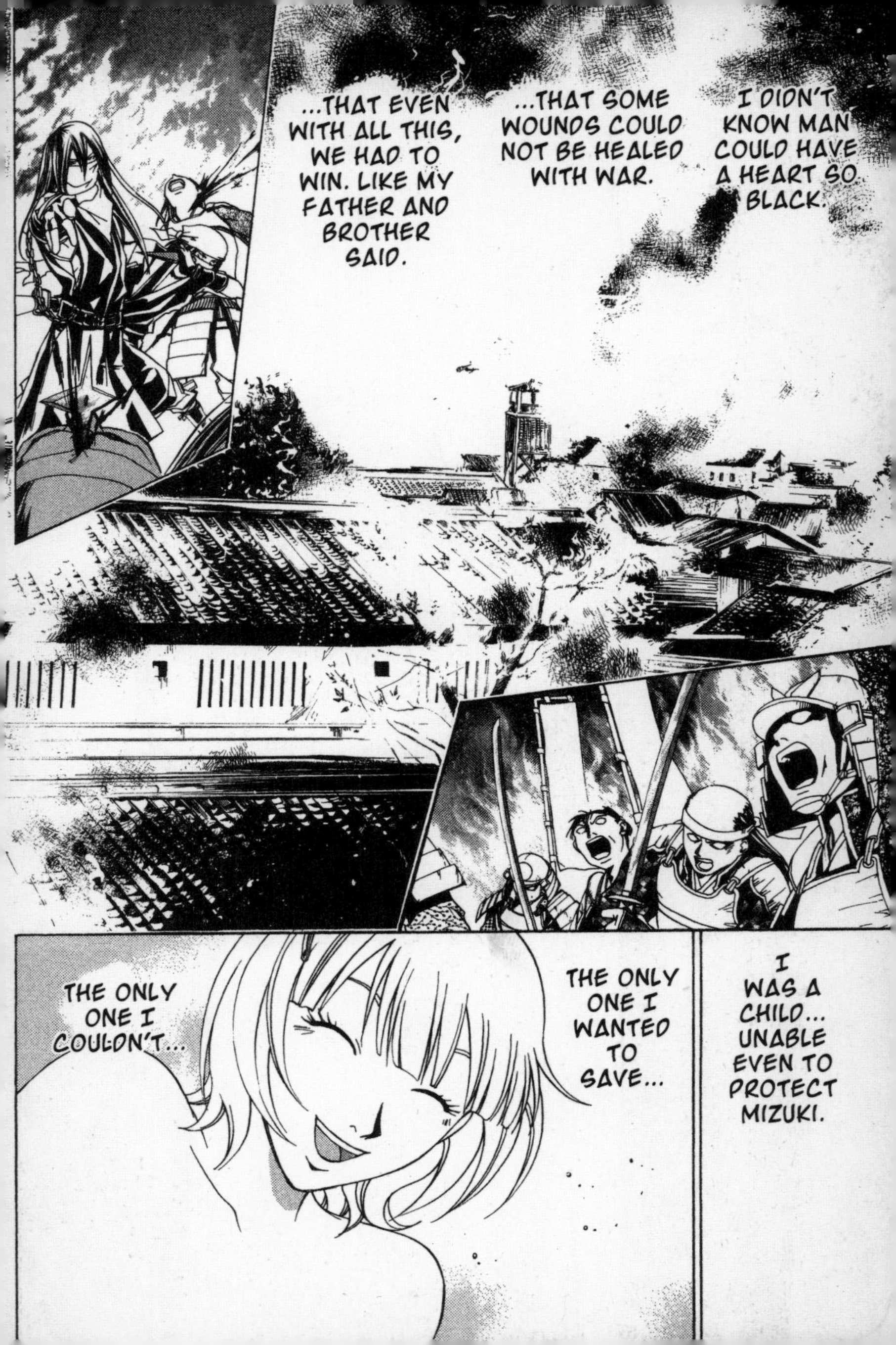
I DIDN'T KNOW MAN COULD HAVE A HEART SO BLACK.
...THAT SOME WOUNDS COULD NOT BE HEALED WITH WAR.
...THAT EVEN WITH ALL THIS, WE HAD TO WIN. LIKE MY FATHER AND BROTHER SAID.
I WAS A CHILD... UNABLE EVEN TO PROTECT MIZUKI.
THE ONLY ONE I WANTED TO SAVE...
THE ONLY ONE I COULDN'T...

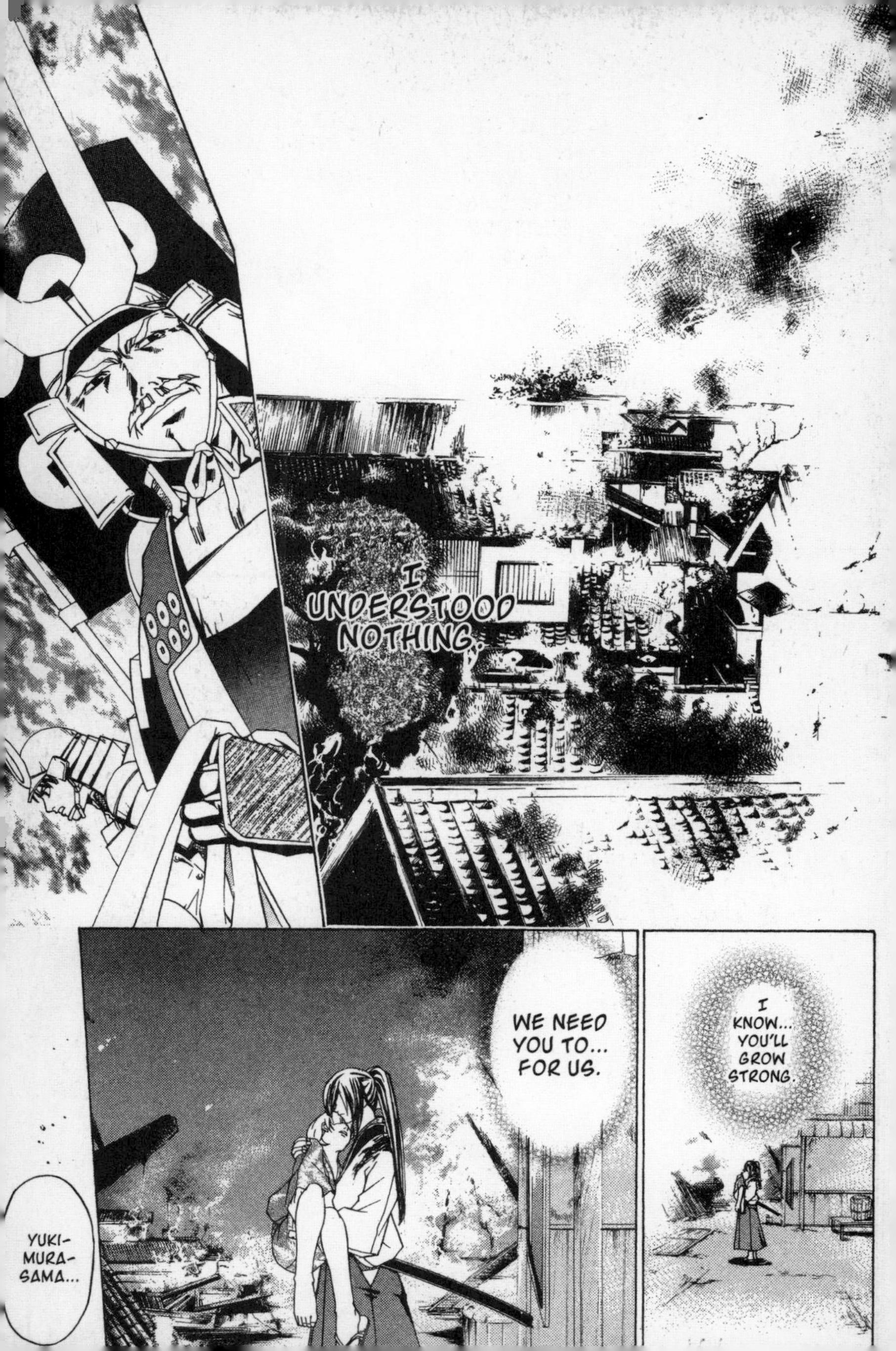
I UNDERSTOOD NOTHING.
I KNOW... YOU'LL GROW STRONG.
WE NEED YOU TO... FOR US.
YUKI-MURA-SAMA...

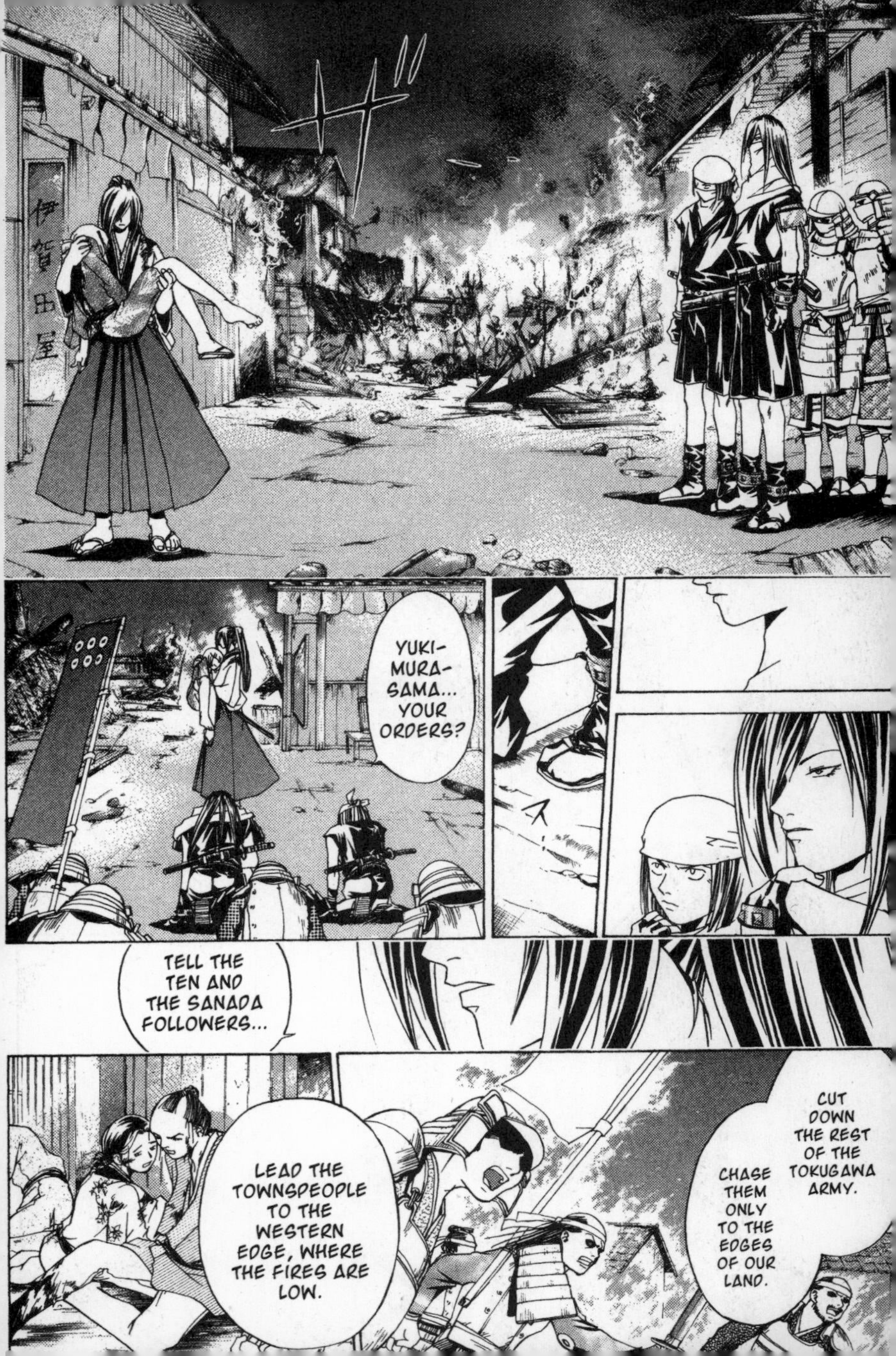
ザッ
YUKI-MURA-SAMA... YOUR ORDERS?
TELL THE TEN AND THE SANADA FOLLOWERS...
CUT DOWN THE REST OF THE TOKUGAWA ARMY.
CHASE THEM ONLY TO THE EDGES OF OUR LAND.
LEAD THE TOWNSPEOPLE TO THE WESTERN EDGE, WHERE THE FIRES ARE LOW.

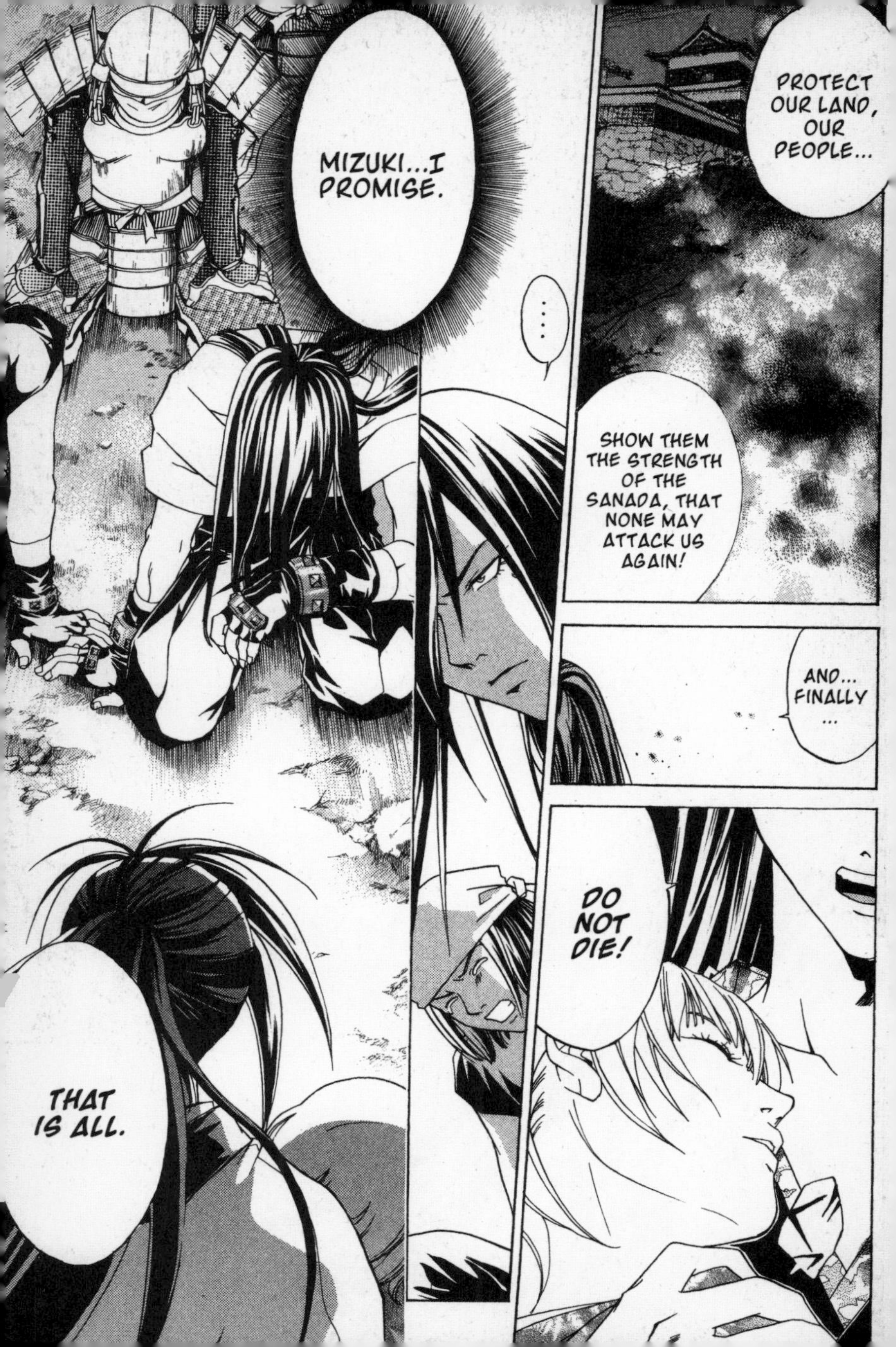
PROTECT OUR LAND, OUR PEOPLE...
SHOW THEM THE STRENGTH OF THE SANADA, THAT NONE MAY ATTACK US AGAIN!
AND... FINALLY ...
DO NOT DIE!
....
MIZUKI...I PROMISE.
THAT IS ALL.

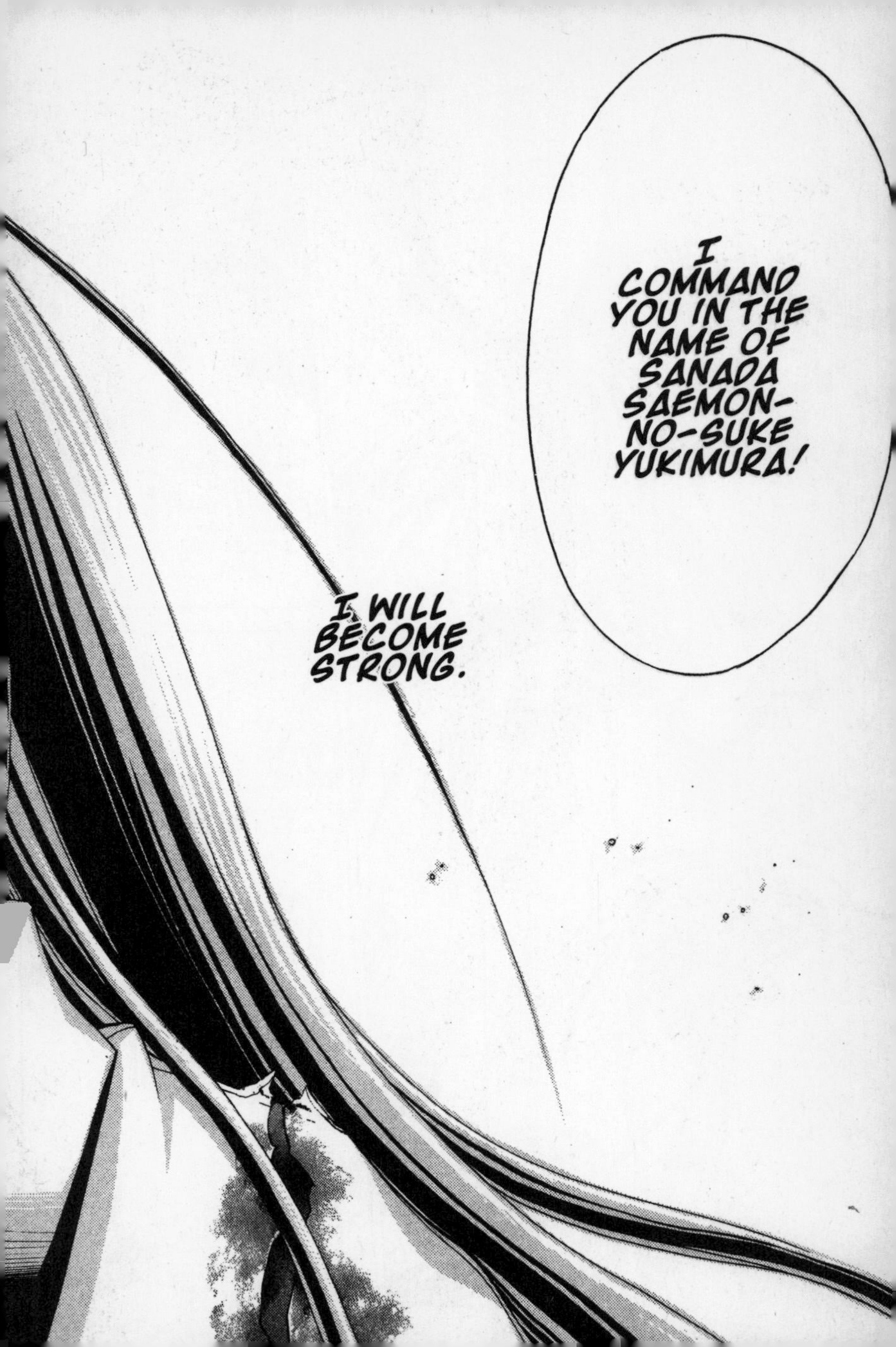
I COMMAND YOU IN THE NAME OF SANADA SAEMON-NO-SUKE YUKIMURA!
I WILL BECOME STRONG.

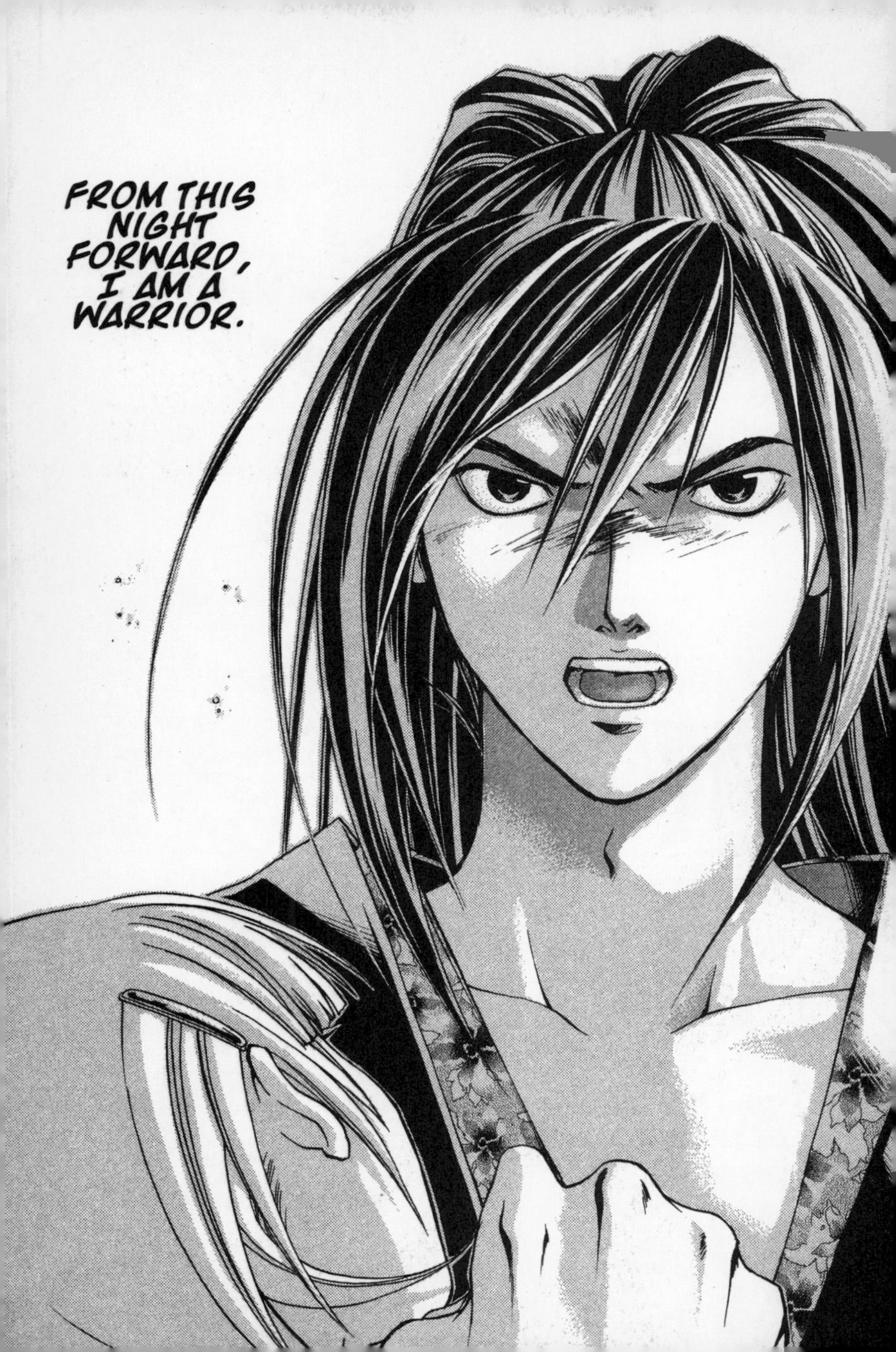
FROM THIS NIGHT FORWARD, I AM A WARRIOR.

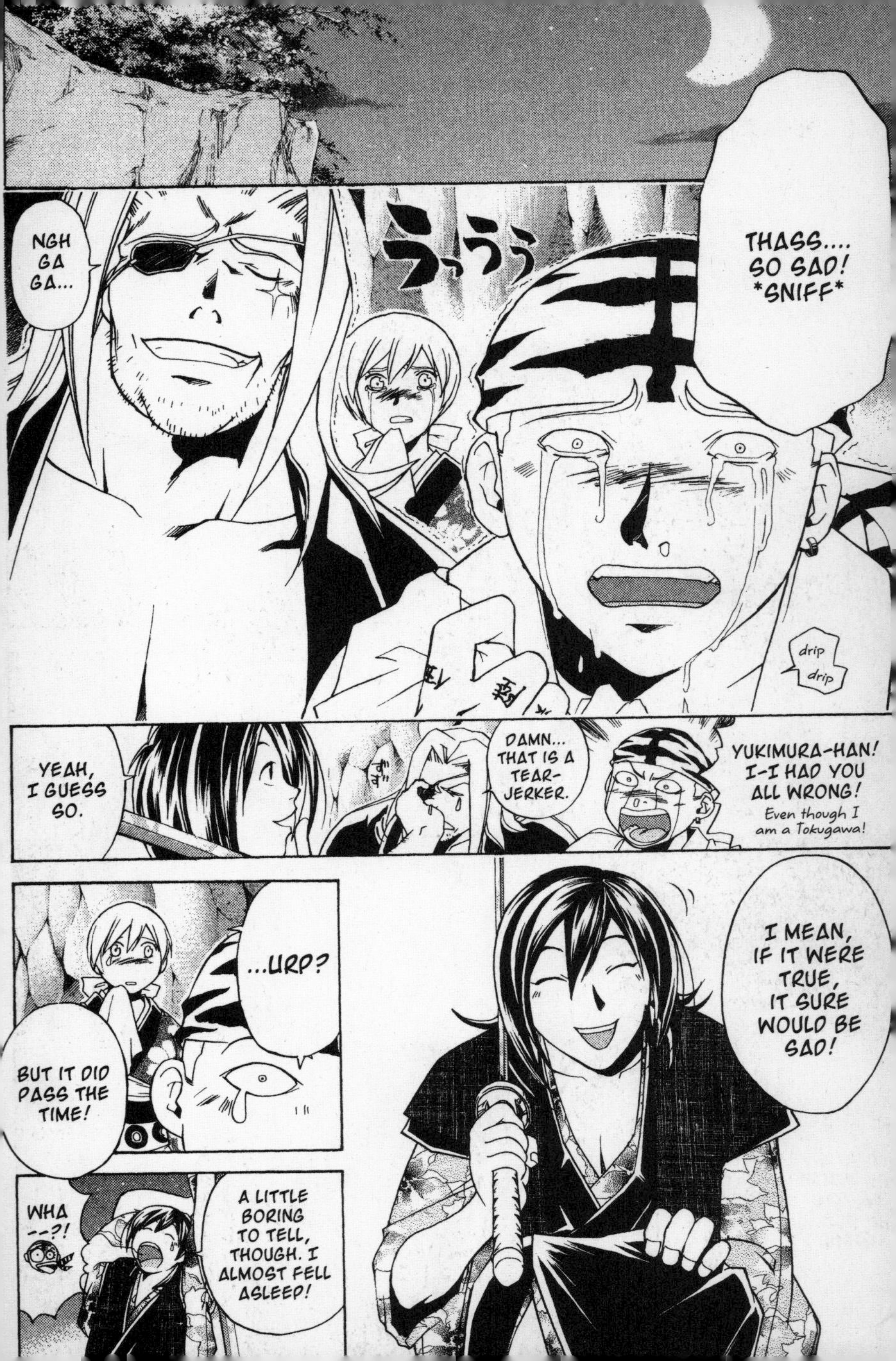
THASS.... SO SAD! *SNIFF*
うっうう
drip drip
NGH GA GA...
YUKIMURA-HAN! I-I HAD YOU ALL WRONG! Even though I am a Tokugawa!
DAMN... THAT IS A TEAR-JERKER.
YEAH, I GUESS SO.
I MEAN, IF IT WERE TRUE, IT SURE WOULD BE SAD!
...URP?
BUT IT DID PASS THE TIME!
A LITTLE BORING TO TELL, THOUGH. I ALMOST FELL ASLEEP!
WHA--?!

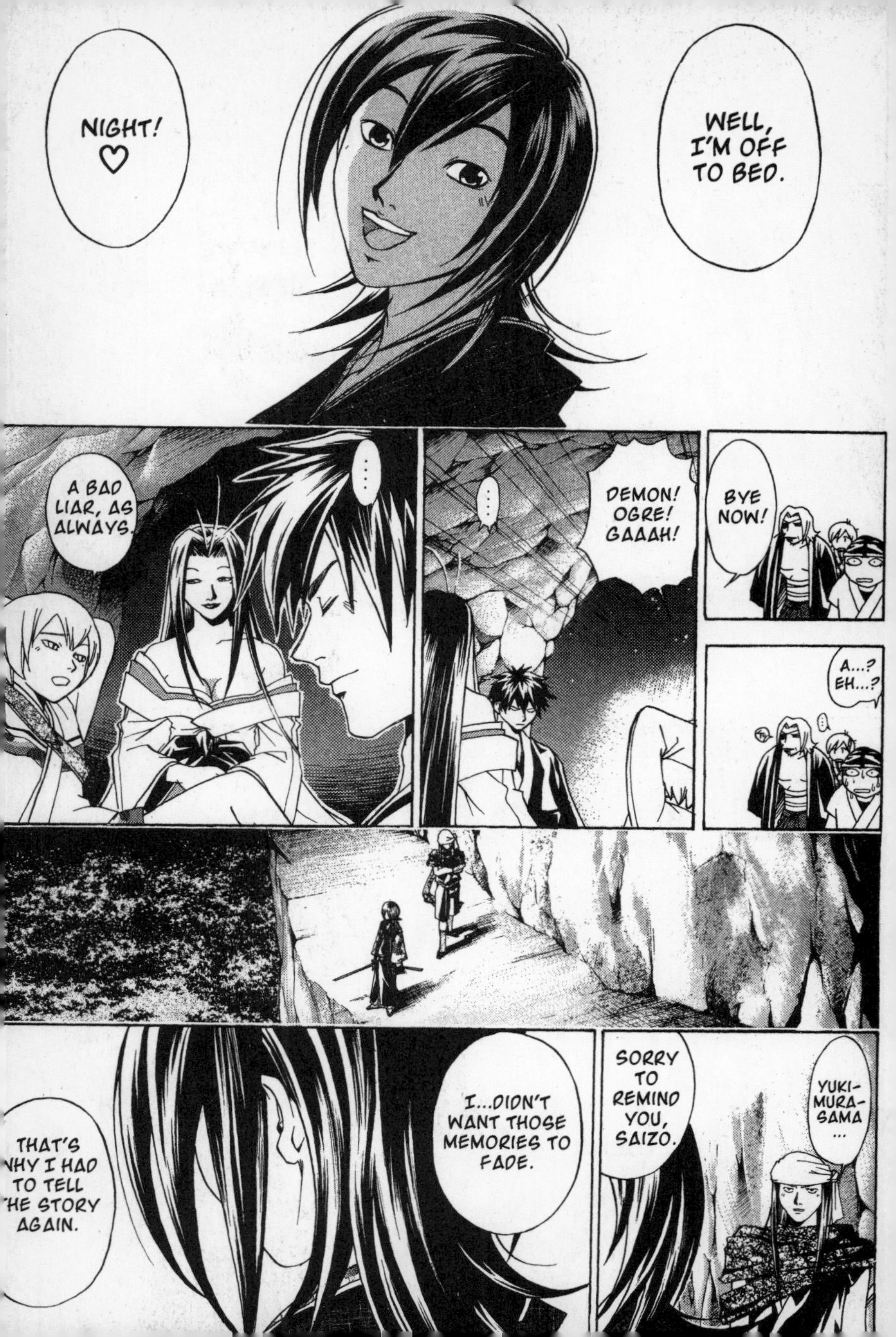
WELL, I'M OFF TO BED.
NIGHT! ♡
BYE NOW!
A...? EH...?
...
DEMON! OGRE! GAAAH!
...
...
A BAD LIAR, AS ALWAYS.
YUKI-MURA-SAMA...
SORRY TO REMIND YOU, SAIZO.
I...DIDN'T WANT THOSE MEMORIES TO FADE.
THAT'S WHY I HAD TO TELL THE STORY AGAIN.

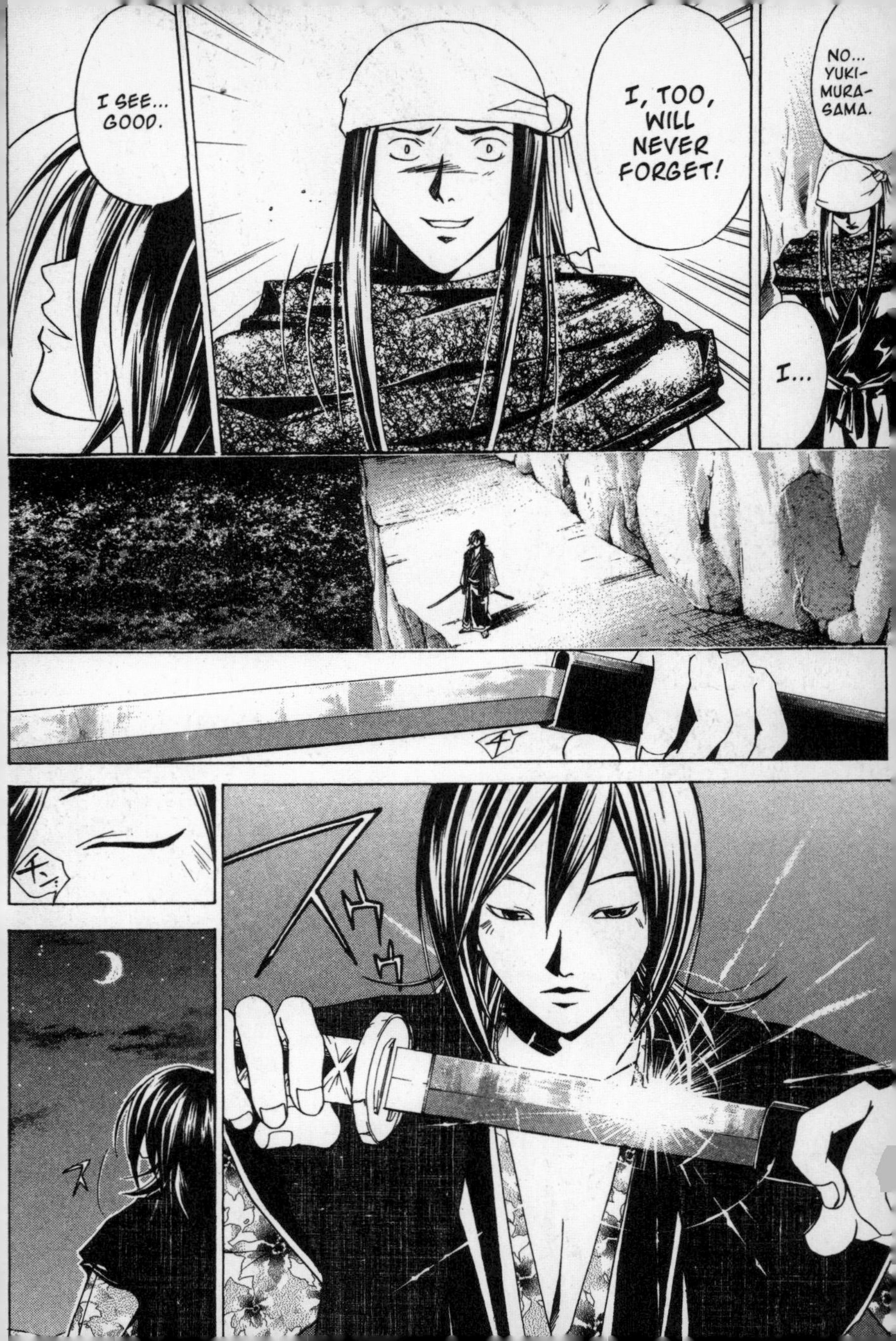
NO... YUKI-MURA-SAMA.
I...
I, TOO, WILL NEVER FORGET!
I SEE... GOOD.

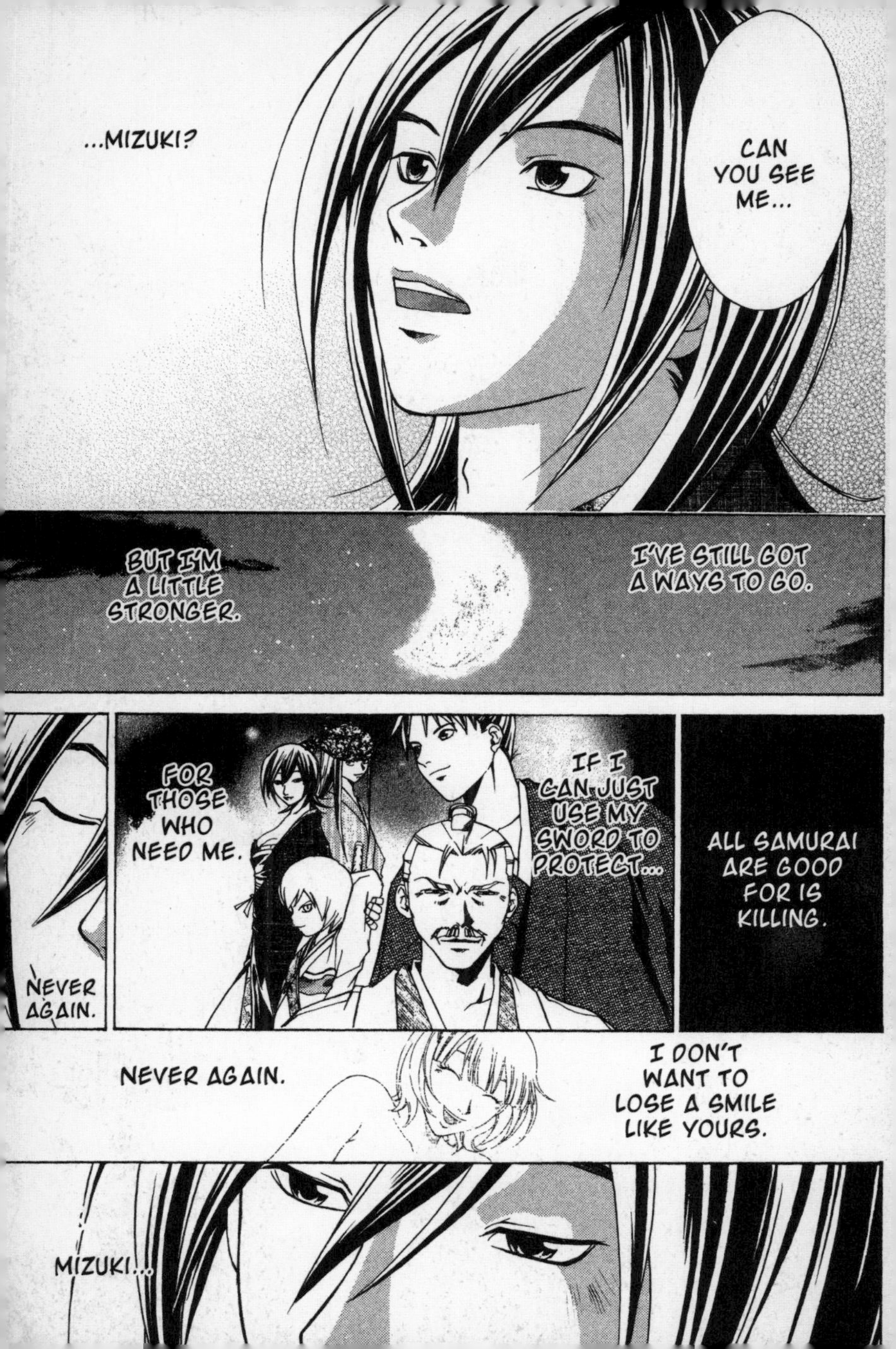

CAN YOU SEE ME...
...MIZUKI?
I'VE STILL GOT A WAYS TO GO.
BUT I'M A LITTLE STRONGER.
ALL SAMURAI ARE GOOD FOR IS KILLING.
IF I CAN JUST USE MY SWORD TO PROTECT...
FOR THOSE WHO NEED ME.
NEVER AGAIN.
I DON'T WANT TO LOSE A SMILE LIKE YOURS.
NEVER AGAIN.
MIZUKI...

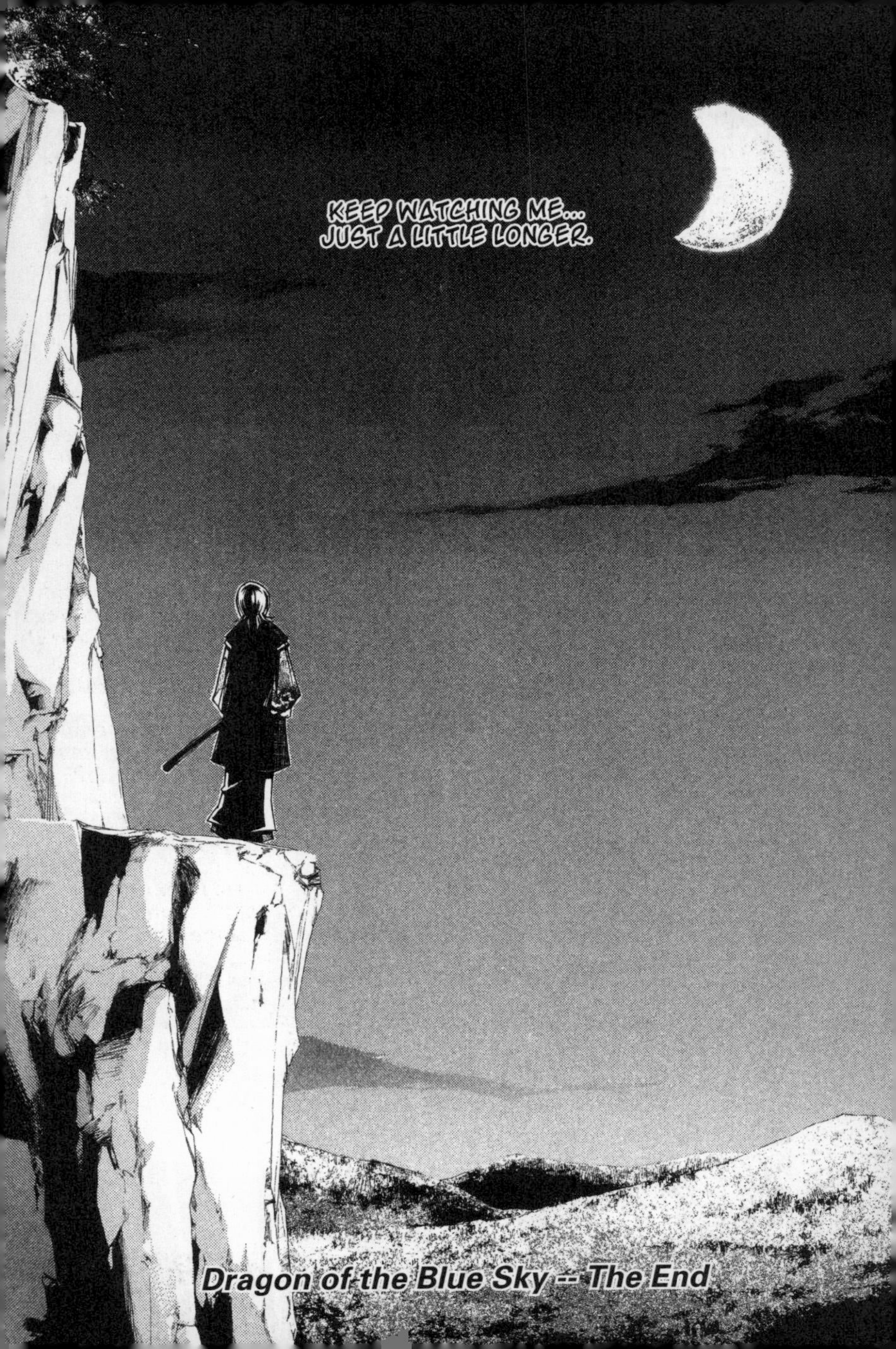
KEEP WATCHING ME...
JUST A LITTLE LONGER.
Dragon of the Blue Sky -- The End

I haven't forgotten Q&A corner either.

☐ **_Howdy! Kamijo here, how's everyone doing? We didn't have a lot of spare room for bonus pages in this issue, so only one page of postcards this time. We'll get them in the next one, though, so keep sending them!_**

☐ **_This volume was half side-story! (Sorry to those who wanted to hear more of the main story!) I thought it was time for a nice, straight, tale. I hope you enjoyed hearing about Yukimura's past!_**

☐ **_I get letters all the time asking "Do you really read all your letters?" I felt exactly the same way as you before I became a manga artist. Now that I am one, I realize what an incredible source of inspiration and energy they are! Really!_**
Think about it--someone I don't know is spending their time, and their 80 yen, and getting all excited, and nervous...all for me! I mean, isn't that AMAZING?!?! (whew)
I read all my letters when I'm feeling down. The letters are the only thing that tell me what my readers are really thinking! It's not all good, of course... Unfortunately, since I can't respond properly to every letter (...sorry, I'm slow!) I try to give back to the readers by making my manga as fun as possible! Thanks for reading!

☐ BIRTH OF BON

Scene: meeting when I decide to draw Bontenmaru
I-I THINK WE SHOULD HAVE A LESS BEAUTIFUL CHARACTER. Like a guy with a big head, or an old lady, or...
OKAY, HOW ABOUT THIS ONE--
Mr. S
HEY!
And then...
A real idiot! Like Masamune, a hero that time forgot! A street punk, with a wooden sword! (poorly shaven!)
And his trade mark'll be... N*ke!
The one-eyed thing seemed a little overdone, so put a mark on the eyepatch...
EH? THE N*KE MARK ?!
Mr. H
THESE TWO ARE OUT OF CONTROL ...
Mr. S
YEAH, THAT SWOOSHY THING!
N*ke
YOU'RE THE IDIOT!
And Bontenmaru was born. (minus the N*ke mark)

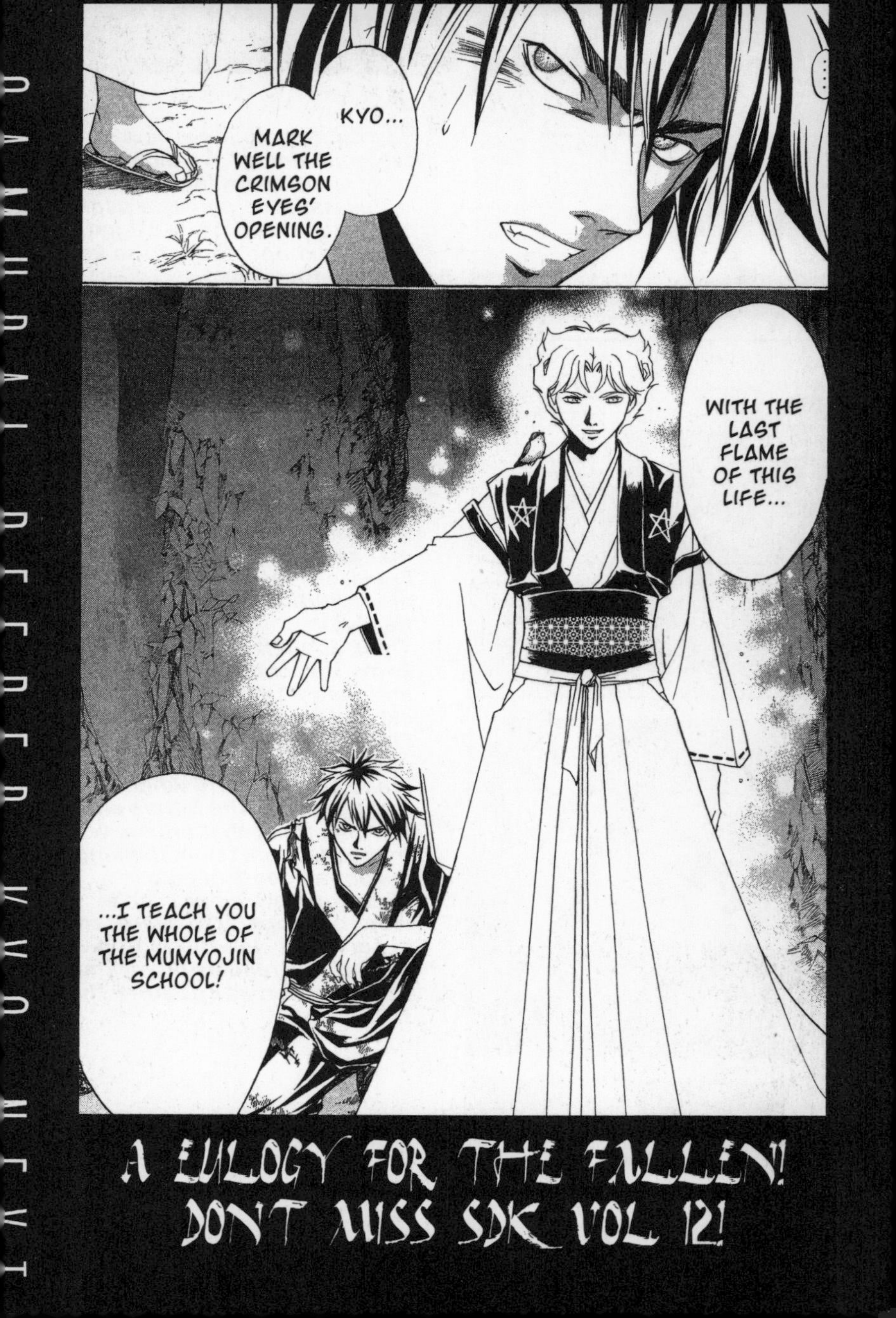
KYO... MARK WELL THE CRIMSON EYES' OPENING.
WITH THE LAST FLAME OF THIS LIFE...
...I TEACH YOU THE WHOLE OF THE MUMYOJIN SCHOOL!

A EULOGY FOR THE FALLEN!
DONT MISS SDK VOL 12!

WARCRAFT
THE SUNWELL TRILOGY

RICHARD A. KNAAK · KIM JAE-HWAN

From the artist of the best-selling *King of Hell* series!

It's an epic quest to save the entire High Elven Kingdom from the forces of the Undead Scourge! Set in the mystical world of Azeroth, *Warcraft: The Sunwell Trilogy* chronicles the adventures of Kalec, a blue dragon who has taken human form to escape deadly forces, and Anveena, a beautiful young maiden with a mysterious power.

EXPERIENCE THE MANGA

TEEN
AGE 13+

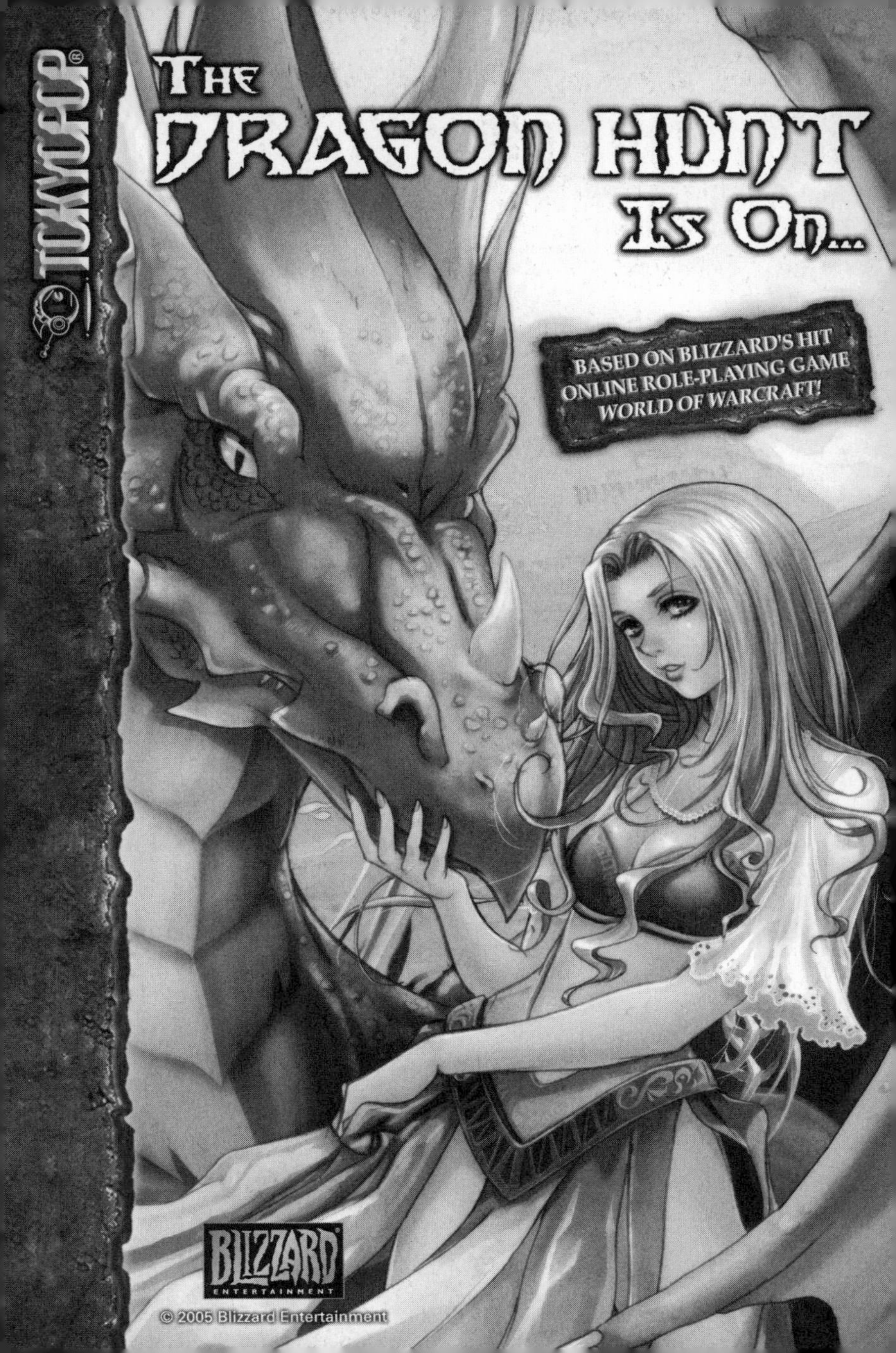
TOKYOPOP
The Dragon Hunt Is On...
BASED ON BLIZZARD'S HIT ONLINE ROLE-PLAYING GAME WORLD OF WARCRAFT!
BLIZZARD ENTERTAINMENT
© 2005 Blizzard Entertainment

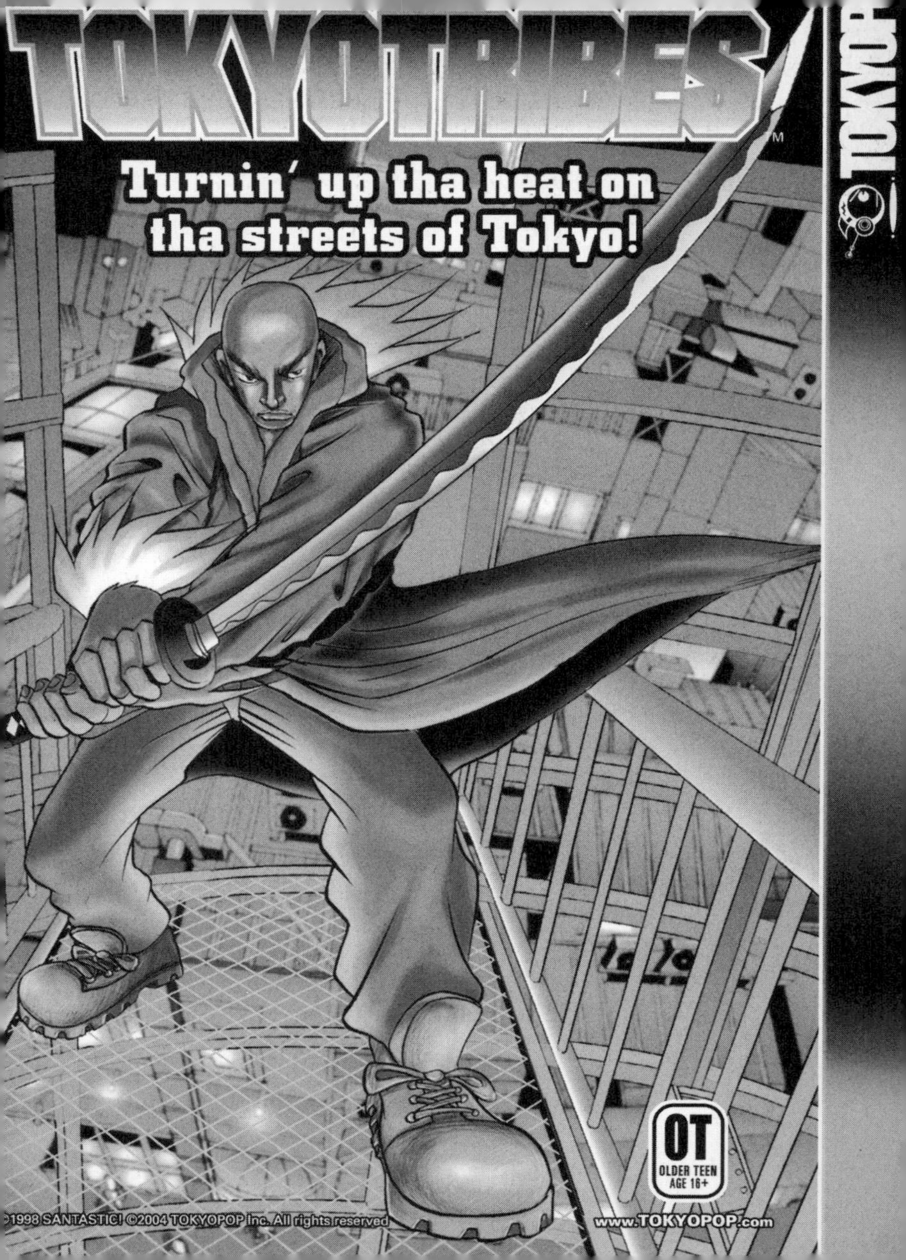
TOKYO TRIBES™
Turnin' up tha heat on
tha streets of Tokyo!
TOKYOPOP
OT
OLDER TEEN
AGE 16+
©1998 SANTASTIC! ©2004 TOKYOPOP Inc. All rights reserved
www.TOKYOPOP.com

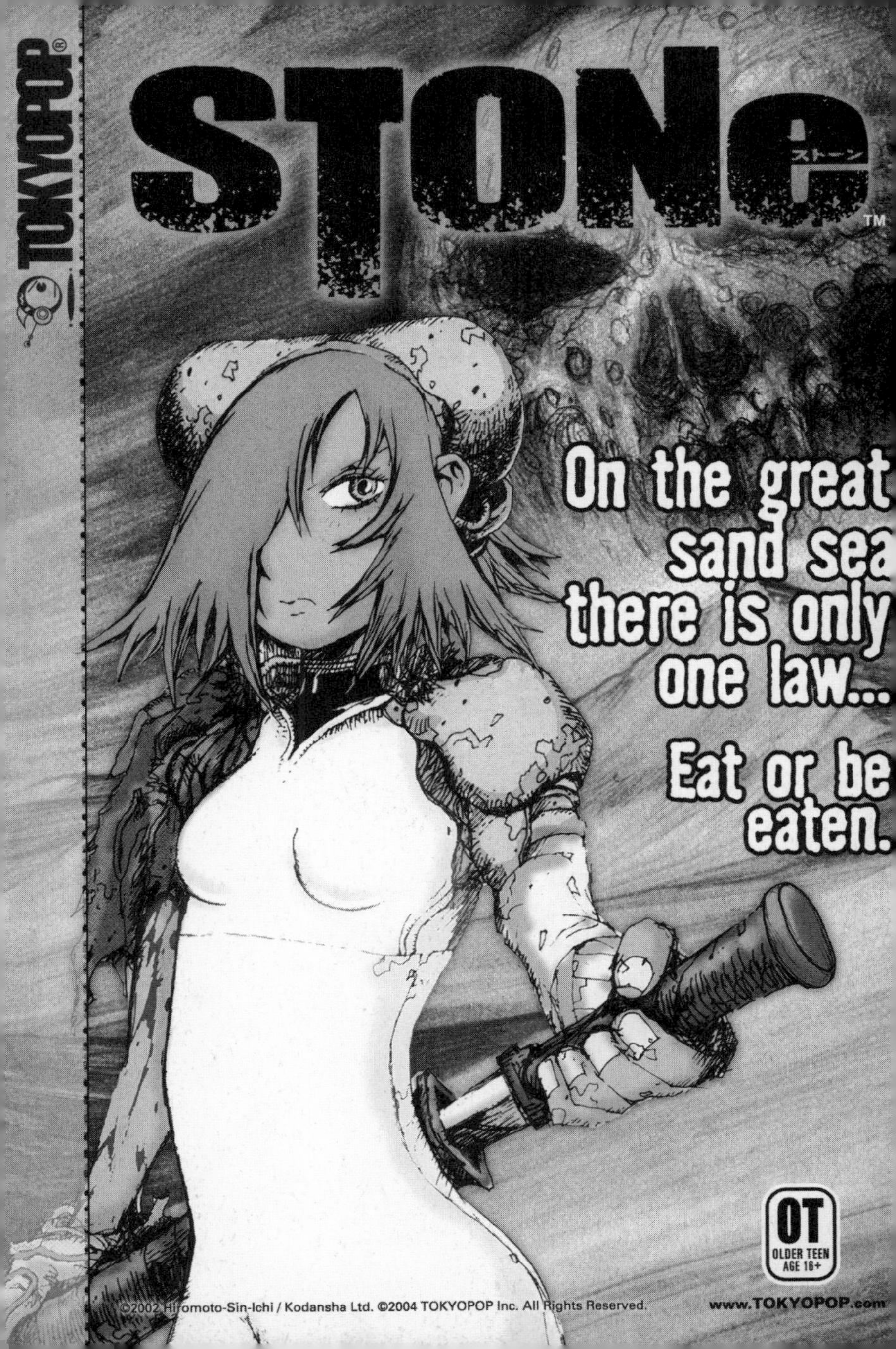
TOKYOPOP®
STONe
ストーン
TM
On the great sand sea there is only one law...
Eat or be eaten.
OT
OLDER TEEN
AGE 16+
©2002 Hiromoto-Sin-Ichi / Kodansha Ltd. ©2004 TOKYOPOP Inc. All Rights Reserved.
www.TOKYOPOP.com

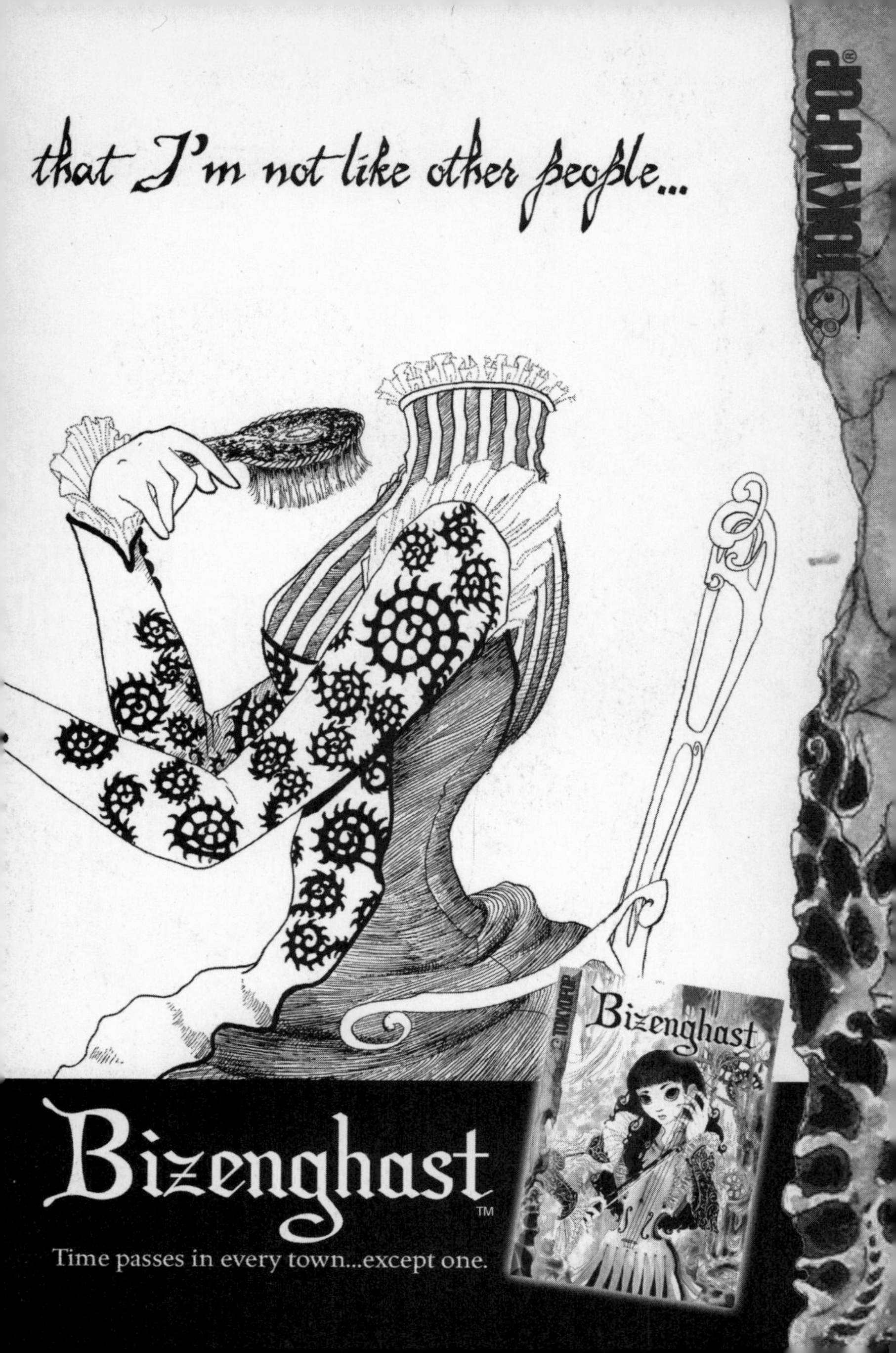
that I'm not like other people...
TOKYOPOP®
Bizenghast
TOKYOPOP
Bizenghast™
Time passes in every town...except one.

Dear Diary,
I'm starting to feel

When a young girl moves to the forgotten town of Bizenghast, she uncovers a terrifying collection of lost souls that leads her to the brink of insanity. One thing becomes painfully clear: The residents of Bizenghast are just dying to come home. © 2005 Mary Alice LeGrow. All Rights Reserved.

STOP!

This is the back of the book.
You wouldn't want to spoil a great ending!

This book is printed "manga-style," in the authentic Japanese right-to-left format. Since none of the artwork has been flipped or altered, readers get to experience the story just as the creator intended. You've been asking for it, so TOKYOPOP® delivered: authentic, hot-off-the-press, and far more fun!

DIRECTIONS

If this is your first time reading manga-style, here's a quick guide to help you understand how it works.

It's easy... just start in the top right panel and follow the numbers. Have fun, and look for more 100% authentic manga from TOKYOPOP®!